The New Western

ALSO EDITED BY SCOTT F. STODDART

Analyzing Mad Men: *Critical Essays on the Television Series* (McFarland, 2011)

The New Western
*Critical Essays on
the Genre Since 9/11*

EDITED BY SCOTT F. STODDART

McFarland & Company, Inc., Publishers
Jefferson, North Carolina

LIBRARY OF CONGRESS CATALOGUING-IN-PUBLICATION DATA

Names: Stoddart, Scott, editor.
Title: The new western : critical essays on the genre since 9/11 / edited by Scott F. Stoddart.
Description: Jefferson, North Carolina : McFarland & Company, Inc., Publishers, 2016 | Includes bibliographical references and index.
Identifiers: LCCN 2015050054 | ISBN 9780786479283 (softcover : acid free paper) ∞
Subjects: LCSH: Western films—United States—History and criticism. | National characteristics, American, in motion pictures.
Classification: LCC PN1995.9.W4 N475 2016 | DDC 791.43/65878—dc23
LC record available at http://lccn.loc.gov/2015050054

BRITISH LIBRARY CATALOGUING DATA ARE AVAILABLE

ISBN (print) 978-0-7864-7928-3
ISBN (ebook) 978-1-4766-2420-4

© 2016 Scott F. Stoddart. All rights reserved

No part of this book may be reproduced or transmitted in any form or by any means, electronic or mechanical, including photocopying or recording, or by any information storage and retrieval system, without permission in writing from the publisher.

Front cover: Jeff Bridges as Rooster Cogburn and Hailee Steinfeld as Mattie Ross in *True Grit*, 2010 (Paramount Pictures/Photofest)

Printed in the United States of America

McFarland & Company, Inc., Publishers
 Box 611, Jefferson, North Carolina 28640
 www.mcfarlandpub.com

*For Tall T,
who, like those pioneers of old,
bravely crossed the prairies and plains
to forge a new life with courage
and determination.*

Table of Contents

Acknowledgments   ix

Introduction   1

Part I. Familiar Landscapes

"Built Ford Tough": The "Sincerity" of John Ford and the Persistence of the American Western
  ARTHUR REDDING   10

"It was justified": Visceral Violence in the New Television Western—*Deadwood, Hell on Wheels* and *Justified*
  PATRICK CONDLIFFE   19

Part II. New Westerns in Dialogue

"Fooling around with Papa's pistol": Avenging Patriarchy in *True Grit*
  JENNA HUNNEF   40

Coen, Coen on the Range: Rooster Cogburn(s) and Domestic Space
  JOSEPH S. WALKER   62

The Beginning and the End: Gay Representations in *Brokeback Mountain* and *3:10 to Yuma*
  VINCENT PITURRO   81

Brokeback Mountain Queering the "Legend": Historical Hegemony and Masculine Memory
  SCOTT F. STODDART   95

Part III. New Frontiers

The Post-9/11 Mohecan: *Avatar* and the Transformation of the "Manifest Apology"
 ANDREW HOWE . . . 116

Security or Freedom: Joss Whedon's Science Fiction Westerns, *Firefly* and *Serenity*
 J.P.C. BROWN . . . 137

Sixguns and the Shadowless Kick: Mythmaking and Generic Hybridization in Westerns and Martial Arts Fantasies
 FONTAINE LIEN . . . 159

Part IV. New Visions

Reclaiming Past, Resisting Progression: Existential Tensions in Rockstar's *Red Dead Redemption*
 MICHAEL SAMUEL . . . 172

Alex Cox and the Hybrid Western
 MATTHEW SORRENTO . . . 188

The Vertical Frontier: Amir Naderi's *Vegas* and the End of American Dream After 9/11
 MARCO GROSOLI . . . 207

Epilogue—New Visions / New Vistas: Christopher Nolan's *Batman* Trilogy and the New Western
 SCOTT F. STODDART . . . 229

About the Contributors . . . 245

Index . . . 247

Acknowledgments

Like my last collection of essays, *Analyzing Mad Men, The New Western* began as a series of conversations that I would have with anyone who would listen. My immediate support network is comprised of colleagues and family who support my efforts in every way imaginable.

Professionally, I have had two homes during the creation of this volume. First, I want to thank Joyce F. Brown, President of the Fashion Institute of Technology, and Giacomo Oliva, Vice President for Academic Affairs, for not only supporting my scholarly efforts, but for championing the liberal arts at a time when the humanities are in a state of crisis. My immediate colleagues are a core group of gifted academics who validate my efforts tirelessly: my appreciation goes to Joanne Arbuckle, Steven Frumkin, Mary Davis, Howard Dillon, Ron Milon and Yasemin Jones.

My immediate team in the School of Liberal Arts continues to be made up of three of the most caring and dedicated professionals I have ever had the good fortune to work with: my thanks to Mary Tsujimoto, Everlina Washington, and Suzanne Richardson for all of their support of my efforts.

Second, I need to thank those at John Jay College, CUNY—my new academic home—who support my continued efforts to be an administrative scholar. My thanks to President Jeremy Travis, Provost Jane Bowers, and my immediate colleagues, Dean Anne Lopes, Dean Anthony Carpi, and Associate Provost Jim Llana for their confidence in my abilities.

Thanks extend to my academic home here at John Jay: my department chair, Professor Allison Pease, and my John Jay team: Katheirne Killoran, Kate Szur, Dan Auld, Michael Rohdin, Dara Bryne, Litna McNickel, Delandra Hunter, Charles Davidson and Nancy Velazquez-Torres and Sumaya Villanueva. Special thanks go to Nikki Hancock-Nicholson, who has been my most valuable source of support this year.

The work presented here is the product of much work and tireless dedication from a group of contributors who have proven to be the utmost professionals. My thanks to them for their efforts—and their patience—as this collection became a reality.

My never-ending thanks go to my parents, Jeanne F. Black and Frederick Stoddart, who have always supported me in my efforts.

I owe so much to Professor Bill Mooney, who will drop anything, any time of day, to sit and talk movies with me. He is a wealth of information and a truly engaged listener, who pushes me to think clearly about my ideas, and supports me to use my voice to focus my attention on my work in film. He is a real inspiration to me.

My surrogate family, James Miller and Madison Ritter, have become a constant source of support since their "adoption." I owe them so many thanks for their love and support, particularly over the past year.

And finally, Tall T … Travis Wicklund rode into my life while this book was in its gestation phase. His love and support have pushed me to remain focused on my work; his love guides me to be the best that I can be. He not only watches all of the films that I feel compelled to watch … no matter the genre … but he openly engages with me after, talking through my own insights, and challenging my ideas with new perspectives. It is to him who I dedicate this labor of love.

Introduction

It started out like every other day in New York City.

I had moved to the city only eight months before, having left my professorship in Fort Lauderdale to pursue an administrative career. After a lonely, arduous job search, I was ready to begin my new job at Marymount Manhattan College as the Executive Director of Special Programs. Today was the start of my third week in this position, and as I made my way through Central Park toward the city's east side, I recall realizing how fortunate I was to be happily employed in "the city that never sleeps."

I remember crossing Park Avenue, the sky a vibrant blue, empty of clouds, the sun shining brightly, indicating that it was going to be another warm day. The leaves had not yet begun to turn; the summer flowers were still in bloom along the medians. Then a plane flew overhead. While a plane flying over the city is nothing that would stand out in one's memory, what struck me, and many of my fellow pedestrians, most was that it was flying so low, the deafening roar of the engines rattling windows of the nearby apartments. An unsettling though not unusual start to that lovely Tuesday morning in New York City.

I wish I could say that I stayed there on that median in the middle of Park Avenue to watch what ultimately happened, but I did not. I did not learn of that plane's fate until I arrived at the college to hear that one of the Twin Towers had been struck by that very plane. And, of course, it was only a matter of minutes before a second plane took a similar path to strike the second tower.

Since that day of dichotomies, I have returned to that same spot on Park Avenue and 72nd Street to ponder what I might have seen had I stayed another seven minutes. Even though I had been in New York for a short time, on that September morning, I know that it was the first day that I believed myself to be a New Yorker—walking back across town with massive crowds later that same morning, stunned and bewildered that someone, some group, could attack our fair metropolis. Returning to our families and homes, we all knew we were part of history, crossing our own frontier, seeking in silence some understanding of this incident so inexplicably horrible.

In the days and years since the attacks on the World Trade Center, many Americans have sought answers to the unanswerable questions raised that day. Politicians talk, commentators postulate and historians offer myriad hypotheses as to what occurred that day, and what it all means. Artists—ever ready to take on a political cause—stylize their commentary through their varied media to help their varied publics make sense of the unspeakable, and to provoke insights as to the causes and effects of this political atrocity.

Hollywood, arguably the greatest capitalistic/artistic enterprise of the twentieth century, took its time to respond to the events of 9/11, and supported only a few efforts to portray the events of that day. However, many filmmakers—taking their lead from the great American auteurs of the early studio days—sought a more covert means of addressing the tragedy of that September morning. *The New Western* explores these films to reveal how these artists used the oldest of Hollywood genres to wrestle with the angst and anguish of the seemingly inexplicable.

A Point of Reflection

Ever since Justus D. Barnes pointed his six-shooter toward an audience of theatre patrons at the end of Edwin S. Porter's *The Great Train Robbery* (1903), the Western has been a part of the American movie mystique. As noted by Mark Harris, "Westerns had long been an essential part of Hollywood's output; as many as 20 percent of the movies produced every year were cowboy films" (52), and the Western has proved to be the most enduring of the Hollywood genres, alongside the melodrama. The popularity of the genre, with the public and with directors, appears to be more cyclical than the melodrama, though; the genre appears to ebb and flow with the times—just as it begins to lose favor, it appears to resurge, influencing another generation of movie lovers.

One commonality highlighted with the backward glance of history underscores that the Western becomes most popular in times of crisis—its brand of action-packed storytelling blended with its patriotic embrace of American values makes it a staple akin to comfort food—artists and their audiences turn to the Western in times of need.

While the Western was always a mainstay, an "ultra-low-budget programmer" that could "generally run under an hour to fill out double bills in rural theatre chains" (Harris 53), the genre was startlingly transformed by John Ford, one of its greatest directors, with his *Stagecoach* (1939), a film that seasoned the genre to become an adult film, taking on the Production Code by elevating a story based on revenge killing, and creating endearing characters from those usually seen as less than noble by Hollywood. Critics have long extolled the place of Ford's film as a hallmark of generic transformation: Andre Bazin found it to be nothing less than "the definitive stage of perfection" (Lusted 153) and Peter Stanfield suggests that the film's blending of idyllic romance with "the film's complex fusion of history, allegory and adult themes" help elevate its reputation as one of the most important films to come out of the 1930s Hollywood.

What has only recently come to light, however, is John Ford's intention in making *Stagecoach*. He and screenwriter Dudley Nichols worked to infuse this simple story of the wild west with palpable political overtones mirroring the brewing political unrest in Europe. As delineated in Mark Harris' *Five Came Back* (2014), Ford was a political activist throughout the 1930s, and he used his stature as an Academy Award-winning director to wrestle control of his films away from the annoying moguls, lacing his products with his personal artistic vision.

Ford's true legacy is that the Hollywood Western could be used to promote personal artistic vision and incite political activity. His Westerns following World War II—*My Darling Clementine* (1946), *Fort Apache* (1948), *She Wore a Yellow Ribbon* (1949), *The Searchers* (1956) and *The Man Who Shot Liberty Valance* (1962)—join those of Howard Hawks (*Red River*, 1948, and *Rio Bravo*, 1959) and Anthony Mann (*Westchester '73*, 1950, and *The Man from Laramie*, 1955) to reformulate the genre, allowing the Western to mature into a genre film that uses American history to both criticize and extoll the virtues that made America a singular world power.

The war in Vietnam pushed the Western into a new territory, causing it to be re-imagined once more by directors following Ford's lead. *Bonnie and Clyde* (Arthur Penn, 1967), a gangster picture that employed Western tropes, broke the final limitations of the Production Code, and made it possible for directors to use genre pictures to openly take on the politics of the day to bring younger audiences angry about the Vietnam War's escalation back to the cinema. Sam Peckinpah, whose earlier Western *Ride the High Country* (1962) tested the boundaries of the Code with its depiction of violence and its focus on "protagonists subject to the destructive and anonymous forces of a changing American society" (Lusted 220), specifically used the Western to take on the contemporary political scene. To the director's way of thinking, *The Wild Bunch* (1969) was not a Western, but a "film about men on horseback" (Kitses 201); regardless, it is an important film in that it brought new expectations to the genre, not only breaking the race barrier, but by blending his use of desensitized violence with the basics of cinematic grammar, pushing the genre to new limits, "allegorizing a fallen nation in flawed protagonists" (Kites 202). Just watch the opening sequence: three tautly cross-cut sections that appear to have no commonality, but that come together in a shoot-out that reveals a disturbing political message. In the first, balanced with the star credits, we are introduced to the Bunch itself, riding into town on horseback to execute their latest haul; in the second, we observe a group of children—white, black and Mexican—hovering over a pair of scorpions being attacked in close-up by a tribe of red ants; and in the third, we see a temperance meeting of devout Christian women, held in the town square that houses the very bank the Bunch are riding to rob. It is only after the Bunch gets to the bank that we observe the local posse of roughnecks, armed and ready to defend the town's honor. As the children ignite the insects with a match and head to the town square, the Temperance meeting turns to a parade, and the Bunch surfaces to intersect with the posse, which opens fire on all three sectors, allowing Peckinpah to use slow-motion, flash cuts and tracking shots to capture the mayhem caused by "the law" trying to control what they see as unlawful. The resulting panning shows the carnage left in the massacre's wake: innocent men and women bleeding in the streets, ending in a close-up of two beautiful children, clasped in terror, standing in the midst of a blood-soaked terrain. As the Bunch rides off, only one member shot, Peckinpah makes his point: the government (represented by the posse) kills innocent victims for the greater good; even though they are anti-heroes, "The Wild Bunch" is a community of men who remain true to the ethical codes of humanity.

Other films followed suit: *Butch Cassidy and the Sundance Kid* (George Roy Hill, 1969); *Midnight Cowboy* (John Schlesinger, 1969) and *Easy Rider* (Dennis Hopper, 1969) each retool the genre by using the Western to directly comment on America's involvement in Vietnam and the culture clash taking place on American campuses in response to the conflict. In this instance, the Western appeared to serve as a cultural stage where fresh commentary regarding American patriotism and ethical responsibility could play out.

Between the 1980s and the turn of the new century, the Western slid from the collective conscience of the American movie-going public. The genre was revisited merely for comedic purposes, in films such as *Blazing Saddles* (Mel Brooks, 1974) and the *City Slicker* series (1991, 1994) because it appeared a part of the Hollywood past, re-freshened for a moment and rendered obsolete.

With the start of the Gulf War two directors returned to the genre, for example Kevin Costner in *Dances with Wolves* (1990)—a film that became the first Western since 1931's *Cimarron* to win the Oscar for Best Picture. *Wolves* has garnered the reputation as being a simple, jingoistic throwback to the Westerns of the 1950s, but—to be fair—it is an important film in its depiction of the Native American experience juxtaposed against the lonesome outsider who learns their language and their ways, aligning himself ultimately with their peaceful, sustainable existence. Seen as a literacy narrative, *Dances with Wolves* shares with Peckinpah a distrust of "civilized" whiteness.

Two years later, another Western more clearly acknowledges the legacy of Peckinpah, and it comes from the man made famous by the Spaghetti Westerns of Sergio Leone: Clint Eastwood. A product of the Reagan/Bush–fueled patriotism surrounding the First Gulf War, Eastwood's *Unforgiven*, from David Webb Peoples' screenplay, uses the Western to play off the nostalgia an audience might have for the Westerns of old, and punctuates the story of William Munny (Eastwood) with the surreal evil embedded in Peckinpah's Westerns, creating a film that seeks a new way of reading the cultural landscape that produced it. Once a cold-blooded killer, Munny lives a good, Christian life on the peaceful plains, raising hogs with his two blond children who appear to be the spitting-image of his now dead wife. Juxtaposed against this serenity, the film captures life at a local bordello, where a dishonest man disfigures one of the women who makes fun of his limited endowments. The women, knowing justice will be denied for "only cutting a whore," raise the money for restitution, and Munny joins forces with a slick-talking wannabe (Jaimz Woolvett) and his old comrade, Ned Logan (Morgan Freeman), to obtain the reward. It is in this delicate balance between male camaraderie on the plains and the tyranny of civilization, represented by a cruelly crooked marshal, Little Bill Daggett (Gene Hackman), that Eastwood parallels the scope and style of Peckinpah. The sequences of violence—mainly the shootout in the rocks, and the ultimate lynching of Ned by Daggett—underscore Eastwood's use of cinematic rhetoric to make the point that the grey areas between right and wrong are not so easily defined. When Munny finally confronts Daggett, shooting him in the face with both barrels of his rifle, the message is clear—we all remain "unforgiven" when we wage war on one another, regardless of how mightily we try and justify the cause.

Since the tragedy of 9/11, the Western has made a remarkable comeback, blending its original, patriotic purpose with its redefinition as a critical commentary on America's place in the global community. *The New Western* is a collection of essays dedicated to analyzing these films in an effort to show how this genre, re-purposed once more, appears to surface in times of crisis.

Riding the Range

The structure of *The New Western* organizes a wide array of films made after 9/11 that use, interrogate and revere the structure and status of the Western as a means of exploring the state of America in the twenty-first century. It is fitting to employ the Western—the oldest of the American film genres—

to explore what it means to be American in this new global world where we now appear vulnerable in the face of such inexplicable violence.

The first part of this book, Familiar Landscapes, opens the collection with Arthur Redding's survey of the Western and the legacy of John Ford. Redding argues that not only is the Western a mainstay of American culture, but its ability to transform itself as genre, adapting to the times that produce it, and addressing the shifting populations it seeks to attract—women, blacks, gay men—is part of how it has remained vital from Owen Wister's days to the present. In surveying the many cultural references that use tropes of the Western, Redding writes, "The message of every Western is this: something has been irretrievably lost or closed within our culture, and, if we are to survive as a nation, we must reckon and honor and mourn that which can no longer persist in order to shape for ourselves from its memory a new culture that can endure the challenges of the present and near future." The Western's ability to morph with the times that produce it heralds its lasting effect on the American psyche.

In a similar fashion, Patrick Condliffe's reading of the recent televised Westerns looks at the HBO series *Deadwood* (2004–06) and the FX series *Hell on Wheels* (2011–the present) and *Justified* (2010–15) in comparison to televised Western dramas of the past, examining how the changing times have allowed this genre to become bolder and more contemporary as it seeks a wider audience. His argument focuses on this escalation: "the violence and visceral nature of its depiction has instead become destabilized as transitioned into a self-fulfilling spectacle, a process that has mostly been critiqued in regard to post-9/11 horror." In examining these contemporary re-visions of the West, Condliffe believes the Western's legacy on television addresses the destabilized feeling Americans had as they wrestled with the shifting world order.

Part II, New Westerns in Dialogue, juxtaposes two readings of several new Westerns against one another, revealing distinct perspectives on the texts. The first concerns the Coen brothers' remake of *True Grit* (2010). Jenna Hunnef goes back to the original source novel by Charles Portis (1968) to focus on the story's feminist origins lost in its initial trip to the screen as a vehicle for John Wayne. Hunnef takes this original focus on Mattie Ross, and reveals how the Coens appear to return to much of the original source as a way of representing "a new variation of an older theme: patriarchy, and its unlikely reestablishment by an adolescent girl, over whom the very system wields power and control, in a society apparently gone 'soft.'"

Joseph S. Walker places the Coen brothers' revisitation among a series of "new" Westerns, namely *Dances with Wolves, Unforgiven, Open Range* (Kevin Costner, 2003) and *The Three Burials of Melquiades Estrada* (Tommy Lee Jones, 2005) to show that the film is not a simple adaptation of the novel, but a revisiting of the John Wayne vehicle itself.

The second part continues with the phenomenon of *Brokeback Mountain* (2005), a film that dominates the cultural discourse of the post 9/11 period. Vincent Piturro seeks to contextualize the film in the progression from covert instances of homosexual imagery in *Bullfighter and the Lady* (Budd Boetticher, 1951), *My Darling Clementine* (John Ford, 1946) and *Butch Cassidy and the Sundance Kid* (George Roy Hill, 1969) through to the present, re-employing a tradition of homosexual innuendo in both the remake of *3:10 to Yuma* (James Mangold, 2007) and *Brokeback*.

Piturro argues that *Brokeback*'s focus on the romance between the two central men makes it more of a "gay love story that happens to be set in the relatively recent American West"—a perspective that I do not concur with in my counter essay, which argues that *Brokeback* is a Western that has been "queered"—much like the way that John Ford "queered" his own iconic *The Man Who Shot Liberty Valance* (John Ford, 1962). The second part of my essay looks at the website sponsored by Focus Features where gay men could write their own stories of lost loves after seeing the film, revealing how the tropes of the American Western resonate to bind men around the Internet campfire.

Part III of the book, New Frontiers, explores a series of films that on the surface would never appear to be of the Western genre; each writer focuses on a particular film to reveal how the imaginary of the Western pervades generic storytelling, allowing us new insights into these varied creations. Andrew Howe, for instance, reads the central conceit of James Cameron's 3-D epic *Avatar* (2009) as a story that has its basis not only in Western films as varied as *Dance with Wolves* and *The Magnificent Seven* (John Sturges, 1960) but in the early nineteenth-century novels of James Fenimore Cooper, whose central character Natty Bumpo first wrestled with the idea of "going native" in order to avoid the corruptions of civilization.

The next essay focuses on Joss Whedon's science fiction television series *Firefly* (2002–03) and its sequel film *Serenity* (2005). By setting the story against the history of the Western, J.P.C. Brown focuses on how the cult series, and its subsequent theatrical sequel, "explores whether an authentic, human individuality can survive the worst that modern science, in the service of an enslaving political system" can do to the American spirit.

Brown's politicized reading provides a nice introduction to Fontaine Lien's essay, which sees a distinct connection between the traditions of the American Western and the Hong Kong martial arts picture. Her argument regarding the "valorization of the outcast life, just violence and heroic codes" helps to create a new understanding between the genres in this post–9/11 age.

Michael Samuel's dissection of *Red Dead Redemption* (Rod Edge and John Zurhellen, 2010) opens the final Part IV, New Visions, seeking to find a critical discourse for exploring the Western's cultural references found in the video experience. Looking at the referents from *Stagecoach* and *Red River* (Howard Hawks, 1948) to *Shane* (George Stevens, 1953), *The Wild Bunch* and *The Assassination of Jesse James by the Coward Robert Ford* (Andrew Dominik, 2007), Samuel shows how the ideology of the video game pushes a message of "individualism, self-reliance and an instinctive commitment to democracy" on to its players, creating a playing field that fuses the real world with the fictionally idyllic.

In 2006, director Alex Cox described the Western as a dead genre; Matthew Sorrento's reading of Cox's vibrant career in the context of the Western tradition provides insight into the filmmaker's *Searchers 2.0* (2007)—his post–9/11 treatise that "agonizes over the loss of a tradition in the film's content, style, and narrative pace." Providing an overview of the director's career through the lens of the Western's contemporary tradition, Sorrento reveals how the genre has been a trope throughout the director's career, celebrating it through his use of new technologies, bringing the genre to a new level of understanding.

Seeking to expose a prescient connection between the Western and contemporary narrative, Marco Grosoli reads Amir Naderi's *Vegas* as a post–9/11 treatise on the demise of the American Dream. Made in 2008, *Vegas* is both a "semantic" and "syntactic" Western that appears to predict the moment of despair experienced by America following the attacks of 9/11 and wallow in the "lost, empty" world "obsessively attached to an ambitious ideology of perpetual growth and expansion that can no longer take place."

I decided to close the collection with an Epilogue focusing on Christopher Nolan's *Batman* trilogy because its use of Western tropes helps us to understand why this re-birthing of the Batman myth was so timely after the 9/11 attacks. Using the broader concepts of the Western to structure the series, Nolan uses space and its relation to the hero to show how the Batman becomes a truly American mythology, a parable for the pioneer fighting the unthinkable in an age where one's home territory—the Wayne legacy of Gotham City—is central to one's identity, and how the struggle against an evil willing to compromise that space is, in essence, a fight for the soul.

In bringing these pieces together, my hope is to share my idea that the Western comes to salvage the American psyche in times of crisis.

Part I
Familiar Landscapes

"Built Ford Tough"
The "Sincerity" of John Ford and the Persistence of the American Western

ARTHUR REDDING

As Lee Clark Mitchell noted in his classic 1996 study of the genre, *Westerns: Making the Man in Fiction and Film*, there is something inherently nostalgic about the American Western. This nostalgia adheres not only *within* the narrative confines of old West-themed books and films, but also marks and shapes the place of the Western in popular culture: "almost the moment westerns emerged, critics hastened to pronounce the last rites, as if a melancholy nostalgia that would come to permeate the genre was almost a part of its reception" (257). In other words, if the Western typically tells a story about values that can be salvaged from a now-past heroic age, it manifests itself as a popular form that salvages, preserves, and makes new the resonant cultural power of a genre that has already been eclipsed: the Western itself. In this essay, I will argue that the Western renews and performs sincerity—a hallmark of John Ford's movie Westerns—in the wake and the wash of ubiquitous postmodern irony.

To identify the pattern, we can look back even earlier than 1902, when Owen Wister's bestselling *The Virginian* appeared, to the very formulation of the concept of the frontier itself. In 1893, when Frederick Jackson Turner promulgated his famous frontier thesis at the Chicago World's Fair meeting of the American Historical Association, he felt compelled to announce that the frontier had "closed" with the 1890 census. The central theme of the Western, as critics from Mitchell to Richard Slotkin have noted, is transition, is the putative death and necessary renewal of an imagined "America" and an imagined American masculinity. The "message" of every Western is this: something has been irretrievably lost or closed within our culture, and, if we are to survive as a nation, we must reckon and honor and mourn that which can no longer persist in order to shape for ourselves from its memory a new culture that can endure the challenges of the present and the near future. Like the American culture itself, "genres must regularly transform themselves, imaginatively manipulating classic givens, if they are to maintain a compelling hold over their audiences" (Mitchell 259).

"What's alive is dead," writes Gregg Rickman in his salutary discussion of Jim Jarmusch's *Dead Man* (1995), "but also what's dead is also alive" (401). Westerns live, but they live always and everywhere a sort of afterlife—they have saturated not just American but global culture. The local television news in Toronto the other night featured a story about a "fast-draw" competition held annually in Japan, wherein now-aging fans of American Western serials (*The Lone Ranger*; *Gunsmoke*) with stony expressions and nicknames like "Tex," dressed like Tom Mix or Clint Eastwood in the Sergio Leone "Spaghetti Westerns," compete to see who can most quickly draw a plastic six-gun from their holster to fire a pellet at a target. When I lived in central Europe during the 1990s, what unified people of a certain age from most countries of the former Soviet Bloc was their shared nostalgia for low-budget German productions (made by Rialto films in the 1960s) of Karl May novels about a gunslinger named "Old Shatterhand" and his wise Apache chief sidekick, Winnetou, which were filmed in Yugoslavia and shown repeatedly on Czech, Hungarian, Romanian, and Russian television during the 1980s. Even while he was president, Ronald Reagan liked to dress up as a Halloween cowboy, and George W. Bush as well was given to invoking Western stereotypes—"Wanted: Dead or Alive," he extemporized notoriously on September 17, 2001, referring to the slippery Osama bin Laden, and thereby reducing the entire war on terror to a dime novel—and likened his own "Texas swagger" to the famously herky-jerky gait of John Wayne. The name and persona of John Wayne is instantly recognized around the world, even—and perhaps especially—by those who have never bothered to sit down and watch a film Wayne starred in. Television commercials for pick-up trucks typically show images of horses and/or men in Stetson hats: in 2006, the country and western singer Toby Keith appeared in Ford television advertising campaign singing "I'm a Ford truck man."

As with the Keith commercials, the Western persists, in large part, as high camp, consciously or less so, lamenting, lampooning, or satirizing the supposed decline in status and power of white American masculinity. Beginning with those by Kevin Costner, heavy-handed, boring, and self-consciously "epic" retreads of classic American Westerns are churned out by Hollywood insistently these days, starring such over-exposed actors as Johnny Depp, Brad Pitt, and Russell Crowe. Costner's include the revisionist Western *Dances with Wolves* (1992), *Wyatt Earp* (1994), and *Open Range* (2003); Pitt, whose film career was launched by his turn as a cowboy in *Thelma & Louise* (1991), starred in *The Assassination of Jesse James by the Coward Robert Ford* (2007), a film whose cumbersome title itself reeks of nostalgia for a patriarchal culture that truly matters; Crowe weighed in with a very silly remake of the classic *3:10 to Yuma* (2007); and Depp, who is doing perhaps the most interesting work in the contemporary genre, starred as William Blake in Jim Jarmusch's aforementioned postmodern Western, *Dead Man* (1995), provided the voice for the recent computer animated Western comedy *Rango* (2011) and played Tonto in Disney's *The Lone Ranger* (2013). The company had earlier pulled the plug on the project, citing spiraling costs and the box-office failure of *Cowboys and Aliens* (2011), which had featured Harrison Ford and Daniel Craig.

"Why," asked Darren Millar, the organizer of a panel on "The Politics of the Western" at the 2010 Northeast Modern Language Association Conference where I originally delivered an earlier version of this essay, "has the Western—unquestionably a uniquely American genre—failed to find a place in the American canon?" My own provisional (but easily documented) answer to this question is simple: the Western *is* the American canon. That is, I would be hard-pressed to name any American text, however subversive or revisionist, that did not in some central way interrogate the thematic concerns, mimic the generic structures, or dramatize (in howsoever a critical fashion) the exceptionalist moral of the American Western, as outlined by such critics as Mitchell, Slotkin, Robert Warshow, or Jane Tompkins. Put another way, if the Western indeed remains a minor or under-appreciated genre within American cultural production, that is simply because the mythic underpinning—the frontier as a nostalgic space wherein individual male competence is tested and the rights to expansion and conquest are proved—is ubiquitous, even elemental: its signatures manifest themselves in everything from reality television (what is *Survivor* but a Western? One series of the show was subtitled "Heroes versus Villains") to contemporary political debates about public healthcare, where protesters act out a farcical recreation of the wild west by bringing their firearms to tea parties and town-hall meetings; such demonstrations perform in decidedly mythicized (if nonetheless cynical) fashion the prized American distrust of big government, which, according to Frederick Jackson Turner, is among the inevitable results of the frontier heritage of self-reliance. The historian Patricia Limerick has testified to the "stickiness" of the frontier myth. At times, the entirety of America feels like *Westworld*, Michael Crichton's 1973 movie about a theme park where android cowboys go crazy and start killing everyone in sight.

In America, for the last decade or so, this technological dystopia seems about right: viral android cowboys took over the government and started shooting everyone in sight. What I hope to provide in this short essay, via a quick trot through the Cold War films of John Ford, whose works provided at least the definitive preamble to the contemporary discursive iconography of the Western, is a few working hypotheses as to why this may be so, and how nimbly the Western continues to adapt to changing social and political circumstances.

In *Gunfighter Nation*, the critic Richard Slotkin argued that, hard upon the heels of the explosive gritty realist cinema of Sam Peckinpah's *The Wild Bunch* (1969) and Peckinpah-inspired Westerns, and following a spate of "revisionist" Westerns in the early 1970s—*Soldier Blue* (Nelson, 1970), *Little Big Man* (Penn, 1970), *Billy Jack* (Laughlin, 1971)—the mythic Western cinema had largely exhausted itself, as the public fallout from the Vietnam war made the structural sincerity of the genre increasingly unpalatable. Elements and features of the Western might thereafter be nostalgically invoked, particularly by such space operas as *Star Wars* (and indeed, the science fiction blockbusters of the 1980s had the same dominant cultural authority and did similar ideological work to the Western of the 1950s); by realist urban thrillers about masculinity in crisis, as with *Fort Apache: The Bronx* (Petrie, 1981), which envisioned urban America as over-run by new ethnic savages with whom the established authorities were no longer equipped or morally authorized to deal; or by such in tongue-in-cheek adventure thrillers as *Raiders of the Lost Ark* (Spielberg, 1981). In various ways, each of these films determinedly dramatizes the decade's deep anxiety about the status and future of white male power.

Alternatively, Western elements were lampooned and recycled in camp subculture: Wayne's hysterical political over-reaching had already made him a self-parody by the mid–1960s, and when members of the disco singing group The Village People dressed up in the role of a cowboy and an Indian (as well as a soldier, a police officer, a construction worker and a biker), the solid masculine authority certified and entrenched by the Western was rendered little more than farcical. This is why, as my student Regi Khokher has pointed out to me, Sylvester Stallone's Rambo films—*First Blood* (Kotcheff, 1982); *Rambo: First Blood Part II* (Cosmatos, 1985); *Rambo III* (MacDonald, 1988)—and anything starring Arnold Schwarzenegger—from *Conan the Barbarian* (Millius, 1982) to *Total Recall* (Verhoeven, 1990)—look and feel like gay porn: they are. During the late 70s, at the same time traditional forms of white masculine authority were perceived to be in crisis, working class gay subculture went upscale and mainstream, stylistically coming to dominate American culture.

But, once again, reports of the Western's death seem to have been greatly exaggerated; as my examples above amply demonstrate, in globalized, post–Cold War, post-camp popular culture, western iconography thrives.

Why?

There are two potential and related—if partial—explanations that I would like to consider in what follows. The first is that what seems to be a fairly limited mythic repertoire of the Western—its available stock of imagery, iconography, tropes and narratives—turn out to be largely inexhaustible, *pace* Slotkin. Indeed, it is the elegant simplicity and the historical reductionism of the Western that allows its features to be pillaged and re-deployed under different and newly pressing social circumstances. As archetypal critics like to point out, the story of the exemplary individual whose mettle and fortitude are to be tested in (and by) a hostile and alien landscape is at least as old as Homer. In the U.S., the myth of the frontier offered a rough historical backdrop that helped the Western to contribute to a national myth—a set of stories that enabled a polyglot nation to reiterate through communal forms of retelling a plastic narrative of origin, collective identity, and destiny, a nostalgic but energizing tale that could be reworked as needed: Owen Wister's 1902 novel, *The Virginian*, as Jane Tompkins has argued, provided the template for male flight, solitude, and re-invigoration, contesting the perceived emasculating effects of a "feminization" of American culture at the turn of the century. By her reading, a threatened patriarchy has to prove itself worthy of patriarchal rights via a usually violent demonstration of male competence before seceding, yet again, social control to woman-dominated institutions—and this gels happily, if not always comfortably, with the leanings of American libertarianism, which is ever-challenged to make a separate peace with collective values. That tension, between the individual and the collective (family, clan, nation) is always at the agonistic heart of the Western, and can only be resolved when men are tested and found-worthy: you only have the right to lay down your arms when you have proven you know how to use them.

Clearly, this theme could be—and was—rescored by such film-makers as Ford and Howard Hawks during the "crisis of masculinity" that historians have documented during the early years of the Cold War, as returning soldiers found their masculine autonomy and homo-social privilege sequestered and over-coded by the post-war corporatization of entrepreneurial capitalism and the feminine domesticity of suburban life. The Cold War Western, typically starring John Wayne, offered a fantasy of a threatened American masculinity redeemed in an all-male world of privilege and action and honor—an ideological conceit that survived, as I have argued elsewhere, until 1963, when it was exposed as hollow by such films as Ford's *The Man Who Shot Liberty Valence*, where the male competence underwriting social power is acknowledged to be entirely a sham.

I am painting this American cultural history in fairly broad strokes, but so far, and however much you may want to quibble with the details, most of this should be familiar to students of the genre. Let me make two more, possibly more contentious or provocative assertions. During the "postmodern" 1980s, I'll venture, it was precisely the lampoonish fraudulence of the Reaganesque reinvigoration of the Western mythos that was key to its success.

Reagan proved to by an effective leader not in spite of the fact that, as a cowboy-hero, he was a fool and a fraud and a poseur but precisely *because* of the hollowness of his imposture. The Reagan presidency had the sheen and production values of gay pornography as well. It was pure camp, pure postmodernism, pure Mickey Mouse, and never pretended to be anything but: this is precisely why he was so beloved. Not because he was the John Wayne hero of our dreams, but because he fell so patently short, because he was a child playing dress-up. It wasn't nostalgia we Americans wanted at the time; it was camp, pretense, or postmodern irony. We—and the whole world—loved the pure sham, the pure ham of the Reagan era.

And today? Contemporary re-fabrications and cultural re-enactments of the Western place a decidedly distinct affect into popular circulation. It is no longer a question of male competence and virility, nor even (certainly) of recapturing masculine authenticity (not to mention authentic masculinity) but simply of mobilizing the re-assuring semblance of male *sincerity*. Critics have spoken of the "new sincerity" in American poetry (Reb Livingston, Joseph Massey, Andrew Mister, and Anthony Robinson), fiction (David Foster Wallace, Colson Whitehead, Junot Diaz), film, popular music and culture in general (radio host Jesse Thorn, in his *New Sincerity Manifesto*, cites the high camp icon Evel Knievel as an exemplar) over the last decade or so. Sincerity, no doubt, is a tricky concept to pin down, but as Ernst van Alphen and Mieke Bal, editors of the excellent anthology *The Rhetoric of Sincerity* (2009), point out, it "traditionally ... concerns a natural enactment of authenticity anchored in and yielding, truth" (1). In the genealogy they derive, Bal and van Alphen demonstrate how sincerity emerged in the sixteenth century, emerging from religious conflicts and alongside modern forms of theater (*Hamlet* is the prime example) that dramatized the difficulty of lining up semblance with motivation, and "that now as then, religious and cultural conflicts take place at the same time that representational idioms and media undergo major transformations" (2). Today, then, they propose to treat sincerity as a "media effect instead of a subjectivity effect" (5) and consider how it is performed and circulated affectively and publicly.

And, for me, this is why John Ford remains intriguing and compelling. My own reading of his work would be that, fundamentally, his movies are predominantly expressive of male sincerity, rather than competence (it is this trait, for example, that effectively distinguishes his work from that of Hawks, the other cinematic paragon of the Cold War Western); typically, the dramatic structure of Ford's films pits a sincere but incompetent man in a struggle for power and patriarchal rights against a competent but cynical (or even criminal) outsider. The drama is resolved when, in a moment of crisis or urgency, cynicism cedes to sincerity, and/or the "sincere" man is duly blessed with a sort of miraculous competence. The redemption of the criminal/cynic/outlaw is a standard and highly clichéd trope of every buddy film, no doubt, from *Casablanca* (Kurtiz, 1942) to *Amos and Andrew* (Frye, 1993).

But clues are to be found everywhere in Ford's work: it is sincerity rather than a capacity for violence or competence that redeems Ransom Stoddard (Jimmy Stewart) at the conclusion of *Liberty Valence*; it is sincerity that was personified in the public persona of the cowboy star, Will Rogers, one of Ford's early leading men, with whom he made three films (none of them, significantly, Westerns). It is sincerity rather than principled abolitionism that motivates Abraham Lincoln's (Henry Fonda) public career as a lawyer in *Young Mr. Lincoln*. It is sincerity that transforms villains into good guys in so many of Ford's films, from the early silent *Three Bad Men* (1926) through to *Stagecoach* (1939) and even in what most critics agree to be his most accomplished film, *The Searchers* (1956), in which Ethan Edwards (John Wayne) reforms himself and emerges transformed from an unspecified criminal past.

Further, according to Ford's vision, the frontier becomes the setting and crucible from which this dialectic of competence and sincerity—the ur-drama of nearly all American public performances of masculinity—emerges. We have Ford's testimony itself as verification, as transcribed in a piece by Bill Libby, titled "The Old Wrangler Rides Again" and published in *Cosmopolitan* in 1964, a veritable list of clichés chock full of "don't give a good god-damn" spiritedness and honest old-fashioned down-to-earth horse-sense. "What were the men of the West really like?" asks Libby.

> The men of the West were like Will Rogers. They were rugged and imperfect men, but many were basically gentle, and most were basically moral and religious, like most people who live with the land.
> They had their own language, but it was not profane. They had a warm rugged natural good humor. Strong people have always been able to laugh at their own hardships and discomforts. Soldiers do it in wartime. The old cowboy did in the Old West. And today, in the hinterlands, in places like Montana and Wyoming, there are working cowboys and they even carry guns, usually .30–30 Winchesters, though for protection against animals, such as coyotes, not to shoot each other [282].

Sincerity, we might say, is for Ford the proper and only ethical mode for a post-ideological, post-political age. Rogers quipped famously that he did not belong to any organized political party; he was a Democrat. Ford too, as he constantly asserted, was more a Democrat than an ideologue, which is why, apart from a sorely tested and sentimental populism, critics have searched in vain for a coherent or consistent political vision in his work. In Ford's own most famous statement—"the most famous understatement in Hollywood history," according to Gaylyn Studlar and Matthew Bernstein— "My name's John Ford. I make westerns," he disarmingly signals an abandonment of Popular Front politics—and, by extension, political posturing—in the name of a homespun horse-sense that trumped ideology. Ford made this comment in 1950, at a Director's Guild meeting during which, according to Studlar and Bernstein, "director Cecil B. DeMille led a right-wing faction in accusing guild president Joseph L. Mankiewicz of being a Communist" (1). Demanding that DeMille and his faction resign and that Mankiewicz be confirmed, so that they "all could go home and get some sleep" (qtd. in Studlar and Bernstein 2), Ford made his political point in a pointedly calculated apolitical way: "We've got some pictures to make tomorrow" (qtd. in Studlar and Bernstein 2). An adulatory profile by Frank S. Nugent that appeared in *The Saturday Evening Post* in 1949 labeled Ford "Hollywood's Favorite Rebel," "rebel" being, in the Cold War discourse of the time, the valorized term for a non-conformist energetic masculinity stripped of any political orientation. For Ford, as the great films he made over the next decade and a half testify, the Western came to occupy the space that opened up in the evaporation, as Daniel Bell termed it in his 1960 book, of ideology. Once again, the frontier functions as a psychic and cinematic refuge from a cloying civilization, where even the director John Ford could go to test and prove himself. That "sincerity" is the most paper-thin of Hollywood sentiments, that his films are infinitely more subtle, complex, and paradoxical than the stereotypes Ford invokes in the Libby interview quoted above, is beside the point, as is the fact that, as Charles J. Maland has documented, John Ford's avuncular, down-to-earth, natural and unaffected American male was entirely impostured, a persona he came to inhabit after many years of playing the aesthete, many years of playing the temperamental working class Irish immigrant: it offered the feel and fabric of righteousness with few of the ethical or political risks. What is at sake is less a codified American set of values or proof of competence than the precise fabulation of character.

    Two brief closing examples from contemporary Westerns may serve to illustrate my point. In Gore Verbinski's recent comic animated Western *Rango*, the titular chameleon, depressed by his own inefficacy, returns to save the day and the old west town of Dirt not through his capacity for violence, but with love, good-humor, and the Heimlich maneuver. Another example of sincerity trumping violence can be witnessed at the very close of Clint Eastwood's 2008 "urban Western," *Gran Torino*, a meditation on aging, ethnic strife, class discontent, and urban violence in contemporary American life, as well as a meta-cinematic reflection on Eastwood's own long career as an actor and director. According to the conventions of the genre, which Eastwood's youthful performances largely helped to cement, virility and thus patriarchal rights are secured through public performances of competence; and competence, in turn, is measured and proven in (successful) acts of violence. Yet, as Drucilla Cornell has argued, the films Eastwood has directed (especially in more recent years) present an "ethical engagement that undoes the familiar story. A central aspect of this challenge is the undoing of our identifying the hero with fantasized phallic masculinity" (186).

> When, as an audience, we settle down before these films, we are comforted not only because we know what to expect, but also because the familiar images and symbols reinforce some of the greatest myths of the imagined "reality of America"—myths that so often now belie the brutal truth of an unjust class structure, racial oppression and, of course, the extra-ordinarily brutal wars of empire.
> The power of Eastwood's movies is that he works within these conventional genres but twists them in such a way that the imaginary of the audience is challenged rather than comforted [186].

At the conclusion of *Gran Torino*, we are offered a revision of the conventional gun fight that concludes every other Eastwood film. Male competence will no longer be performed as violence, but as self-surrender. In a vision that imagines a new multi-ethnic America rising from the slums of the rust-belt inner city, the hero, Walt Kowalski (Eastwood) faces the villains unarmed, and it is his act of martyrdom that renews and restructures a complex of American values, reinvigorated by contemporary Hmong immigrants, for the twenty-first century.

In a formula that I have always very much liked, the American philosopher and psychologist William James made the rather counter-intuitive claim that emotions are the consequence rather than the cause of physical expressions. That is, it is not a feeling of sadness that produces tears, but rather the physical act of crying that makes one sad. Perhaps this is what is being hoped for in the endlessly stylized performance of the Western affect of masculine sincerity.

WORKS CITED

Cornell, Drucilla. *Clint Eastwood and Issues of American Masculinity*. New York: Fordham, 2009.
Kitses, Jim, and Gregg Rickman, eds. *The Western Reader*. New York: Limelight, 1998.
Libby, Bill. "The Old Wrangler Rides Again." Studlar and Bernstein, 277–88.
Maland, Charles J. "From Aesthete to Pappy: The Evolution of John Ford's Public Reception." Studlar and Bernstein, 220–52.
Mitchell, Lee Clark. *Westerns: Making the Man in Fiction and Film*. Chicago: University of Chicago Press, 1996.
Rickman, Gregg. "The Western Under Erasure: *Dead Man*." Kitses and Rickman, 381–404.
Slotkin, Richard. *Gunfighter Nation: The Myth of the Frontier in Twentieth Century America*. New York: Atheneum, 1992.
Studlar, Gaylyn, and Matthew Bernstein. Introduction. Studlar and Bernstein, 1–20.
_____, and _____, eds. *John Ford Made Westerns*. Bloomington: Indiana University Press, 2001.
Tompkins, Jane. *West of Everything: The Inner Life of Westerns*. New York: Oxford University Press, 1993.
Van Alphen, Ernst, and Mieke Bal. Introduction. Van Alphen and Bal, 1–16.
_____, and _____. *The Rhetoric of Sincerity*. Stanford: Stanford University Press, 2009.

"It was justified"
Visceral Violence in the New Television Western—Deadwood, Hell on Wheels, *and* Justified

Patrick Condliffe

> Profanity purges language of meaning, and this is why it's necessary.—David Milch[1]

> If horror cinema can be a machine of good, sacrificial violence, then "torture porn" represented that machine breaking down. And it seems these new Westerns are breaking down in the same way.—Jason Archbold[2]

> To raze the English language—down to the ground, down to the harsh syllables of profanity—is to break free.—David Milch[3]

The Western as a genre is representative of something broader than a romanticized notion of American frontiers of and around the period of the United States Civil War: it is not the temporal location that is so fascinating, but instead the broader narratives of frontiers and civilization. People in civilized places act and behave in far different manners than those in places that are in the process of being civilized. The viewing of Westerns has developed into a ritual: it reacquaints the audience with the Myth of the Frontier, while dissipating our personal need to enact violence. Westerns have been characterized as a means of justifying and representing American exceptionalism, most famously by Richard Slotkin in *Gunfighter Nation*, who saw the rise of the Western as the bedrock for interventionist policies in Vietnam, its predecessors, and beyond. Slotkin characterizes this well in the assertion that "violence is central to both the historical development of the Frontier and its

Newspaper advertisement for *Deadwood*. An HBO Series for Television, 2004.

mythic representation. The Anglo-American colonies grew by displacing Amerindian societies and enslaving Africans to advance the fortunes of White colonists" (Slotkin 11). And this is a point that will be revisited in my discussion of the dual depictions of race and violence in *Hell on Wheels*. Sergio Leone, in the revivalist period of Spaghetti Westerns, used his caricatured characters as a condemnation of such an argument; classic scenes such as the prisoner-of-war camp in *Il Buono, il Brutto, il Cattivo / The Good, the Bad and the Ugly* (1966) were stinging rebukes of the myth of the American frontier, rebukes that fed into the zeitgeist of young educated urban filmgoers who were disenchanted with such narrative excuses as had been propagated by Hollywood since its inception. The 1990s saw a lull in the American desire for the Western, and though this particular drought was punctuated by the clichéd and formulaic *Unforgiven* (1992), its four Oscars failed to revive the format in theatres. It is only in recent years that the Western has seen a successful resurgence with the likes of the Coen brothers' adaptation of *No Country for Old Men* (2007), *3:10 to Yuma* (Mangold, 2007), *Django Unchained* (Tarantino, 2012), and the chameleon that is *Rango* (Verbinski, 2011). *No Country for Old Men* and *Django Unchained* have both been heavily criticized for their violence, while their cable counterparts have largely escaped such critical lynch-mobs. What is forgotten in these critiques of contemporary Westerns is the mythical import of violence to the genre in the first instance. The Frontier is a lawless place at the outpost of civilization where external force, usually in the form of violence, is used as a form of regulating governance and this occurs regardless of depiction; be that depiction *Bonanza* and other traditional Westerns of the 1960s or variations such as *Buck Rogers* and *Star Trek*. The Frontier according to myth is a place constructed on a bedrock of violence and bloodletting and as such, contrary to Foucault, violence was justified as the most immediately effective form of population control and civilization.[4] What this essay seeks to examine is the place and representation of such violence in the New Television Western. I will argue that what has its origins in a founding American myth has diverged from its ritual purpose and, instead of acting as a form of catharsis, the violence and the visceral nature of its depiction has instead become destabilized and transitioned into self-fulfilling spectacle, a process that has most recently been critiqued in regard to post–9/11 horror.[5] At the heart of this argument is a shift away from the revisionist sparse violence of *Deadwood* and its disruptive use of language back towards the traditional myths of American exceptionalism and masculinity embodied by "standing one's ground" and extra-judicial killing, which characterize both *Hell on Wheels* and *Justified*; a pair of shows that have, albeit entertainingly, engaged in an "arms race" of violence and gore, while disregarding the recovery of catharsis that lay at the center of *Deadwood*'s corpulent heart.

"Them's fightin' words"

It is hard to envision profanity as something liberating, and it is initially difficult to realize it through the Greek Orthodox notion of catharsis, or regeneration through purgation, let alone to consider that the violence and emptiness of the affective utterance of something such as the roughhousing, whoring, bar-room-brawl consonance of "cocksucka" could serve the ritual release that violence should enact. But it does, and somewhat ironically, the perceived "lowbrow" format of the television serial has achieved this with the, equally ill-perceived, language of those who are and have been imagined to eke out, subserviently, a life and living on the fringes, and in the borderlands of the Frontier. Over three seasons *Deadwood* demonstrated the limits of language while redefining the Western as a genre. The ritual violence of the gunfight was usurped through what could be conceived as the antithesis of action for the genre—language. This not to say that *Deadwood* is without its moments of horrifying violence, as it has more than its fair share. But much of the powerful brutality of the town and its inhabitants is not only imbued through its judicious use of extra-judicial slaughter and beatings, but further, and more effectively so, through its use of profanity.[6] This is at odds with the traditions of the genre.

There is, I would argue, an inherent relationship between violence and profanity, one wherein the cathartic violence of the act can be replaced with the catharsis of the profanity. This is largely why the balance between language and obscenity was so successful and effective in HBO's *Deadwood*. The most universal experience of this can be found simply within the act of injuring oneself and then uttering, or shouting, a curse—be it "fuck," "cunt," or "damn"—the (violent) outburst functions as a release, a purging that helps relativize and process the pain. On a social level violence has long been tied to the notion of *catharsis*, which has its ideological roots in Aristotelian theatre, but is from a semantic standpoint most accurately anchored in the Greek Orthodox tradition. René Girard notes that "[i]t's a religious word. It really means 'the purge' as purification. In the Orthodox Church.... *Katharos* means purification. It's the word that expresses the positive effect of religion. The purge makes you pure. This is what religion is supposed to do, and it does it with sacrifice" (Girard and Doran 24). Society requires catharsis, to restrict violent urges within the larger populace. In this reckoning, the appropriate use of profanity serves to substitute for what Devin McKinney calls "strong" violence, thus enabling an audience to overcome their need to enact violence on another (McKinney 16). Girard sees this as being linked to man's awareness of the dangers of cyclical violence such as revenge.[7] And to counter this we need ritual where

> [r]itual sacrifices ... are multiple, endlessly repeated. All those aspects of the original act that had escaped man's control—the choice of time and place, the

selection of the victim—are now premeditated and fixed by custom. The ritual process aims at removing all element of chance and seeks to extract from the original violence some technique of cathartic appeasement. The diluted force of sacrificial ritual cannot be attributed to imperfections in its imitative technique. After all, the rite is designed to function during periods of relative calm, as we have seen, its role is not curative, but preventative [Girard 102].

The ritual of repeated violence is used to hold off society and its members from enacting more violence. This is not a new idea, and catharsis has been linked to violence in the films of Martin Scorsese and Francis Ford Coppola from the 1960s and 1970s, when discussions surrounding the level of violence in cinema, as part of a continuing cycle of discussion about the subject, reared up among critics, academics, film-makers, and the public. I would suggest that there is a link between this and the more affective examinations of violence in the media that are the focus of study today, and that, furthermore, the discussions of visceral reactions to the spectacle on the screen—be it the mega-screen of the contemporary multiplex or the cable-ready flat-screen now colonizing many living rooms—serve to remind audiences of the effect and ritual importance of iterable, non-damaging violence. McKinney characterizes violence as falling into two broad categories, the "strong" and the "weak." "Strong" violence serves to function as a form of release, it is unsettling, unpleasant, and often traumatic to experience—McKinney begins his discussion with reference to his physical illness in the aftermath of watching *Taxi Driver* as a young adolescent—and orients this effect in the reactions of the audience where "strong" violence "leaves an audience feeling dead inside, yet, somehow, more alive than it was two hours before" (McKinney 17, 19). This is the catharsis of ritual that is the focus of Girard's work. And the important parallel between McKinney and Girard is the failure of the "weak" violence or over-iterated ritual to allow for catharsis or release. Only with "strong" violence does the watching present us with suitable substitutes, and as long as the "violence is *committed*—as most movie violence is not—because it demands commitments of those who are living" (17), the unpleasant experience of the viewing, however harrowing, functions as purge, release, and transference. The violence when it occurs, as it does sporadically, in *Deadwood* functions as this form of "strong" violence; and so too does the use of profanity.

The opening scenes of *Deadwood* are cumulatively unsettling: in the pilot episode (1:1) the protagonist, Seth Bullock (Timothy Olyphant), strings up and hangs a man before he can be attacked, beaten, and lynched by a mob of drunken workers led by their incensed and equally inebriated employer. The condemned man passes a letter to Bullock to give to the man's sister, and then Bullock hangs him from the veranda of the sheriff's office, pulling on his legs to ensure that the alleged horse rustler's neck is broken before then departing the town in a wagon with Sol Star (John Hawkes), who has been holding off the mob with the threat of a shotgun. The violence of the scene is disturbing, not in its explicitness—there is no bloodshed—but in the matter-of-fact manner in which it all unfolds. Here, not death, but rather the collapse of law and order that is mob rule is the threat. The hanging of the rustler, therefore, maintains the rule of law, the "strong" violence ensures that there is an emotional and social burden raised through the sacrifice. There are two other instances of this from the first and second season that I wish to explore in the sense of "strong" violence before illustrating how that translates to what I will call, to borrow from and bastardize profanely Rudolph Otto, "The cocksucka of things." Otto saw that in language there was a word to encapsulate wonder and release, and that in certain situations we must express our cosmic wonder such

> that in whose presence we must exclaim "aaah!" and one cannot illustrate the numinous character of this "aaah" by any better analogy than that of the lightning here given. The unexpectedness and suddenness of the lightning-flash, its dreadful weirdness, its overpoweringness and dazzling splendour, the fright and the delight of it, give it an almost numinous impressiveness, and indeed often do produce an actual numinous impression on the mind [Otto 191–2].

My use of this phrase, then, tries to identify the usurping (and inverting) of the universal transcendence of the "aaah" he posited in *The Idea of the Holy* (Otto), so that instead of an exclamation of wonder and release, it is a purging and expunging of that which tries to compel us to violence.

Following the lynching in the opening scene, Al Swearengen (Ian McShane), the proprietor of the Gem Saloon, which functions as the town's primary bar and brothel, is interrupted from enjoying his drink by the sound of screaming heard out-of-shot, and proclaims to his offsider, "That's her Derringer.... I warned you about that loopy cunt!" In the next scene Trixie (Paula Malcomson) is shown cowering and bloodied in a corner while Doc Cochran (Brad Dourif) tends to the victim, who is still alive, despite having been shot horizontally through the forehead. Viscerally, Cochran takes a metal probe and pokes it through the wound, much to the dismay of Swearengen's henchmen. The prospector had been beating her, and her response, in self-defense, is to shoot him with her concealed weapon. The lingering death—which Cochran tells us has taken "20 minutes"—and the shaken figure of the beaten and traumatized whore serve to emphasize the gravitas of what has occurred. The actual violence, the act and image of shooting is, in fact, not shown, merely its aftermath. The lobotomized and babbling, near-dead man, coming to terms with his final moments, and Trixie, witnessing these final moments as the agent responsible, are both images that serve to locate the audience as party to the executioner, for whom the victim is sacrificed. The violent act of the sacrifice is, however, replaced by Swearengen's use of obscenity immediately following the diegetic sound of the shot. The misogynistic utterance of "that loopy cunt" in fact replaces the violent image; preceded by the adjective loopy, "cunt" affects a dual purpose, becoming the "cocksucka of things" and channeling Swearengen's rage, and also, simultaneously, replacing the "strong" violence of witnessing the actual murder itself.

Contrastingly, "Suffer the Little Children" (1:08) concludes with Cy Tolliver (Powers Booth), owner of the Gem's competition—The Bella Union—brutally beating a pair of siblings, the superficially innocent Miles (Greg Snipes) and Flora Anderson (Kristen Bell), while cursing incessantly. In this uncomfortable scene the beating is protracted and visceral, the frame rate is slowed and it is shot out of focus to emphasize Flora's dazed and brain-damaged state; her face is heavily bloodied and swollen, and it is only at this point that the beating begins. Cy hits her repeatedly in the head and face before turning to her brother Miles. After ordering Joanie Stubbs (Kim Dickens), his madam, to stand "on [his] sinister side [left]" Cy then begins the following monologue as he beats the young teenage boy:

> Are you awake, Miles? Don't be fucking passing out, youngster. The next fucking breath you draw the smell of fucking sulfur is liable to be strong in your nose. Where's your fucking nose anyway? Fuck it, Miles. [strikes him] You are now found guilty of being a cunt. I'm hereby passing judgment. If you let this little bitch push you around and tell you what to do when you're supposed to be a man and show her the fucking ropes … [strikes him] Hear me, Miles? Instead of being the cunt you are now, before you could have been a man, done your fucking part, you little shit [shoots him].

This again is "strong" violence promoting a cathartic response, but it is contrasted with "weak" violence in the form of Cy's obscene monologue. Arguably, he attempts to emasculate the boy by calling him a "cunt"—a term usually used to refer to both the whores of Deadwood and the singular orifice which makes their pimp's income—but this utterance lacks the violence of, say, Swearengen's earlier ejaculation over Trixie. Instead, this scene is reflective of what McKinney terms a "sterile contradiction: it reduces bloodshed to its barest components, then inflates them with hot, stylized air" (McKinney 19). There is no violence to Tolliver's speech; it is merely exsufflicate and blown air punctuating the syntax of his strikes.

The characterization of Bullock as the stereotypical silent hero is best demonstrated in *Deadwood*. In this scene Bullock and Star are negotiating with Swearengen, when in response to one of his inciting questions concerning his earlier shooting of a "road agent" with Wild Bill Hickok (Keith Carradine) the following exchange occurs:

> BULLOCK: [To Star] What business of that is his?
> SWEARENGEN: You mean what business of mine is that.
> BULLOCK: [Furious] Don't tell me what the fuck I mean!

In correcting, grammatically, Bullock's statements Swearengen teases out "his barely constrained propensity for violence even when it sabotages his interests" (Jacobs 12). And, furthermore, it is this barely constrained violence that comes through as "strong" violence in the preposition "fuck." The profanity punctuates the sentence and stands in demonstrable contrast to Bullock's usual reticence with words, and unlike Tolliver and Swearengen, a reliance on profanity in only the direst of situations. In fact, Bullock is very much the Western cliché of the series, in a manner that *Deadwood* usually eschews. He is the typical Western hero; he distrusts language and prefers to save his words, lest they lose meaning. Jane Tompkins in *West of Everything* argues that "the men who are the Western's heroes don't have the large vocabularies an expensive education can buy." And that because of this,

> Westerns distrust language in part because language tends to be wielded most skilfully by people who possess a certain kind of power: class privilege, political clout, financial strength.... In order to exist, the Western has to use words or visual images, but these images are precisely what it fears. As a medium, the Western has to pretend that it doesn't exist at all, its words and pictures, just a window on the truth, not really there [Tompkins 49].

Silence is then the hero's natural mode, his side arm his preferred mode of communication when brooding silence is incapable. But unlike the extreme caricature by Leone of *Man with No Name* (Clint Eastwood), from his Spaghetti Westerns, Bullock can resort to speech if it will avert violence, albeit at the cost of unmasking him as a man who relies on violence and has the ready sense of violence that all people do if the ritual of catharsis is broken. This "fuck," then, is exemplary of the "cocksucka of things," as it is the violent reaction to a slight that takes the place of violence, while fulfilling the audience's need for catharsis.

There is a correlation, then, in this use of profanity by Bullock and the famous use of it to communicate by Mr. Wu. Mr. Wu (Keone Young) is the unofficial head of the Chinese immigrant community in Deadwood, the "Celestials"; he has two businesses that he runs for Swearengen behind his front of running a butchery: the first is disposing of the bodies that have expired at the Gem—through means both fair and foul; the second is the sale of opium to Swearengen for both the drug trade amongst the miners but also for his whores. In "Mister Wu" (1:10), Swearengen and Wu have their first onscreen dialogue of any substance. It is incredibly telling, not only of the power of language, but of how it positions Mr. Wu's most useful word. Rather than entering the Gem through the back door, normally reserved for Asians and African Americans, Wu storms up the stairs, into Swearengen's office, then produces a sheet of parchment and charcoal from inside his jacket. He then begins to draw, and speaking in Cantonese, which Swearengen cannot understand, the following dialogue occurs:

MR. WU: Bok Gwai Lo ... cocksucka!
SWEARENGEN: Yeah, glad I taught you that fuckin' word. These are whites, huh?
MR. WU: White cocksucka! [shows empty bag]
SWEARENGEN: Two white cocksuckers killed him and stole the dope that he was bringing to you.
MR. WU: White cocksucka! You, Swedgin.
SWEARENGEN: [suddenly enraged] The dope that you were gonna fuckin' sell to me?
MR. WU: White cocksucka.
SWEARENGEN: These two white cocksuckers? Who the fuck did it?
MR. WU: Wu?
SWEARENGEN: "Who," you ignorant fuckin' chink!
MR. WU: Wu!
SWEARENGEN: Who? Who? Who stole the fucking dope?
MR. WU: Cocksucka!

"Cocksucka," here, functions in two ways; it is a noun and also a cathartic release. And it is from this scene that I draw the notion of "cocksucka of things." Otto's conception of the "aaah of things" is based upon that which cannot be explicated, what seems to be the work of the divine and strips us of our ability to communicate except in the most rudimentary form.[8] It is the inverse which we might term the "cocksucka of things," rather than having what could be termed the superlatives of that which we find of no value, those things which are entirely antithetical to any sense of what we might want to possess or experience. What comes through most consistently about Wu's use of the word is both the sense of anger and profundity with which it is used. Milch, talking about his use of vocabulary and reliance upon the term in a later episode from Season 2, states his belief that "at a very fundamental level ... words are electrical," and that furthermore,

> the generation of words is an expression of electrical energy. The reason storytelling engages us perhaps more fully than other kinds of communication is because the words in a story can mean in different ways. They contain their opposites. In that scene—"Swearengen!" "Cocksucker!"—we understand how provisional the meaning of a word is and that its fundamental meaning is contingent upon the energy with which it's endowed by the speaker [Singer].

Words, such as Wu's "cocksucka," in this manner reflect not only the flexibility of English and language as a whole, but also the ideal mode of expressing energy, so that when it is invested with negative energy the desire for release is discernible as is its vehemence. Ergo, the responder can feel it, can understand it, and appreciates both aspects of the utterance at the same time. What is unique amongst the new television Westerns is that in *Deadwood* the violence functions successfully as catharsis, but interestingly and, I would argue, uniquely, so too can "strong" profanity.

Hell on Screen

AMC's *Hell on Wheels* is not inundated with violence, but it has a visceral nature that is not really seen in *Deadwood*. This show is set in the mobile series of camps that followed—in an itinerant manner—the construction of the Trans-Pacific Railway by the Union Pacific Railroad Company. In many ways it is a traditional Western: its main protagonist, Cullen Bohannon (Anson Mount) is silent and brooding, a "man who knows Indians" and who fears language; the Cheyenne are presented, largely in the stereotypical mode of the traditional Western—full of savagery and violence and noble ignorance about technological progress. Men are silent and women talk, and men come to the Frontier for profit or for escape. It is redemptive in how it attempts to negotiate race and the boundary between cultures, but it ultimately fails and falls into caricature through its use of violence and gore.

The pilot begins (1:1) with a Union soldier making his way through Washington, D.C., to a church where, during confession, Bohannon guns him down while posing as a priest. This is presumably representative of the prologue statement that in "Washington, D.C., 1865, the war is over, Lincoln is dead; The nation is an open wound." We are positioned to see the opening scene of violence as emblematic of the divisions still visible in a post–Civil War America, as well as an act of vengeance and attempt at failed catharsis. Initially we know not why Bohannon guns the man down in a holy space, only that by stating that "we opened a door and let the devil in" he is marking himself as a villain, creating in the process the traditional dichotomy between villain and hero that so characterizes the genre. Additionally, in the process of locating himself as in league with the devil, the soldier absolves in the viewer's mind the ethical dilemmas that should be raised through such an act of violence. Instead, the victim is positioned as evil and beyond redemption, the hero must have his reasons, his vengeance must be justified. This is juxtaposed against the Cheyenne raid that takes place on the forward surveying camp of Robert (Robert Moloney) and Lilly Bell (Dominique McElligott). In this scene, Cheyenne sneak up on the camp, first shooting a surveyor through the chest with an arrow in stereotypical fashion and then beginning to slaughter and scalp all of the whites in the camp. Robert and Lilly escape into the woods, a lone warrior in pursuit. Robert is struck down by the "brave" who subsequently fires an arrow into Lilly, pinning her hand to her shoulder, and then, after a subsequent scuffle in which Robert is fatally wounded, Lilly attacks the warrior with the now-removed arrow, pinning him to the ground and inserting it upwards through his jaw and into his brain. The two striking pieces of violence are caught in close-up and then extreme close-up. The shocking pinning of the hand is the prelude to the

Fulcian gore of the Indian's subsequent impalement.[9] The former is used to justify the latter, the violence against women and the slaughtering of a husband is provocation for the audience's desire to agree to, and support, the harm enacted upon the Indian. I would argue that the Indian's body is actually the subject of the most traumatic and violent abuse in the series. It functions not as catharsis, but more as "weak" violence, a reiteration of the traditions of violence brought forward to the modern expectations of cable television, and the resurgence of the grindhouse aesthetic to a generation who can afford cable, and emblematic of Archbold's statement that I use as epigraph above.

Elam (Common) is probably the most interesting figure in the series. He is a liminal figure who crosses boundaries: on one level he is a foil to Bohannon, serving as a conscientious objector to much of his behavior; yet, as a freeman, released from slavery with the close of the war, Elam is in a difficult social position. He wants the opportunities to generate income beyond what he can earn as a laborer, albeit one in a managerial position, yet he does not want to forgo or break the link between himself and his African American colleagues and brothers. It is the characterization of Elam, and his descent into a world of questionable ethics and behaviors that should be so compelling and engaging, when it occurs in "Timshel" (1:9). Having tracked some Cheyenne, Bohannon, Elam, and some Marshalls are ambushed by them and have to fight for their lives. The fight sequence which opens the episode, after the closing expository "cliff-hanger" of the previous episode, begins as a typical Western sequence, the white men—with their superior firearms—versus the Indians—with their greater savagery—until it unfurls into a fierce melee between desperate men. Many are shot, stabbed, or hit with arrows; Elam drowns a man face-down in a puddle while Bohannon beats a Cheyenne to death with a deer antler. This last shot is mid-close-up, in the mode of Leone, framing part of Bohannon's face but situated so as not to reveal the supposedly crushed skull of his victim, merely the blood spatter across Bohannon's face. Subsequent to their victory, Elam and Bohannon, who are here uneasy allies, converse over the bounty available for Cheyenne scalps. Elam decides to do what Bohannon refuses to do, to take the scalps of their vanquished foes.

In a scene reminiscent of Tarantino's *Inglorious Basterds* (2009), Elam, framed in a mid-shot, genuflects and begins to remove the scalp of the first Cheyenne. The scalping itself is seen in a series of cut shots alternating between the mid of Elam and the close up of the scalping. We see the scalp removed over two shots, and then see Elam regard it questioningly after he has removed it. There is then a cut to Bohannon who shakes his head; he is the "man that knows Indians" and can locate his own act of brutality in a different moral sphere to that of Elam. The sequence is problematic for multiple reasons. Outside of the racial and cultural considerations raised by this scene—and the overarching themes of the series (which I will not digress into here)—there is the issue of how violence is depicted. The non-diegetic soundtrack is the song "Timshel" performed by Mumford & Sons; the lyrics to this song reinforce the notion of brotherhood with the refrain obviously binding the disparate band of men together: an African American, a former Confederate soldier, former Union soldiers, and a Christian Cheyenne who straddles the liminal space between both cultures. The message here being that violence unites these men and through this particular crucible of arrows and fire they will forge bonds. The word itself is Hebrew and, like much from the Talmud, among its contested definitions are "thou mayest rule" and "thou mayest triumph over sin." The episode is obviously attempting to achieve two things: to play on the cliché of war as a unifying force: and to present how engaging in violence is a slippery slope that is deeply corrupting. In this reading Elam is something of a *tabula rasa*: as a freeman he is new to the possibilities of sin and the ethics of behavior and given his travails as a slave his action of scalping is completely understandable as both a reaction to war and also as a desire for income, especially based on the high monetary value that has been placed on the scalps. The writers have, therefore, attempted to create a dichotomy between what they are trying to present as "good" violence, that is, the slaughtering of the Cheyenne at all costs by this brigade of brothers, and "bad" violence, the scalping of the dead and the desecration of bodies. Presumably the semantics of the episode's title are intended to be ironic in consideration of this.

However, if we contextualize this against the representation of violence in *Deadwood*'s "Suffer the Little Children" (1:8) we can begin to see the binary which McKinney introduces. The death of Flora and Miles, because of Jodie having to fire the shot that dispatches Flora, acts in the mode of McKinney's "strong" violence. In these deaths and this act there is an obligation placed upon Jodie, as the living. She must live so that Flora cannot, she must ensure that Cy has no more opportunities for such brutality, and ultimately, it informs her character arc as a caring brothel madam. This is the cathartic trade-off that the audience does not enjoy but understands, and functions in the manner of sacrifice that Girard postulates—the ritual sacrifice is made in effigy such that society need not make it in reality. In "Timshel" this catharsis does not occur, there is no responsibility, not in this scene. Any responsibility generated through the violence is negated through its portrayal and reliance on stereotypical tropes which emphasize the barbaric clichéd myth: the Indian and the morally corrupted black man are rendered inferior by the ethical superiority of the white man "who knows Indians." The repetition of this lacks catharsis and plays into myth, and supports myths, such as that the Frontier was born of blood and violence and that it is indelible in the American psyche, but necessary to allow America's ongoing success nationally and internationally, the very same argument that Slotkin critiques so well in *Gunfighter Nation*.

There is a moment in the first season of *Hell on Wheels* ("Immoral Mathematics," 1:02) when it seems that it is becoming self-aware of how it represents the Western as a genre as well as of the stereotypes upon which it relies for its narrative. Thomas Durant (Colm Meaney) rides in to the survey camp to try to find the surveyors' maps that Robert and Lilly were trying to save. The Union Pacific workers are in the process of placing the corpses of the surveyors onto a wagon and a journalist from the *Chicago Tribune* is photographing the massacre. Durant rides in and realizes the opportunity is ripe for a narrative. "But one body will not do," he states, before commanding, "put these bodies back where you found them. I want an unblinking look at the horror perpetrated here. More arrows, we need more arrows." At this point Durant scours the site and proceeds to collect arrows before stabbing them into the fallen corpses, much to the journalist's horror. Included in the sequence is another ubiquitous close-up shot of a weapon penetrating the body, not dissimilar to the first discussed above. The series is making, what seems to be, a Baudrillardian comment on the way fiction is mistaken for reality through the lens of the media. The framing and artistry applied to the image by Durant stands as the difference between reality and its representation. Yet, this in itself is deeply ironic, as the violence enacted on the corpse here and earlier by Elam attest to the fact that, in using "weak" violence which lacks the cathartic qualities which so imbue the interplay between violence and profanity in *Deadwood*, the series falls into the trap it seeks to avoid— the violence machine has derailed itself. *Hell on Wheels* takes a somewhat unique perspective on race in its treatment of the Cheyenne and former slaves and their roles in post–Civil War U.S. society, albeit one that has been criticized for its failure to include the Chinese workers who were essential to the railway's construction.[10] In it racial lines are somewhat blurred and more contested; Elam, for instance, becomes an unofficial sheriff and Durant's dogsbody. For all of this, though, its framing of the historic and mythical narrative becomes more subject to accuracy, which the reliance on "weak" violence instead subverts to continue the myths and stereotypes of how the West was won, or in this case industrialized on bloody rails.

Justifiable Violence?

Justified, broadcast on FX, is critically acclaimed and also immensely popular. It is loosely based on characters created by the late Elmore Leonard for a short story, "Fire in the Hole." The series' protagonist, Raylan Givens (Timothy Olyphant), is a U.S. Marshall in contemporary Kentucky. He is an anti-hero and much of the show's appeal resides in the fact that he is a walking anachronism; he wears a big white cowboy hat, is strong and silent, and has a penchant for shooting to kill when drawn upon. The show, as Justin Joyce notes, plays into many of the traditional stereotypes of the Western; Givens is even accused of having too much swagger, and the only change is that the traditional antagonists have become "skinheads" instead of rustlers and thieves, and "hillbillies" have usurped the Indians as the savages of the hills (Joyce). How *Justified* differs most prominently from the other series mentioned here is its return to the villain-of-the-week formula. Givens is a Marshall, and so, while there are overarching narratives throughout the four seasons, there is a cavalcade of fleeting episodic villains, who allow the protagonist to fit the traditional role of Western lawman. His fast-draw fixes the law where it is broken and also rectifies and allays any fears about the fallibility or failure of the law. Joyce suggests that "the popularity of the show demonstrates our continued dependence on this deeply cherished personal liberty, the right to stand our ground and kill an assailant; in short, our right to justifiably kill another" (179). Obviously, this has more recent cultural relevance with the trial of George Zimmerman and the death of Trayvon Martin and there is a small relation between these issues and *Justified*, not only because the show begins in Florida, the site of Martin's death at the hands of Zimmerman, but also because of Givens' reliance on the "stand your ground" law as an excuse for his continued search for justice by means of an empty holster. Joyce has made much of the connection between "stand your ground" and *Justified*, such that it would be redundant to go into it in any further detail here, but his assertion that *Justified*'s "tapestry, then, is inherently conservative, deeply continuous of the traditional triumphalist Western's glorification of individuals taking justice into their own hands" (180) provides a good point reference for my discussion of the ritual uses of violence and the potentialities of their collapse.

One of the core ideas in Girard's paradigm of Sacrifice is that it has to be iterable, yet meaningful. The interchange of sacrificial victims must not become devoid of value and degenerate because

> [a]s the ritualistic aspects of the festival dwindle it degenerates into a communal "letting off steam"—the very idea of the festival held dear by modern scholars. The gradual loss of ritualistic structure and the constantly increasing misunderstandings surrounding the festival seem to go hand in hand. The disintegration of myths and rituals, and indeed of religious thought in general, leads not to genuine demythologizing, but to the outbreak of a new sacrificial crisis [Girard 125].

I see an inherent breakdown between the causes for the "sacrificial crises" and the difference between McKinney's "strong" and "weak" forms of violence. What is central to McKinney's reading of "strong" violence is that "the audience is both acted upon and made to act by acknowledging its role in the fulfillment of a wish it barely knew it had: it is both victimizer and victim" (22). The semantic use of victim suggesting an affective experience of the act of violence, the audience wants to see the violence enacted—to suffer through it—but also to feel the catharsis of the representation of sacrifice as long as there is a responsibility in its final estimation.

Justified's allure, as Joyce has noted, lies in the regularity and predictability of the show's structure. It is heavily ritualized and reliant on the myths and stereotypes of the Western to a surprising degree. Although remarked on by Joyce, it is worth detailing the opening scenes of the pilot ("Fire in the Hole," 1:1). Givens, dressed in a suit with his trademark Stetson Beaver, approaches Thomas Buckley (Peter Greene)—a Miami gangster—on a hotel veranda; to situate this in the contemporary era the guests are dressed in bikinis and swimsuits and lounging by the pool (a modern-day saloon). Givens has given Buckley twenty-four hours to leave town or he "will shoot [him] on sight" (1:1). The camera work follows the traditional formula of the Western, switching back and forth between close-ups of Givens and Buckley before both men draw, Givens shooting the man twice before pausing and hitting him with a third shot. When approached by his superiors about the public shooting he argues that "he shot first." Givens is here marked as a "man that knows Indians," because as Slotkin argues,

> as the "man who knows Indians," the frontier hero stands between the opposed worlds of savagery and civilization, acting sometimes as a mediator or interpreter between races and cultures but more often as civilization's most effective instrument against Savagery—a man who knows how to think and fight like an Indian, to turn their own methods against them. In the "Indian-hater" whose suffering at savage hands has made him correspondingly savage, an avenger determined at all costs to "exterminate the brutes" [16].

Givens' anger is directed not at Indians, but gangsters, villains, hillbillies, and his father, and he wants to exterminate these brutes too. As figures beyond the law he is more than willing to cross the line to bring them to justice, as long as it comes in a metal casing and is justified. Most episodes, in fact, result in the death, mostly by firearm, of at least one character; because of this the show begins to suffer in a manner similar to that in which Miller suggests the genre as a whole has suffered, because "[t]he Western as a form seems incapable of coping with the social problems it is asked to resolve, and one of its central premises—that violence is legitimate in certain circumstances when all else fails—is gradually undone through its own excess" (Mitchell 188). Yet, in spite of this the show itself has received critical acclaim, with the second season garnering an Emmy for Margo Martindale who played Mags Bennett, a ruthless but seemingly caring matriarch of a family of hillbilly criminals. The season presents an interesting story arc, with two deaths that could possibly be figured as "strong" violence; yet, the third season, on which

I wish to focus here, takes a decidedly nastier, more violent turn towards "weak" violence. The season villain is Robert Quarles (Neal McDonough), a Chicago mobster who has been sent to Kentucky to set up an OxyContin racket. The season continues with the structure of an overarching villain complemented by an irregular bad guy of the week. The season finale, "Slaughterhouse" (3:13), has its climax in the combination piggery and barbecue restaurant owned by Ellstin Limehouse (Mykelti Williamson). In a tense standoff between Quarles, Givens, and Limehouse, one of Limehouse's associates walks in and shoots Quarles, causing a distraction that leads to Quarles having his arm cut off by Limehouse. The scene is bloody and visceral, and while it has an attempt at humor—when Quarles reaches for his arm Givens pulls it further away—it is devoid of pathos, responsibility, or ritual satisfaction as Quarles bleeds to death on the slaughterhouse floor. I would suggest that this scene has echoes of the notorious scene in *Reservoir Dogs* (1992) where Mr. Blonde (Michael Madsen) cuts off a policeman's ear. The slow dance and play with the severed limb is close to the implications of sadism where Mr. Blonde speaks into the ear "Hey, can you hear me, what's going on?" McKinney cites the scene from *Reservoir Dogs* as a perfect example of "weak" violence. The violence and death is there for the sake of violence and entertainment; there is no catharsis, and instead of the violence serving the story it is the reverse (McKinney 21). Not only does *Justified* have as its foundation serialized "weak" violence, it is also succumbs to violence that is meant to be a kick to a desensitized audience. This reversion to gore is not limited to the third season, but also appears in episodes from the fourth ("Kin," 4:5) and fifth ("Foot Chase," 4:6), which feature the vivid and gory depiction of a man's severed limb being used as a mechanism of torture. While I don't wish to wade into the political ramifications of Joyce's argument in the wake of the death of Trayvon Martin, I do believe it is plain to see a correlation between the use of weak violence in *Justified* and the necessity it places on crossing legal boundaries for the correct outcome, and Slotkin's characterization of American foreign policy as led by the Frontier Myth.

As I write my conclusion to this, America is in a tense standoff with Syria over chemical weapons and is proposing a military strike. How it will be resolved is yet to be seen, but there is a striking similarity between the rhetoric being used by President Obama, where the use of chemical weapons would be crossing "a red line…. That would change my calculus…. That would change my equation" (Barak Obama as quoted in Kessler), and Slotkin's argument about the Frontier Myth in American foreign policy and its place at the heart of American exceptionalism. The use of violence in the new television Western seems, then, to be playing a peculiar societal role. Where the violence in *Deadwood* was never "weak," that role being taken instead by "weak" utterance, both *Hell on Wheels* and *Justified* rely on "weak" violence to generate narrative. They do not provide catharsis and there is no purging. While *Hell on Wheels* does have its moments of catharsis (such as the Season 1 finale where the town preacher kills a Marshall to protect his son) it is largely devoid of any sense of responsibility or ritual purging, it only maintains the stereotypical ritual without investment. Furthermore, I would argue that *Justified*'s more recent seasons are reactionary to the stakes raised by *Hell on Wheels* and that the first season of the latter sparked a kind of "arms race," the end result of which mirrors the larger trend of disarming people about U.S. involvement in foreign conflict, much as Slotkin saw this at play in the Vietnam and Gulf wars. Arguably the post–9/11 litany of international conflicts seems to be desensitizing and tiring and is representative of a "sacrificial crisis." Perhaps, then, we require a return to the aesthetic of *Deadwood,* where Milch has argued that the use of profanity is, "as language is for all of us, the instrument of accommodating those contradictions and still functioning.... It is verbal meditation" (Milch 17). The fact that words and utterance can in fact replace violence and the violent act, can stand in lieu of our need to commit violence, is too readily forgotten. In this way violent language can be as "strong" as "strong" violence can be, allowing for the sacrifice to be made without spilling blood or emptying a six-shooter. That is, a mediation in response to life and away from violence, and so rather than the constant iteration and reiteration of "drawing" on an opponent, it might instead be better, functionally cathartic, to mediate and meditate for a moment and call them a "cocksucka" instead.

Notes

1. Milch, "And Mr. Wu: To the Celestial Is Given the Last Word," 213.
2. Spoken in an inspirational conversation in a dank Sydney saloon.
3. Milch, "The Language of Men: Lies, Profanity, and Greed, and How Words Can Lead Us to the Apprehension of Our Common Existence," 15.
4. Foucault argues that "[t]o govern ... is to structure the possible field of action of others. The relationship proper to power would not therefore be sought on the side of violence or of struggle, nor on that of voluntary linking (all of which can, at best, only be the instruments of power), but rather in the area of the singular mode of action, neither warlike nor juridical, which is government." And so in this estimation true power is wielded without force (Foucault 225).
5. See, for instance, *Post 9/11 Horror* (Wetmore Jr.) or *Horror after 9/11* (Briefel and Miller).
6. I use the term profanity over "cursing," "swearing," or "obscenity" because of the link between the term and the notion of disrupting the sacred. Furthermore, David Milch has stated that he intentionally chose modern vernacular for such profanity because, largely, the earlier, obscenity would have been profanity such as "goddamn," etc. (see Singer and Benz 256).
7. Girard writes, "Only violence can put an end to violence, and that is why self-propagating. Everyone wants to strike the last blow, and reprisal can thus follow reprisal without any true conclusion ever being reached" (26).

8. Eilidh St. John argues the characterization of this "is simple if not simplistic. It goes some something like this: 'The essence of the thing which elicits the "aaah" must logically be greater, more significant, more powerful, more sagacious, more valuable, than anything we know which does not elicit the "aaah." Let us, therefore, attribute to the "aaah of things" the superlatives of that which we do value'" (John 187).

9. Lucio Fulci, while not the first to stylize gore (that would be Buñuel in *Un Chien Andalou/An Andalusian Dog*), is probably most well remembered as the director of "gore pornos" such as *Zombi 2* (1979) and *L'aldilà/The Beyond* (1981) which were remarkable for their over-the-top use of, for the time, realistic gore. Most are unfamiliar with his early work *I Quattro dell'apocalisse/Four of the Apocalypse* (1975) which was arguably one of the best and most innovative Spaghetti Westerns.

10. http://www.washingtonpost.com/lifestyle/style/tv-column/2011/07/28/gIQA2FczfI_story.html.

Works Cited

L'aldilà/The Beyond. Dir. Lucio Fulci. Medusa Distribuzione, 1983.
Benz, Brad. "*Deadwood* and the English Language." *Great Plains Quarterly* 27.4 (2007): 239–51. Print.
Briefel, Aviva, and Sam J. Miller, eds. *Horror After 9/11: World of Fear, Cinema of Terror*. Austin: University of Texas Press, 2011. Print.
Il Bruno, Il Bruto, Il Cativo/The Good, the Bad, and the Ugly. Dir. Sergio Leone. United Artists, 1966.
de Moraes, Lisa. "AMC at a Loss for Words Over 'The Killing' and 'Hell on Wheels.'" *Washington Post* July 29, 2011, sec. Style: n. pag. Online. http://www.washingtonpost.com/lifestyle/style/tv-column/2011/07/28/gIQA2FczfI_story.html (accessed September 23, 2013).
"Deadwood." *Deadwood: The Complete Series*. Dir. Walter Hill. HBO Video, 2008.
Django Unchained. Dir. Quentin Tarantino. The Weinstein Company, 2012.
"Fire in the Hole." *Justified: The Complete First Season*. Dir. Michael Dinner. Sony Home Entertainment, 2011.
"Footchase." *Justified: The Complete 4th Season*. Dir. Peter Werner. Sony Home Entertainment, 2013.
Foucault, Michel. "The Subject and Power." *Beyond Structuralism and Hermeneutics*, 2d ed. Ed. Hubert L. Dreyfus and Paul Rabinow. Chicago: University of Chicago Press, 1982. Print.
Girard, René. *Violence and the Sacred*. Trans. Patrick Gregory. Baltimore: Johns Hopkins University Press, 1978. Print.
Girard, René, and Robert Doran. "Apocalyptic Thinking After 9/11: An Interview with René Girard." *SubStance* 37.115 (2008): 20–32. Print.
"Immoral Mathematics." *Hell on Wheels: The Complete First Season*. Dir. David Von Ancken. Entertainment One, 2012.
Inglorious Basterds. Dir. Quentin Tarantino. The Weinstein Company, 2009.
Jacobs, Jason. "Al Swearengen: Philosopher King." *Reading Deadwood: A Western to Swear By*. Ed. David Lavery. London: I.B. Tauris, 2006. Print.
Joyce, Justin A. "The Warp, Woof, and Weave of the Story's Tapestry Would Foster the Illusion of Further Progress: Justified and the Evolution of Western Violence." *Western American Literature* 47.2 (2012): 175–99. Print.
Kessler, Glenn. "President Obama and the 'Red Line' on Syria's Chemical Weapons." Blog, *Washington Post*, June 9, 2013. Print.

"Kin." *Justified: The Complete 4th Season.* Dir. Peter Werer. Sony Home Entertainment, 2013.
Leonard, Elmore. "Fire in the Hole." *Fire in the Hole: Stories,* reprint ed. Ed. Elmore Leonard. New York: William Morrow Paperbacks, 2012. Print.
McKinney, Devin. "Violence: The Strong and the Weak." *Film Quarterly* 46.4 (1993): 16–22. Print.
Milch, David. "And Mr. Wu: To the Celestial Is Given the Last Word." *Deadwood: Stories of the Black Hills.* Ed. David Milch. New York: Melcher Media, 2006. 207–13. Print.
_____. "The Language of Men: Lies, Profanity, and Greed, and How Words Can Lead Us to the Apprehension of Our Common Existence." *Deadwood: Stories of the Black Hills.* Ed. David Milch. New York: Melcher Media, 2006. 14–35. Print.
"Mister Wu." *Deadwood: The Complete Series* Dir. Dan Minahan. HBO Video, 2008.
Mitchell, Lee Clark. "Violence in the Film Western." *Violence and American Cinema.* Ed. J. David Slocum. London: Routledge, 2001. Print.
Mumford and Sons. "Timshel." *Sigh No More.* London: Island Records, 2009. Print.
No Country for Old Men. Dir. Joel Coen and Ethan Coen. Miramax Films, 2007.
Otto, Rudolph. *The Idea of the Holy: An Inquiry into the Non-Rational Factor in the Idea of the Divine and Its Relation to the Rational.* Trans. John W. Harvey. Oxford: Oxford University Press, 1950. Print.
"Pilot." *Hell on Wheels: The Complete First Season.* Dir. David Von Ancken. Entertainment One, 2012.
I Quattro Dell'apocalisse/Four of the Apocalypse. Dir. Lucio Fulci. Anchor Bay Entertainment, 1975.
Rango. Dir. Gore Verbinski. Paramount Pictures, 2011.
Reservoir Dogs. Dir. Quentin Tarantino. Miramax Films, 1992.
Saint John, Eilidh. "The Sacred and Sacrilege—Ethics Not Metaphysics." *Negotiating the Sacred: Blasphemy and Sacrilige in a Multicultural Society.* Ed. Elizabeth Burns Coleman and Kevin White. Canberra: Australian National University Press, 2006. Print.
Singer, Mark. "The Misfit." *New Yorker,* February 14, 2005, 19. Online. http://www.newyorker.com/archive/2005/02/14/050214fa_fact_singer (accessed December 8, 2013).
"Slaughterhouse." *Justified: The Complete Third Season.* Dir. Dean Parisot. Sony Home Entertainment, 2012.
Slotkin, Richard. *Gunfighter Nation: The Myth of the Frontier in 20th Century America.* Norman: Oklahoma University Press, 1998. Print.
"Suffer the Little Children." *Deadwood: The Complete Series.* Dir. Dan Minahan. HBO Video, 2008.
3:10 to Yuma. Dir. James Mangold. Lionsgate Films, 2007.
"Timshel." *Hell on Wheels: The Complete First Season.* Dir. John Shiban. Entertainment One, 2012.
Tompkins, Jane. *West of Everything: The Secret Life of Westerns.* Oxford: Oxford University Press, 1992. Print.
Unforgiven. Dir. Clint Eastwood. Warner Bros., 1992.
Wetmore, K. J., Jr. *Post 9/11 Horror in American Cinema.* New York: Continuum, 2012. Print.
Zombi 2/Zombie. Dir. Lucio Fulci. The Jerry Gross Organization, 1979.

Part II
New Westerns in Dialogue

"Fooling around with Papa's pistol"
Avenging Patriarchy in True Grit

Jenna Hunnef

Since its first appearance in print, Charles Portis's *True Grit* (1968) has experienced two cinematic reincarnations, first in Henry Hathaway's 1969 feature-length film of the same name, and then in Joel and Ethan Coen's 2010 interpretation. Over the last forty-five years, scholarship on the novel and its films has been conspicuously absent, and, where it does exist, is widely divergent in opinion. Many critics have fixated on generic debates in an attempt to locate the novel within a particular literary tradition. Most obviously, it is a Western, but the question remains as to whether it upholds those conventions or subverts them. Others have suggested that *True Grit* is a love story, a buddy comedy (Blount 315), an *entwicklungsroman* (Shuman 367), a revenge narrative (Cieply, Doherty), a feminist text (Maher, Keegan), or that it is a story about loyalty (McMurtry and Ossana), redemption (Scott Rudin qtd. in McMurtry and Ossana), or willpower (Tipton Cortner 57). The small body of scholarship and criticism on the *True Grit* franchise has tended to conceptualize it as a kind of "new" Western, both for how it appears to signal "the end of heroic individualism" (McLuhan 136), especially in John Wayne's iconic performance as Rooster Cogburn, and for its endorsement of what appears to be a feminist heroine. Contrary to these popular interpretations, I suggest that the "newness" with which the *True Grit* narrative appears to confront its audience (whether in 1968 or 2010) is not actually new at all; rather, it represents a new variation on an older theme: patriarchy, and its unlikely reestablishment by an adolescent girl, over whom that very system wields power and control, in a society apparently gone "soft."[1]

Set in Fort Smith, Arkansas, and the Indian Territory in 1878, Portis's

Poster for *True Grit*. An Amblin Entertainment release, directed by Joel and Ethan Coen, 2010.

novel is told from the first-person perspective of its protagonist, Mattie Ross, a sexagenarian woman who narrates the events of her fourteenth year when she travelled into the Choctaw Nation in the company of a U.S. Marshal and a Texas Ranger to exact blood revenge from her father's murderer. The events in the novel take place twelve years prior to what is arguably the first crucial decade in the history of anxious American masculinity, a period when rugged male individualism was supposedly still alive and well, but was beginning to show signs of wear and vulnerability. As such, Portis's *True Grit* emblematizes what many historians have identified as a massive shift in the ideology of the American heroic character that began just prior to the 1890s, the decade in which James Gilbert and others claim "the anguished beginnings of modern masculinity" have their origin (22).[2] Gilbert suggests that the 1890s' rapid increase in urbanization and the concomitant transformation of labor made it difficult for men to realize older ideologies of self-reliance, individualism, and "manliness" (16). The contemporary response to this shift is witnessed, for example, in the enthusiastic reception of Theodore Roosevelt's advocacy of "the strenuous life" and the popularity of his Rough Riders. Not incidentally, the "first" Western, Owen Wister's *The Virginian* (1902), was not only published in the wake of this shift, but was also dedicated to Roosevelt. It is significant that the intensification of this first palpable crisis in American masculinity coincides with the same decade during which Frederick Jackson Turner famously announced the closing of the frontier, and, by extension, the obsolescence of those rugged, individualistic heroes inspired by national fantasy. Gilbert identifies the 1950s as the period during which this gendered "crisis" reached its zenith; however, the intensity of both periods' crises of masculinity have since been equaled during two subsequent periods: the Vietnam War and the decade after 9/11.

The visual aesthetics and thematic concerns of each incarnation of *True Grit* attempt to navigate the chronological divide between the time of the narrative's setting and the time of material production in the present; moreover, each incarnation is reflective of what Stephen J. Ducat calls "anxious masculinity." In Ducat's terms, "anxious masculinity" is not simply "the fear of being feminized," but more fundamentally, "the fear of being feminine" (1, 5). In other words, the latent fear expressed in a variety of cultural media that American men are being feminized by external forces "is really an unconscious defense that is employed to keep out of mind something even more disturbing—an *identification* with women," or "the sense that they are not 'real' men" (1).[3] Appropriately, then, the characterization of men in Portis's novel and in its 1969 big-screen adaptation is a coded response to the failures of the ongoing conflict in Vietnam and the growth of the women's movement in the 1960s. Likewise, the 2010 film engages in a subdued conversation with the crises in masculinity brought about by the trauma of the terrorist attacks on the World Trade Center in New York on September 11, 2001. As both Ducat and Susan Faludi have observed, the events of 9/11 cast doubt upon American men's ability to defend the nation from harmful external forces.[4] However, despite the fact that the novel and each of its adaptations demonstrate the fluctuating nature of masculinity as a cultural category, their revisions nonetheless recapitulate a masculine hegemony according to their contemporary interests and needs.

Both of the films emerged during major American armed conflicts abroad, one aimed at containing the spread of communism, and the other motivated by the threat of terrorism. These movies emerged long after their respective conflicts began, but at crucial moments when civilian support and national morale were flagging. If, as Faludi suggests, both of these periods demonstrate "the suspicion that the nation and its men had gone 'soft'" (8), then it is no wonder that the male characters in the novel and its adaptations suffer from an emasculated characterization that is conventionally *un*characteristic of the story's frontier setting. However, despite the incongruous effect created by Mattie Ross's stern implacability and the unmanly ineptitude evinced by the story's male characters, the novel and its films are nonetheless designed to restore our confidence in the potent American male. Indeed, the perceived incapacity of the central male characters and their improbable triumph obfuscate the ambivalent, vicarious nature of modern masculinity in order to reassert male social dominance in light of present ills and threats. Notwithstanding what amounts to the sheer brokenness and mockery of the story's male protagonists—evident in Rooster Cogburn's age, visual impairment, and girth, and in LaBoeuf's Boy Scout–like characterization—these imperfect men nevertheless prove themselves "bully" shots and eternally capable of rescuing the vulnerable from danger and of decimating the bad guys.

Prior to its publication in book form by Simon & Schuster in late 1968, Portis's novel was condensed and serialized in three parts in the May 18, June 1, and June 15 issues of *The Saturday Evening Post*. Not only was the story serialized during the most devastating year for American casualties in Vietnam, but the two-week interim between the publication of the story's second and third installments witnessed the assassination of U.S. presidential candidate Robert F. Kennedy. Although many critics have suggested the novel signals the twilight of heroic individualism and the demythologization of the frontier (and thus the subversion of the Western's generic conventions),[5] *True Grit*'s appearance in *The Saturday Evening Post*—even in 1968, just months before the magazine's financial collapse—nevertheless reveals the tale's kinship with the fundamentally conservative ideologies to which the *Post* typically subscribed. Jan Cohn suggests that George Horace Lorimer, editor of the *Post* during its most influential period (1899–1936), actively set out to create and shape America in the pages of the magazine (5). Lorimer's vision of the twentieth-century United States combined "traditional values inherited from the nineteenth century," such as pragmatism, self-reliance, hard work, thrift, and a sense of civic responsibility, with "the culture of the emerging world of business" (8, 10). Mattie Ross just might be the kind of "representative American" Lorimer had in mind. Cohn insists, "Even those stories most innocent of 'intention' were partners in the job of constructing America for the *Post* audience; westerns, historical romances, sports fiction were all spun out of the collective web of a comprehensible society, a society built on fair play and individual initiative and common sense" (7). Although *True Grit* was not published under the leadership of George Lorimer, the ideals and values it espouses nonetheless reflect the magazine's ontogeny even as it gasped its dying breaths. *True Grit's* first appearance in the pages of *The Saturday Evening Post* during the waning days of that formerly powerful publication is, in fact, analogous to the triumph of masculinity-despite-infirmity described above. After all, *True Grit* may have seen its first publication in a failing medium, but it nonetheless went on to achieve commercial and critical success as a best-seller and then as a box-office hit, not merely once but twice.

The difficulty of categorizing this particular text originates in the eclipse of the novel by the long shadow of John Wayne, who starred in the role of Rooster Cogburn in Hathaway's 1969 production of *True Grit*. In fact, most critical discussions of *True Grit* are couched within larger monographs on Wayne's role and influence in American culture. Recent scholarship on Wayne's career attempts to recast it in a more ambivalent light. Jonathan Lethem suggests that Wayne's admirers and detractors alike have hidden behind his "brute Republicanism" as a way to avoid "the awful contradictions he represents." Wayne's biographers, Lethem complains, focus on the actor's personal life rather than his most resonant films in which, he maintains, "Wayne stands simply as the most persuasive and overwhelming embodiment of our ambivalence about American manhood. His persona gathers in one place ... all those things that reside unspoken at the center of our sense of what it means to be a man in America." Russell Meeuf echoes Lethem in his suggestion that Wayne's films of the 1950s "offered a sense of masculinity and individuality that was dark, ambivalent, and often contradictory" (63).

Perhaps surprisingly, these counter-readings of the ideological influence of Wayne's career are less applicable to his role in *True Grit* than to his most famous postwar roles. What is more, they have had little effect on the actor's popular reception. Prior to the release of the 2010 film, conservative columnist Lisa Fabrizio asked in *The American Spectator*, "Who in his right mind would dare remake *True Grit*?" and proceeded to characterize the heroes of classic Hollywood Westerns as "real men confronted by the complexity of western expansion." Fabrizio praises the Western genre for the connections it forges between Americans and "their predecessors who were brave, bold and free, and mostly contemptuous of government nonsense: men like Rooster Cogburn." In his homage to John Wayne in *The New American*, R. Cort Kirkwood gushes, "Many of [Wayne's] films aren't just good, they are masterpieces of moral storytelling that uplift heart and soul by imparting through historical fact and fiction, useful lessons about masculinity, love, loyalty, friendship, forgiveness, reconciliation, and courage" (38). Uncharacteristically, the Coen brothers' interpretation of Portis's novel subscribes to a parallel conservative philosophy and aesthetic. For a filmmaking duo known for its quirkiness and subversion of generic and cultural conventions (cf. *Fargo*, 1996; *No Country for Old Men*, 2007), their vision of *True Grit* is staunchly conservative. Kevin Maher comments, "[W]hat strikes you is not how radically different [the Coens' *True Grit*] is from past Western traditions, but just how strictly it obeys their conventions." In a similarly astonished tone, Roger Ebert praises the film "for what it is, a splendid western," and elaborates, "This is the first straight genre exercise in [the Coens'] career. It's a loving one." Echoing the prophetic diction of the Jeremiad tradition, Ebert adds, "The cinematography by Roger Deakins reminds us of the glory that was, and can still be, the Western."

Although *True Grit*'s characterization and dialogue are what generate the novel's lasting appeal, it is the opacity of those characters—their motivations, their doubts, their loyalties—and their precise, almost biblical diction that present readers with the greatest interpretive challenge. The inscrutability of Portis's characters combined with a deceptively simple plot have contributed the most to the mistaken impression that *True Grit* endorses a feminist hero. Are we to take Mattie's pedantry seriously, or is the joke on her—the blowhard in pigtails? Portis, in *True Grit* and elsewhere, keeps us guessing. In a 2001 interview for the *Arkansas Gazette* Project, Portis reflects on his employment in the 1950s as a legal correspondent and editor for the *Northwest Arkansas Times*. During his tenure there, he says, "I edited the country correspondence from these lady stringers in Goshen and Elkins.... My job was to edit out all the life and charm from these homely reports. Some fine old country expression, or a nice turn of phrase—out they went. We probably thought we were doing the readers a favor" (294–5). Ed Park speculates that Portis actively created Mattie Ross "as penance for these early deletions" (324). However, if Portis's other representations of older women can be levied as evidence, he expressed as much criticism of their eccentricities as he did respect and sentimentality for their "homely" ways. In the first chapter of Portis's third novel, *The Dog of the South* (1979), Ray Midge provides a caricature of his mother-in-law and the other elderly women of the town:

> On certain days of the week she and several hundred other biddies would meet at [the big shopping centers] and get their assignments, first having taken care to park their [cars] across the painted lines and thus taking up two parking spaces,

sometimes three. Then they would spread out over town. Some would go to the supermarkets and stall the checkout lines with purse-fumbling and check-writing. Others would wait for the noon rush at cafeterias and there bring the serving lines to a crawl with long deliberative stops at the pie station. The rest were on motor patrol and they would poke along on the inside lanes of busy streets and stop cold for left turns whenever they saw a good chance to stack up traffic [26–7].

Midge wryly casts these elderly women's maladroitness as evidence of malice aforethought; consequently, the analogical gap between these women's *gauche* behavior and Mattie's in *True Grit* is sufficiently narrow to call into question Park's hopeful speculation that Portis pays homage to an extinct generation of "biddies" in his most famous novel. Other evidence similarly refutes Park's speculation; for example, both *True Grit* and *The Dog of the South* contain evidence of a deep and abiding mistrust of women. In *True Grit*, Rooster Cogburn freely voices his doubts about women's fairness as employers, and expostulates to no one in particular, "There is no generosity in women. They want everything coming in and nothing going out.... A man will not work for a woman, not unless he has clabber for brains" (166–7). Whether or not Rooster is cognizant of the irony of this statement is unclear. Similarly, Ray Midge, the pathetic hero of *The Dog of the South*, attributes his and his male acquaintances' lack of vigor to the women in their lives, lamenting, "[We] had all contrived to get ourselves into the power of women and I could see no clear move for any one of us" (166).

In the same way that Portis has been likened favorably to certain notable literary antecedents, including Mark Twain and Geoffrey Chaucer, Mattie Ross has been likened to other literary and cinematic heroines, including Ree Dolly (*Winter's Bone*, 2010), Mindy Macready/Hit-Girl (*Kick-Ass*, 2010), the eponymous sixteen-year-old assassin of *Hanna* (2011), and Katniss Everdeen (*The Hunger Games*, 2012). Rebecca Keegan voices these connections in an article for the *Los Angeles Times* in which she lavishes praise on Hailee Steinfeld's portrayal of Mattie Ross in the Coen brothers' film and characterizes her as a "new kind of teen heroine":

> She's the product of a film industry in which young women are infiltrating traditionally male genres like action films; female directors and producers are wielding increasing creative influence, and the culture is moving from a sexed-up, dumbed-down model of female adolescence to one marked by smarts, strength and scrap.

Keegan's assessment of this "new" role for women and girls in popular culture is echoed in John Ditsky's 1973 assessment of *True Grit*, and more recently by Kerry Fine. Ditsky argues that the quality of "grit" embodied by Mattie Ross is not only what *True Grit* is all about, but that it is specific to a "type" of frontier woman, one who "adopt[s] certain masculine traits out of a need to survive" (19). Fine makes a similar statement, albeit in a different context, in her examination of two television series set in the western United States, *Sons of Anarchy* and *In Plain Sight*, both of which feature strong female leads amidst ensemble casts consisting mostly of men. Fine suggests that Western literature and film have traditionally depicted heroic power as inherently masculine, but that by creating female characters who wield this kind of heroic power, these television dramas call into question the masculine nature of heroism and redefine the parameters that delimit who is permitted to exercise that power (153). Fine bases her discussion on notions of frontier heroism, defined, she claims, by toughness and aggression, which are "characteristics of the heroic" (154). Fine further distinguishes "expressive" from "instrumental" aggression. Instrumental aggression, she says, "is the form of aggression most explicitly linked with the masculine," and notes that it is typically premeditated and purposeful—like Mattie's vengeful quest (155). The hitch in Fine's argument is her claim that Gemma Teller Morrow of *Sons of Anarchy* and federal Marshal Mary Shannon of *In Plain Sight* are "heroic" in this *masculine* sense and that this somehow makes them *feminist* characters. However, a woman who simply acts like a typically "heroic" man does not a feminist make, a point overlooked by Keegan, Ditsky, and Fine alike. In a video review of *True Grit* (2010) on FeministFrequency.com, Anita Sarkeesian articulates this particular trap of feminist thinking more eloquently, making specific reference to the popular and problematic identification of Mattie Ross as "feminist":

> [S]ince we live in a male-dominated, male-centered society, traits stereotypically identified as masculine are most valued and consequently more celebrated by Hollywood while traits stereotypically identified as feminine are undervalued and often denigrated. This may be one of the reasons why people are quick to adopt Mattie as a feminist character and other female pop culture characters who are considered strong and tough. The feminism I subscribe to and work for involves more than women and our fictional representations simply acting like men or unquestioningly replicating archetypal male values.... In *True Grit*, Mattie is certainly subverting expected gender roles by being witty and smart and competent and independent, yet she's not challenging the set of patriarchal archetypal male values ever-present in most mass media narratives—she's actually adopting them.

More pointedly, Mattie herself observes the conventions of her gender both when it is to her advantage and when she feels it is proper. She frequently uses her subject position as a legitimate means of hiding behind the safety of "law" in order to achieve her goals. When the stockbroker, Colonel Stonehill, refuses to buy back the ponies her father had purchased, Mattie vows to take it up with the law, threatening, "We will see if a widow and her three small children can get fair treatment in the courts of this city" (Portis, *True Grit* 32). Hathaway's film reproduces the scene in the novel where Mattie asks

Rooster to walk her back to the Monarch boardinghouse because it is dark and she does not know the way (60). When a drunken, belligerent Rooster refuses to accede to her demands, she says, "I got up and walked out thinking I would shame him into coming along and seeing that I got home all right but he did not follow" (63). Although Rooster's refusal to acquiesce to Mattie's demands in the novel may represent a moment of gender nonconformity, the concluding scene of the 1969 film nonetheless corrects his lack of gallantry in a manner that subtly invokes the famous conclusion of another Wayne film, John Ford's *The Searchers* (1956). Mattie requests Rooster as a chaperone once she is well enough to return home after her ordeal in the Winding Stair Mountains. This time, the Marshal gives her what she wants and returns her to the safety of her domestic circle. Notably, Rooster acquiesces to her request only *after* Mattie relinquishes her "grit" and bluster in recognition of her greater need to be rescued. Moreover, although she never marries (claiming, "I never had time to fool with it" [215]), and she certainly does not mince her words around men, Mattie nonetheless expects gendered etiquette to be observed by others, if not herself. At the end of the novel she snaps at Frank James, "Keep your seat, trash!" because he neither stands nor removes his hat in her presence (214). Finally, Mattie's attention to class (evident in her frequent use of the epithet "trash" to characterize those whom she deems low or improper) and her successful navigation of the new economic order of the early twentieth century (evident in her success as a businesswoman and as proprietor of a bank) support the capitalist socioeconomic system developed and controlled almost exclusively by white men in the U.S. Furthermore, Mattie's acquisition of wealth specifically by means of money-lending, a profession to which negative associations have frequently been attached throughout the history of Christianity, casts doubt upon the legitimacy of her success according to the Christian capitalist framework in which she attempts to conduct her business.

Also contributing to the popular notion that *True Grit* signals the emergence of a "new" kind of Western is the novel's depiction of worn and vulnerable masculinity, which upsets the stability of "traditional" gender norms in popular culture. This apparent destabilization reflects what Christina D. Weber identifies as the "shifting" forms of hegemonic masculinity that American soldiers returning from Vietnam were forced to confront when, suddenly, "[r]ituals and experiences such as participating in war and fighting for the country did not provide a clear path into manhood" (341). Appropriately, many of Portis' male characters demonstrate stereotypically "feminine" qualities: Rooster chatters incessantly and loves sweets and candy; LaBoeuf is vain about his appearance; Colonel Stonehill blames others for his woes, and his malarial complaint likens him to Mattie who is similarly ill with a head cold. These men do not immediately present readers/viewers with the kind of potent masculine imagery that Charles R. Acland criticizes for its contribution to flawed textual critique in global cultural studies. Acland is particularly critical of those who interpret images of power as powerful images, and asks, "What if we were to see exactly the inverse, arguing that the popularity of the archetypal form and function of a figure like Schwarzenegger, with its exaggerated emphasis on an image of strength, is a symptom of weakness, of frailty, and of dwindling possibility?" He suggests that "[s]uch figures can be a way to compensate for the overall vulnerability people feel in a global system, hence, paradoxically, they refer to people's sense of inconsequentiality and puniness" (37–8). But what if the masculine figure is already "weakened"? The evacuation of exaggerated images of strength from Portis's novel before the action of the story even takes place—evident in LaBoeuf's fruitless four-month search for Chaney and in Cogburn's previously unsuccessful attempt to apprehend Lucky Ned Pepper (not to mention his string of failed businesses and romantic dealings before he became a Marshal)—relieves these characters of lofty expectations. Counter to Acland's formulation of the male heroic figure, and contrary to Thomas Doherty's characterization of *True Grit*'s landscape as "a plain of broken dreams and dead ends," the blatant "inconsequentiality" of the story's male heroes, coupled with their unlikely triumph, predicts an optimistic forecast for "softened" masculinity regardless of context.

In a brilliant ideological sleight of hand, the novel's tendency to characterize men as overgrown children when they are at leisure only heightens their masculinity when they engage in conflict. Mattie's descriptions of her male acquaintances are often infantilizing in nature; for example, she notes how the bandit Lucky Ned Pepper writes his name in "childish characters" (187), and how, while dividing the spoils of the gang's latest train robbery, he reminds her of a child on Christmas morning (185). Similarly, the novel's hero, the U.S. Marshal Rooster Cogburn, is initially depicted as little more than a self-indulgent child. When Mattie joins Cogburn for dinner, she watches as he spreads butter and jam all over his honey cake "like a small child" (58). Unlike the 2010 adaptation's complete dismissal of this characteristic (which reflects the Coens' conscious excision of unmanly traits from Jeff Bridges' portrayal of the Marshal), the 1969 film briefly alludes to Cogburn's child-like propensity for sweet treats when he shows Mattie the provisions he has purchased for their trip, which include a sack of taffy. Notwithstanding Hathaway's faithful infantilization of Cogburn, however, the 1969 film elevates him to a more heroic and potent level than he ever achieves in the novel. Indeed, the conclusion of the 1969 film presents viewers with a Mattie Ross whose arm—bound in a splint, but still whole—has only been *broken* by her descent into the snake pit, but was not amputated as a result of snakebite, indicating that Cogburn's efforts to save her life were not only successful, but actually exceed the compromise of the novel's conclusion in which he rides all night to get her to a doctor, saving her life at the cost of losing her arm.

An examination of the differences and similarities of the scenes in which Mattie first meets Cogburn and the Texas Ranger LaBoeuf, likewise illuminates the ways in which these men's vulnerabilities are merely red herrings intended to defer the revelation of their heroic capabilities in order to achieve maximum dramatic and emotional effect. The 2010 film heightens this effect beyond the level of the 1969 film, the latter of which initially imbues Rooster Cogburn with some degree of competence. In Hathaway's film, Cogburn first appears in a distinctly legal setting: he arrives at Judge Parker's courthouse towing a wagonload of captured criminals. The insertion of this otherwise extraneous scene into the 1969 production immediately establishes Cogburn's ruthless potency as an agent of justice. Similarly, the final image we have of Cogburn in the film is of him riding off into a wintry sunset after having escorted Mattie back to her home in Arkansas.

Our introduction to Rooster Cogburn in the Coen brothers' film likewise represents an improvisation, but unlike Hathaway's production, he does not initially appear as a representative of the law; instead, we do not *see* him at all, but, rather, we hear his voice through the walls of the saloon outhouse where Mattie first confronts him. In this scene, Cogburn's capacities—in all respects—are, to say the least, diminished. Although the scene is treated with characteristic Coen brothers humor, it nevertheless renders Cogburn vulnerable: he is, presumably, seated while Mattie stands erect outside the outhouse door in a position of authority over him, having caught him, literally, with his pants down. The uneven and unconventional distribution of power in this scene will, however, be smoothed out and made orthodox by the film's conclusion when Mattie must be rescued from the snake pit and carried through the night to safety.

Taking its cue from Portis's novel, in the 1969 film Mattie's introduction to the Texas Ranger, LaBoeuf (Glen Campbell), unfolds in the very public setting of the dining room at the Monarch boardinghouse where they are seated, like equals, across a table from one another. In contrast, Mattie's initial encounter with LaBoeuf (Matt Damon) in the Coen brothers' film heightens her feminine vulnerability because it does *not* take place in the security of a public setting, but rather in the intimacy of her own bedchamber. This disturbing confrontation plays upon the sexual threats an unchaperoned young woman on the western border of Arkansas might have expected to face in 1878. The 2010 film heightens beyond the level ever achieved by either of its predecessors the inherent threat of rape that Mattie faces throughout her journey. While in Fort Smith, Mattie awakens one morning to discover a strange man watching her from the foot of her bed. After receiving several acid-tongued gibes from the girl in reply to his queries, LaBoeuf advances several steps toward where she lies prostrate and, towering over her, threatens, "While I sat there watching you, I gave some thought to stealing a kiss, though you are very young, and sick, and unattractive to boot." Although this little speech is delivered almost verbatim from the text in the novel, the Coen brothers' decision to place Mattie in bed emphasizes her consistently vulnerable position that will become most crucial in the film's final scenes when she is rendered utterly helpless and dependent upon Cogburn's paternal assistance and heroic rescue.

Even though *True Grit* was made into a movie just one year after it was published, the continuity between the 1968 novel and the 1969 film is nevertheless inconsistent. In the novel, an aged Mattie Ross retrospectively narrates the entire sequence of events, beginning with a description of her father's murder. Hathaway's 1969 film significantly alters not only the sequence of expository events, but also—and crucially—the entire narrative perspective to the effect that the stable nuclear family under the father's control becomes the film's first image, and the only narrative perspective to which we have access is that of the camera's lens. As such, Mattie's voice and her agential role are significantly diminished in this film, and the focus that would otherwise be directed upon her is instead deflected to the film's male characters. The first scene depicts Frank Ross's leave-taking of his wife and three children as he prepares to depart for Fort Smith, Arkansas (it should be noted that no such scene of quaint domesticity takes place in the novel). As he kisses his wife goodbye, Ross asks, "Where's Mattie?" Mattie's face appears behind a window in the front of the family's home, and she replies, "I'm in here, Papa." The film begins, then, with the presentation of an intact nuclear family whose eldest child, a girl, is properly framed within the confines of the domestic abode, albeit she *is* in a somewhat unlikely position as her father's bookkeeper. The stability of this nuclear family is destroyed by the murderous intervention of Chaney, a twenty-five-year-old bachelor—that is, a man who has, thus far, refused to submit to the social stability supposedly wrought by heteronormative coupling. Mattie's quest for vengeance effectively seeks retribution for the unmarried man's insurrection against the stability of the nuclear family.

The novel delivers frequent reminders of Mattie's authority over her narrative. In contrast, both filmic adaptations of the novel sacrifice Mattie's central role in favor of profiling their male leads. In large block letters beneath the tagline "Punishment comes one way or another," the 2010 promotional poster bills, in order, Jeff Bridges, Matt Damon, and Josh Brolin (Chaney) as its headlining stars. Hailee Steinfeld's name only appears in the list of credits at the bottom of the poster, and even then she is second in line, sandwiched between Barry Pepper (Lucky Ned) and Carter Burwell, the composer of the film's musical score.

For his performance as Rooster Cogburn, Jeff Bridges was nominated for Best Actor at the eighty-third annual Academy Awards; Hailee Steinfeld received a Best Supporting Actress nod at both the Oscars and the annual Screen Actors Guild awards. In her December 2010 entry in the *Los Angeles Times* weblog, Nicole Sperling probes the politics behind SAG's decision to nominate Steinfeld in a category that does not acknowledge her leading role. Steinfeld was nominated in the same category as several veteran actresses, but, Sperling observes, what sets Steinfeld's role apart from these notable women's is that "her character is in almost every scene of the film. So why is she a *supporting* actress?" In her talks with a Paramount award consultant, Sperling learned that the studio, the Coen brothers, Steinfeld's parents, and the movie's producers collectively decided to submit her name for nomination in the supporting actress category in recognition of the young woman's age and inexperience. "Of course," Sperling adds, "SAG, and the Academy of Motion Picture Arts and Sciences, can choose to nominate her in whatever category they wish, though clearly SAG didn't balk at the supporting distinction," and neither did the Academy when the list of nominees for the 2011 Oscars was released a short time after Sperling's article went online. Given Steinfeld's youth and lack of training, these nominations were surely a recognition of the vivacity and "grit" she brought to her portrayal of Mattie Ross, but the residual doubt concerns the Academy's designation of that role as "supporting" rather than primary in and of itself. John Wayne was the only cast member from the 1969 film to receive an Oscar nomination. He won the award for Best Actor, his first and only Academy Award, which many people have suggested was bestowed in recognition of his career as a whole, rather than for his singular performance in *True Grit*. I have already alluded to the manner in which the ensemble cast of the 1969 film was quickly overshadowed by John Wayne's dominating persona. Consequently, both films differ from Portis' novel in one crucial respect: they shift the focus from Mattie to her male co-stars in a manner that deprives viewers of her keen tongue and strips her of authoritative control over her own narrative.

The films superficially mitigate Mattie's loss of control by maintaining her possession of the two props most necessary for the realization and success of the Western hero: a horse and a gun. However much the *True Grit* franchise negotiates contemporary gender concerns by suggesting that women are sufficiently—even superlatively—competent to transact what were once traditionally "men's affairs," inevitably, these films suggest, it is still up to men to fulfill the world's truly "gritty" tasks, such as Cogburn's unfortunate but necessary euthanization of Little Blackie, Mattie's plucky pony, in the 2010 film. In the novel and in the 1969 adaptation, Cogburn uses the little pony as his first means of transporting the snake-bitten Mattie to safety. In each of these incarnations, Little Blackie simply drops dead, exhausted and "played out" by the heavy burden and rigorous ride imposed on him. Cogburn carries Mattie in his arms until he is able to commandeer, at gunpoint, a horse-drawn wagon from a party of hunters. In the novel, Cogburn ultimately exchanges the wagon for a buggy that he borrows from "a wealthy Indian farmer" (208). Not only does the Coen brothers' version omit Rooster's appeal to a wealthy Indian for help, but it also aggrandizes beyond the level of the 1969 film the Marshal's heroic individualism in its depiction of Mattie's rescue as the product of Rooster's solitary sacrifice. The Coens' altered version of Rooster's sacrifice contains both a racial element, in its emphasis on the lawman's specifically *white* heroic individualism (to which Hathaway's film also subscribes, though to a lesser extent), *and* a gendered element in its decision to have Rooster shoot Little Blackie in the head, rather than allow the poor pony to die of its own volition.[6]

Throughout the narrative, Little Blackie functions as a visual symbol of Mattie's gender non-conformity, business acumen, and grit. According to Jane Tompkins, horses "are the place where everything in the [Western] is hidden. Besides doing all the work in a literal sense ... they do double, triple, quadruple work in a symbolic sense" (90). In addition, Mattie's blatant affection for and partnership with Little Blackie represents a potentially destabilizing threat to the Western's generic conventions. Tompkins comments on the phenomenon of horses' relative invisibility in Western films, and she notes the specificity of horses in the genre as "ridden by men" (90, 93). Not only is Little Blackie *not* ridden by a man for most of the story, but some might even say he stars in a supporting role. Mattie purchases Little Blackie from Colonel Stonehill in what is perhaps the novel's most blatant example of her ability to triumph over adult men: she buys the pony back from Stonehill for two dollars less than she sold it to him earlier that same day (Portis, *True Grit* 87–8). Furthermore, the 2010 film makes it appear as though Mattie is successful in her attempt to purchase the pony for ten dollars, half of what Stonehill paid for each pony in the morning, thereby increasing the tenor of her success. The triumph of her business acumen over Colonel Stonehill's is thus emblematic of her agency as both a child in an adult's world and a woman in a man's world. Later, in defiance of Cogburn's and LaBoeuf's attempt to prevent her from boarding the Poteau River ferry and thus accompanying them into the Choctaw Nation, Mattie urges Little Blackie into the river's icy current, swimming its breadth, and arriving triumphantly on the other side in advance of the ferry carrying the men (103). In both of the adaptations, when Mattie confronts the men on the other side of the river, an astonished Cogburn utters an impressed variation of "That's some horse," the admiration of which obviously extends to Mattie herself. However, by the end of the film, Little Blackie has been commandeered by Rooster Cogburn, a male rider, who must sacrifice the pony's life in order to save the girl's. Chillingly, then, the painful scene in which Jeff Bridges as Rooster Cogburn towers over the dying pony and fires a bullet into its brain represents the willful, albeit humane, destruction of the symbolic representation of Mattie's transgressive gender nonconformity and "grit." What is more, Little Blackie is one of the only living beings for which Mattie exhibits a deep and abiding affection (in the 2010 film she sobs hysterically at his death, tears that were not similarly shed for her own dear father), and Rooster kills it.

In each of *True Grit*'s incarnations, moreover, it is clear that this momentous event in Mattie's life represents an aberration from her past conduct and will not repeat itself in her future affairs. Portis presents us with a controversial heroine whose admirable qualities will later become simply the eccentricities of a "cranky old maid" (214). She harbors no illusions about her motivations, either: when Ned Pepper asks her, "Most girls like play pretties, but you like guns, don't you?" she emphatically replies, "I don't care a thing in the world about guns. If I did I would have one that worked" (178). Mattie is fully aware of the temporary nature of her gender nonconformity. Effectively, once she has achieved her vengeful purpose, she *immediately* becomes a helpless, defenseless little girl once again when the kickback from the gunshot that wounds Chaney propels her backward into the pit where she is bitten by a venomous rattlesnake, and must ultimately be rescued. Ditsky suggests that Mattie "surrender[s]" her femininity in order to achieve her vengeful purpose, adding,

> [She] never marries, the changes wrought upon her by her experiences presumably having made such a step impossible.... [She] is ... a pitiable creature who surrenders her womanhood in order to do a man's work, and whose character is frozen at the moment of her attainment of "manhood" through trial: through the crisis engendered by her use of her Papa's pistol [29–30].

Significantly, Mattie uses her father's gun to exact her revenge, a gun that belonged to a man who, as Mattie herself reveals in the novel's first chapter, is "soft," who makes poor personal and business decisions, and who does not exercise good judgment or common sense. The first chapter characterizes Frank Ross as too gentle for his environment; Mattie admits, "If Papa had a failing it was his kindly disposition" (10). Mattie describes her father's decision to go to Fort Smith to buy some Texas mustang ponies for hunting and breeding purposes as a "scheme," a description that establishes his willingness to engage in risky, speculative behavior that ultimately threatens the well-being and stability of his family. Instead of travelling to Fort Smith by steamboat or train, Ross decides to go on horseback with the intention of walking the ponies back home. As Mattie notes, "Not only would it be cheaper but it would be a pleasant outing for him and a good ride. Nobody loved to gad about on a prancing steed more than Papa," a description that somewhat anachronistically characterizes her father as a kind of "weekend warrior" (11).

Although financially responsible, Ross's decision is unpractical, especially when he arrives in Fort Smith and discovers that the ponies he intended to breed are all geldings. Perhaps to assuage his wounded pride or to deny his foolishness, Ross purchases four of the ponies anyway, a decision that Mattie vehemently defends, arguing, "It was a good enough buy" (13). Later, when Mattie sells the ponies back to Stonehill in that gloriously comic scene, not only does she pragmatically unburden her diminished family of the unnecessary ponies, but she also *corrects* her father's prideful error in judgment. In the Hathaway film, Mattie explicitly notes the fact that the ponies are gelded and so they are not suitable for breeding purposes (in the novel she simply tells Stonehill, "We don't need them" [31]), which simultaneously highlights her father's poor business sense and her own superior judgment. Because his death occurs during his (literally) fruitless trip to buy gelded ponies, Frank Ross is irrevocably linked to sterility, which parallels his lack of *cojones* at the moment of his death when confronted by Chaney in front of the Monarch boardinghouse. During this confrontation, Ross tries to convince Chaney to take his complaint of having been cheated at cards to the law; Ross is a man of recourse, rather than action. Moreover, Ross's decision to venture onto the streets of Fort Smith, a border-town, "unarmed," as Mattie tells us, indicates a lack of common sense (14). Again, Mattie anticipates and takes a defensive posture against those naysayers who might doubt the legitimacy of her father's actions: "[H]e was trying to do that short devil a good turn. Chaney was a tenant and Papa felt responsibility. He was his brother's keeper. Does that answer your question?" Frank Ross was no "heroic individual"; he was too concerned with the affairs of others, and too willing to let those affairs be handled by legal authorities. This is the man whose life Mattie sets out to avenge.

Mattie's deontological quest for vengeance is motivated as much by her desire to see her father's killer killed as it is by her need to address the "anxious masculinity" she experiences on his behalf, that is, her fear that he is not a "real" man (Ducat 1). Consequently, she resolves to array herself in her father's clothes and "traps" (his slicker, hat, and saddle), and to use his pre–Civil War-era Colt's Dragoon revolver to lay low the life of Tom Chaney (96–7).[7] Outfitting herself in her father's accoutrements—the physical talismans of his essence—brings her as close as possible to being able to turn back time and achieve what her father ought to have done in the first place: shoot and kill Chaney instead of being shot himself.

If the symbolic power of the gun in the West has developed an almost clichéd reputation as a metaphorical representation of the phallus or of male sexuality (cf. Grant 69, Tompkins 33), then the failure of Mattie's father's gun not only when she needs it most but also when she uses it to discharge her fatal purpose is significant on two levels. At the same time that it condemns "softened" masculinity, it condemns even further a woman's attempt to wield the phallic power represented by the gun, even if that power has been substantially diminished or "gelded."[8] The improvised domestic scene that commences the 1969 film immediately calls into question the relevance and reliability of Frank Ross's pistol—and, by proxy, its owner—when Mattie questions her father's decision to take it with him on his journey. "Papa," she ventures, "that gun's old-fashioned. Why don't you buy a new one in Fort Smith?" To which Ross replies, "It certainly worked at Chickamauga. It's got a long way to go yet." The Hathaway production neglects to mention, however, that Frank Ross was badly injured—almost fatally—during the Battle of Chickamauga in 1863 (Portis, *True Grit* 11). In the novel, Rooster gives Mattie the opportunity to exchange her father's aging firearm for a "like new" "Ladies' Companion," a "twenty-two pepper-box that shoots five times," but Mattie refuses, insisting on using "Papa's gun" herself (62). In all three versions of *True Grit*, "Papa's gun" misfires on Mattie when she first encounters Chaney at the river. Her first shot injures him when the bullet grazes his ribs, but when she attempts a second and a third shot, "the hammer snap[s] on a bad percussion cap" previously loaded into the gun by Cogburn, or so Mattie claims (172). Given the fact that Chaney has to remind her to cock the hammer before firing, it stands to reason that Mattie's failure with the gun is just as likely the result of her own inexperience with firearms or the result of the gun's age and history of disuse. Again, Mattie's reliability as a narrator is characteristically impenetrable not only because of the retrospective, first-person nature of the tale, but also because of Portis's trademark opacity.

In the novel as in the 1969 film, her Papa's pistol betrays Mattie once more when she uses it on Chaney for the last time at the scene of the bandits' camp. At the very instant she successfully sends "a lead ball of justice, too long delayed, into the criminal head of Tom Chaney," the kickback from the big pistol sends her reeling into an open pit behind her (195). It is in this pit that Mattie encounters the rattlesnakes, one of which bites her broken left arm and necessitates Rooster's wild ride to get her to safety. To heap insult upon injury, Mattie's "lead ball of justice" does not achieve its purpose: she only succeeds in wounding Chaney, rather than killing him. It is not until Rooster strikes Chaney dead that the villain finally expires. The significance of the gun as a phallic object in Hathaway's film achieves its fullest expression in the improvised final scene when Mattie hands her father's revolver over to Rooster, saying, "I think it's only right that you have Papa's gun; it might keep you alive." Despite the questionable functionality of the gun and its ability to prevent personal injury, Mattie's symbolic act restores the phallus to its proper place in the hands of the patriarch.

The 2010 film does not emphasize Frank Ross's shortcomings in the same way as the Hathaway production; instead, it finds other ways to undermine the value of the man she avenges and the transgressive power she attempts to wield. In the Coen brothers' version, Mattie is allowed to take credit for Chaney's death, but notably she does not use her father's pistol to blast him over the cliff's edge. She grabs LaBoeuf's Sharps carbine rifle after the Texas Ranger is knocked unconscious by a blow to the head from Chaney, and blasts the latter squarely in the center of his abdomen, sending him over the cliff's edge and into oblivion. Even though the recoil from LaBoeuf's powerful rifle likewise sends Mattie reeling backward into the pit of snakes, it is significant that she does so using a phallic object belonging to a more suitably "masculine" man, capable of hitting his mark from "four hundred yards at least," rather than the impotent Dragoon revolver belonging to her father.

The 2010 film also revises Mattie's appearance throughout the drama in a manner that is both truer to the novel than the 1969 version and more punitive in its condemnation of her usurpation of her father's role. Due to the nature of the novel's first-person narrative, we get very little physical description of Mattie except as she is criticized by other characters as being "unattractive," "bony," and "spindly" (72, 116, 202). Consequently, her appearance differs significantly between the two films. In Hathaway's production, Mattie (Kim Darby) sports a short bob hairstyle, a cute bowler hat, and wide-legged gender-appropriate pants that simulate the appearance of a skirt; moreover, at the time of the film's release, Kim Darby was twenty-two years old. In Hathaway's film, Mattie is neither terribly likeable nor terribly childlike. In many ways, her 1969 incarnation can be construed as a stereotyped reflection of the "women's libbers" contemporary with the film's release: she is shrill and argumentative, she demands the recognition of the men around her, she possesses business-savvy, and she is educated beyond the level of many of the men in the film. The use of an adult actress narrows the age gap between the film's protagonists, further suggesting that Mattie's feminine independence represents a potentially destabilizing threat to the world inhabited by men. In contrast, in the Coen brothers' film, Mattie's hair is styled in two braided pigtails, and throughout most of the movie she wears her father's coat and hat, and carries his revolver, all of which are obviously much too large for her child's body and function to emphasize her youth and inexperience. At the time of filming, Hailee Steinfeld was thirteen years old, much closer in age and appearance to the character she plays than Darby was forty years earlier. The cartoonish appearance she strikes with her too-large coat, hat, and gun presents us with the image of a pigtailed damsel, who, although toting a gun rather than a ragdoll, nevertheless requires the aid of a male avenger to return her to the safety of the domestic sphere. The image of "the pigtailed damsel," Faludi suggests, became the iconic image of the post–9/11 world in the U.S., an image that resulted, she says, from the ascendance of "a new John Wayne masculinity" in American gender ideology (7, 4). Perhaps even more insidiously, Mattie's appearance throughout the 2010 film recalls

Angus's famous utterance in reference to the ill-fated Scottish king in Shakespeare's *Macbeth*, "Now does he feel his title / Hang loose upon him, like a giant's robe / Upon a dwarfish thief" (V. ii. 20–22). Clearly, Mattie's thievery is not limited to her usurpation of the father's domain, but more pertinently, the masculine domain, and she pays dearly for her "crime." Rife with Old Testament imagery—that era of grand patriarchs—the scene in which Mattie falls into the pit and is bitten by a venomous rattlesnake produces dramatic results: in what can only be viewed as a symbolic castration, Mattie's left arm is amputated to save her life, its absence a lifelong reminder of her ordeal and of the consequences of a woman's folly in usurping a man's role.

In what is perhaps their most obviously conservative effort, both cinematic adaptations conclude Mattie's narrative in ways that significantly revise that of the novel. These revisions consciously perpetuate the trope of the timeless Western hero. The conclusion of Portis's novel differs from the conventional expectations of the stock Western popular in the 1950s and 1960s. Wyn Wachhorst locates the underlying motivation for these conventions in "the complex realities of modern life," which "dictate that the hero of simple solutions, after giving us our moment on the screen, must ride off, having outlived his time and usefulness in both fact and fiction" (20). In contrast, Portis's *True Grit* concludes some three or four decades after the events in the novel have taken place. An elderly Mattie Ross recounts the sequence of events that transpired after she lost consciousness from the effects of the snake venom (208). Mattie's epilogue endows Rooster with an afterlife, a dubious distinction rarely bestowed upon the Western hero. Notably, Rooster's foray into the Choctaw Nation with Mattie and LaBoeuf does not positively influence his future trajectory, as Mattie reveals in her postscript:

> Not three weeks after we had returned from the Winding Stair Mountains, Rooster found himself in trouble over a gun duel he fought in Fort Gibson, Cherokee Nation. He shot and killed Odus Wharton in the duel.... Rooster shot two other men that were with Wharton and killed one of them.... [T]hey were not wanted by the law at that time and Rooster was criticized.... Pressure was brought and Rooster made to surrender his Federal badge [210–1].

Rooster later absconded to Wyoming where he became a hired gun for the Stock Growers Association. Mattie admits, "It was a sorry business, I am told, and I fear Rooster did himself no credit there in what they called *The Johnson County War*" (211). Not only does Portis give Rooster an afterlife rare for the Western hero, but he makes it rarer still in its criminal inflection.

Neither of the novel's cinematic adaptations faithfully represents its conclusion. In its most significant departure from Portis' novel, the Hathaway adaptation imagines a very different fate for the concerned parties, one that restores the stock conventions of popular postwar Westerns. In the Hathaway film, LaBoeuf succumbs to his wounds; Mattie merely breaks her left arm, a temporary rather than permanent injury; and the film's conclusion envisions the eternal youthfulness of Mattie and the virile triumph of Rooster Cogburn as the one-eyed fat man jumps his horse over a four-rail fence and rides off into the distance, hale and hearty for all time.[9] The Coen brothers' version is more faithful to Portis' novel than its 1969 predecessor, but in addition to several minor alterations to Mattie's concluding monologue, it significantly excises any mention of Rooster's dubious activities in the aftermath of his heroic nighttime rescue.

The conservative theme of the films is not an innovation; in fact, both cinematic adaptations actively support and even exceed the novel's conservative ideology in response to their respective contexts of national crisis that shook the foundations of what it meant to be a man in America. The franchise navigates contemporary gender anxieties by remarking on how to be a man in less-than-ideal circumstances, on how *not* to be a man, and on the potentially devastating consequences for women who are too smart for their own good. However, even in spite of their staid conservatism, the hidden depths of this deceptively straightforward novel and its two very different cinematic adaptations continue to challenge successive generations of readers and viewers. The consistent attention that this story has received over the last forty-five years illustrates a perpetual fascination with the triumphant man of impaired abilities, a theme that clearly has lasting appeal and not simply because of its sardonic wit or its grit, but because it keeps us guessing, replete with doubt, at every new viewing and re-reading.

Notes

1. Susan Jeffords's definition of patriarchy as not only "male dominance over women," but also "the socialized domination of masculine over feminine" contributes to an enhanced understanding of how masculinity ("the set of images, values, interests, and activities held important to a successful achievement of male adulthood in American cultures") functions as a means of establishing and maintaining a gendered social hierarchy that also enables the "feminization" of other groups of men defined by varying categories of difference who are similarly made vulnerable to domination and control (xii).

2. See also John Higham, "The Reorientation of American Culture in the 1890s," *Writing American History: Essays on Modern Scholarship* (Bloomington: Indiana University Press, 2003: 227–56); Warren Susman, *Culture as History: The Transformation of American Society in the Twentieth Century* (New York: Pantheon, 1984).

3. As examples of these forces, Ducat lists gay men in the military, feminists in the civilian home, and women in the marketplace (1).

4. Faludi notes how political and cultural commentaries that emerged in the weeks, months, and years after 9/11 "were riddled with apprehensions that America was lacking in masculine fortitude, that the masses of weak-chinned BlackBerry clutchers had left the nation open to attack and wouldn't have the cojones for the confrontations ahead" (8).

5. Cf. McLuhan, Doherty, Simmons, Connaughton.

6. The 2010 version eliminates the scene where Rooster parleys with Captain Boots Finch of the Choctaw Light Horse Police in McAlester; both versions omit Finch's presence during the comic "corndodger massacre" sequence, which the 1969 film omits altogether (Portis, *True Grit* 163–4). These omissions, along with several other omissions of Portis's representations of Indigeneity in his novel, efface the presence of an Indigenous masculinity from Mattie's narrative in favor of emphasizing the *white* heroic individualism of Cogburn and LaBoeuf.

7. There is a larger argument to be made about Mattie's choice of an archaic, malfunctioning firearm given Portis's reputed familiarity with and affinity for guns (cf. Park 321).

8. Ducat broadly defines the phallus, and thus phallic power, as "the mythic, permanently erect archetypal monolith of masculine omnipotence that signifies untrammeled growth, invulnerability, and freedom from all dependency" (2).

9. The altered conclusion of the 1969 film also left open the possibility for a sequel, which was eventually realized in the 1975 film, *Rooster Cogburn*, starring John Wayne and Katherine Hepburn in a plot remarkably similar to *True Grit*. Another sequel, *True Grit: A Further Adventure*, starring Warren Oates and Lisa Pelikan, aired in 1978 as a made-for-television movie, which, as the title aptly suggests, depicted the further adventures of Rooster Cogburn and Mattie Ross. Both of these sequels revise and extend the *True Grit* mythos beyond Portis's original vision.

WORKS CITED

Acland, Charles R. *Screen Traffic: Movies, Multiplexes, and Global Culture.* Durham: Duke University Press, 2003. *Scholars Portal Books.* Web. 6 Aug. 2013.

Blount, Roy, Jr. "Comedy in Earnest." Portis, *Escape Velocity* 313–6. Print.

Cieply, Michael. "Coen Brothers Saddle Up a Revenge Story (or Two)." *New York Times* 3 Dec. 2010. Web. 7 Aug. 2013.

Cohn, Jan. *Creating America: George Horace Lorimer and the Saturday Evening Post.* Pittsburgh: University of Pittsburgh Press, 1989. Print.

Connaughton, Michael E. "Charles (McColl) Portis." *American Novelists Since World War II, Second Series.* Ed. James E. Kibler. Detroit: Gale Research, 1980. *Gale Literature Resource Center.* Web. 27 July 2013.

Ditsky, John. "True 'Grit' and 'True Grit.'" *ARIEL* 4.2 (1973): 18–31. Print.

Doherty, Thomas. "The Duke and the Dude: The Remake of 'True Grit' Shows the Enduring Power of a Genre." *The Chronicle Review* 2 Jan. 2011. Web. 30 May 2012.

Ducat, Stephen J. *The Wimp Factor: Gender Gaps, Holy Wars, and the Politics of Anxious Masculinity.* Boston: Beacon, 2004. Print.

Ebert, Roger. "True Grit." Rev. of *True Grit.* RogerEbert.com 21 Dec. 2010. Web. 12 Aug. 2013.

Fabrizio, Lisa. "Nothing But Grit." *The American Spectator* 24 Nov. 2010. Web. 7 Aug. 2013.

Faludi, Susan. *The Terror Dream: Fear and Fantasy in Post–9/11 America.* New York: Metropolitan, 2007. Print.

Fine, Kerry. "She Hits Like a Man, But She Kisses Like a Girl: TV Heroines, Femininity, Violence, and Intimacy." *Western American Literature* 47.2 (2012): 153–73. Print.

Gilbert, James. *Men in the Middle: Searching for Masculinity in the 1950s.* Chicago: University of Chicago Press, 2005. Print.

Grant, Barry Keith. *Shadows of Doubt: Negotiations of Masculinity in American Genre Films.* Detroit: Wayne State, 2011. Print.

Jeffords, Susan. *The Remasculinization of America: Gender and the Vietnam War.* Bloomington: Indiana University Press, 1989. Print.
Keegan, Rebecca. "Teen Girls in Film Showcase True Grit." *Los Angeles Times* 9 Jan. 2011. Web. 7 Aug. 2013.
Kirkwood, R. Cort. "John Wayne: Mr. America." *The New American* 23.11 (2007): 35–38. *ProQuest.* Web. 6 August 2013.
Lethem, Jonathan. "The Darkest Side of John Wayne." Salon.com 11 Aug. 1997. Web. 7 Aug. 2013.
Maher, Kevin. "True Grit." *The National* 17 Feb. 2011. Web. 7 Aug. 2013.
McLuhan, Marshall. "The Popular Hero and Anti-Hero." *Heroes of Popular Culture.* Eds. Ray B. Browne and Marshall W. Fishwick. Bowling Green: Bowling Green University Popular Press, 1972. 135–7. Print.
McMurtry, Larry, and Diana Ossana. "Talking About 'True Grit.'" *New York Review of Books Blog* 8 Feb. 2011. Web. 19 Sept. 2012.
Meeuf, Russell. "Shouldering the Weight of the World: The Sensational and Global Appeal of John Wayne's Body." *Journal of Popular Film and Television* 39.2 (2011): 59–70. Print.
Park, Ed. "Like Cormac McCarthy, but Funny." Portis, *Escape Velocity* 317–36. Print.
Portis, Charles. *The Dog of the South.* 1979. New York: Overlook, 1999. Print.
_____. *Escape Velocity: A Charles Portis Miscellany.* Ed. Jay Jennings. Little Rock: Butler Center Books, 2012. Print.
_____. "*Gazette* Project Interview with Charles Portis." Interview by Roy Reed. Little Rock, AR, 31 May 2001. Portis, *Escape Velocity* 285–309. Print.
_____. *True Grit.* 1968. London: Bloomsbury, 2005. Print.
Sarkeesian, Anita. "*True Grit*, Mattie Ross, and Feminism?" *FeministFrequency.com* 9 Mar. 2011. Web. 11 Aug. 2013.
Shakespeare, William. "Macbeth." *The Oxford Shakespeare: The Complete Works.* Oxford: Clarendon, 1998. 975–999. Print.
Shuman, R. Baird. "Portis' *True Grit*: Adventure Story or *Entwicklungsroman*?" *The English Journal* 59.3 (1970): 367–70. JSTOR. Web. 20 Aug. 2013.
Simmons, David. "The Countercultural Cowboy: Rereading the 1960s Novels of Doctorow, Herlihy, and Portis in a Marcusian Framework." *Westerns: Paperback Novels and Movies from Hollywood.* Ed. Paul Varner. Newcastle, UK: Cambridge Scholars, 2007. 215–27. Print.
Sperling, Nicole. "Why is 'True Grit's' Hailee Steinfeld in SAG's Supporting Actress Category?" *Los Angeles Times Blog* 17 Dec. 2010. Web. 18 Aug. 2013.
Tipton Cortner, Amy. "Why the America of Mattie Ross Needs to Read Hariette Simpson Arnow." *Appalachian Heritage* 40.2 (2012): 56–8. Print.
Tompkins, Jane. *West of Everything: The Inner Life of Westerns.* New York: Oxford University Press, 1993. Print.
True Grit. Dir. Henry Hathaway. Perf. John Wayne, Glen Campbell, and Kim Darby. Paramount Pictures, 1969. Film.
True Grit. Dir. Joel and Ethan Coen. Perf. Jeff Bridges, Matt Damon, Hailee Steinfeld, and Josh Brolin. Paramount Pictures, 2010. Film.
Wachhorst, Wyn. "Come Back, Shane! The National Nostalgia." *Southwest Review* 98.1 (2013): 12–25. *ProQuest.* Web. 6 August 2013.
Weber, Christina D. "'I Mean It's Awkward Anxiety': Exploring the Role of Sociohistorical Context in Men's Negotiation of Masculine Subjectivity." *Cultural Studies ⇔ Critical Methodologies* 10.4 (2010): 337–46. SAGE. Web. 5 Aug. 2013.

Coen, Coen on the Range
Rooster Cogburn(s) and Domestic Space

JOSEPH S. WALKER

> *There is no knowing what is in a man's heart.*—Mattie Ross in Charles Portis's *True Grit* (1968)
>
> *Who knows what's in a man's heart?*—Mattie Ross in *True Grit* (1969), screenplay Marguerite Roberts
>
> *I do not know this man.*—Rooster Cogburn in *True Grit* (2010), screenplay Joel & Ethan Coen

We can't help but be a little embarrassed by the Western. It is the souvenir of a national adolescence we would like to believe we have outgrown. It is racist, sexist, homophobic, reactionary, perhaps even fascist. It celebrates an outmoded form of masculinity distinguished by the artful wielding of phallic force and the automatic, unchallenged assumption of male primacy and superiority. It relegates racial others to the marginalized roles of mindless savages or servile sidekicks. It dismisses animals and the other forms of an undisciplined natural world as commodities to be used or destroyed in the name of selfish gain or simple pleasure. It romanticizes gunplay and brute violence as not merely the solutions to immediate problems, but the necessary foundations upon which all civilization is built. As a narrative form it is frequently formulaic and childishly simplistic, relying upon a rigidly ritualistic set of icons and conventions which inhibit artistic innovation. It depends upon a simple binary construction of morality dividing the world into "good guys" and "bad guys." It legitimizes the militaristic assumption of national authority and privilege that licensed the Cold War and our disastrous adventures in Asia. It is part and parcel with the nationalist narrative of Manifest Destiny, a phrase our era can no longer articulate in an innocent way.

And yet, like the boy calling out at the end of *Shane*, we can't stop calling upon the Western to come back to us, which is to say we can't stop coming back to it. In terms of the sheer number of movies, TV shows, novels and magazine stories produced, the Western went into a severe decline in response to the disillusioning failure of the American project in Vietnam, but in the decades since it has been "mythologized, demythologized, romanticized, deromanticized, spoofed, mongrelized, inflated, deflated, politicized, allegorized—transmogrified in every conceivable way" (Minus 83). We might add to this list contemporized, motorized, globalized, commodified, sci-fied, horrified, steampunked, feminized, queered, inverted, deconstructed, and, of course, analyzed and theorized. Whatever is done to it, however, the Western endures, though our level of comfort with it and the things we seek within it shift. In the arena of film particularly, it seemed for a time that the primary project of new Westerns was the reconsideration and attempted rehabilitation of the Western form itself. Thus, Kevin Costner's 1990 *Dances with Wolves* revisited the conflict between Native Americans and the cavalry, familiar from the iconic Westerns of John Ford, to depict the whites as destructive invaders, though somewhat problematically still presenting a white man as the film's messianic hero. In a similarly self-reflective mode Clint Eastwood's 1992 *Unforgiven* drew upon the star's own long history in the genre and questioned the value and the long-term effects of the violence so frequently represented as immediately and completely solving all problems in the Western.

It is telling that both of these films were directed by actors and won multiple Oscars, indicating the film industry's stamp of approval. There are few things Hollywood loves more than stories about itself, and *Dances with Wolves* and *Unforgiven* are self-consciously movies about movies, more than they are movies about any real set of historical circumstances and personalities. To a degree, of course, this is true of any Western. The earliest forms of the Western myth—newspaper stories and dime novels celebrating the exciting and profitable expansion of the nation toward the Pacific—appeared concurrently with the actual historical movement they recorded, but the form came into its own with the creation of the motion picture, which coincided almost precisely with the disappearance of the Wild West itself into the realm of nostalgia and myth. Certainly the significance of Edwin Porter's twelve-minute 1903 film *The Great Train Robbery* has been extensively documented and discussed. The West is always already a field of memory, and increasingly over the course of the 20th century those memories were of actors and films, not "real" people or events. Robert Stam has suggested that, when a novel is adapted into film many times, "the diverse prior adaptations ... form a larger, cumulative hypotext available to the filmmaker who comes relatively 'late' in the series" (31). Similarly, the context which gives any specific new Western film its greatest depth of meaning and impact is its relationship to the collective body of Western films and the cultural history of their reception taken as a whole. The outcome, too, is similar, in that new Westerns "are caught up in the ongoing whirl of intertextual reference and transformation, of texts generating other texts in an endless process of recycling, transformation, and transmutation, with no clear point of origin" (31). If this was particularly true of the highly praised revisionist Westerns of the 1990s, it was possible at the time to see this as a way of closing the books, a reflection upon a cultural form taking its last bow. The Cold War was over, after all, and in a world in which America stood as the last superpower and seemed likely to preside over an age of increasing global prosperity and peace, it appeared that it was time for the cowboy to hang up his gun belt.

Today, of course, it's plain that these attempts to eulogize the Western were as premature as the notion that America itself was no longer open to challenge or confrontation. There have certainly been more big-screen Westerns produced since the turn of the century (and, crucially, since the attacks of 9/11) than in the comparable number of years preceding it, particularly if films set in modern times which employ the trappings and the conventions of the Western (*Brokeback Mountain* and *No Country for Old Men*, for example) are included in the count. As they always have, these films reflect a complexly intertwined matrix of influences, contexts and references. In part the Western continues to be animated by a simple sense of nostalgia—nostalgia less for the historical period it represents (which is, after all, now beyond living memory) than for a time when the films themselves could be received and enjoyed in something like a spirit of innocence. This nostalgia is in part fueled by, but often coexists uneasily with, concurrent attempts through the Western to come to terms with a new global reality, where America is confronted by enemies who are difficult to identify and successfully confront, and where America itself is implicated to some degree in the conflicts which define the age. The Western has always been an allegorical representation of America's understanding of itself, and in the post–9/11 era America has struggled to achieve any such understanding. Whatever version of reality the Bush administration may have wished to impose upon the world conversation through its "cowboy diplomacy" (and it's certainly clear what conventions Bush was drawing on when he invited terrorists to "bring it on"), it has been impossible in the years since 9/11 to completely ignore such inconvenient truths as the long-standing amorality of America's involvement in the Middle East, our willful disregard for the opinions and desires of the rest of the world, or our transparent fabrications used in the name of launching a war. America can no longer simply don a white hat and declare itself the "good guy."

The desire to do so is, however, still visible in some of the more straightforward Westerns of the new century. Consider, for example, Kevin Costner's 2003 return to the genre as director and actor in *Open Range*. Here, Costner and Robert Duvall are Charley Waite and Boss Spearman, a pair of free-range cowboys drawn into battle with a wealthy, corrupt rancher who seeks to kill them and claim their cattle for his own. In accordance with many previous variations on the same narrative, the rancher, Denton Baxter, is the ruling force in the small frontier town where the conflict occurs, using his money and his control of the local sheriff to assemble overwhelming force against the two heroes. Coming less than two years after the attacks of 9/11, *Open Range* is shamelessly explicit in representing Waite and Spearman as symbols of American bravery, values and virtue. Spearman tells Waite that he may not be willing to die for a few cows, but that "one man telling another man where he can go in this country, that's something else." Later, Spearman makes a similarly principled speech to the people of the town gathered in a café, declaring his intention to oppose the sheriff and asserting that he and Waite have a right to protect their lives and their property that transcends the law. The complications and ambiguities of *Unforgiven* or *Dances with Wolves* have vanished here; though Waite is allowed some guilt over his violent actions earlier in life, he and Spearman are essentially the kind of unvarnished, straight-shooting heroes rarely seen in the Western since the stylized, nihilistic films of Sergio Leone and Sam Peckinpah undermined the simplest conventions of the genre. The film even attempts to elide the most unsavory elements of the historical record by erasing Native Americans entirely from the film (there is but one brief mention, by Baxter, of the townspeople having "run off the Indians" years previously).

All this is familiar enough, if startlingly retrograde. There are any number of Western films which depict the good guy riding into a corrupt town, being drawn into a conflict which allows him to cleanse and purify it, and then riding off into the sunset ("riding off" is a theme I will return to). What pushes *Open Range* still further in the direction of post–9/11 wish fulfillment is that the townspeople themselves, in the inevitable gun battle which provides the film's climax, rise up against their own economic interests to assist Waite and Spearman and oppose Baxter. It bears emphasis that this is not a case of cowed villagers learning to defend themselves from demonized invaders (as in, for example, *The Magnificent Seven*), but rather an entire town choosing to, in essence, participate in the assassination of its wealthiest citizen because his values are insufficiently American (played by the English actor Michael Gambon, Baxter, alone among the townspeople, has a foreign accent). There is a longing here for community and unity which is difficult to imagine in a film made, say, five years earlier. In perhaps the most remarkable scene of the film, Waite, wounded in the final battle and resting against a water trough, watches some townspeople in a field chase down one of the last of Baxter's enforcers, now unarmed, and kill him with a volley of gunfire as he stumbles and falls. We are apparently meant to take this execution as an indication of the town's redemption and virtue—as good an indication as any of the political atmosphere in the years following 9/11. It's significant, too, that our heroes, having won the day, do not now ride off to return to their lives as wandering "free rangers"; instead they decide to remain and become residents of the town, with Spearman buying a saloon and Waite marrying the town doctor's sister (Annette Bening). This preference for a fantasia of communal unity, with even the element of violence integrated into the whole, over the valorization of the heroic but self-exiled individual marks the only point where *Open Range* departs from the Western in its most traditional and conservative forms.

The Western, then, provided a field to respond to the new realities of 21st century America and its place in the world with visions of comforting, reassuring nostalgia. It also, however, offered more complex, challenging responses, through texts that reflect the confusion, ambiguity, and anxiety that have marked the age of the War on Terror. Such an approach characterizes, for example, Tommy Lee Jones's *The Three Burials of Melquiades Estrada* (2005), a film with a contemporary setting that uses the tropes of the classical Western to examine America's troubled relationships with the rest of the world. Once again here, an actor already associated with the Western (most famously the TV miniseries *Lonesome Dove*) directs himself in a story that draws upon the conventions of the Western form in innovative ways. Jones's character here is Pete Perkins, a ranch hand in the border regions of contemporary Texas whose best friend and fellow cowboy, the titular Melquiades Estrada (Julio Cedilo), is an illegal immigrant from Mexico. Flashbacks scattered throughout the film show the two meeting and eventually developing a strong relationship, but the film's narrative proper begins with the discovery of Estrada's body in the desert. Mike Norton (Barry Pepper), a young member of the Border Patrol, kills Estrada, who he mistakenly believed was firing on him, instead of the coyote he was trying to kill. Norton, depicted violently assaulting other illegals in fulfilling his duties, initially conceals the killing, then confesses after the body is found, but is not punished by either local law enforcement, uninterested in a dead "wetback," or the Border Patrol itself, which primarily seeks to avoid embarrassment. Realizing this, the grief-stricken Perkins kidnaps Norton, then forces him to disinter Estrada and accompany him on a horseback mission to return the body to Estrada's home south of the border.

Perkins's quest for a form of justice and revenge defined and enacted by himself is firmly within the accepted set of motivations for Western heroes, and in many ways he acts morally and considerately, in contrast to most of the other major characters. Having tied up Norton's wife, for example, he covers her with a blanket in case the night gets chilly. He is shown to be skilled and experienced in horse riding, shooting, and the other accomplishments we expect of our cowboys. Unlike all the other white men in the film he seems to be completely free of prejudice, accepting Estrada as an equal and friend immediately, treating other Mexicans with respect and kindness, expressing himself fluently in both Spanish and English, and regarding the border as a bureaucratic nuisance rather than a real division between distinct kinds of people. It becomes increasingly clear, however, that he is also mentally unbalanced. This is evident first in the odd combination of tenderness and rough practicality with which he treats the body of Estrada, already half mummified and rotting following its first two burials (first by Norton in an unmarked, shallow pit in the desert, then by the state in a pauper's grave) and regarded by every other character who encounters it with gagging disgust. Perkins cares for the body with the fondness he felt for his living friend, but he is also capable of setting it on fire to deter ants from eating it, and pouring antifreeze down its throat in an effort to further preserve it. Seen in the context of these acts, Perkins' taciturn nature and straightforward employment of violence to achieve his goal come to seem less like the traditional attributes of the self-reliant Western hero and more like the deranged actions of a man driven mad by grief.

Then again, perhaps being driven mad by grief is the only reasonable response to the post–9/11 world. *Three Burials* departs from the traditional Western not only in its troubled hero, but also in its representation of a troubled reality where even the security of traditional narrative forms fails to hold. We expect, for example, that much of the structure of the film will be provided through a personal pursuit of Perkins by the local sheriff, Frank Belmont (Dwight Yoakam), who has several tense confrontations with Perkins early in the film over the failure to investigate the murder. In fact, however, Belmont almost immediately locates Perkins and his captive in the desert and has the opportunity to shoot Perkins from across a canyon, but cannot bring himself to pull the trigger; instead, he takes a cell phone call from the married woman he is seeing, who tells him to buy her a package of Kotex before their next illicit assignation. Belmont is never seen in the film again, though we learn he has gone on vacation to Sea World, saying the affair is strictly between Perkins and the Border Patrol. The Patrol itself, however, is completely ineffective, and never comes close to stopping or even locating Perkins. Nor does Norton ever provide Perkins with real opposition; though he runs away at one point, Perkins easily recaptures him after a rattlesnake bites him, and the two never have a significant physical confrontation. Denied the satisfactions of a conventional conflict, we are also denied any satisfactory romantic plot; Rachel (Melissa Leo), the woman both Perkins and Belmont have been sexually involved with, tells Perkins that she loves him, but when he calls her from Mexico and asks her to marry him, she brusquely tells him that she is staying with Bob, her husband, an elderly short-order cook we never see outside his kitchen. Rachel, like Belmont, simply disappears from the film after this. The film's vision of romantic love is perhaps best expressed by an early scene in which Norton copulates with his wife from behind in their kitchen while she, ignoring him completely, continues to watch a bland soap opera scene on TV. When Norton is kidnapped she gets on a bus and leaves town without ever learning if he lives or dies.

The cowboy tradition is inadequate to a world in which plots routinely fizzle out rather than reaching any definitive resolution; it can respond only with confusion. Such confusion is visible, too, in a scene where Perkins and Norton encounter a blind old man in an isolated cabin. He gives them food and supplies, but asks them a favor: to kill him. He is on the verge of an unavoidable, painful, lonesome death, but he does not wish to offend God by killing himself. Perkins, baffled by a request he can understand but never accommodate, can only say that he does not wish to offend God either and ride away, leaving the man to suffer.

The film's destabilization of Western tropes and Perkins' madness both reach their apex in the film's final moments, when Perkins and Norton reach their destination. In an earlier flashback Estrada had proudly shown Perkins a picture of his wife and children and drawn a map of how to find his idyllic hometown of Jimenez, making Perkins promise to take his body there if he dies. Now, however, Perkins discovers that none of this was accurate; the town of Jimenez, he is told repeatedly, does not exist. He finds the woman from Estrada's picture, but she is married to another man and angrily denies knowing Estrada at all. Norton loudly points out that Estrada was clearly lying, but Perkins refuses to accept this, and the film never provides a satisfying explanation of Estrada's origins, his real relationship with the woman, or his reasons for concocting his elaborate tales. Coming across an abandoned ruin—really no more than a few crumbling stone walls—Perkins declares that this is, in fact, Jimenez, and that it's "just like Mel said it was." He points out a nonexistent garden and yard, and even gestures, smiling, to another ruined building further off: "store's right over yonder." He holds up Estrada's picture to prove the identification to Norton, not realizing that he is holding it sideways. Norton, who by now has come to feel sorry for Perkins, can only agree. The two men put a makeshift roof on the ruin before Perkins forces Norton to dig Estrada's final grave and then tearfully—and to all appearances sincerely—apologize for killing him. The following morning Perkins releases Norton (who, speaking for the audience trained by conventional narrative forms, says, "I always thought that you'd end up killing me"), telling him, "You can keep the horse, son," and riding off alone. The film ends with Norton, looking after Perkins's retreating figure, yelling out, "You gonna be all right?" There is, of course, no response. Both knowledge and action have failed, and the hero can only choose to believe in a reality he knows to be false.

In its self-conscious deployment of Western tradition, its concurrent refusal of conventional narrative form and resolution, its depiction of a world bereft of meaning and logic, and most of all its failure to locate the promised, idyllic domestic space, *Three Burials* provides a fitting companion and prelude to another film which embodies the internal contradictions of the post–9/11 Western: Joel and Ethan Coens' *True Grit* (2010). Here we arrive at a film in which the tensions, pressures and influences of previous works is so overdetermined that any statement about meaning, intent or even tone can only be made with the greatest possible caution and provisions. We have already seen how Westerns are always already movies about movies, films which inevitably draw upon a well-established body of tropes and conventions which, by now, have only loose connections to any historical reality. This is all the more true of this particular Western, an adaptation of a Charles Portis novel previously filmed in 1969 by Henry Hathaway with John Wayne, the most iconic of all Western stars, in the central role of Rooster Cogburn. The first *True Grit* is a flawed film, but it won Wayne his only Oscar and the image of him wearing Cogburn's eye patch dominates any consideration of the final years of his career. Though the Coens insisted that their film was an adaptation of the novel rather than a remake of the earlier film, it's impossible to watch the 2010 version of Mattie Ross's story without some consciousness of Wayne's considerable shadow hanging over it.

These considerations are multiplied and complicated by the identity of the filmmakers behind the second version of *True Grit*, because critics and audiences are, not without cause, suspicious of the Coen brothers. Anthony Lane has described them as "artists who have settled for making films about films," and is one of many critics who accuse them of not merely choosing style over substance, but of mocking the very idea that a film can contain substance. David Lavery describes the Coens' style as "cine-mendacity" and calls them "inspired confidence men (I mean this as a compliment)" (145). I myself have written elsewhere of the pervasive, uneasy suspicion that the brothers' films "add up to little more than a collection of quotation marks" and suggested that "what makes analyzing the films of the Coen brothers particularly challenging is a fear that, on some level, we viewers are simply not in on the joke" (5–6). Moments of apparent sincerity and characters of depth and appeal occur in Coen films, but they are almost always accompanied and undercut by scenes or ideas of excessive absurdity, by narrative stunts, by spectacle employed in the service of self-conscious irony. Thus, for example, the deeply human, sympathetic characters and tragic situations in *Fargo* (1996) must compete for our attention with cartoonishly exaggerated Midwestern "accents," with the grotesque violence of a body shoved into a wood chipper, and with a distracting "true story" framework that is, in fact, entirely false. The superficially realistic sufferings of Larry Gopnik in *A Seri-*

ous Man (2009) are bookended by a prologue which appears to be a supernatural fable and an ending in which an unnaturally large tornado threatens his entire community. The noirish *The Man Who Wasn't There* (2001) ends with a dream of flying saucers. The slapstick plotting and acting of *Burn After Reading* (2008) erupts into unexpectedly graphic, deadly violence. The Coens routinely make it difficult, if not impossible, for audiences to judge how to react to their films.

For such idiosyncratic filmmakers to adapt a narrative that, in its previous incarnation, was one of the screen's most conservative and uncomplicated Westerns is already a difficult choice to fathom. As Garry Wills has pointed out, the 1969 *True Grit* is most significant as the beginning of the cycle of films marking the end of John Wayne's career, a cycle during which "he recognized that his success would now depend on becoming a living anachronism." The film came only a year after the disastrous failure of *The Green Berets*, which "had shown what a dead end he had reached in pursuing the imperial certitudes of the Ford cavalry pictures" (287). In the Age of Vietnam, the simplistic patriotism and hypermasculinity which had made Wayne a star were giving way to the fetishized violence of Sam Peckinpah's *The Wild Bunch* (1969), the stylized nihilism of Sergio Leone's Man Without a Name trilogy, the complete deconstruction of Robert Altman's *McCabe and Mrs. Miller* (1971). In the successful Westerns remaining to him (*True Grit*, its sequel *Rooster Cogburn* [1975], *Big Jake* [1971], *The Shootist* [1976]), Wayne could only draw upon "his self-consciousness as a living monument" (288), acknowledging that he had essentially become a figure out of step with time, though still deserving of respect.

True Grit was the ideal vehicle to allow Wayne to transition into this final phase. Portis's novel is narrated, in her later years, by Mattie Ross, who relates her adventures as a teenage girl who traveled to Ft. Smith, Arkansas to claim the body of her father and seek vengeance upon Tom Chaney, the man who killed and robbed him. She hires a U.S. Marshal, Reuben "Rooster" Cogburn, and accompanied by a Texas Ranger named LaBoeuf they pursue Chaney into the Indian Territory (now Oklahoma), where he has joined a bandit band led by "Lucky" Ned Pepper. After an initial skirmish Mattie is captured, but LaBoeuf rescues her and Cogburn successfully defeats the rest of the gang. A rattlesnake bites Mattie during the final confrontation, and Cogburn delivers her to a doctor in time to save her life, though her arm is amputated. She never sees Cogburn again, but she does recover his body decades later, when he dies while touring with a Wild West show, and has him buried in her family plot. The great appeal of the book rests in Mattie's shrewd, smart, determined character and her honest, carefully precise voice. The actual narrative is a straightforward conflict between upright virtue and craven villainy, with none of the moral ambiguities or political implications that Wayne's image could no longer support. Although he was decades older than the book's Cogburn, the role allowed him to present himself as a comforting, semi-comic, but still heroic figure; Rooster is a greedy, lazy drunk, but it is he who has the "true grit" of the title, as exemplified by the famous scene—taken, like most of the film, directly from the book—in which he charges alone at four outlaws, the reins between his teeth and two guns blazing.

Hathaway's film is, indeed, remarkably true to the novel, even preserving much of the charmingly stilted, formal dialogue Mattie (Kim Darby) puts in the mouth of every character, including hardened criminals and murderers. Events are streamlined, but every significant sequence in the film, and much of the dialogue, is taken directly from the book. The only significant exceptions to this come at the end of the film. LaBoeuf (Glen Campbell) dies in the film from the same wound he survives in the book, while the movie's Rooster succeeds in getting Mattie to a doctor in time to save both her life and her arm. The book's coda, in which a much older Mattie who has been financially successful but has never married or had children recovers Rooster's body, is replaced by a sequence where Rooster accompanies Mattie back to her family's homestead at the end of their adventure. Mattie shows Rooster the family cemetery, pointing out the plot she intends him to have next to hers, and he indicates that he is touched by the gesture but not yet prepared to take his place in a grave. In response to his boasts about his new horse, Mattie tells him that he is too old and fat to be jumping horses. "Well, come see a fat old man sometime!" he responds in the film's final line of dialogue, spurring his horse into a leap over a fence as heroic music swells. The changes here are clearly intended to emphasize Rooster's—which is to say, Wayne's—heroism and vitality, erasing his death from the narrative in order to leave the living monument alive (and, in fact, prepared for a sequel, though it would not arrive for several years).

Tellingly, the 2010 version of *True Grit* restores an ending which is, in most details, much more faithful to the original novel, and in consequence much bleaker and more meditative. At the end of the final conflict with the film's villains, LaBoeuf (Matt Damon) is alive, but left behind in Rooster's (Jeff Bridges) race to get Mattie (Hailee Steinfeld) to a doctor, and not seen again in the film. The journey to save Mattie's life is more extended and more painful here. In both films Rooster runs Mattie's horse—the only one available after his own mount is killed by the outlaws—to death, and is forced to carry her on foot. Wayne's Rooster, however, quickly locates and steals a wagon to complete the trip; this incident does appear in the novel, making it noteworthy that the Coens choose instead to force their Rooster to continue on foot until he finally comes in sight of a homestead, whereupon he collapses to the ground and fires his pistol to attract attention. "I've grown old," he pants as he waits for help; this is his last line of dialogue and the last time he is seen in the film, a marked contrast to Wayne's triumphant final leap and invitation. Mattie is by this point unconscious, and, as in the book, she never sees Rooster again. The film now jumps forward to her older, one-armed self, traveling to a Wild West show to see Rooster and learning from real-life outlaw Cole Younger (Don Pirl) that he had passed days previously. As in the book, Mattie accepts this news stoically while snarling at Frank James to "keep your seat, trash." The film ends with Mattie at her family plot, looking down at the grave marker proclaiming Rooster to have been "a resolute officer of Parker's court." In a voiceover taken largely from Portis's novel she acknowledges that she is considered a strange old woman for visiting the grave, wonders whether LaBoeuf is still alive, and concludes, "Time just gets away from us." The film fades to black as she walks away from the grave and the camera, toward the featureless horizon.

Where the Hathaway film looks to the future and celebrates the continuity of Wayne's iconic status, the Coen film—like the novel—can only lament the inevitable losses and separations imposed by time. This alone makes the film more suitable to a post–9/11 world in which the Western can no longer signal America's steady march to dominance, but the changes to the setting of the final scene are also significant in this regard. Where the cemetery in Hathaway's film was on a small rise directly above the Ross home, which is visible throughout the final sequence, the Coens' cemetery is isolated in the middle of an unmarked prairie, with the graves gathered under the bare branches of the only visible tree in a light snowfall. What is missing here is Mattie's home. It is absent, too, from the beginning of the film. Hathaway's *True Grit* opens with Frank Ross leaving his home to travel to Fort Smith; we see him bidding farewell to his wife and children, including Mattie, and we see his neat, well-maintained home. In the Coen version, a title card giving a Bible verse ("The wicked flee when none pursueth. *Proverbs 28:1*") immediately follows the title, then a fade-in to an image of Ross's body lying in the snow outside the boarding house where he died as his killer gallops past to escape, Mattie's voiceover drily explaining the circumstances of his murder. It's worth noting that the inclusion of the Bible verse here as an epigraph to the film is a typical example of the kind of game critics accuse the Coens of playing with their films. Portis's Mattie does quote the verse, but only in passing, as a biting comment on the townspeople who allowed her father's killer to escape. It seems deliberately misleading to seek to apply the sentiment to a narrative concerned in its entirety with a very real pursuit of the wicked, something akin to the title card falsely claiming *Fargo* is based on a true story; it puts the film within a framework that does not quite fit. Be that as it may, the key point here is that the actual Ross home is entirely erased from the Coens' film. We first see their Mattie on the train to claim her father's body, and we never see her home or any other member of her family.

This might seem like little more than a device to more quickly launch the central narrative of the film, but this erasure of domestic space is in fact epidemic in Westerns of the post–9/11 era. It is not only the loss of the Ross home that is significant here. The boarding house where Mattie stays before setting off with Rooster is, in the Hathaway film, a lively, bright, welcoming place where Mattie is warmly welcomed and comfortable; in the Coen film it is dark and cold, and Mattie's discomfort and eagerness to leave are emphasized. Unlike in the Hathaway film, we never see her take a meal there. Indeed, Mattie doesn't even go to the boarding house until her second day in Fort Smith, after tending to her father's business and securing some cash; in a characteristically macabre addition to the narrative by the Coens, she must spend her first night in town sleeping in a coffin in the undertaker's back room, surrounded by dead bodies. A similar change is made in Rooster's living arrangements. In Portis's novel Rooster lives in the back room of a Chinese grocery, and has a cat named General Sterling Price; he invites Mattie there to have supper with him and discuss her proposal. The Hathaway film retains these elements, adding a joke: Mattie says she would like to meet Rooster's family, and when they arrive at the grocery he introduces "my father Chen Lee, and my nephew General Sterling Price." The claimed relationships might be a jest, but there is a sense that the place is a genuine home for Rooster; it is roomy and comfortable, and he and Chen Lee chat companionably and share a meal with Mattie at his table before engaging in a game of cards. Little of this is retained in the Coen film. The cat is entirely absent, and Chen Lee is seen only briefly, and never together with Rooster. Rooster's room is cramped, dirty and uncomfortable—he stumbles around it bumping into things and pushing them aside—and he never actually invites Mattie there, though she arrives of her own accord. The Coens' *True Grit* is a film in which domestic space is almost nonexistent.

Of course, domestic space—perhaps more accurately, domesticated space—has always been threatened in the Western. Much of the logic of the form is built around the dangers which surround vulnerable, isolated homes built on the frontier, and the heroes of the Western have traditionally been men who are more contented riding alone on the range than sitting by the fire. There has always been, however, a sense that the domestication of space is an inevitability, and in the final analysis a good. Western heroes may not like being confined to the walls of a home, but they fight to make it possible for others to build such homes and, ultimately, communities. Consider one of the undisputed classics of the genre, John Ford's 1956 *The Searchers*. Discussions of the film usually center on John Wayne's portrayal of Ethan Edwards, the violent, racist former Confederate officer who spends years looking for his niece Debbie (Natalie Wood) after she is taken by Comanche raiders. Edwards is a compelling figure, and it's easy to focus on, for example, his discomfort at being inside in the film's earliest scenes, when Ford's camera angles emphasize the way the ceilings seem to squeeze Wayne painfully. In the film's justly famous final shot Edwards is left outside while the rest of the reunited family happily goes inside their home; he turns and walks toward the horizon as a song on the soundtrack mournfully intones "Ride away, ride away," and the door ultimately closes on him. There is, apparently, no place for him in the home he has made possible.

This apparent alienation from domestic space, however, should be balanced against Edward's final spoken line in the film: "Let's go home, Debbie" (indeed, this would be the final dialogue in the film if not for a woefully misplaced "humorous" scene about a wound Captain Clayton has received to his posterior). Again, readings of this scene usually focus on the surprisingly facile resolution of narrative tension, since Edwards has often indicated that Debbie has been despoiled and should be killed. His easy invocation of "home" should not be ignored, however. Edwards may not personally be comfortable in a home, but he does not doubt that there is a home to go to. Indeed, while most of Edwards' family is killed and their homestead destroyed in the early moments of the film, *The Searchers* deliberately presents this as an aberration. For the most part the community the settlers have built is secure, productive and happy, and even as Edwards continues his quest we return frequently, by way of contrast, to the settled, peaceful life he has turned his back on. The Comanche who serve as the film's villains never seriously threaten the security of the community as a whole; they can only harass those on its margins, and their power to do even this is shown to be on the wane. Even when one character laments that the wild land they inhabit has caused the death of his son, his wife corrects him: "Someday this country's gonna be a fine, good place to be. Maybe it needs our bones in the ground before that time can come." *The Searchers*, like the vast majority of traditional Westerns, accepts this notion that the domestication of Western space is both inevitable and good, and never doubts that there will be a home to return to.

This is frequently no longer the case in Westerns made in the new century. Domestic space is not merely threatened, but entirely absent, as in *True Grit*, or even completely illusory, as in *The Three Burials of Melquiades Estrada*. Homes are no longer only threatened by outside evils that can be confronted and defeated; they are shown to be inherently insecure, unbalanced, transitory, unable to bear the weight of faith or desire invested in them. It is not accidental that Andrew Dominik's elegiac *The Assassination of Jesse James by the Coward Robert Ford* (2007) so strongly emphasizes Jesse's repeatedly frustrated desire to establish a stable home; his death at the hands of Ford while he is in the midst of the seemingly safe domestic task of hanging a picture is ironic, as is Ford's subsequent, tortured movement from place to place seeking to find a setting where he will not be condemned for his act. The theme finds expression even in a film like Ed Harris' *Appaloosa* (2008), which is in most respects a completely traditional Western. Much of the narrative tension in the film, however, derives not from the confrontations between the virtuous gunslingers and friends Virgil (Ed Harris) and Everett (Viggo Mortensen) and the evil rancher Randall Bragg (Jeremy Irons), but from the tendency of Everett's beloved, Allison (Renée Zellweger), to make herself available to any dominant male available, including Bragg. Everett—having declined Allison's advances himself—must ultimately kill Bragg and ride away, sacrificing his own friendship with Virgil, not because Bragg threatens his or Virgil's life but because his presence threatens to undermine Virgil's marriage through Allison's infidelity, an infidelity the film represents as unavoidable. Domesticated space can be understood in the conventions of the traditional Western as being defined by the presence and safety of (white) women, but *Appaloosa* suggests that women can no longer provide such a space and that, even when protected from external threats, the home and family are internally insecure.

Returning to the 2010 *True Grit*, it is worth noting the other ways in which the film differs from Hathaway's version of the story. Many of these changes are, like those at the end of the film, designed to bring the film closer to the source novel. For example, Portis's novel is explicitly set in the winter, but the 1969 film places its events in the middle of the summer, setting the chases and gunfights in lush, green scenery which contributes significantly to the film's relatively light, comic tone. The Coens restore the winter setting, with frequent snowfall and harsh winds, resulting in a much darker, more barren look that emphasizes the danger and inhospitality of the landscape. This is part of a visual strategy emphasizing darkness, dirtiness and drabness that creates a very distinct contrast between the look of the two films. Hathaway's characters—even the outlaws—are clean and dressed in bright, well-maintained clothing; the Coens' are visibly unwashed and clad in worn, earth-toned, makeshift gear. Hathaway's Fort Smith is an open, green, cheerfully well-established community; the Coens' is muddy and dank, with buildings that often seem on the verge of collapse. It's difficult to see Western expansion as a grand project based on the visual evidence the Coens provide.

Still more telling are the alterations and additions the Coens do make to the source novel. In Portis's telling, Rooster and LaBoeuf frequently bicker, but once they and Mattie have entered the Indian Territory in pursuit of Chaney the three do not part. The Coens change this, having LaBoeuf grow so annoyed with Rooster that he parts company with the others not once but twice, intending to pursue the mission on his own. On both occasions the group is reunited by a violent confrontation with Lucky Ned Pepper's (Barry Pepper) gang, but during the first of these separations the Coens insert a sequence which seems to borrow less from Portis's novel or the Western tradition generally than from the skewed universe of their own body of films.

Rooster and Mattie are riding through the woods, with Rooster narrating the story of his long and eventful life (much of his story is taken verbatim from the novel, though there he tells the story in response to Mattie's probing questions while the Coens present him as simply enjoying the pleasure of hearing himself speak). They come across a man who has been hanged, his body dangling some twenty-five or thirty feet directly above the path they are taking. They are unable to determine if the man is Chaney, so Rooster has Mattie climb the tree—as he continues to tell the story of his time as a buffalo hunter—and cut the body down. When she wonders why he was hanged so high, Rooster can only speculate that it was "possibly in the belief it'd make him more dead." Once the man is on the ground Rooster fails to recognize him, but at that moment an Indian wearing a top hat rides up. Looking down from Mattie's point of view we do not hear Rooster's conversation with the Indian, but by the time she climbs down the Indian has taken the body and ridden off, since it might be "worth something in trade."

In the next scene, Rooster and Mattie hear a distant gunshot, which Rooster takes as the Indian's agreed-upon sign that they are being followed. He assumes the follower is LaBoeuf, but when he and Mattie stand and wait they see, emerging from the woods, what initially appears to be a bear riding a horse. This turns out to be a dentist named Forrester (Ed Corbin), wearing a bearskin, who provides medical services throughout the territory for "those humans that will sit still for it." Heavily bearded, with wild eyes and a deep, halting voice, Forrester has now, in his own turn, acquired the dead body from the Indian and extracted its teeth; he asks if Mattie and Rooster would like to trade for the rest. Rooster declines but asks about shelter, and Forrester directs him to the dugout where, that night, they will encounter Lucky Ned's gang for the first time. Significantly, in both the Portis novel and the Hathaway film Rooster is already well acquainted with the dugout; here he must be directed to it, as though the land is suddenly strange to him, though we have heard his familiarity with the territory heavily touted.

Perhaps his disorientation results from the fact that he is no longer in the Indian Territory, but rather in what might be called Coenland. The encounters with the hanged man and Forrester occur nowhere in Portis's novel; they are the only significant events in the Coens' film of which this can be said. Both encounters are bizarre and dreamlike, with grotesque details (like the buzzard feeding on the hanged man when he is first seen) and obscure hints of darker, unnamed implications (like the repeated references to the dead body as an object of trade). Neither encounter has any real bearing on the central plot of the film; there is never any identification of the dead man or any explanation of why he was hanged, or why (or even how) he was hanged so high. The sequence seems to exist solely to undermine any possibility of seeing this version of *True Grit* as a return to the traditional Western, instead asserting an absurdity and ambiguity which echo strongly with the disjointed, uneasy tone of *Three Burials* and, still more, with the Coens' previous foray into Western territory, 2007's *No Country for Old Men*. *No Country*, with its villain motivated by chance more than greed, its hero who fails to defeat or even come face-to-face with his enemy, and its lack of normative closure, has been widely understood as a film in which "the moral map that was used in the traditional western narrative has faded, leaving viewers without a clear moral compass to determine what is right and wrong, thereby forcing the western tradition to collapse into moral nihilism" (Devlin 222). For some critics, the Coens' *True Grit*, with its more conventional narrative and apparent triumph of good over evil, marked a retreat from this challenge to Western tradition: "there is no mystery at the end of *True Grit*, a bloodlusting vigilante story with a mightily smug and tidy conclusion" (Welsh 81). Even if this is an accurate reading of the ending of the film, however (and surely the Coens provide an ending which is a good deal less smug and tidy than that crafted by Hathaway), it is a mistake to look only to the ending of a film to discover the ways in which it represents the world. The hanged man / Forrester sequence, no less than anything on offer in *No Country*, depicts a world in which uncanny violence without reason can appear at any moment, a world bereft of normative markers of morality, a world that "is no longer a place for the western hero" (Devlin 230). The Coens' Rooster, after all, does end up under a tombstone, after having subjected himself to the indignity of becoming a sideshow attraction. Even if only in this one sequence, the 2010 *True Grit* surely participates in the contemporary Western's trend of presenting the world as a confusing, hostile place where even identity has become uncertain and there is no home to return to.

This trend, I would suggest, reaches an apex in Kelly Reichardt's *Meek's Cutoff* (2010) a film that merits consideration alongside *Stagecoach* (Ford, 1939) or *The Good, the Bad and the Ugly* (Leone, 1966) as a text with the potential to significantly alter the trajectory of the Western genre. Set in Oregon in 1845, and loosely based upon a real historical incident, the film follows a small wagon train of three families trying to reach the promised riches and bounty of the Pacific coast. They are guided by Stephen Meek (Bruce Greenwood), a flamboyant, confident figure straight out of Western convention who repeatedly assures them of their ultimate safety and prosperity while spinning tales of his own prowess. He has led them onto a side trail splitting aside from the main path, the cutoff of the title. Despite his assurances, however, the families he is guiding suspect that they are lost, and as their water supply dwindles they become increasingly desperate and pessimistic about their plight. They even consider hanging Meek, but decide their only hope is to continue to follow his direction.

The film is remarkable, first, for its highly unconventional look and sound. Westerns have traditionally highlighted the open expanses and limitless horizons of the frontier as spectacles of beauty and freedom, often by employing widescreen formats to their full potential. *Meek's Cutoff*, however, is shot in a 1.33:1 ratio which has been used by very few theatrical releases in the last fifty years, since Hollywood turned to size in an attempt to counter the appeal of the box-screened television. The nearly square image is, according to Reichardt, intended to evoke the restricted, boxed-off view of women wearing bonnets, as the female members of the wagon train frequently do. The effect is startling, eliminating the romantic appeal of the boundless Western landscape and replacing it with a sense of restriction, limitation, and futility; no matter how doggedly the families move forward, there is no sign of any significant change in the barren, endless plains that contain them. In effect the very emptiness of the land becomes a kind of prison. The sound of the film reinforces the sense of alienation and hopelessness. There is virtually no music in the film, and most dialogue is heard only in distant snatches and incomplete conversations. For the most part, the only sound is the near-constant wind. Much of the film is taken up with sequences of the three wagons and the handful of desperate humans and animals simply plodding forward, and every incident that seems to relieve the building tension proves to be temporary and illusory: they find water but it is alkaline and undrinkable, a boy finds gold nuggets but they have no time to look for more and no way to meaningfully mark the place.

The narrative focus of the film is on the three women in the party, particularly Emily Tetherow (Michelle Williams). Although her husband is the nominal leader of the group, it becomes clear over the course of the narrative that he relies so heavily upon her for advice that her decisions are actually those which will be abided by. Most of her time, however—and that of the other wives—is spent in a futile effort to make the wagons function as homes, and here *Meek's Cutoff* joins other recent Westerns in making the domestication of Western space essentially impossible. The chores the women do become increasingly impossible and meaningless as their supplies of water and food decline, and the possessions they have brought across the continent—a pet bird, valued furniture, family heirlooms—must be abandoned, often simply thrown out of the back of one of the wagons as they proceed. The futility of their gestures is fully brought home when one of the wagons, while being lowered down a steep grade, irreparably crashes, cruelly exposing the fragility of the domestic illusion.

The key narrative event in the film occurs when the group captures a Native American man (Rod Rondeaux). Meek, offering as evidence several colorful examples of atrocities committed by Indians, advocates killing the man immediately, though he cannot even identify with any certainty what tribe the man belongs to (a crucial question in fixing not only his possible intentions and resources, but also their location). The majority of the group, however—led by Emily—chooses to follow the man, believing he must of necessity know where water can be found. They make numerous attempts to communicate their desires, offering pleas, beatings, and trade, but there is never any indication that the native man understands them; his own language is unknown to them, and it is not translated for the audience. When he begins to walk, the group has no choice but to follow.

A lesser film—or a more traditional Western—would complete this narrative arc by forming a bond between Emily and the native man, perhaps having them communicate through signs and drawings and ultimately save the group through their cross-cultural friendship. Emily does try to form such a relationship; she repairs the man's moccasin, and when a frustrated Meek decides to kill the man after the wreck of the wagon, she points a rifle at Meek and insists that he relent. *Meek's Cutoff*, however, declines to reward her efforts; the native remains irreducibly unknown and unknowable, showing no particular reaction to any of her efforts, even when she obviously saves his life. His tribe is never identified; he is never given a name. His actions, like the features of the land, offer neither meaning nor hope. Are his nighttime chants prayers, or signals to unseen listeners? Is the pile of rocks he walks past, as one of the other women insists in a panic, a sign from his tribesmen to lead them into slaughter? Is he guiding them towards salvation or ruin?

What marks *Meek's Cutoff* as perhaps the ultimate example of the post–9/11 Western is its refusal to answer these questions. Once, Westerns were given context and meaning by the inevitability of the American project; no matter the fate of individual characters, the Pacific would be reached, the natives would be conquered, the nation would fulfill its destiny. The final moments of *Meek's Cutoff* embody a new American context in which there can be no such certainty. Coming over a ridge which they had hoped—based on little more than optimistic readings of the native's direction—concealed water, the wagon train encounters only a solitary, half-dead tree in the middle of the endless scrub, and yet another ridge beyond. The party's one child hesitantly offers the belief that the tree cannot grow without water, but clearly no salvation has yet been found. They can only choose, once again, whether to continue following the native, with still no indication of his intentions or thoughts. Meek defers, pointedly, to Emily, who turns to look at the native. In the film's final shot, we see him from her point of view, framed between some branches of the tree, as he turns and begins to walk away.

In many ways the shot returns to one of the iconic gestures of the conventional Western: the closing shot of the figure retreating into the distance. Think, again, of Shane, dwindling away even as the boy calls after him, or Ethan Edwards, his back to us as we close the door of the film upon him. Many conventional Westerns have ended in this way, with the hero perhaps moving into solitude, but still moving, still exhibiting the fundamental freedom that is basic to the form. In the new Western, however, the shot has changed. Pete Perkins rides away from us, but we know he has nowhere to ride to; his former captive calls after him not hoping for his return, but to enquire anxiously about his welfare. Mattie Ross walks away from us into a cold, darkening world, toward a home we never see. The native in *Meek's Cutoff* walks away toward we know not what, and we cannot know, either, whether to follow will bring disaster or survival, or even if following is possible. His is the emblematic figure of the new Western, the marker of all the things we cannot know and all the places we cannot tame.

WORKS CITED

Devlin, William J. "*No Country for Old Men*: The Decline of Ethics and the West(ern)." *The Philosophy of the Western*. Ed. Jennifer L. McMahon and B. Steve Csaki. Lexington: University Press of Kentucky, 2010. 221–240.
Lane, Anthony. "Heists: 'The Ladykillers'; 'Intermission.'" *The New Yorker* 80.7 (2004): 89.
Lavery, David. "'Secret Shit': The Uncertainty Principle, Lying, Deviations, and the Movie Creativity of the Coen Brothers." *Post Script* 27.2 (Winter/Spring 2008): 141–153.
Minus, Ed. "Westerns." *Sewanee Review* 118.1 (Winter 2010): 82–90.
Stam, Robert. "Introduction: The Theory and Practice of Adaptation." *Literature and Film: A Guide to the Theory and Practice of Film Adaptation*. Ed. Robert Stam and Alessandra Raengo. Malden, MA: Blackwell, 2005. 1–52.
Walker, Joseph S., and Keith Perry. "Introduction: 'If You Think We're Alive, You Ought To Speak.'" *Post Script* 27.2 (Winter/Spring 2008): 3–7.
Welsh, Jim. "Don Graham Does Cormac Doing Oprah." *Cormac McCarthy Journal* 8.1 (Fall 2010): 80–81.
Wills, Garry. *John Wayne's America*. New York: Simon & Schuster, 1997.

The Beginning and the End
Gay Representations in Brokeback Mountain *and* 3:10 to Yuma

Vincent Piturro

In 1950, the great Budd Boetticher was still a young, struggling director intent on making Westerns. His big break came that year with *Bullfighter and the Lady*, a film that was being produced by Republic Pictures with help from John Wayne. Wayne had been moonlighting as a producer for Republic, and the Boetticher film was a project in which he was very interested. Wayne asked John Ford for help with the final cut, and Ford subsequently called Boetticher to arrange a screening. Ford loved the picture, and he immediately forged an agreement with Boetticher to give Ford final cut rights; Ford told Boetticher that he would win Boetticher an Oscar! Ford cut the film from its original 124 minutes to 87 minutes, telling Boetticher,

> "You've got forty-two minutes of real chichi shit in this thing. This relationship between [Robert] Stack and [Gilbert] Roland. They're a couple of queers. They love each other." Boetticher replied that men can love each other without being homosexuals. "That's a lot of bullshit," Ford replied [Eyman 395–396].

The story ends with Ford's cut being released, and Boetticher forever angry at him for what he thought was "hacking up his film." The film was nominated for one Academy Award and helped Boetticher establish himself as an A-list director.

There are several illuminating points to take from this vignette: first, Ford was well aware of the homosexual subtext in the Western; second, Ford was obviously uncomfortable with portraying overt homosexuality in the Western; and finally, what constitutes a gay interpretation of male relationships in Westerns is debatable, especially among the directors. But both Ford and Boetticher were obviously aware that homosexual relationships in the

Poster for *Brokeback Mountain*. A Focus Features release, directed by Ang Lee, 2005.

Western were real possibilities, and they were consciously trying to either tame them or get rid of them completely. The evidence is not only in the conversation between two iconic directors of the Western, but also in the films themselves. The history of homosexuality parallels, to a certain extent, the history of homosexuality in all film. When dealing with such a definitive and prominent genre such as Westerns, however, the stakes are a bit higher: Westerns were the face of Hollywood for the bulk of its formative years, and the Western defined classic Hollywood cinema, helping examine the fundamental aspects of our country at the time of its expansion as well as the years in which the Westerns were produced. The Western was also the standard for masculinity and a space in which "men could be men," particularly in the emasculating years after World War II. The Western became a male refuge. A short survey of early Westerns can illuminate how homosexuality in the Western became fertile ground for discussion and analysis.

Charting the representation of gay men in Westerns begins in the early days of cinema straight through the halcyon years of the 30s–50s to the more recent Westerns such as the remake of *3:10 to Yuma* (Mangold, 2007). A discussion of *Brokeback Mountain* (Lee, 2005) is also required, although for reasons that will be discussed later, the film stands outside the Western genre. *Brokeback Mountain* attracted the most attention because of the centrality of the gay relationship, rather than the subtextual status of such relationships depicted in other Westerns. *Brokeback Mountain* would garner impressive reviews for its daring (for Hollywood!) portrayal of the love story between two men, and would be called everything from the "gay Western" (Clark), to a "gay cowboy movie" (Stein; Clarke), to "genre bending" (A. Thompson). While *3:10 to Yuma* features a gay character in the more traditional mold of the Western in Ben Foster's Charlie Prince, it received little or no attention when it was released just over a year later. Hollywood quickly and easily slipped back into the old representations after the supposed cathartic experience of *Brokeback Mountain* and the discussion around homosexuality immediately disappeared. Roger Ebert made passing reference to Prince's character, and David Denby noticed as well, but there was little to no critical discussion surrounding the issue of homosexuality and/or gay representations in Westerns. What started as a verdant conversation around *Brokeback Mountain* also ended there.

In one sense, *Brokeback Mountain* let Westerns off the hook when it comes to homosexuality: it places that behavior into a finite space from which the rest of the genre can distance itself. The problem is in the formalism: it is not necessarily a Western about homosexuality, but rather a gay love story that happens to be set in the relatively recent American West. That more recent setting allows time and distance from earlier Westerns, thereby differentiating itself as modern and uninhibited. In other words, the gay storyline of *Brokeback Mountain is rendered as a sign of the times rather than an inherent characteristic of the genre.

This essay argues that the treatment of homosexuality in the remake of *3:10 to Yuma* follows from earlier Westerns and allows a more open space for discussion, investigation, and ultimately, deconstruction. *3:10 to Yuma* takes the gay subtexts of previous Westerns to a more logical extension than does *Brokeback Mountain*. That subtext, which sometimes seeped into primary text, was there from the very beginning.

The Broncho Billy film series, which would set the standard for most Westerns to follow, portrayed a gay theme in the very early days of cinema. *The Buried Letters* (1910) tells the story of how a jealous prospector divides Billy from his wife by concealing letters between the two. Once the letters are revealed and Billy forgives his friend, as David Lusted notes, "the two men die with a clear conscience" (87). Comparing that film to an earlier Broncho Billy film where there is a male/female reconciliation, Lusted states, "That the first reunion is between heterosexual partners and the second between homosocial friends suggests that the early Western incorporates a range of intimate gender relations. This variety is clearly connected to the variety of the varied aesthetic traditions the Western draws upon" (87). The final sentence of Lusted's assessment points toward the inclusion of melodrama as one of the aesthetic traditions, one more aspect of the Western's formation that speaks to varied types of relationships and themes. The other important point from Lusted's argument is that it connects directly to the Ford/Boetticher story. It is certainly possible, as Boetticher points out, that men can love each other in a non-sexual manner. Certainly the Western genre is based on homosocial spaces and close relationships among men, and not all of them will be sexual relationships. But can some of them be? The logical conclusion is not all relationships will be platonic and conversely, not all relationships will be sexual. The truth probably resides somewhere in the middle, and such a dynamic played out from the early days of cinema and the formation of the genre.

It would continue throughout the life of the Western. The Code Westerns could not show blatant gay sex acts, but they were full of innuendo. Ford's own *My Darling Clementine* (1946) is one of the most prominent; the mutual admiration between Henry Fonda's Wyatt Earp and Victor Mature's Doc Holliday straddles that line between homosocial space and homosexual longing. As Edward Buscombe notes,

> The bond between Wyatt Earp and Doc Holliday is based on the principle that opposites attract. Earp is upright and uncomplicated, and with strong family ties who is committed to law and order. Holliday is essentially a loner, an educated man who has tried to lose himself in the frontier and run away from civilization and its discontents [4].

The mutual attraction begins as Earp and Holliday meet, at a bar, early in the film. Earp is the newly-appointed Marshal and Holliday runs the gambling house in Tombstone. There is initial friction between the two at their first meeting and beyond. When Holliday is insulted by Earp in their initial meeting, he challenges Earp to draw his gun. Earp coolly pulls back his jacket to reveal he is not carrying a gun. They work out their differences after that first meeting and eventually forge an uneasy friendship. Yet Earp is immediately smitten with Holliday and sees a cultured, intelligent person who is a natural ladies' man; conversely, Holliday sees a calm and grounded soul in Earp. Both want what the other has, and even though women are present, namely the wild and promiscuous Chihuahua (Linda Darnell) with whom Holliday has mated, the men still drift toward each other and the women become secondary.

Earp also exhibits stereotypically gay traits in his fastidious appearance, his meticulous attention to detail when it comes to his cleanliness, and at one point, spraying himself with flowers—much to the surprise/dismay of his brother. In his first foray into Tombstone, Earp simply wants a shave after being out on the road. Contrast that to his brothers, who have no such craving, and we see an Earp who is clearly differentiated from his brothers in appearance, personal hygiene, and actions. While these qualities don't necessarily make him gay, they do stray from the typical portrayal of the masculine hero in the Western. The most telling scene, however, is when Earp and Holliday rescue a Shakespearean actor from the evil clutches of the rival Clanton gang (who have abducted the actor and forced him to perform). As the actor struggles to finish a soliloquy, Holliday steps in and recites it from memory. Earp is mesmerized, and in that moment, he touchingly gazes on Holliday with a lovely sparkle in his eye that speaks more than any dialogue. Soon after, when Clementine (Cathy Downs) (Holliday's ex from the east coast) appears in Tombstone and is rebuffed by Holliday, Earp steps in to take Holliday's place. As he awkwardly speaks to Clementine, she responds by saying, "I don't think you know too much about a women's feelings, Marshal." Obviously, he is more comfortable in the company of men. And finally, as Buscombe concludes, "In allowing Holliday to join in what is in effect a family quarrel at the OK Corral, Earp offers [Holliday] a symbolic celebration of their bond. And Earp's engagement to Clementine after Holliday's death can be read as evidence of his desire to preserve the relationship beyond the grave" (4). Buscombe makes a logical assertion here that Earp wishes to continue his bond with Holliday posthumously, and in Clementine he sees the same qualities that he saw in Holliday: cultured, intelligent, and attractive. But we can go further. There is no evidence of any "engagement" between Clementine and Earp, and the film ends as Earp leaves Clementine behind in Tombstone, promising—thinly, it seems—to return to her someday. At the perfect moment for a Hollywood three-point-lighting, good-bye kiss between the two principal stars, Earp abstains and rides away; it is a curious ending and a curious lack of action by the supposed masculine hero Earp. Based on the evidence given in the film, however, the conclusion points to a yearning and mourning for his real love, Doc Holliday. Certainly during this very strict Code era, a gay love story would never have been an option, but a kiss between the male and female lead would have been standard. It is not here. And remember that it was only just a few years later that Ford gave his advice to Boetticher about getting rid of the "queer" material; he was obviously sensitive to it after his own *My Darling Clementine* displayed such an obvious love affair between men.

Late Code films would also display such attraction between men. *Ride the High Country* (1962), Sam Peckinpah's breakthrough film, chronicled a close relationship between Gil Westrum (Randolph Scott) and Steve Judd (Joel McCrea) that had an unexplained past and a tumultuous present. As they plan to steal gold they have been entrusted to guard, they see one last job and a way out. As Buscombe relates, "Neither Steve nor Gil has a sexual relationship in the film and their pairing seems to occupy all the emotional energy. In the final scene, when Gil suggests the two stand up together against the bad guys, he calls Steve 'partner'—a common term of affection in the Western, but significant even so" (3). They are an aging "couple," they have drifted apart, they have their differences about what to do and when to do it, yet they recognize their unbreakable bond and wish to go out together—good or bad. We can argue that not only are they are a couple, but they are a strong example of a gay couple.

The homosexual undertones were not exclusive to the Code-era films; they continued on after the death of the Code. *Butch Cassidy and the Sundance Kid* (Hill, 1969) portrays one of the closest male-male relationships in all of cinema. Their bond is obvious from the beginning, and the film takes pains to establish their closeness not only through the narrative but through the cinematography and editing, placing the pair next to each other or isolated from other males and then cutting back and forth between the two—cinematically pairing them. When the gang disbands, it is Butch and Sundance (Paul Newman, Robert Redford) that stay together. Even the introduction of Etta, Sundance's girl, it seems, comes later in the film after Butch and Sundance have already been established as a couple. And when Sundance and Etta are together, Butch always intervenes and comes between them. The famous "Raindrops Keep Falling on My Head" sequence is an intimate moment between Butch and Etta, not Sundance and Etta. In his analysis of the boys' relationship, Buscombe sees more than just buddies:

> Every time Sundance talks to Etta, Butch seems to pop up nearby, as if monitoring their conversations. Butch is friendly to Etta but there's never any sense that it's a *ménage a trois*: the two boys are too wrapped up in each other for that. Just before they discuss Bolivia, Butch and Sundance have leaped over the cliff

together into the raging torrent below, if not quite holding hands then all but. In their relationship they seem to take on stereotypical male and female roles: Butch is the thinker and decision-maker and Sundance the intuitive one who waits for Butch to take the initiative. In the freeze frame that ends the picture the two are still together, united in death as in life [3–4].

Buscombe makes a very strong case for a gay couple here. And resistance to this reading can be explained by Star Theory: Redford and Newman were very much the sex-symbol male stars of their day; Newman was in the middle of his career and Redford was near the beginning of his. A reading of the pair as a couple would have been seen as blasphemous, but that theoretical tack can also explain exactly why they *can be read* as a gay couple: taken so far out of their comfort zones as the typical male Hollywood starring roles and Western heroes, it makes the pairing more palatable to the general audiences. But the evidence for the coupling is logical and extensive.

There are many other examples of gay couples/pairings throughout the history of the Western. Buscombe also briefly details *Monte Walsh* (Fraker, 1970), and *Open Range* (Costner, 2003) and their close, male relationships. Of course, Buscombe's (nor any other's) list is not exhaustive and it may be exclusive, but if nothing else, it supports the notion that where there are close homosocial spaces, there are certainly male-male relationships as well. And that brings us to *Brokeback Mountain*.

Based on the 1997 short story by Annie Proulx, Ang Lee's film tells the story of two male ranch hands who fall in love and begin an intermittent affair that lasts for eighteen years. As the film begins and the two are hired as sheep herders, they spend a great deal of time alone together in the mountains. Initially, Ennis del Mar (Heath Ledger) sleeps outside the tent and Jack Twist (Jake Gyllenhall) sleeps inside. But on one particularly cold night, Jack invites Ennis to sleep in the tent. Later that night the men have sex. Ennis is initially reticent to discuss it or repeat it, and he displays a cold, violent side to Jack. But Jack persists and the affair blossoms, away from the eyes of society—save for the binoculars of their boss. When Jack speaks of the two of them moving onto a ranch together, Ennis gives a foreboding speech about a man who was killed because of a similar affair. The story serves to foreshadow Jack's death as well as ground the film in its time period and the period's attitudes about same-sex couples. Ennis understands that theirs is a forbidden love that society would not accept. As Thomas Piontek describes, this idea of "tragic love" is exactly what makes the film palatable to heterosexual audiences:

> What makes the film both "relatable" and convenient for straight audiences is that they can feel good about feeling bad for the gay characters on screen and their "private" suffering while simultaneously resting assured that the cowboys' touching story poses no threat to their heterosexual privilege or the social

order that requires that the movie's gay love story be "tragic" in the first place [130].

The film is thus rhetorically brilliant: it spoke to both a gay audience that had never seen such explicit sexual relations between Western men, and it spoke to heterosexual audiences while allowing them a safe distance from any real-life implications.

Ennis and Jack leave the mountain as new lovers, but they go their separate ways. Both men marry and live their separate lives, yet they come back to each other often and carry on their affair away from the eyes of civilization. Ennis and Jack are two lovestruck cowboys that were perhaps born in the wrong era or even the wrong part of the country. Ennis in particular understands they cannot live their life together in public, and in the end, Jack is seemingly killed because he is gay.

Brokeback Mountain is thus a melodramatic love story set in the American West; it is not a Western. Curiously, even Ang Lee said that he did not consider the film a Western, but rather, a "love story." Piontek sees that disavowal as a calculated marketing move. By calling the film a "love story" rather than a Western, the distribution company Focus Features was looking for a broader audience outside the gay community. The film was thus marketed heavily toward women, the target market for romance and love stories. The strategy worked, and the film's popularity with women was a major reason for its box-office success (126).

Yet many still believed the film to be a Western, and the critical community in general embraced the label. Robin Wood, in his effusive and positive review of the film in "On and Around *Brokeback Mountain*," says of director Ang Lee: "He has made one other film about a gay couple and one other Western" (29). The simple categorization seems strange for such a venerable critic, but his review was focused on a historical context for the film and not a genre discussion. Even noted Western scholar Edward Buscombe flatly labels the film a Western in the first sentence of his article "Man to Man" in a Western special edition of *Sight and Sound*: "Brokeback Mountain is the latest in a long tradition of Westerns to explore the intense, unspoken and physical bond between its two male heroes" (34). Again, this oversimplified classification misses the dense history of the Western and how films are categorized into the genre.

The Western is one of the best-defined genres in the history of American cinema, even by the slippery standards of genre study and genre theory. If we examine the bulk of Westerns throughout history, we find solid ground: most are set in the American west during the period directly following the Civil War, from 1865 to the "closing of the west" in 1890. And as I have noted elsewhere, many of the genre characteristics are fairly well agreed upon:

For Richard Slotkin a "regeneration through violence" has been a central characteristic of the Western. For Jim Kitses, the aesthetic of the West was an important characteristic: the openness, the possibility, and the coexistence of beauty and violence were paramount aesthetic concerns. Kitses also saw class warfare and the search for identity as essential thematic concerns [Piturro 113].

Now all this business about whether or not the film is a Western may seem slightly reductive, dogmatic, or even irrelevant. But if the film is analyzed and then classified as a Western, it then stands in relation to all other Westerns before and after it. And that categorization has grave implications for the film itself and the rest of the genre. So we have to take that business seriously.

Whatever the classification, however, *Brokeback Mountain* is still highly problematic, particularly in its portrayal of gay men and the consequences of their sexual relationship. Both Ennis and Jack are prone to violence outside their relationship with one another; Ennis in particular is shown to have a short fuse and many times that violence is either directed toward his wife Alma (Michelle Williams) or occurs when she is around. They fight inside their home; Ennis fights with nearby drunkards at a Fourth of July celebration; and their break-up/blowout at the Thanksgiving dinner ends in violence. Jack has his share of outbursts too. The film conveys that the repression leads to the violence, yet there are several scenes that call such an oversimplified assertion into question: at one point when Ennis and Jack are herding the sheep near the beginning of the film, they end up in a fistfight; their sex is always rough and coded as a violent act; and their last meeting together ends up in violence as well. So is it merely the repressed homosexuality that leads to the violence? Or is it something more inherent in the presentation in this and other films?

This same dynamic was present in Maggie Greenwald's *The Ballad of Little Jo* (1992). A story about a woman who is excommunicated from her wealthy family in the east and remakes herself as a man in the West, there is one obviously coded gay character in the town, Percy (Ian McKellan), who also has violent tendencies. As I have argued elsewhere,

> His homosexuality also has dual implications: Percy's repressed urges eventually lead him to act out violently against two separate women in the film—the traveling prostitute as well as Jo herself (after Percy reads a letter and discovers Jo's secret). Percy's actions will lead to his banishment from the town. On the genre level, Percy highlights the implicit homoeroticism of many Westerns throughout the history of the genre.... Through Percy, *The Ballad of Little Jo* suggests that one possible underlying reason for violence in the Western is this repressed sexuality in the middle of such a male-centered West [Piturro 117].

Perhaps it is more than just a simple matter of the repression that leads to violence, however, since other recent gay characters—such as Charlie Prince in *3:10 to Yuma*—were also violent, quick on the trigger, unremorseful, and end up banished or dead. None lived a happy, fulfilling existence with their partner, and the films did not even give an option for such an outcome; it had to end badly. This same dynamic haunts *Brokeback Mountain*: Jack's death is the punishment for his sexuality, and even Ennis' reluctance to live with Jack because he is aware of the societal biases shows how the character who "knows his place" is rewarded by being allowed to live, albeit alone.

When deconstructing *Brokeback Mountain*, simply portraying an overtly gay male-male relationship does not go far enough in reversing the degrading representations of Hollywood; the stakes of that partnership lead to a different reading. As Thomas Piontek notes, "it is not groundbreaking in any respect. On the contrary; the film's inability to imagine love between two men as anything but a tragedy that gets at least one of the lovers killed in the last reel links it to one of the darkest chapters in the history of gay men and lesbians in Hollywood.... In a straight cowboy town like Hollywood, many considered this progress—and rightly so" (131). And once progress is achieved, there is no need to look back.

Therein lies the problem with *Brokeback Mountain*: it ended the conversation on homosexuality in Western film. In an era when gay relations between men on film have finally become explicit, the conversation around this film substitutes for a larger conversation about homosexuality in the Western and therefore abrogates the discussion. We never deconstructed the long-view of the issue; we simply took this film as evidence that "it was there" and moved on. The problem becomes that we never fully examined the underlying representations and presentations of gays in the Western and pawn it all off on *Brokeback Mountain*. As mentioned before, however, *Brokeback Mountain* is not a true Western, the representations are ultimately negative, and it falls into the stereotypical presentations of many gay characters as repressed, violent, quick-tempered, unremorseful, and/or fatalistic. The questions of why such representations are prevalent and what they tell us about the genre have never been fully examined, and that is why the genre discussion/labeling is so important. If critics such as Robin Wood not only call it a Western but also see it as progressive, then the discussion of gay characters in other Westerns becomes superfluous: *Brokeback Mountain* exposed the truth and absolved the Western of its sins. But it is not that simple.

The character of Charlie Prince (Ben Foster) in *3:10 to Yuma* provides a better canvas on which to examine the portrayal of homosexuality in the Western. The film chronicles fugitive Ben Wade (Russell Crowe), who is captured after a stagecoach raid and transported to the town of Contention where he will board a train to Yuma prison. Wade is the leader/father figure of a ruthless gang of thieves. When he is captured, the Marshal forms a ragtag group to transport Wade, a group that includes poor, handicapped rancher

Dan Evans (Christian Bale). Charlie Prince is the perhaps one of the most vile, violent characters in all of Western cinema. As the henchman to gang leader Ben Wade, Prince carries out his boss' plans with economy and ferocity. We meet him in the second sequence of the film, as the gang hijacks the stagecoach. Once the stagecoach is upended and the guards crawl away in agony, Prince slowly stalks them as a predator stalks its prey. After shooting one of the guards, another man, Byron McElroy (Peter Fonda), tries to crawl away but comes under the foot of Prince. "You might of heard of me, Pinkerton; Charlie Prince?" Prince squeals as he loads his gun; McElroy responds, "I heard of a balled-up whore named Charlie Princess." Enraged, Prince shoots him in the stomach—not to kill him but only to make him suffer. And so before we are able to make our own judgments about Prince, the film delivers a judgment for us, pre-packaged and opened in the first reel. The reference to "whore" is an obvious emasculation; the "balled-up" speaks to the repressed homosexuality; and the "Princess" puts the nail in the coffin. There is no subtext here: Prince's homosexuality becomes part of the central narrative from the beginning of the film.

The film continues the gay character development very quickly, as Carol MacCurdy notes, "After the stagecoach robbery, an infatuated Charlie introduces the star outlaw to Dan, 'careful, rancher, that's Ben Wade you're talking to'" (286). Soon after the raid, the gang heads to town and takes over the saloon. As they split up their money, Wade becomes entranced with the beautiful bartender. Prince looks on, watching intently and jealously, as his attraction to Wade is visualized—he looks upon Wade the same way Wade looks upon the bartender. He exhorts Wade to leave in advance of the marshal returning, but Wade stays with the girl. As Prince leaves, he tells Wade that he will meet him just over the Mexican border: "I'll wait for you," he says, with all the force of unrequited love—the "wait" taking on double meaning. But Wade stays too long with the girl and is caught by the marshal. As MacCurdy notes, "Ben is so secure in Charlie's loyalty that he is unconcerned when caught by the law. He knows Charlie will inevitably rescue him" (287). We understand that this episode has happened before.

Tellingly, Prince never leaves for Mexico; rather, he stays and watches as Wade is taken away, all the while screaming vengeance on the town. When another gang member objects to springing Wade because of Wade's own inept behavior, Prince violently threatens him too. When Wade's captors trick the gang and send off a decoy stagecoach, Wade burns the decoy alive. When the gang realizes they are a day's ride—80 miles—behind the real Wade caravan, Prince vows to ride the horses till they die and then get new ones. When he happens upon a posse that is looking for Wade, he shoots them on the spot. He has a singular, psychopathic drive to save his beloved, and he allows no one to get in his way. Or they die. As MacCurdy describes,

Charlie's worship of Ben unmistakably takes on homoerotic elements, a point only a handful of reviewers made. Ben Foster's androgynous looks, his character's dress, the dialogue, and plays on the name "Charlie Prince" all speak to the character's passionate love for Ben Wade. Although not classically handsome like Richard Jaeckel, who plays the 1957 Charlie, Foster presents a man who is conscious of his looks; with his platinum blonde hair and piercing blue eyes, his flashy orange rawhide pants with slits for boots, and unconventional cream leather jacket with double-breasted brass buttons [287].

Contrast that costuming to the more classical, rugged look of Crowe's Wade, who wears darker colors, a more contemporary sport coat over an open-collared shirt, and a fashionable hat that could be a hipster's accoutrement on a Saturday night out, and we see Wade tracking closer to what Martin Pumphrey describes as the conventional look of the Western hero. As David Lusted notes, "Pumphrey suggests that the Western hero can rarely be seen out of Western uniform, separated from the conventional dress and armoury of the fictional cowboy and gunfighter, for fear of feminizing his body and appearing to offer it for a sexualized look" (31). Wade also has a sensitive side but he only shows that when alone or when in the company of a woman. He beds the bartender that leads to his capture, but he also sweet talks Dan's wife Alice (Gretchen Mol) at dinner before the group sets out on their journey. The cinematography even highlights their attraction through a shot/reverse-shot sequence that isolates the two. Alice is clearly aroused by the smooth Wade, and finally Dan has to intervene. Ben is the Alpha-male in every respect, and he is therefore offered up as both subject of the film and objectified body for the spectator, the two women in the film, and for his partner Prince. Contrasted to Prince's flashy outfit and actions, Ben is the typical male hero of the Western while Prince is feminized through his wardrobe and behavior, a feminization that is made literal by the very contrast to Wade.

Finally, as MacCurdy notes, Prince is "a creature of flamboyant will, he struts across the landscape, holds his lean body erect, and fires his long barreled pistols with frightening brio" (287). This rendering of Prince is quite different from the 1957 version of the film, where Richard Jaeckel is simply the typical sidekick for the hero; the change is quite telling, as MacCurdy notes, "The 2007 film dramatically transforms the character, showing Charlie's unconcealed love for Ben, his devotion to Ben's celebrity status, and his willingness to take loyalty to a frightening level. As devoted son and passionate lover of Ben Wade, Charlie Prince is willing to die to preserve Ben's masculine omnipotence" (287). To go further, he is also willing to die to try and prove his own masculinity, a masculinity that was overtaken by his homosexuality and seemingly manifests itself in overt violence. Finally, that brings us to the central question of this study.

At issue here is the *why?* of the representation. Why is Prince portrayed as he is? Why is he feminized and coded as gay? There are several possible answers to this question, and most are disturbing. First, consider that such a representation may serve to be reflexive—showing how earlier Westerns portrayed gay characters and highlighting the negative representations therein. Similar to a Tarantino-esque representation of race relations, making the portrayal overt can serve to illuminate the negativity inherent in Westerns. But there is no real evidence of reflexivity, and in fact, the film makes pains to present its subjects and settings as highly realistic.

Another possibility is that the representation is negative because of an institutional homophobia when it comes to the Western genre and Hollywood cinema in general. Prince's character has no redeeming qualities, he is a bitter loner, he is extremely violent, and he dies a violent death at the hand of his beloved. It is hard to extract anything positive from that portrayal, and it follows directly from other gay representations in Westerns and other films in general. If we look at Piontek's reading of *Brokeback Mountain* as a fatalistic gay love story—when most generally regarded it as a groundbreaking film—then it is virtually impossible to construct a positive reading of any gay relationships in the Western. There is certainly more evidence for this latter reading than the first option.

The end result is that recent Hollywood Westerns have made little or no progress in the portrayal of gay men or same sex partnerships. In fact, by deconstructing the representations in *Brokeback Mountain* and *3:10 to Yuma*, we have clearly moved backward; since the current era allows for more explicit portrayals and the public has become increasingly more tolerant outside the theater, the representations on screen are even more regressive than at first glance. Simply showing a same sex couple, as in *Brokeback Mountain*, should not be enough to end the conversation and it certainly should not let Hollywood off the hook. In a country where thirteen states have legalized gay marriage and seven others have legalized some form of civil union, Hollywood is embarrassingly behind the times. Most national polls now show a majority in favor of gay marriage, so it seems only a matter of time before it becomes a law of the land. For Hollywood, the conversation should not end with *Brokeback Mountain*; it needs to begin there.

Filmography

The Ballad of Little Jo. Dir. Maggie Greenwald. Joco and PolyGram, 1993. DVD.
Brokeback Mountain. Dir. Ang Lee. Focus Features, 2005. DVD.
Bullfighter and the Lady. Dir. Budd Boetticher. Republic Pictures, 1951. DVD.
The Buried Letters/Broncho Billy and the Buried Letters. Dir. G.M. Anderson, 1910.
Butch Cassidy and the Sundance Kid. Dir. George Roy Hill. Twentieth Century Fox, 1969. DVD.
Monte Walsh. Dir. Simon Wincer. Turner Network Television, 2003. DVD.
My Darling Clementine. Dir. John Ford. Twentieth Century–Fox, 1946. DVD.

Open Range. Dir. Kevin Costner. Touchstone Pictures, 2003. DVD.
Ride the High Country. Dir. Sam Peckinpah. MGM, 1962. DVD.
3:10 to Yuma. Dir. James Mangold. Lionsgate, 2007. DVD.

WORKS CITED

Brower, Sue. "They'd Kill Us if They Knew: Transgression and the Western." *Journal of Film and Video* 62.4 (2010): 47–57. *General One File.* Web. 23 August 2013.
Busombe, Edward. "Man to Man." *Sight and Sound* 16.1 (2006): 34–36. *Film and Television Literature Index with Full Text.* Web. 25 June 2013.
Clark, Mike. "'Brokeback' Opens New Vistas: Review of *Brokeback Mountain.*" *USA Today* 9 December 2005. Web. 25 June 2013.
Clarke, Roger. "Lonesome Cowboys." *Sight and Sound* 16.1 (2006): 28–32. *Film and Television Literature Index with Full Text.* Web. 25 June 2013.
Denby, David. "Eastern, Western." Review of *3:10 to Yuma. The New Yorker* 3 September 2007. Web. 25 June 2013.
Ebert, Roger. "Review of '3:10 to Yuma'" *Chicago Sun Times* 7 September 2007. Web. 25 June 2013.
Eyman, Scott. *Print the Legend.* New York: Simon & Schuster, 1999. Print.
Hoberman, J. "Still Waiting for the Train." Review of *3:10 to Yuma. Village Voice* 28 August 2007. Web. 25 June 2013.
Lusted, David. *The Western.* Harlow, England: Pearson Education Limited, 2003. Print.
MacCurdy, Carol. "Masculinity in 3:10 to Yuma." *Quarterly Review of Film and Video* 26.4 (2009): 280–292. Web. 26 August 2013.
Piontek, Thomas. "Tears for Queers: Ang Lee's *Brokeback Mountain,* Hollywood, and American Attitudes toward Homosexuality." *Journal of American Culture* 35.2 (2012): 123–134. Web. 25 June 2013.
Piturro, Vincent. "Reverse Transvestism and the Classic Hero: *The Ballad of Little Jo* and the Archetypal Western (Fe)Male." *Love in Western Film and Television: Lonely Hearts and Happy Trails.* Ed. Sue Matheson. New York: Palgrave Macmillan, 2013. 111–124. Print.
Stein, Ruthe. "Ang Lee Reworks the Classic Western and Gives 'Pardner' a New Meaning—Two Straight Actors Learn to be Lovers." *San Francisco Chronicle* 30 November 2005, final ed.: E1. Web. 25 June 2013.
Thompson, Anne. "'Brokeback' Explores Last Frontier." *Hollywood Reporter* 17 November 2005. Web. 25 June 2013.
Travers, Peter. "Review of *3:10 to Yuma.*" *Rolling Stone* 19 September 2007. Web. 25 June 2013.
Wood, Robin. "On and Around *Brokeback Mountain.*" *Film Quarterly* 60.3 (2007): 28–31. *JSTOR.* Web. 23 July 2013.

Brokeback Mountain
Queering the "Legend"
Historical Hegemony and Masculine Memory

SCOTT F. STODDART

In adapting and expanding *Brokeback Mountain* from Annie Proulx's short story, Ang Lee's film of the McMurtry/Ossana screenplay pays homage to a number of Hollywood Westerns: *Red River* (Hawks, 1948), *Shane* (Stevens, 1954), *The Searchers* (Ford, 1956), and *Rio Bravo* (Hawks, 1959)—each one a Western that emphasizes particular facets of American masculinity. Where the film truly evokes the spirit of the Hollywood Western is in its emphasis on the romanticized notion of the dichotomy between the wilderness that brings Ennis (Heath Ledger) and Jack (Jake Gyllenhaal) together and the civilized worlds of family and home that try to domesticate the men. However, Lee's direction, partnered with the cinematography of Rodrigo Prieto, curiously subverts the broad vistas of the genre, using close-ups of the men to reveal the anguish brought on by the freedom of this natural retreat. While the wilds of Brokeback Mountain permit the lovers to be together, it inevitably forces both to articulate their desires—a thing that generic cowboys never have the need to do.

This essay has two specific purposes. First, it reads *Brokeback Mountain* against John Ford's *The Man Who Shot Liberty Valance* (1962), itself a queer Western in its use of tropes associated with the genre. Second, it examines responses to the film via its website: I believe it is Lee's notions of Hollywood tradition that helped to make this film so pertinent in the lives of its spectators, causing gay and straight men from 50 states and over 30 countries, to flood the film's website with stories of past loves that dared not speak before. *Brokeback* became a masculine phenomenon—a film steeped in the varieties of masculinity common to the Western tradition, while subverting it, as evidenced in the interaction of these men with their inner desires, and their struggle to articulate what their new connection means. It is not simply the love between these two men that subverts the genre; it is their struggle to articulate that love—to put it into a language that they both can understand and live with—that subverts the characterization of the traditional cowboy.

Looking Backwards: Ford and Lee

John Ford's *The Man Who Shot Liberty Valance* (1962), made the phrase "print the legend" famous, and it comes to have a significant meaning at the end of the film when Ransom Stoddard (James Stewart) admits that the deed that made him famous—the shooting of the famed outlaw Liberty Valance (Lee Marvin)—was not of his doing. In admitting that his male protector Tom Doniphon (John Wayne) covered his back that night and shot Valance, Stoddard clears his conscience, but finds that he cannot erase the legend of his own virility.

The act of secreting legend marks the ending of Ang Lee's *Brokeback Mountain* (2005) when the tight-lipped Ennis Del Mar opens his closet door to reveal his personal treasure: an old shirt of his, once taken by his lover of ten years, Jack Twist, hanging over a shirt that belonged to Twist—a token of their first summer of love and, more importantly, a totem of their secret passion—one that runs counter to the prevailing myths of masculinity on America's open range.

Most critics of Ford would scoff to think of the auteur of the American West might be a melodramatist, insisting instead on comparing *Brokeback* to one of Ford's more "typical" Westerns, such as *The Searchers* (as A. O. Scott did in the *New York Times*). However, the melodramatic qualities of *Liberty Valance* (ironically released in the very year—1962—*Brokeback*'s Ennis and Jack consummate their relations) attest to what makes both films Westerns. In examining *Brokeback Mountain* from a male-centered, melodramatic standpoint, I want to argue that Lee adapts the techniques of the standard Western, stylizing his film of Annie Proulx's short story to ally itself alongside the complexities of this particular Fordian melodrama—queering the cowboy film in a distinct manner.

Melodrama has not been an examined sensibility in respect to male-dominated genres such as the Western. While Thomas Elsaesser's work on the family melodrama is crucial toward understanding the tropes of the form, it was Peter Brooks's *The Melodramatic Imagination* that first argued melodrama was more of a sensibility than a genre. As such, the melodramatic sensibilities highlight distinctive narrative and aesthetic effects that reveal its ideological intent: a forceful use of pathos to forge an emotional connection with the audience, and a relation to the real world that correlates toward an historical tradition. Responding to this, Christine Gledhill argues that "melodrama insists on the realities of life in a bourgeois democracy while recognizing limits of conventional representation" (79), exposing, for instance, the limits of language. Given these definitions, it is easy to see that a melodramatic insight operates beneath and behind the repressed and unthinkable, allowing music, *mise-en-scène*, and gesture to carry the weight of meaning (Mercer 80).

Following this logic, the sensibility conveyed in the Western is not that of simple binaries to reflect the psychology of the characters, but relies instead on the internal, engaging the spectator through the external (such as action, movement, gesture, décor, lighting, editing)—a specific trope of the Western, routinely peopled with men who barely articulate a thought.

When Ford's *The Man Who Shot Liberty Valance* was released in 1962, most critics scoffed at the director's decision to film a tale of the West in such a non–Western fashion. A. H. Weiler of the *New York Times* found the film "creaky" and *Daily Variety* simply labeled it "unsophisticated." Brendan Gill of the *New Yorker* found it "a parody of Mr. Ford's best work, and Bosley Crowther, in a second review in the *Times*, found it "a strangely synthetic sort of film, an almost slapdash entertainment that is a bit of a baffling oddity"—in other words, the mainstream press found the film a queer one from the master of the Western genre. Ford even embraced this distinction, writing to Crowther that "the film was deliberately stylized like a silent Western—and, this point appears to have sailed over your head" (McBride 624–25). Ford knew he was departing from the norms of the Western genre with this film.

In a similar vein, contemporary critics struggled to find a generic home for *Brokeback*. While the releasing studios appeared to favor the term "gay cowboy movie," Roger Ebert felt the phrase demeaning and limiting; referring to the film as a "gay Western," J. Hoberman uses quotation marks around the phrase to avoid calling it a "gay weepie," the subtitle to his *Village Voice* review. Kenneth Turan emphasizes that the film insists on being considered "a romance like any other," separating it wholly from the Western genre. Academic critics, such as Harry Brod, call the film a "bi-sexual shepherd narrative," getting more particular. Even the director himself in an interview with the *San Francisco Chronicle* termed it a "gay love story. Calling it a gay cowboy movie sounds like *Blazing Saddles*." What these shifting labels reveal is the discomfort that critics have with generic forms because they limit the approach to reading the film, leaving the door open to read cowboy movies that involve bonds of love and redefinitions of masculinity to be read as both Westerns and as melodramas.

Even though the stories of each film take place sixty years apart, there are a number of similarities between the two texts to form the basis for a comparative exploration. Both films tell stories of a secret bond between two men—men caught up in the culture's definition of what it means to be masculine. In each, a secret threatens the societal standing of one of the men—both men bound to secrecy in order to maintain their standing in the tight-lipped mainstream community. In *Valance*, the outsider is a man of the world, able to articulate his desires to others without shame; in *Brokeback*, the outsider is a more worldly man than the quiet local, and he articulates his desires repeatedly.

The ideology of each mainstream culture dictates the morality of manhood that forces each couple into secrecy—and, it is this same culture that mandates that after the death of one man (Tom and Jack) the survivors (Ransom and Ennis) are forced to maintain the secret, preserving the status quo. Each secret involves a bond between the men that holds the key to their masculine identity. In *Valance*, the "legend" secures the masculine ideal of Ransom so much he is elected to as the territory's first Senator on the slogan "Elect the Man Who Shot Liberty Valance!" However, during the course of the film, Stoddard's recounting of the facts behind the legend, he cannot get his constituents to print the truth because it flies in the face of their own identities as a land of virile power.

This is mainly because when Stoddard reveals the "truth," it is a humiliating depiction not only of himself but also of the Shinbone community that permitted Liberty's brand of violence to run rampant. Valance and Stoddard meet when Liberty's posse robs a stagecoach that is bringing the lawyer to Shinbone and the savage beating that Ransom suffers as a result of helping a female passenger makes him seem weak—unfit for the world he has now entered. His continued rebuking of guns and violence—set in the kitchen of Pete Ericson's saloon (John Qualen) where he wears an apron to pay his debt—sets him in contrast to Tom, who is not only the strong, silent loner of the range—but the country's masculine ideal.

Both films maintain women on the boundaries of each narrative, securing the notion that both are truly love stories between the men. The initial meeting between Ennis and Jack positions both men as opposites without the aid of an apron. While Ennis maintains his demeanor with reserved quiet, speaking only when provoked, Jack is demonstratively chatty, constantly voicing his opinions in much the way Ransom voices his—questioning the life that permits injustice. One sly bit that Lee employs to reveal Jack's inner desire is the male gaze: While shaving the morning of their first interview, Jack adjusts his rear view mirror, not to get a better angle for shaving—but for a secretive glance at Ennis, who he sizes up immediately as a kindred spirit. This brand of hero worship is a component of both films as the representative types from outside the culture (Jack and Ransom) identify that the archetypes of quiet virility (Ennis and Tom) are really sentimental softies who desire an emotional connection.

Dress plays a key role in a melodramatic reading of these films because it quickly labels the men. As stated earlier, after the hold up of the stagecoach, Ransom is attired in a long apron for half the film, working off his indebtedness at Pete's restaurant, where he becomes, in essence, the domestic goddess. Halle (Vera Miles) appears more of a man, barking orders to maintain the chaos throughout this typical Saturday night. When Tom enters, dressed for a night on the town, he still sports his gun belt, affirming his masculinity even while bearing a cactus rose for his girl. Ransom's apron becomes the source of his public humiliation as Liberty refers to him as a "waitress," and trips him as he attempts to serve Tom his dinner. This second bullying sets the stage for the big showdown, when Ransom confronts Liberty on the Shinbone streets to restore order. Still wearing the apron, Ransom hardly looks the cowboy, Ford shooting the confrontation in noir-ish shadows that call attention to the feminized lawyer. Liberty taunts his victim, shooting the gun from his hand, and shooting at it in order to prevent its retrieval. Ultimately, no one seems more surprised than Stoddard when in response to Liberty's final taunt, he fires his weapon and shoots the villain dead.

Brokeback's use of cowboy garb similarly toys with the image of masculinity as it follows Jack and Ennis' developing relationship. While Ennis wears the blue denim and fur-lined flannels naturally, Jack's attire always appears too new, signaling that he really does not belong to the landscape. One item that Jack proudly exhibits is his ostentatious belt buckle, won in a rodeo contest—the shiny bauble a constant reminder that "real men" do not need to brag to exhibit their virile skills. This costuming feminizes Jack in a similar fashion to Ransom, and carries through the film, as Jack adopts the later 1960s and early 1970s adaptations of Western wear—bolo ties, polyester blend shirts, crisper, tighter fitting jeans—that convey a faux cowboy masculinity, particularly in comparison to the worn, lived-in feel of Ennis' limited wardrobe. In essence, the attire in both films places Jack and Ransom in emasculated positions within the community, Ransom holding forth as a book-reading scholar (running the local school in an effort to teach the community to read), and Jack becoming a salesman in his father-in-law's tractor company, his wife Lureen (Anne Hathaway) appearing to be the real brains behind the business, just as Hallie appears to be true driving force at Ransom's school.

These gendered roles get to the heart of how both films defy the Western tropes as they take on serious considerations of the law—law in the West, intrinsically linked to the "Law of the Father," a Lacanian term that brings sexuality into the mix. The foundation of both films is a deconstruction of this law—predicated on the notion that violence is the way to maintain order in a civilized world. Ford's melodramatic take reveals that the gun that Ransom/Tom uses to rid the streets of Shinbone of Liberty's violence is an impotent tool, as the pervasive myth that Stoddard is the hero not only wins him the girl, but his career as a politician. In essence, the world that Tom knows and controls—exhibited in the pedagogical lesson he gives Ransom in the art of gun-slinging that turns into a showcase for his own acumen—is destroyed by the lie that provides Ranse with his faux manhood. Stoddard, representing a new law based in falsehood, erodes the Law of the Father, leaving Tom to die disconnected from society—alone and forgotten.

In essence, *Brokeback*'s undermining of the Law of the Father and its traditions is similarly shattered by a falsehood. Jack's lifelong desire to maintain a life in the wilderness with his lover is constantly rebuked by the quiet Ennis, who may desire a richer emotional life, but his connection to the majority culture renders him impotent. When Jack finally articulates his dream of a home with his man, Ennis bursts his bubble violently, telling of how his old man brought him as a child to the scene of a murder, where two men who lived as a married couple were mutilated by the bullying violence privileged as law—in much the same manner that Liberty's bullying of Ranse is considered "just his way." Jack's final plea, "I don't know how to quit you" (83), haunts the rest of the film as Jack meets a violent end at the hands of bullies who seek to maintain the Law of the Father. Death leaves the survivors, Ransom and Ennis, to end their narratives in stifled mutterings, leaving their secrets literally sealed away in closets; knowing that their truths will set them free, both men are impotent in the face of the legend—the accepted history.

Lee's film pays homage to Ford's film through its appropriation of narrative tone and melodramatic sensibility and each film becomes a melodramatic Western that emphasizes a particular western masculinity. Both films evoke the spirit of the Hollywood Western in their emphasis on the romanticized notion of manhood: how the dichotomy operates between the wilderness that brings men together and the civilized worlds of family and home that try to domesticate and silence them.

However, Ford's direction, partnered with the black-and-white cinematography of William H. Clothier and Lee's direction, partnered with cinematography of Rodrigo Prieto, curiously subvert the broad vistas of the traditional Western, using close-ups, *mise-en-scène*, and gesture to reveal the anguish brought on by the freedom of the world outside the familiar. While the wilds of *Brokeback Mountain* permit the lovers to be together, it inevitably forces both men to articulate their inner desires—a thing that generic cowboys never appear to have reason to do. Similarly, Ransom and Tom only truly speak to one another outside the confines of the town, Tom allowing Ransom a dignity that the bookish lawyer cannot exude in the village.

While Ford did not consciously "queer" the Western, his *The Man Who Shot Liberty Valance* is a queer Western in that it defies the traditional tropes of the genre, employing melodramatic sensibilities to articulate a new brand of Western; his film paved the way for Lee's *Brokeback Mountain*, a decidedly queer Western in its subject and in its execution.

Momentary Reflection: The Virtual Campfire

The website established by Focus Features for advertising *Brokeback Mountain* (Lee, 2004) hit a nerve with men—both gay and straight. At the site, a feature called "Share Your Story" asks those who patronized the film to relate a personal story that was brought to mind after screening the film. Given the fact that men, traditionally, are strong and silent—just like that mythical John Wayne—the site became a repository for over one thousand tales of lost male loves. In this section, I explore why this film sparked so many men to tell such beautiful stories of men who "got away" and to discuss how these individual stories relate to the film's notions of masculinity—a form that is decidedly based in the Hollywood Western.

On-line forums and gay-identified men's roles in respect to them remains one subject of many social critiques; critics theorize that the Internet has not galvanized the queer community in the same way that it helped other minority groups to bond. As Andrew Holleran says, "The computer has tightened the bonds of every other minority group—from Al Qaeda to the KKK—but gay men have only used it to look for dick" (12). While a bit harsh, Holleran's notion that "the computer came along at a time when gay politics were exhausted" (12) rings true. Cyberspace has attained for gay men a safe method of seeking sex—cruising sites such as Grindr and Scruff without the fear of face-to-face rejection: Send your pic, if there is no "connection" there is no harm done, send it out again. Other M4M sites such as Adam4Adam and gaydar.com reveal that gay men are using the Internet for connection—a replacement for community in its political sense. However, it appears that the anonymity and the accessibility of the Internet create more sexual networks. According to a study by Dew and Chaney, "the Internet allows gay and bisexual men the opportunity to express their sexuality without fear of persecution ... the number of sexual minority males who access the Internet numbers 16.8 million" (260) and continues to grow each year. In their study, men, particularly bisexual men, are now more reluctant to visit bars, clubs or other social venues because of the persistent availability of sexual partners on the Internet (261).

While these discussions (and many others) conclude that the Internet is doing more to fragment the gay community than to bring it together, one, by Brown, Maycock and Burns in a study of the Internet in Australia, disagrees. The team argues that the Internet's conversational aspects allow gay men a sense of control over their self-presentation, creating a very positive effect. In their conclusion, they believe that on-line connections "facilitate and encourage up-front discussion either through public or private chat, resulting in shared expectations and possibly increasing the sense of safety and control" (70). While many of the men in their study revealed that they used the Internet for sexual trysts, many more found that it serves as a vital link to a socialization process denied them because of geographic location and because of fear of rejection.

It is this positive socialization facet that most resonates at the *Brokeback* site as the men struggle to share *Brokeback* memories in order to articulate what this past event meant to them, and how they believe it figures into their current masculine identity. The process as a whole reflects the Western itself: the anonymous community of strangers enters a new frontier, becoming an open space for reflection. Once around the Internet campfire, often in the dark, they swap experiences, so both gay- and straight-identified men benefit from the male camaraderie of shared experience. In general, the stories are written by either a gay/straight narrator who identifies as Jack Twist, or by a gay/straight narrator who identifies as Ennis Del Mar. Most often, the story recounts a sexual encounter between men, and each story recounts how screening the film has either assisted him in coming to terms with his sexuality, or triggers questions regarding their perceived straightness. Of course, there is some blending of these borders, but the majority of the stories reveal a necessary reason for responding to the film and/or to one another. The website, in essence, becomes a communal diary, recounting the shared pain and grief of personal experiences without losing a sense of one's masculine ideal.

The men that identify as Jack Twist generally recount stories where their Ennis did not respond to their overtures—or who responded with a sex act but refused to read it as "queer." Often, these sad tales reveal Jack's coming to terms with his sexuality while their Ennis never does; rarely are these stories happy. George from Alabama recounts his experience in a "small-town college":

> [We] were like brothers who had somehow never met before. Both from the rural South ... I knew I was gay; not many other people did. I told him; he didn't care. We were insep[a]rable.
> A few months later we were being boys, drinking bourbon, lamenting our love lives. He moved closer to me, and then it all happened. We never talked about it afterwards. Then he got sick, had to leave school.... I know some of that was my fault.
> I used to visit him, a seven hour drive each way. We would sleep in the same bed, under the covers, undressed, just this or that patch of skin touching. I still remember waking those mornings. I remember watching him climb out of bed, standing in the chill to smoke a Camel with him and stare out over the Virginia mountains. I still remember feeling so perfectly content.

> I was best man at his wedding, even though by that time we hadn't seen each other in god knows how long. We talk now and then. Most days I don't think of him. I know love comes and goes, like everything in this life.

What is most telling in George's story is the guilt that he feels because his Ennis did not understand his own feelings. This scenario pervades the Jack Twist narrative, the narrator feeling that his own predatory instinct forced Ennis to behave in an unnatural manner. Levi in Chicago recounts an experience of seeing the film with his Ennis—a man who understands his feelings, but refuses to reciprocate them.

> I went and saw the film with a good friend who I've been in love with for about a year. He knows I love him, but doesn't want it to go any further than friendship. I was crying while in the theatre because I was putting myself in the boots of Jack. It's wonderful to have a friend who you can share so much with, but so painful for reality and fantasy to live side by side. Even though you know nothing can or will come of it, you still cling to the hope that one day you'll get your little ranch in the country with him.

In this scenario, the Jack narrator is obviously looking for self-worth from his budding Ennis, and the desperation of his situation: "Even though you know nothing will come of it, you still cling to the hope," mirrors the way that many spectators have viewed Hollywood films since their inception as escapist fairy stories of ideologies that resolve happily within the film's two-hour time frame. In another, Joseph of Florence, Alabama, tells of his experience seeing the film at a midnight screening:

> My story happened much the same as the movie when myself and Tim were in our early 20s. We too didn't know what to call what was happening to us and just called it "friendship." It lasted only nine months, and then life took over. His solution to our situation was for he and I to both marry, our wives would be friends, and so would our kids. This would leave opportunities for us to go camping and fishing for as much as a week at a time, with no one being the wiser. I loved him (but never could really verbalize it) and I honestly considered his "solution" several times. In the end, however, I just couldn't bring myself to fake a life with some unsuspecting woman, even for such a love. So I went on my own sep[a]rate journey. To this day, I do not know whatever became of him. (Tim: "Where ever you are.... Thank you for giving me a "love that will never grow old." I love you.... Whew.... I finally said it!) Also a big "Thank you" to the couple that consoled me outside the Grove Theatre after the movie ended. I really needed those shoulders. It's too late for me and Tim, but I hope this movie will help others see that you should always follow your heart.

The heartening detail is that Joe speaks of not allowing himself to live a lie at the call of his Ennis. However, the diction of the story shows that this Jack was made to feel that he was the one with the problem—Ennis, in this instance, would be happy living a lie. All these years later, it is obvious that Joe not only carries a torch for his married love, but that he continues to feel that he is undeserving of happiness ("It's too late for me and Tim"), compelling him to even "thank" a couple who reached out to console him as the film washed over his conscience to reveal the memories obscured by his own self-loathing.

Cracking Open the Closet

Oddly enough, those men that identify themselves as Ennis character types in their stories find the site a comfort—a place that allows them to articulate feelings that have been closeted inside for many years. Often, these men appear to be articulating their experiences for the first time—many of them identify as married with children, but in these stories they often wonder about the fate of their "Jack" who left because of their inner–Ennis' unwillingness to come to terms with their sexuality. In Los Angeles, Joe details the frustrations as he recognizes that his inner–Ennis prevented him from taking personal risks:

> I realize that the reason I connected so strongly with the characters was that there is a great deal of both Ennis and Jack in me (and I think the same may be true for a great many people). In some situations I have been just like Ennis— afraid to take the risk of acting on my feelings and in the process losing out on what could have been a great relationship. At other times I have been just like Jack—trying to convince someone to take the leap along with me, but unable to do so, and having to walk away, but in the end never quite forgetting what could have been. The only things I regret in life are the chances I did not take.

Recognizing the bi-polar quality of his life, Joe acknowledges both the fear of acting on his feelings and the need for someone to join him in his own "leap" toward happiness. The paralysis evident in this pointed response to the film reveals Joe's sincere disappointment in his own inability to take control of his life.

In another response to the film, K of Portland recounts his own *Brokeback* tale—a story of how fear emotionally handicaps his inner–Ennis:

> It was my Freshman year of college, and his name was Tom. They called us twins because we wore the same clothes, and did everything together.
> The hug by the fire in the movie, for me, is a trip down the mountain in Palm Springs, during that Freshman summer, driving a summer camp truck, and taking the rest of the day off to spend with Tom. It was hot, and his room in the dorm was cool, and we just reveled in our friendship. We never did touch each other, or verbalize what was happening. And I've never spoken to him since about what I experienced.
> But in this human experience, perhaps he knows. Perhaps he'll see this film and remember. In any event, I will love him forever.

What is most interesting about this Ennis narrative is the fact that K admits that "we never did touch each other, or verbalize what was happening"—in other words, both men recognized that something special was building between them, and neither had the language to articulate meaning until seeing the film. This speech-act is an amazing realization of how Hollywood film can assist in the self-awareness of a spectator.

Sadly, more typical of the Ennis stories are those that end with the death of the Jack figure. For instance, Damien of Albuquerque recounts his story of his lost love—one that still haunts him many years later.

> I met Brandon when I was 16.... We became real close and made each other laugh. When he smiled he looked at me in a way that made my heart flutter, and left me in a state of awe.
> There were no secrets between us; we wore our hearts on our sleeve. One magical night everything that we were both feeling came together and we made love for the first time. This was the beginning of the most amazing relationship that anyone could ever imagine. We shared our hearts and souls. We laughed and we cried. We made plans for the future together by applying for schools, looking to move to California.... It wasn't a dirty little secret, it was something pure and precious that just belonged to us. We completed each other. He was my soul, my heart and life.
> In my 19th year I lost him. There was a horrible car accident that stole him away from me. For months I could barely function. People realized that I was grieving, but they could never know how much.... I learned to have the happy face, although my heart still yearned for him.
> Nine years later I met someone that I thought was pretty good. We shared a lot together and had some fun, but it wasn't the same. I never told him about Brandon, but I was still in a lot of pain. Bless his heart he and I tried so hard, but it ended after two hard years.
> After that I think I gave up. Everything was wonderful with Brandon, and even if things in my life were going well, it was never complete. In the last seven years I think I have closed off myself from everything that can really make me feel. I have only a few friends, and at some point my self image has sunk to a level that seems unsalvageable. I have no passion anymore for anything. I am only going through the motions, and although I recognize this, I don't know how to break the surface.

Damien begins by speaking defensively about his relations with Brandon: "It wasn't a dirty little secret, it was something pure and precious." In pouring out his soul, his inner–Ennis naturally sees that what was kept as "secret" had shameful implications—particularly when he says that he never told the man he subsequently lived with for two years. What is remarkable in this self-reflection is the final, sad paragraph: the articulation of his present state of mind, realizing that his emotional catatonia is a result of his love for his now dead Jack. His Ennis-psyche has been crushed by his Jack's death, and, he acknowledges that he will continue to experience a fate similar to Ennis'— "going through the motions" without knowing how to "break the surface" of his grief over his now dead friend.

In a similar vein, Jim from Boston (presumably still heterosexual), speaks of his lost "soul mate," a man lost in the attacks on the Twin Towers on 9/11.

I can't remember the last time I cried. I so need to move on but don't know how. I just need some inspiration.

We all have our *Brokeback Mountain* story. I was married at the time when I met my first true soul mate. He was a wonderful, caring, and kind person. *Brokeback Mountian* parallels my story in many ways. You see I met my first true love much like the two young men met. Our lives were somewhat complicated as we both were in relationships, I was married, he was partnered. But that did not stop our friendship. We were inseparable until 9/11. 9/11 changed all of our lives, but it changed mine in many ways. I lost the one soul mate that I felt so connected to and so loved by. We learned from each other and grew to love one another. Our friendship forged into a loving relationship that only two soul mates would understand. He taught me that the best love was the kind that weakened the soul. I always felt that our love planted a fire in our hearts when we saw one another and always brought peace to our minds. That's what he gave to me and that's what I would have hoped to have given to him forever had he not tragically passed away. He will always live on in my memory.

In reading *Brokeback* as a post–9/11 Western, Jim reveals that for him the film becomes a site of "inspiration," and the website is a seen as a communal campfire where he can join his fellow cowboys in safely recounting a sad personal story that reflects the on-screen tragedy. Jim's philosophical closing, articulating (perhaps for the very first time) just what this male loving meant to him highlights the sadness he experiences in his effort to articulate his grief. Like Ennis, Joe is left to conjecture how his life might have proceeded had death not taken his lover: Would they have remained a clandestine couple? Might his "soul mate" convinced him to break away to find that ranch of his dreams?

J of Oklahoma uses the site to confess his own culpability in terminating his relationship with his Jack. In his story, as in others, internalized homophobia forces the Ennis character to take an action that he later regrets:

[The film] has opened up wounds I thought were finally healed. Over 20 years ago I met a young man while going to college. We were just two guys in college doing typical guy stuff and friendship grew stronger and stronger. One night while when we had been drinking our relationship went to "the physical level." The next morning we were both afraid we had gone too far, but we realized we were OK with it ... more than OK ... it felt good, and right, and happy.... His grades fell and his parents pulled him out of school. He would come visit me at school every month or so. One time I heard his voice in the hall and jumped up to meet him. He was there with a young woman he introduced as his fiancé. It felt like I had been punched in the stomach. That was the last time I saw him for over 10 years. We both got married and started families. As fate would have it, he came to work for the same company I worked at, reporting to me. At first it was great.... As time passed however we both realized we were drifting towards each other again. It scared me. As a result I pulled away and had him tra[n]sferred to another area. He wound up leaving the company. When he came to say goodbye, I didn't even turn around in my chair to look at him.

Less than a year after that, I received a message that he has taken his own life. A big part of my heart died that day.

> I've been married to the same woman since college and will probably stay married, because I can't bear the thought of betraying the trust she put in me so many years ago when I was too cowardly to be the man I really am. If nothing else, I pray that this movie will help others to embrace who they really are, and not live out their existence on this planet in pain and loneliness.

What is most painful about this story is the fact that J's internalized homophobia forces him to continue living a lie. Interestingly, he uses a public website as a place to confess not only his role in his companion's misery, but his own acknowledgement that he has known all along that he "was too cowardly to be the man I really am." The way that the *Brokeback* site emerges as confessional site for married men is a testament to the connection men felt in screening the film.

In another type of Ennis-identified story, Michael, a man who now lives in New York, recounts his growing up in New Mexico with his friend, Clark, a man who helped him to experience a *Brokeback* brand of love.

> Homosexuality was not an option. Clark, my best friend in high school was a close friend, we performed music together, went drinking together, talked constantly about life and philosophy and history and politics, double-dated girls together.
> We went our separate ways for a couple of years, me away to college and him getting married and going to college at home. When I came home after two years away and decided to go to college at home, I met my future wife and we were married and started having babies. He and his wife lived in married housing next door to us (a total coincidence) and we started hanging out together again, falling easily back into our old friendship.
> At that point, we went jackrabbit hunting one night in the desert, got pretty drunk, and made love for the first time. It was quite wonderful for both of us, but we never really spoke of it. We were both happy with our marriages and loved our children, and we continued an irregular love affair on the side over the next ten years, until I left for New York to work.
> We spoke on the phone for long sessions many times over the years and got together again twice, went out into the desert and made love both times, very tenderly and lovingly.
> Clark died last year of lung cancer, and his wife sent me his favorite pipe. She was afraid to call me, because she was afraid of how devastated I would be. I didn't think our wives knew about our relationship at the time, but now I think they did. It was a great friendship/love affair, with no tragic overtones until his death, which did indeed devastate me.

Mike's story serves as a reminder of how complex the closet can be. In the film, the closet is literal (where both Jack and Ennis hide the physical evidence of their love—the entwined shirts) and figurative—an ever-present reminder of the boundaries that restrict male love. In our post-closet existence, where young men declare their sexuality earlier, louder and prouder than before, it is difficult to imagine not only that the closet was an ever-present phenomenon, but that it is still a convenient way to hide away the persistent evil of homosexuality. These Ennis-like stories constantly draw on the pain of secrets that these men locked away; the film, in essence, unhinges the doors of these closets, disinfecting these psyches with the sunlight of acknowledgment.

Coming Together

As mentioned before, there are some happy stories recounted at the website showing that Jacks and Ennises do come together in some versions. These stories play off the notion that the lovers are now "remaking" the *Brokeback* saga—rewriting the fable of the doomed cowboy lovers. For instance, Ed of Glouster, Massachusetts, recounts his own story of meeting his Jack in the Army during World War II:

> I met him while in the Army in Germany. It was a friendship at first then on my 20th birthday we drank a wee bit too much. We shared many thoughts and talked all night and started to get physical but stopped.
> I was afraid for a week after that, that he'd turn me in, that I wouldn't have him for a friend, that'd he'd reveal my secret and shame me.... Instead, he looked into my eyes and kissed me.
> For a year we stole time to be together. Here. There. On the train with 1000 other soldiers on maneuvers, secretly, quietly, gently, we loved each other. We had to keep our secret. We kept it from our friends and our families. We decided that we wanted to stay together. That was twenty years ago. I love him more now than ever before. My love, my life, the one who loves me. Vince, I still love you.

For those of us who are cultural historians, students of D'Emilio's *Coming Out Under Fire* (1990) and Randy Shilts' *Conduct Unbecoming* (1997), Ed's story of his twenty-year partnership sweetly reminds us of the courage that it took for these two soldiers to defy the scorn of others to simply embrace in a time of horror, and live to share a life together during a time of almost universal hatred against homosexuality.

Screening the film gave some men the courage to use the site in an effort to reconnect with their man who got away. Brian Raab of San Antonio used his story to not only reflect on what happened to his Ennis, but to reach out to him, asking his Ennis to return to take their *Brokeback* relationship to another level:

> Me and Stephen have a story just like *Brokeback Mountain*. We go fishing together, four-wheeling, and popping snowmen. After a night of alcohol we like to snuggle up in the bed of one of our trucks and make love. I felt so connected with this movie because I wish he could realize that were meant to be together. He has a girl friend and I always stand back wishing that I was in his arms instead of that girl. Stephen, if you read this, marry me?

There is no way of knowing if Brian's wishes came true, but the communal atmosphere of the site provides a sense of hope for these men who desired to reconnect with their former lovers. Kaleb, another writer from California, not only explained how his situation mirrored the film, but he spoke of how the film inspired him to change his own Jack-like existence:

> This film had a huge impact on me. I couldn't help but relate to Jake Gyllenhaal's character. I was involved in a relationship with a man who honestly loved me but couldn't allow himself to do so. I love him with all my heart. We share a unique bond, much like Heath Ledger & Jake Gyllenhaal's characters. Nothing can seem to tear this bond apart. Sometimes I wish something would.
> Recently my "Ennis" realized what we shared and wants me back. If it were not for this film I would possibly be making the biggest mistake of my life. I guess I can give him one more chance. If this risk means I can end up with my soul mate and live the life Jack and Ennis could have it's more than worth it.
> Maybe Bri and I can live the life Jack and Ennis could have.

Again, the comfort of the Hollywood Western and the identification that the narrator finds in Jack and Ennis appears to inspire him in overcoming societal limitations, regardless of the consequences.

Straight-Forward Reflection

The stories written by straight men that identify as Ennis, who remain married, and who now—after seeing the film—realize that they made a mistake in letting their Jack get away are, by far, the saddest. These tales—and there are quite a few—often end with the Jack figure dying; the Ennis narrator suffering—all while the film leads to a crisis of conscience, reflecting what might have been. Even more torturous, these men only now question their sexuality, confronting their own homophobia many years after the fact. Luke, from Santa Monica, tells a story that is similar to most of these—understanding too late that his love got away. The film, it appears, inspires him to act differently the next time.

Brokeback Mountain shares a love story that is as achingly raw as it is profoundly tragic. Unfortunately, the world we live in, no matter the location or decade, often dictates to others that they have no right to love or even be loved.

Such was my experience. My partner and I weren't cowboys but more, college students twelve years ago. We weren't in Wyoming but rural Ohio, which can be equally exclusionary and judgmental in its ultra conservative attitudes.

For five years we shared every part of our lives. We traveled, exchanged gifts and loved each other on every level. The problem: I couldn't SAY the words, "I love you." That would have made it "real." We were just "best friends" who happened to have a sexual and romantically-inclined relationship.... Being from a conservative Christian fundamentalist household, the "programming" in my brain was just too strong.... Identifying with Ennis and his regret and pain from start to finish in *Brokeback Mountain* left me struggling to catch my breath at times.

My partner lovingly and patiently tried to coax me into the life we deserved to live but I just couldn't go there. After five years, he finally found someone who could offer him a life where they could live and love each other openly.

> It is because of losing him that I have grown tremendously and now look forward to participating fully in a loving relationship with my next partner. The tragedy, as with *Brokeback Mountain*, is that I often feel that I have lost the one chance at the "love of my life." He is gone and I cannot get him back. It's been six years and it still seems like yesterday sometimes.
>
> How do you unlove someone? I don't think you ever do. All I know is that I will take his gifts and his love into my next relationship and live fully for the first time in my life.

Luke identifies his background as "conservative Christian fundamentalist" a barrier that appears too steep to overcome, even with a patient and loving partner. As he openly identifies with Ennis' "regret and pain" he, too, realizes that his love left him behind. The tragedy of a story like Luke's is the suffering that is behind each word that he uses, not only regret but crippling loneliness.

Jay from Minnesota speaks of an adolescent action that still haunts him; the film brought this memory to the forefront, and the site offered the opportunity to deal with his confusion.

> I am a 25-year-old married man. When I was 10, I thought a girl next door was cute. I thought her brother was cuter. I never told him how I felt—he was a cool kid and I didn't know what he would say at school. I tried to contain my feelings for boys my age throughout high school. One night when I was 17, Kevin came over. He was a good friend of mine. We drank a few drinks that night and he fell asleep on my bed. I was excited have an attractive man in my bed with me. He woke up as I was touching him. He didn't stop me but lay back instead. We had sex that night. A first for both of us. Throughout that school year, we acted as if nothing happened. I haven't seen him since 1999. Now, I have been seeing a young man for six months. I can't break it to my wife but I feel more with him than her. What do I do? This taboo of homosexual relationships affects everyone in some way. Thanks for this opportunity.

The interesting aspect of Jay's story is that he never identifies as "queer" (another Ennis-like quality in many of these stories), even though this high school tryst profoundly affected his sexual development. Now married, he deceitfully carries on a queer relationship behind his wife's back. This is the real power of the *Brokeback* site—the community forged by not only screening the film, but the myriad of stories shared allows the Internet to become a group therapy session—no one judges or offers solutions, but the personal becomes political as it is rendered public.

Kevin from Minnesota tells another sad story after a screening of the film. Although he does not confess to having sex, Kevin obviously has come to grips with his feelings after seeing Ennis' life of inaction.

> A decade ago I lived in a small town in Iowa, and worked at an office with a man who fast became my friend. With real tenderness we formed a friendship that was solid. We both wanted to make something of our feelings for each other, but I did not dare. He was willing but I held back. He was a married man, and had two small children who sometimes ran through the office to see their

> dad. I was afraid of a married man and what our actions would do to his family. The business we worked for became troubled—I was let go before it folded. I moved away and never saw him again. This film has torn my heart open, and all the pain floods me again. God how I miss him and still love him—his friendship and his warmth. I am troubled now with all the thoughts of what might have been.
>
> I don't understand how life can be so unfair. I don't understand how love can hurt so much. There he stood, right before me. But I was afraid of the only thing I ever wanted. I was afraid that if I loved him I would hurt him.

Again, the conventions of society prevent the natural course of love; however, Kevin's experience of the film now causes him to question his former actions. The pain he writes of—the "unfair" quality of life's decisions—comes through ten years later. Wrestling with these matters on-line helps these men to recognize the fuller impact of their actions—the film becomes a catalyst for personal responsibility.

Another Kevin, from New York City, speaks of being raised in the south as an athlete where "the good ol' boy system" still mandates particular codes of masculinity that carry a man into adulthood.

> I was known as the most promising Hockey player to come from our area since most could remember and as a starting varsity quarterback, I was compared to all the greats. I had offers to Duke, Princeton, UCLA, Texas and Oklahoma State just to name a few. I play the most physically demanding sports around and excelled at everything but my connections to my feelings.... Most athletes will tell that there is all types of practical joking and hazing in the locker room, most will deny that it is even the least bit homo sexual. 250 linemen dry humping the sophomore place kicker is not gay it's just fooling around. But when the Star quarterback, is caught shirtless passed out with another guy of considerable popularity it is cause for a total breakdown in the good ol' boy system. I was drunk he was drunk we both live openly gay lives now (separately) but what transpired that night no one witnessed. The mere thought of me being gay was too much. I went to college a year and half later on an academic scholarship, my coach made sure I would not play ball anywhere on his recommendation. It didn't stop him from using me to win his 11th state title my junior year and his 12th my senior year. Needless to say my college career was uneventful, I was an emotional wreck and though I managed to graduate with a degree in Human Sexuality and Family Development, my life was a bit of a let down during that period.
>
> I saw *Brokeback Mountain* ... and it was a total shock to my system. It brought back such vivid and gut wrenchingly painful memories I was forced to let go of the silence that had been killing me. Not of my current life but of the life I relived in my dreams and memories, always trying to correct and modify as if it would alter my present existence.

Even though Kevin now lives a "gay life" separately from his former team mate (also identified as gay), Kevin's painful conditioning as a young man surfaces as a result of seeing the movie, and it still affects his daily interactions. It frightens me personally to think of him as a "Human Sexuality and Family Development" counselor; however, he is at least still wrestling with his suppressed desires that were squelched by a homophobic coach. Many of the men recount tales of athletic indoctrination and the sexually charged atmosphere of the locker room; Kevin's story is a little more than that as he wrestles with a culture that has made him feel diseased and unnatural since his act of passion became public.

Another type of response to the film is found in a remark made by Justin from Louisiana. His comments are most typical of the Ennis-identified narrator—a man who restrained his feelings because of fear, and who now, after seeing the film, fears that these unexplored feelings will incapacitate him once more.

> The longing for intimacy, closeness and oneness is a basic human yearning. Suddenly the heart gets a signal—its force unfathomable. Caution simply doesn't seem to work. For me it all started at a wrong place, at a wrong time and with a wrong person—over 20 years ago. This powerful feeling for oneness just overpowered me. After intense heartbreak I was determined to put those feelings in a bottle and cap it tightly—so that it would never escape and overpower me again. The cap popped open with utmost ferocity while I was seeing the movie—I felt like Ennis—trying to cope with it all over again. I could hardly walk back home. It is a powerful movie. I am not sure if I can recap this feeling before it consumes me and incapacitates me as it did 20 years ago.

Perhaps it is the closeted nature of his continued Southern existence that prevents him from exploring his emotions, but Justin's story is typical of the effect *Brokeback* had on closeted men who identified as straight by "cap[ping] it tightly" to prevent their secret from exposure. Openly identifying with Ennis is a step in the right direction for these men, but the tragedy is that they will probably end up like Ennis—emotionally paralyzed, never really coming to terms with their sexuality. For such men, the site is a place to read similar stories and to realize theirs is not an isolated instance but a common masculine experience—much like the Hollywood Western.

I set out to prove that *Brokeback Mountain* was a film that struck a particular chord with American men—both gay and straight. Reading the many stories shared at the *Brokeback* site proves that the Internet environment, similar to any other social or sexual space, can be a site for personal and communal change. The many stories, regardless of their narrative perspective, reveal commonalities in the male experience that link to the notions of masculinity that are tightly interwoven within the texture of the Hollywood Western. While Lee and his filmic team may have set out to break new ground by screening a male love story for the mainstream, little did they know that their film could charter new frontier by creating a website that would create a safe space for communal sharing—a campsite for men to swap stories with other men, a place for bonding and communal healing. Every man has their own *Brokeback* story—every man is welcome to sit for a spell at the fireside and take part in this most spiritual experience.

WORKS CITED

Brod, Harry. "They're Bi Shepherds, Not Gay Cowboys: The Misframing of *Brokeback Mountain*." *Journal of Men's Studies* 14.2 (Spring 2006): 252–53.
Brokeback Mountain. Dir. Ang Lee. Perf. Heath Ledger, Jake Gyllenhaal. Focus, 2005.
Brooks, Peter. *The Melodramatic Imagination: Balzac, Henry James, Melodrama and the Mode of Excess*. New Haven: Yale University Press, 1976.
Brown, Graham, Bruce Maycock and Sharyn Burns. "Your Picture Is Your Bait: Use and Meaning of Cyberspace Among Gay Men." *Journal of Sex Research* 42.1 (2005): 63–73.
"Dating on AOL: You've Got Males" *Time* 155.6 (14 February 2000): 74.
D'Emilio, John. *Coming Out Under Fire*. New York: Free Press, 1990.
Dew, Brian J., and Michael P. Chaney. "The Relationship Among Sexual Compulsivity, Internalized Homophobia, and HIV Risk Sexual Behavior in Gay and Bisexual Male Users of Internet Chat Rooms." *Sexual Addiction and Compulsivity* 12 (2005). 259–73.
Ebert, Roger. Rev. of *Brokeback Mountain*. Dir. Ang Lee. *Chicago Sun Times Online* 16 December 2005. 16 December 2005. http://rogerebert.suntimes.com/apps/pbcs.dll/article?AID=/20051215/REVIEWS/html.
Elsaesser, Thomas. "Tales of Sound and Fury: Observations on the Family Melodrama." *Film Genre Reader II*, ed. Barry Keith Grant. Austin: University of Texas Press, 1995.
Gledhill, Christine. *Home Is Where the Heart Is: Studies in Melodrama and the Woman's Film*. London: British Film Institute, 1987.
Hoberman, J. "*Blazing Saddles*." *Village Voice* 29 November 2005. 12 December 2005. http://villagevoice.com/generic/showprint.php?id=70461&page=hoberman&issue.html.
Holleran, Andrew. "Laptops and Loneliness." *The Gay and Lesbian Review* 12–13.
The Man Who Shot Liberty Valance. Dir. John Ford. Perf. James Stewart, John Wayne, Lee Marvin. Paramount, 1962.
McBride, Joseph. *Searching for John Ford*. New York: St. Martin's, 2001.
Mercer, John, and Martin Shingler. *Melodrama: Genre, Style and Sensibility*. London: Wallflower, 2004.
Scott, A. O. "*The Searchers*: How the Western Was Begun." *New York Times Online* 11 June 2006. 14 June 2006. http://www.nytimes.com/2006/06/11/movies/11scot.html.
Shilts, Randy. *Conduct Unbecoming*. Los Angeles: World Publications, 1997.
Stein, Ruthe. "Ang Lee Reworks the Classic Western and Gives 'Pardner' a New Meaning." SFGate.com. 15 December 2005. 16 December 2005. http://www.sfgate.com/cgi-bin/article.cgi.html.
Turan, Kenneth. Rev. of *Brokeback Mountain*. Dir. Ang Lee. *Los Angeles Times Online* 9 December 2005. 15 December 2005. http://www.calendarlive.com/movies/reviews/cl-et-brokeback9dec09,0,7500247.html.

Part III
New Frontiers

The Post–9/11 Mohican
Avatar *and the Transformation of the "Manifest Apology"*

ANDREW HOWE

For all of its visual innovation, James Cameron's 2009 blockbuster *Avatar* is a very familiar story. In this film, former Marine Corps corporal Jake Sully (Sam Worthington) journeys to a moon called Pandora in order to begin a new life. Hired by the Resources Development Administration (RDA), which mines the moon for the element unobtanium, Sully's consciousness will combine with an alien body known as an "avatar" grown for his use in communicating with the indigenous population, the tribal Na'vi. Although he initially participates in the program, Sully soon notes how human greed has resulted in encroachment upon Na'vi territory, becoming radicalized when he witnesses their victimization. From that moment forward, he joins the Na'vi resistance against the human colonizers. *Avatar*'s central conceit of "going native" in an attempt to protect the culture and resources of an invaded peoples is nothing new in American fiction, extending back through *Dances with Wolves* (Costner, 1990) and other films to the nineteenth century tales of James Fenimore Cooper. *Avatar* is very much about the greedy qualities and genocidal dimensions of manifest destiny, with space exploration standing in for westward continental expansion, the Na'vi replacing groups such as the Lakota Sioux, and unobtanium symbolizing gold and other precious resources. And much as *Dances with Wolves* has been criticized for its lionization of the character John Dunbar (Kevin Costner), *Avatar* has been similarly served for suggesting that it takes an enlightened white man to lead an oppressed group to freedom.

There are key differences with *Avatar*, however, separating it from its predecessors in the translation of Cooper to contemporary times. For over forty years, the Vietnam War and all of its excesses have been formative in

The Post-9/11 Mohican (Howe) 117

Poster for *Avatar*. A 20th Century Fox release, directed by James Cameron, 2009.

revising the cultural landscape of the Western, from *The Wild Bunch* (Peckinpah, 1969) and *Butch Cassidy and the Sundance Kid* (Hill, 1969) through *Dances with Wolves* and later. In the sequel to his landmark study of the Western, *The Six Gun Mystique*, John Cawelti acknowledges the manner in which the Vietnam War forever changed the racial politics of the Western:

> The impact of the Vietnam War and the ending of the Cold War deeply eroded the Western's acceptability as a myth of America's role on the international scene. The obsessive pursuit of victory in Vietnam, allegorically associated in later Westerns like *Little Big Man* and *Dances with Wolves* with the destruction of Native Americans, made the idea of the Winning of the West seem increasingly ironic [117–118].

There are several different reasons why the American frontier myth, which had been first articulated by Frederick Jackson Turner in the late nineteenth century, was no longer viable after Vietnam.[1] Richard Slotkin notes that the evolution of Vietnam into a war of pointless attrition matched a similar evolution of public sentiment regarding American foreign policy (561). John Lenihan, however, cites a gradual shift in public perception regarding the ideological underpinnings governing involvement. According to Lenihan, "The Vietnam War subsequently shifted debate from the issue of how best to respond to alleged communist expansion to the question of America's own expansionist impulses" (47). For these reasons and others, narratives that championed the successes of manifest destiny were out of touch with the prevailing attitudes of the times, which also included new ideas about race that did not gel with traditional Hollywood representations of Native Americans. Although *Avatar* definitely fits into this post–Vietnam lineage, the film refreshes the metaphor for the post–9/11 era, particularly in regard to America's engagement in unpopular and expensive conflicts in Afghanistan and Iraq. Albeit in simplistic terms, the film underscores the lie in manifest destiny, one that resonates with *Heart of Darkness* (1903) and other notable works of colonial regret: there *are* no empty spaces left to explore, as one group or another already lives there! Expansion is thus exploration in name only and can be more accurately described as the selfish acquisition of resources. Bringing civilization to the Na'vi is as hollow and constructed a goal as bringing democracy to the Iraqi people.[2] The real goal involves securing resources at all costs, whether that resource be oil or security or unobtanium. The events of 9/11, along with the subsequent conflicts in Afghanistan and Iraq, served to change the landscape of the Western, allowing for the expression of moral turbulence in films such as *No Country for Old Men* (Coen, 2007). However, these events also made possible the transformation of the "Manifest Apology."[3] Despite its lack of subtlety and simplistic divisions between good and evil, *Avatar* is a culturally important text in that it suggests that post–9/11 American excesses in foreign policy have finally replaced Vietnam with regard to the modern prism through which we apologize about the genocidal nation-building of the nineteenth century.

Aside from its metaphorical concern over the concept of manifest destiny, there are many genre features that qualify *Avatar* as a Western. At its core, the film involves a technologically dominant culture and its attempts to tame a savage wilderness. Immediately after Sully's arrival on Pandora, Colonel Miles Quaritch (Stephen Lang), head of security and an ex–Colonel in the Marine Corps, warns the new arrivals of the dangers that await by stating that "beyond that fence, every living thing that crawls, flies, or squats in the mud wants to kill you and eat your eyes for jujubes." Quaritch later claims he received his disfiguring facial scar during his first mission on Pandora. Ironically, Sully's first foray into the jungle introduces him to three potentially lethal animals, two of which try and kill him. Clearly, Pandora is a dangerous place, further evidence of which appears in the form of arrows protruding from the tires of RDA's mining vehicles. Critics of the Western genre have long noted the manner in which the landscape is constructed as dangerous, necessitating a project of domestication. As Deborah Carmichael notes, "Both for Turner and us today, westward expansion and the conquest of western land remains embedded in our national myth. Turner's 'meeting point between savagery and civilization' defined the American relationship with a natural world discovered and exploited in the name of progress" (3). Unlike most pre–Vietnam Westerns, the narrative sympathy in *Avatar* rests with the colonized Na'vi who, due to their biological relationship with the environment, are technologically disadvantaged and therefore vulnerable. Aside from this key difference in the Western formula, many of the other usual suspects in the genre are present: action and repose, the importance of individualism, regeneration through violence, a protagonist without familial ties, conflict tinged with racial components, practical expediency, the importance of resources, and others.[4] It is easy to see why a genre that, at its core, revolves around expansion, violence, race, and resources would find refreshment due to American involvement in Vietnam in the 1960s and Afghanistan and Iraq following 9/11.

Avatar belongs to a specific subgenre of the Western, one that is ready-made for a critique of American expansionist impulses: the Western transplanted into space.[5] Extending back through Jules Verne and H. G. Wells to Mary Shelley's 1818 masterpiece *Frankenstein* (and as Shelley notes in this novel's after-title, in distant ancestry to Greek mythology and the Promethean theft of fire), the frontiers of human knowledge and the exploration required to expand them have proven fertile grounds for fiction. In more recent history, the prevalence of science fiction following World War II can be traced to numerous technological advancements in medicine, weaponry, and engineering that took place during the conflict, culminating in the birth of the atomic age at Alamogordo on July 16, 1945. Despite a prevailing pessimism regarding rapid scientific advancement, evident in the cultural products of the Cold War period (bomb shelters, the advent of UFO culture, and monster movies with creatures made freakishly large due to radiation), the next fifty years were typified by radical progress in numerous fields, culminating in such widely diverse advancements as the desktop computer, the human DNA project, and most notably the space race. The latter stands out as perhaps the most amazing scientific feat in human achievement. On October 4, 1957, the Soviet Union launched the first man-made satellite into space. Known as *Sputnik*, this satellite initiated a race of epic proportions, as mathematicians, engineers, and astrophysicists flocked to government contract work much like prospectors to a new gold strike.[6] The United States fully committed to this program; President John F. Kennedy elucidated the goal, a manned lunar landing, in his famed "Special Message to the Congress on Urgent National Needs," delivered on May 25, 1961.[7] Astonishingly, just over 4300 days after *Sputnik*'s launch, Neil Armstrong and Buzz Aldrin of the Apollo 11 mission set foot on the moon.[8] Armstrong's "giant leap for mankind," a phrase uttered as he took his first step onto the lunar surface, was just that; space was now a frontier for subsequent steps.

In the popular imagination, the frontiers of science that had created such harmful technologies as nuclear weaponry now offered new possibilities, initiating a wave of cultural texts that sought to mine this vein. Included among them were numerous films, many of which resonated with a society that, facing internal turmoil due to protests over the Vietnam War, urban decay, and later on Watergate, inflation, and the oil crisis, was increasingly willing to look to the heavens for hope. These films, direct predecessors of *Avatar*, included the following notables: *Star Wars: A New Hope* (Lucas, 1977) and its follow-up *The Empire Strikes Back* (Kershner, 1980), *Outland* (Hyams, 1981), and *Star Trek V: The Final Frontier* (Shatner, 1989). George Lucas' *Star Wars* trilogy enjoyed tremendous critical, popular, and financial success. Indeed, the series was so popular that the Strategic Defense Initiative, proposed by President Ronald Reagan in 1983 just two months prior to *Return of the Jedi* (Marquand, 1983), was popularly known as "Star Wars." Although not nearly as popular, Peter Hyams' *Outland* was notable in its imitation of plot and characters from *High Noon* (Zinnemann, 1952). Despite lacking its predecessors resonance with the Red Scare, Hyam's film demonstrated that settings could be interchangeable in Westerns as long as they kept their frontier status, and that the genre still very much resonated with the American public. And finally, Gene Roddenberry apocryphally pitched his concept for the original *Star Trek* series to television executives as "*Wagon Train* to the Stars."[9] Each of the five live action *Star Trek* television series contained elements of the Western, including episodes directly linked to Western themes, even specific films.[10] Indeed, the entire concept of *Deep Space Nine* was based around mid-to-late nineteenth century Western towns of commerce and trade. From Quark's bar, with its gambling and drinking, to Odo's frontier constable and the occasional showdown on the Promenade, the station's main thoroughfare, the entire show was structured like a Western frontier town set in space.

The blending of science fiction and Western genres concurrent with and in the period following Vietnam provided for James Cameron a cultural inheritance, one that he debatably mined in *The Terminator* (1984) and *The Abyss* (1989). Although not Westerns, these science fiction narratives do evidence anxiety regarding frontiers, perhaps providing context for the filmmaker's later work. *Avatar*, however, came at a time when the space Western was in decline. Following David Twohy's *Pitch Black* (2000) and John Carpenter's *Ghosts of Mars*, which although released late in 2001 would have been in post-production by 9/11, few space Westerns were released. One noteworthy exception was Joss Whedon's short-lived television series *Firefly*, canceled after a brief run in the fall of 2002. Although marketed as science fiction, the accouterments of the Western can be seen *everywhere* in this series: from the gunfight in "Serenity" to the saloon brawl and train robbery in "The Train Job," from the holdup of a covered wagon in "Our Mrs. Reynolds" to ship members who smuggle cattle and play horseshoes in their spare time, the series is steeped in the plots, characters, and settings of the Western. One episode, "Heart of Gold," is in its entirety a tribute to *The Magnificent Seven* (Sturges, 1960). Despite the popularity of this series, which eventually resulted in *Serenity* (Whedon, 2005), a cinematic release with toned down Western qualities, the series was canceled and some of the original episodes never even aired on television.[11]

Avatar was thus released during a period where, unlike in the aftermath of the Vietnam War, the space Western was not as culturally resonant with the American public. Ironically, the sub-genre began to lose currency following the moonwalk and, despite the ability to find new possibilities for exploration with the Hubble Telescope, the 1986 destruction of the Challenger space shuttle and the dissolution of the Soviet Union five years later served to close the door on hopes to send manned missions to Mars.[12] Although the immediate aftermath of 9/11 witnessed the proliferation of the crime procedural (particularly the ever-expanding *Law & Order* and *CSI* franchises) and the continued ascendancy of reality television, there were signs that the American public was slowly but surely re-gaining their appetite for science fiction.[13] Although the Sci-Fi Channel was in its tenth year by 2001, it was largely a niche cable channel with much of its content recycled from the television shows of previous eras.[14] However, in acquiring rights to the new season of cult favorite *Stargate SG-1* and airing the critically acclaimed mini-series

Taken in 2002, and in green-lighting the landmark series *Battlestar Galactica* a year later, the SciFi channel broadened its profile and appeal. Still, despite the growing acceptance of science fiction, *Avatar* probably would not have worked so well had it appeared several years before its 2009 release. The film's timeliness has been noted vis-à-vis the innovation of cutting edge, computer-generated imagery and ability to present attractive third-dimensionality. Additionally, there was definitely a war fatigue factor that contributed to its 2009 success. In presenting a tale of hope and redemption for its ex-marine protagonist, *Avatar* hit the right note, as the anger and frustration over the events of 9/11 that had led to support for intervention in Afghanistan and Iraq had long since transformed into anger and frustration over the inability to either prevail or extract ourselves from these conflicts.[15] Furthermore, the erosion of personal freedoms that resulted were hard to accept, from minor inconveniences at airport security checkpoints to major consequences for due process with the Patriot Act. As Elisabeth Anker points out, "The most dangerous implication of the melodramatic national identity during September 11 was that it took power away from citizens by encouraging them to assume that state power was an unquestionable moral imperative in fighting the eternal battle between good and evil" (36). Although in many ways the American public willingly accepted this brave new world, by 2009 there was much dissatisfaction. Released at the end of a year that had begun with the inauguration of President Barak Obama, who had vowed to return the troops home at the earliest possible moment, American audiences were ready to stand up and cheer a film that allowed for the redemption of a single character at the expense of an imperialistic, resource-driven foe distinctly reminiscent of the United States of America. Tapping into the baggage of American perceptions regarding their own foreign policy, with extensions back through 9/11 to the Vietnam War and beyond, Cameron introduced an added element to the space Western sure to magnify the impact of the guilt cinema that was on display: Bring back the Indian![16]

From the earliest moments of European colonialism on the continent, indigenous Americans have played a central role in depictions of the frontier. The early settlers in what would become known as Massachusetts wrote about interactions both positive and negative, from the mutual sharing of the first Thanksgiving to the terrible conflicts of King Philip's War, including Mary Rowlandson's famous captivity narrative. Indeed, several stories have become so engrained into the national narrative that they have been reconstituted in tales involving different cultures and peoples. In *Avatar*, Sully's incorporation into the Na'vi and his subsequent romance with Neytiri (Zoe Saldana) combine two of the most powerful myths of the American frontier experience: the Pocahontas and Mohican stories.[17] The latter narrative and its numerous progeny involve a savior figure from the dominant (often white) culture who brings his expertise to the developing culture, often eschewing his own heritage but finding redemption through restitution or revenge (Anker 25). In 1823 with the publication of *The Pioneers*, James Fenimore Cooper introduced the character Natty Bumppo, a white hero gone completely native who, friend to native and European alike, roams the American wilderness saving others. This book and its sequel, *The Last of the Mohicans* (1826), were so popular that the "Mohican Syndrome" became a prevalent trope depicting white interactions with other cultures.[18] As Karl Kroeber notes, these books evidenced a nostalgia for frontiers both physical and cultural, a theme that would be applicable to future generations: "Cooper's work spawned literally thousands of stories–right down to the film *Dances with Wolves*, an almost exact replica of the Cooper paradigm, especially its underlying nostalgia: the red man, like the wilderness, is inevitably being extinguished by the inexorable advance of Western civilization" (4). Cooper's narrative descendants would initially focus upon internal cultures such as the Iroquois and the Sioux but eventually progress to external cultures during post–World War II American imperialism.

The most enduring of Cooper's series is undoubtedly *The Last of the Mohicans*, which has seen over twenty American versions since 1911. Most of these were released theatrically or as television mini-series, although there have also been versions adapted for the radio, drawn as comic novels, and performed on stage as operas. It is interesting to note that six of the sixteen film and television versions were released between 1965 and 1975, suggesting that this narrative was attractive to an American public preoccupied with Vietnam. In addition to concerns over the nature of the frontier, the racial politics evident in Cooper's book would have been highlighted during the late Civil Rights era. Natty Bumppo is biologically white but was raised from a young age by Chingachgook, fated to be the last Mohican following the death of his son, Uncas. Bumppo views Chingachgook as father and Uncas as brother; these three see no problem in the bond they have formed, but nearly everyone else does, as is evidenced by the variety of names by which Bumppo is called throughout the series. The English, French, and indigenous groups who interact with Bumppo all call him by a different name: "Nathaniel," "Hawkeye," "Pathfinder," "Deerslayer," "Leatherstocking," "Long Rifle," and "Le Longue Carabine," among others. The text indicates tremendous anxiety in the manner in which the various groups on the frontier attempt to construct Bumppo's identity as a white man raised by Indians. Cooper's complex identity politics are not reserved solely for Bumppo, however. Uncas and Cora, the older daughter of Colonel Munro, a Scottish officer in command of the British fort, develop an attraction for one another during the course of the story.[19] As a character, Cora herself evidences some of the racial and ethnic tensions present in the British Empire during the colonial period. She is Scottish, which in and of itself is unusual for such a heroine. However, her mother, whom Colonel Munro met while stationed in the Caribbean, was a mulatto.[20]

Of the more popular and mainstream versions of this narrative (the 1920 and 1992 film versions and the 1957 television series), it is the earliest one that most closely maintains these racial tensions. The 1920 version, directed by Clarence Brown and Maurice Tourneur, is one of few visual renderings to maintain the sexual chemistry between Cora and Uncas. The film is racially problematic, as Magua's threat to Cora is largely sexual in nature and the dedication, "To the memory of those unknown women, THE MOTHERS OF A NATION.... Whose love was stronger than the perils of the wilderness...." implicitly invokes Native Americans as agents of peril, and probably rape, who are linked to the conquest of wilderness. Appearing in 1920, this version existed within the cinematic gravity well of *Birth of a Nation* (Griffith, 1915) and its troubling racial politics and, at only two years removed from the end of World War I, it was only natural that in the public imagination nation building would be linked to fears regarding white female sexuality. In addition to linking race to sexuality, the film perpetuates stereotypes ("An Indian lost in the woods? Impossible!"), employs redface, and adheres to the bizarre rule that all indigenous villains must speak of themselves in the third person ("Magua does not kill his prisoners-he tortures them!").[21] Despite these problems, the 1920 version was much edgier than subsequent versions, many of which elided the sexual tension altogether (George Seitz's 1936 version) or transferred it to Bumppo (Michael Mann's 1992 version), the latter of which represents a cultural but not a biological act of miscegenation. For its era, Cooper's early nineteenth-century tale was quite progressive with Scottish, Indian, and an Indian-raised white serving as protagonists. However, the racially interesting implications that saturate this Western have proven difficult to maintain. The trope he established would soon be perverted by nineteenth-century attitudes regarding white supremacy.

The switch in romantic focus from Uncas to Bumppo, most pronounced in Michael Mann's 1992 version of the tale, accompanied new interpretations of manifest destiny. Although by the early nineteenth century it was obvious the degree to which European colonialism had devastated the indigenous populations, Cooper was writing before the full ramifications of the Trail of Tears and the Indian Wars had been realized.[22] His was a more romantic notion of a disappearing culture lacking many of the racist attributes that would mar latter depictions. As Kroeber notes, these books implicate Europeans as the agents of cultural destruction: "Cooper's romanticizing of Indians was entangled with enough realistic criticism of white Americans to dramatize some parts of the essential tragedy of the Indians' victimization and that victimization's counter-effects upon the Indian's destroyers" (4). Cooper began his writing career during the late Enlightenment period, and as such would have been influenced by the prevailing views of indigenous groups throughout the European-colonized world. Indeed, *The Last of the Mohicans* very much reflects the concept of *tabula rasa*, which held that primitive groups reflected a true human nature untroubled by the unnatural modifications of technology and civilization. An outgrowth of this concept was the "noble savage," which Peter Bayers links implicitly to Cooper and explicitly to Pocahontas.

> The other long-standing tradition in Euro-American representations of Natives is to depict them sympathetically as "good" or "noble savages." The male Noble Savage is dignified, brave, and virtuous because of his closeness to nature. In this tradition, the Indian is not inherently violent but rather peaceful, and is only too willing to welcome and aid whites. The female version of the noble savage follows a similar vein, and is best exemplified by Pocahontas or the Indian princess figure, who willingly sides with and protects whites from the violence of her fellow Indians [Bayers 41–42].

Late twentieth century adaptations of the Mohican formula have adapted the concept of the "noble savage" not as an exercise in romantic regret, but to expiate guilt over genocidal nation building. The struggle of a white protagonist to preserve an indigenous culture from the colonial impulse has proven attractive to audiences raised on guilt-inducing images of racial violence from the American South. Several decades later, discussions over the 500th anniversary of the European "discovery" of the New World also factored into this re-examination. However, for the most part the Manifest Apology can be situated within the excesses of American foreign policy during the Vietnam conflict, with Westerns such as *Butch Cassidy and the Sundance Kid* and *The Wild Bunch* criticizing policies of foreign intervention, and Westerns such as *Little Big Man* (Penn, 1970) and *A Man Called Horse* (Silverstein, 1970) serving as thinly veiled metaphors for going native in Southeast Asia.[23] Western studies by Cawelti (1971), Wright (1975), Fenin (1977), Cameron & Pye (1996), and Kitses & Rickman (1998) all cite the importance of the Vietnam War in the changing nature of race and violence in the west.

Before *Avatar*, arguably the most well known of these films modifying the Mohican formula was *Dances with Wolves*. Peter Bayers situates this film within a larger project of Western revision: "More recently a cultural resurgence of interest in Natives in the early '90s aimed at 'rewriting' the national story of the frontier. For instance, films such as *Dances with Wolves* (1990), *The Last of the Mohicans* (Mann, 1992), and *Geronimo: An American Legend* (Hill, 1993), reengaged the myth of the frontier in an attempt to show sympathy for Natives" (Bayers, "Larry Watson's" 36). *Dances with Wolves* was thus a product of a greater trend, although due to the film's popularity it, in turn, helped to shape narratives that followed. The story itself is fairly simple, not nearly as involved as the plot in *The Last of the Mohicans*. After leaving behind the chaos of the Civil War, John Dunbar hopes to see the West before it disappears, requesting a post to a frontier inhabited by the Pawnee and the Sioux. He subsequently befriends a group of the latter, eventually becoming a member of their tribe and helping them resist not only their traditional Pawnee enemies, but also more pronounced and serious incursions by the U.S. Army. By this point, he has completely given himself over to the Sioux culture that he now embraces, and that embraces him. *Dances with Wolves* shares an important similarity with *Avatar*; the protagonist is an *adult* convert to the indigenous culture. This was not the case in Cooper's tale, or in many of the narrative descendants that followed. For instance, two films that preceded *Dances with Wolves* and perhaps influenced Costner, *The Emerald Forest* (Boorman, 1985) and *Clan of the Cave Bear* (Chapman, 1986), involve protagonists who were integrated at a young age into their adoptive societies. In *The Emerald Forest*, Tommy (Charley Boorman) is taken at a very young age by an Amazonian tribe. When his biological father, having mounted expedition after expedition into the upper reaches of the Amazon, discovers him a decade later, Tommy is in no way culturally western. Indeed, any memories of his previous life he attributes to dreams. He may be biologically Caucasian, but in all other regards he belongs to the tribe known as "the Invisible People." *Clan of the Cave Bear* takes things even further back into narrative history, exploring a young Cro-Magnon girl raised by Neanderthals. Ayla (Daryl Hannah) is no more than two years old when her parents are killed during an earthquake. As they are the only adults attending her, she carries with her no appreciable cultural past. Any ties to her ancestry are strictly biological, although it should be noted that this heritage does convey upon her increased intelligence, superior linguistic capabilities, and a greater facility with tools. Regardless of whether or not the conversion to another culture is made as a child or as an adult, these tales often end up demonstrating the superiority of the original culture. Bayers notes that "despite their efforts, these narratives unwittingly reinscribe what they seek to challenge, which is to say they reinforce white colonial hegemony, either through their method of telling of frontier 'history' or representation of Natives or both" (Bayers, "Larry Watson's" 35). Although narratives from *The Last of the Mohicans* to *Avatar* may appear progressive and even contain progressive elements, the narrative device of a white savior undermines the story and perpetuates the division of native populations into villainous or helpless.

In the post–Vietnam War period, *Dances with Wolves* enjoyed the highest profile of such films, also serving to re-invigorate the Western. The twin successes of this film and the television mini-series *Lonesome Dove* (Wincer, 1989) initiated a decade filled with Westerns.[24] Despite this resurgence of the genre, one which saw *Unforgiven* (Eastwood, 1992) win the Academy Award for Best Picture, very few of these specifically mined the Mohican formula, perhaps in part due to an increased distance from Vietnam. However, the events of 9/11 and the subsequent invasions of Afghanistan and Iraq set the stage for this trope's resuscitation, and *Avatar* was released during a time of critical examination of American foreign policy. Upon its release, *Avatar* was derided as a shallow reworking of the Mohican myth, often linked specifically to *Dances with Wolves* in this regard. Annalee Newiz suggests that, at its core, *Avatar* fits into a heritage of white guilt cinema:

> These are movies about white guilt. Our main white characters realize that they are complicit in a system which is destroying aliens, AKA people of color.... The whites realize this when they begin to assimilate into the "alien" cultures and see things from a new perspective. To purge their overwhelming sense of guilt, they switch sides, become "race traitors," and fight against their old comrades. But then they go beyond assimilation and become leaders of the people they once oppressed. This is the essence of the white guilt fantasy, laid bare. It's not just a wish to be absolved of the crimes whites have committed against people of color; it's not just a wish to join the side of moral justice in battle. It's a wish to lead people of color from the inside rather than from the (oppressive, white) outside.

Her analysis, which could apply to *Dances with Wolves* just as well as *Avatar*, is as devastating as it is accurate. This film fits into a troubling racial legacy extending back at least as far as *Last of the Mohicans*. However, what all critics missed in their rush to point to the film's racial dimensions was an important historical shift. Cameron's film suggests a move beyond Vietnam as a controlling metaphor for Westerns seeking to translate the excesses of manifest destiny, establishing in American fiction a new referent that serves to collapse identity markers including religion (Islam), geography (the Middle East), and ethnicity (Arab).[25] In introducing the MacGuffin of unobtainium, an element that sells for $20 million a kilogram due to its electro-magnetic properties, Cameron situates the specific project of colonialism as one of stripmining physical resources, unlike previous narratives such as *Dances with Wolves* with their closer ties to the Vietnam War and conflicts more purely ideological in nature.[26]

In placing a physical resource at the center of the narrative, Cameron also departs from Cooper's original vision. *The Last of the Mohicans* was set during the Seven-Years War, during which the campaigns contested in the Americas have largely been referred to as the French-Indian War. This conflict can be considered the first true "World War" as most of the major European powers were fighting over the future of the non–European world. England's victory over France allowed the former to inherit the mantle of colonial dominance throughout the world, most notably eastern North America. The conflict as it appears in Cooper's narrative involves ideological resources: the right to expand into colonies on one hand, for preserving freedom and culture on the other. The same can be said of Vietnam, which was very much a war fought over the perceived spread of communism. The Vietnamese viewed American involvement as an extension of the colonial battle they had long fought with the French. From the American perspective, the resulting proxy war was waged over different ideological resources: American troops fought for freedom for the South Vietnamese and to make America safe by stopping the spread of communism.[27] It can be argued that the wars in Afghanistan and Iraq involve a similar resource: freedom from fear of terror. However, there is one physical resource that has clearly driven American foreign policy in the Middle East: Oil.

Avatar thus joins a select few Mohican stories that revolve around physical resources; these include Frank Herbert's novel *Dune* (1965) and its resource, the spice mélange (also coded as oil), as well as the forest itself in *The Emerald Forest*.[28] Unobtanium is symbolic of any resource that has served as justification for the removal or outright destruction of a culture that stands in the way. In American history, this resource could have been gold in the 1870s in the Black Hills of South Dakota or uranium a hundred years later in the Badlands region of the same state.[29] *Avatar*'s unobtanium is specifically symbolic of oil, however, in that it is a resource used for transportation. Indeed, the implication in Cameron's universe is that this material replaces fossil fuels. As stated in Maria Wilhelm and Dirk Mathison's exploration of the *Avatar* universe (James Cameron sanctioned), unobtanium rewrites what is possible with regard to commuting.

> Within a few decades, the company had the stature to propose the construction of a world-spanning rapid transit system that would allow entire population groups to conveniently commute hundreds or even thousands of kilometers to perform work where it was needed, without impinging on the cultural values of host populations. This led to the current global network of maglev trains that require the superconductor unobtanium for their continued operation [147].[30]

In allowing the servant class to live at great distance from their employers, the element serves to separate groups of people along lines based upon class and race. The thirst for power is thus subtly linked to xenophobia (or at least cultural intolerance), apropos of American involvement in the Middle East. Although it has a distinctly American feel, the RDA is never identified in the film as affiliated with any specific nationality. Americans during the late Vietnam War period could not ignore the international nature of the oil industry with the ascendancy of OPEC, and were beginning to observe the rise of the multi-national corporation. Due to forces as diverse as the 1970s oil crisis to the environmental damage caused by the Exxon Valdez oil spill in 1989 to the first Gulf War, Americans viewing *Avatar* in 2009 would have recognized in RDA and Parker Selfridge (Giovanni Ribisi) some of the shadier dimensions of big business. The manner in which the film constructs the destruction of culture, originating from an executive in a corner office, combines with the nature of the resource to link this tale, not to Vietnam, but the Middle East and American dependence upon cheap oil.

Aside from the film's focus upon resources, there are other strong indicators that 9/11 has achieved cultural ascendancy in *Avatar*, eclipsing Vietnam as the metaphor exerting the largest cultural influence. A central theme in the film is very much rooted in a fear of terrorism in the post–9/11 era. The fear of infiltration is acknowledged the moment Sully sets foot into the Na'vi camp. The notion that an individual can take on the mantle of the other causes anxiety on both sides; although the Na'vi are initially suspicious, later on RDA begins to view Sully's status with the tribe as a liability, believing him to have gone native. Although there may have been American troops that went native in Vietnam, the problem of infiltration was not really an issue as the war was fought overseas and without any avenue for the Viet Cong to strike at the American homeland. This was not the case with 9/11, however, where the twenty men tasked with commandeering the planes were careful to dress, speak, and act in such a way as to attract minimal attention.[31] The nature of infiltration is even more complex when it involves the infiltration of ideas. In the years following 9/11, the occasional American citizen would be taken into custody for aligning themselves with groups such as the Taliban or Al Qaeda, including some individuals who enjoyed a privileged upbringing, such as John Walker Lindh. Indeed, one of the more sensationalized cases involved "Jihad Jane" (Colleen LaRose), whose capture was revealed to the American public two months prior to the release of *Avatar*. Traditional notions of the American Dream were difficult to champion during a decade that had witnessed stalemate in two wars and the beginnings of a far-reaching global recession. American audiences were thus more finely attuned to stories of those who might choose to reject their parent culture for one reason or another. Combining with concerns over infiltration was anxiety over how religious identity can trump national affiliation. The fact that the 9/11 terrorists acted not on behalf of a nation, but instead upon interpretations of religious ideology, made the enemy that much harder to envision or combat. By 2001, Americans were accustomed to wars with well-delineated boundaries. For instance, American intervention in Korea and Vietnam was relatively easy to understand, with American troops sent to the south of each country to stop the advances from the north. After 9/11, however, American foreign policy could not be broken down along such clean lines, with America at war with the Taliban but not the Northern Alliance, and with Al-Qaeda and the remnants of the Ba'ath Party but not the Kurds. Although *Avatar* presents a conflict with very few gray areas, the wars to which it metaphorically links itself do not enjoy such clean lines.

It is visually, however, that *Avatar* establishes its most visceral ties to 9/11. The demise of the home tree resulting from the cruelty of corporate enterprise stands as the central image of the film. The collapse of the Twin Towers on 9/11 provided the singular, imagistic centering point for that particular narrative, more so than the plane crashes an hour earlier. This fact suggested that the real tragedy for Americans, as magnified by the media, was less about the attacks themselves and more about the notion of a "fall," both the physical demise of the towers and the evaporation of American innocence and security. The fall of the home tree similarly provides a narrative focal point for the Na'vi, with the loss of domestic security and potential threat of cultural genocide taking center stage. Ironically, it is a threat to the Na'vi (and a symbol of terror) around which they rally following the destruction of the home tree. Knowing that he will not be accepted or listened to unless he makes a grand entrance, Sully biologically links with Toruk, a dragon-like creature, subsequently appearing in dramatic fashion to dismount and deliver to the stunned Na'vi his own version of the St. Crispin's Day speech (Mahoney 77). Translated into English, Toruk means "Last Shadow," suggesting not only a link to Vietnam (helicopters and "death from above") but also to the victims on the upper floors of the World Trade Center (some of whom must have seen the plane rapidly approaching), as well as from subsequent bombing campaigns carried out by the United States Air Force in both Afghanistan and Iraq.[32] In linking with this fearsome creature, Sully hijacks the symbol of aerial terror and transforms it to his own uses, thus robbing it of its power. Another symbolic aspect of Toruk is referenced in Sully's voice-over prior to his linking. In denoting Toruk "the baddest cat in the sky" and suggesting that due to his aerial dominance he never worries about potential danger, *Avatar* establishes yet another metaphor for American foreign policy. An important dimension of 9/11's swift incorporation into the American psyche was the fact that most found the event to be unexpected. Considering the bombing of the USS Cole and the prior attack on the World Trade Center, the event should not have been too surprising. However, the effect of nearly sixty years of primacy in global politics resulted in a nation that, much like Toruk, paid little attention to new threats. Toruk is thus a loaded sign, simultaneously representing American complacency immediately prior to 9/11 and the aerial nature of the attacks against the United States as well as Afghanistan and Iraq!

The changing complexion of the American frontier has, on several occasions, led to the imagined demise of the Western, only to see that genre find new and novel means of expression. Patrick McGee links the beginning of this trend to the late Vietnam period: "Periodically, since the early seventies, the Western has been pronounced dead only to be resurrected by some particular reinvention of the genre" (235). The frontier of space allowed for an easy revision during the post–Vietnam period, offering audiences familiar narratives in exciting new settings. One thing that was not so familiar, however, was the new relationship to manifest destiny, with characters from the position of privilege self-marginalizing in order to aid or even lead the resistance of the oppressed. The final battle scene in *Avatar* is a prime example of this impulse for rewriting history. This battle, following the devastating loss of the home tree, stands as an inversion of history, almost as if the events of Wounded Knee (1890) preceded those of Little Big Horn (1876). With help from the animals of the forest, Sully leads the Na'vi to victory, a fantasy rewriting of history akin to the unlikely event of the grizzlies and raccoons of South Dakota rising up against the United States Cavalry. The modern Manifest Apology, of which *Avatar* is the most recent example, has a new symbolic register: the events of 9/11 and subsequent aggression in American foreign policy. In many ways, 9/11 was a game changer for the American public, who in five short years transitioned from a naïve sense of security to a moral rage akin to Pearl Harbor to renewed frustrations over America's tendency to get involved in expensive, unpopular, and by all counts unwinnable military conflicts. Throughout all of the challenges to the genre, from the chaos and turbulence of the 1970s to the conflicted sentiments of the present day, the Mohican trope has served as a familiar harbor. Across generations of racial strife following James Fenimore Cooper's "Leatherstocking" series, this narrative has remained culturally resonant with the American people, who have faced tensions due to wave after wave of foreign immigration from one part of the world or another. *Avatar* raises to new heights the ability of a privileged white character to pass as the other, offering Sully and others the possibility of physically becoming Na'vi, which serves to facilitate the more difficult cultural transition. Many critics note the racially insensitive dimensions of such a plot device, although the Mohican narrative as transplanted to Pandora suggests something interesting about contemporary American culture. James Cameron adapts a familiar trope from the distant past to explore the uncertainties of the present. The events of 9/11 and subsequent wars in Afghanistan and Iraq are thus the latest cultural backdrop by which the United States, at least cinematically, explores and apologizes for its colonial origins on the North American continent.

NOTES

1. For more information on Turner's "Frontier Thesis" and the concept of manifest destiny, see *History, Frontier, and Section*, a collection of his public talks on the subject. Turner saw the American frontier as a "meeting point between savagery and civilization" (60), one where people of different backgrounds were brought together, often with violent repercussions. The Louisiana Purchase of 1803 and the Lewis & Clark Expedition a few years later established the Pacific Ocean as the goal for westward expansion, implicating all of the native groups across the continent in the drama

that was to follow. For a different vision of American conceptions of the frontier and its effects upon those already living there, see Dee Brown's *Bury My Heart at Wounded Knee*.

2. Kevin Mahoney sees British prime minister Tony Blair in RDA administrator Parker Selfridge in that the former publicly expressed the desire for a peaceful solution to the post–9/11 situation in Iraq while privately supporting American plans for war (27). Indeed, some view the film as more of an indictment of European imperialism in Asia and Africa in that the human presence on Pandora comes in the form of an enclave built to support the wholesale theft of resources. However, this reading ignores the fact that military enclaves built across the North American continent during the eighteenth and nineteenth centuries were often situated so as to support trapping, logging, mining, and other operations. Furthermore, nearly all of cultural referents in this film enjoy resonance with historical conflicts between indigenous Americans and European settlers as well as their descendants.

3. In this essay I employ the term "Manifest Apology" rather than the somewhat clunky "anti-Manifest Destiny film," as technically the former is more precise. It should be noted that these "apology" films allow a protagonist who is able to resist the agendas of his cultural hegemony to find redemption through resistance.

4. There are many works that provide structural analyses of the Western genre. Although dated, John Cawelti's *The Six-Gun Mystique* and its sequel are standouts.

5. Most critical works on the Western pay little attention to this sub-genre. Indeed, two essay collections from 2004 suggest that discourses regarding science-fiction are more likely to point to this linkage than those regarding the Western. *The Science Fiction Reader* makes more overt references to this genre hybridity than *The Western Reader*. Ironically, both of these collections were edited by Gregg Rickman (the latter along with Jim Kitses).

6. NASA openly acknowledges the numerous ways in which *Sputnik* was important to the course of America's post–World War II development (history.nasa.gov/sputnik), not the least of which was the formation of that organization a year later.

7. President Kennedy's speech in its entirety can be found in the online archives of the John F. Kennedy Presidential Library and Museum (www.jfklibrary.org).

8. The "Moonwalk" took place on July 20, 1969, almost eighteenth months before the goal set by President Kennedy for landing a man safely.

9. Pocket Books, publishers of sanctioned *Star Trek* fiction, capitalized on this catchy phrase by releasing a series of fictional books under this title, beginning with *New Earth* in 2000.

10. Four such episodes are "Spectre of the Gun" (*Star Trek*), "A Fistful of Datas" (*The Next Generation*), "The Magnificent Ferengi" (*Deep Space Nine*), and "North Star" (*Enterprise*). *Voyager* is the only live-action series to lack a Western-themed episode.

11. For insight into a wide range of issues regarding *Firefly*, including a discussion of its cancelation, see *Finding Serenity*, edited by series writer Jane Espenson.

12. In their online history (www.nasa.gov/50th/50th_magazine/10presidents.html), NASA discusses the forces that contributed to smaller budgets throughout the 1990s.

13. Although published too soon after the events of 9/11 to fully appreciate long-term trends, Wheeler Winston Dixon's edited collection *Film and Television After 9/11* examines the complexity of 9/11's influence upon the film and television industries.

14. These series included *The Twilight Zone* and *Lost in Space*. The early years of the channel are analyzed by Averil Chase in the online journal *The Thunder Child*.

15. Also contributing to this fatigue was the media saturation of 9/11 and 9/11-

related stories. For discourse regarding the role of the media in constructing the 9/11 narrative, see Noam Chomsky's *9–11*.

  16. Although occasionally suggested as denoting Africans, the Na'vi are usually glossed as Native American, although in some cases from South America. Joshua Clover discusses the complexity of assigning to the Na'vi human correlates:

> The blue anthro-feline Na'vi, three meters tall, are not so much any indigenous people, but rather any number thereof: Native Americans in their natural harmony, or the Urarina of the Amazon rainforest—but no more these than, say, Iraqi natives (cued bluntly by the phrase "shock and awe"). Among these shifts, the oddest is when paraplegic corporate mercenary/incipient race traitor Jake Sully muses over how they are unlikely to throw over their world for "lite beer and jeans," and the Na'vi seem to be ... East Germans? [6].

All humor aside, Clover makes the point that the Na'vi resist a singular interpretation as to symbolic alignment with a specific group. However, in that *Avatar* exists as a Western metaphorically exploring the concept of manifest destiny, the Na'vi are best viewed as metaphors for the native groups of the North American plains, most notably the Sioux.

  17. This section is concerned primarily with *Avatar* and the manner in which it adapts the Mohican narrative to fit with post–9/11 concerns. However, the Pocahantas myth has powerful resonance with Cameron's film. Although Neytiri's first impulse is to kill Sully, she does decide to save his life from a pack of viperwolves and the two begin a relationship. The trope of a native girl intervening on behalf of a white soldier or soldier of fortune and their subsequent taboo romance has been updated for several eras. Although owing a very loose allegiance to the Pocahantas myth, the opera *Madame Butterfly* and the musical *Miss Saigon* transplanted concerns over race and American expansion to, respectively, Japan and Vietnam. Such tales are often difficult to identify, with textual codings blending into those of William Shakespeare's *Romeo & Juliet*. However, the enduring nature of the Pocahontas myth cannot be denied, although there has yet to be such a tale involving American involvement in either Afghanistan or Iraq, at least that has risen to the level of cultural prominence. It may be too soon for such a tale, with such conflicts still so fresh in cultural memory. However, there may also be other factors, such as the restrictive nature of Islam when it comes to female sexuality.

  18. According to Roger Nichols, Cooper's success was not limited to domestic markets. When *The Deerslayer* was published in America in 1841, thirty German publishers competed for the rights to the German-language translation.

  19. Cora and Uncas are both fated for death, dying at the hands of Magua. For their death scenes and funeral, see *The Last of the Mohicans* (Project Gutenberg), Chapter 33.

  20. Ibid., Chapter 16.

  21. John Saunders briefly discusses redface (93), a cousin of the more infamous blackface, in his study *The Western Genre*. In this practice, a white actor is given makeup so that he or she can play the role of a Native American.

  22. Dee Brown's aforementioned study *Bury My Heart at Wounded Knee* contains much information on the Trail of Tears and the Indian Wars.

  23. Vietnam-era Westerns such as these perform a very important critique of expansionist ideology. These films, many of them set south of the border, lament the loss of freedom that has accompanied the domestication of previously empty spaces. In *Butch Cassidy*, this loss is signaled by the super-posse, a faceless entity that grows ever closer to the protagonists. In *The Wild Bunch*, it is technologies such as the

machine gun and the telegraph that threaten to make the outlaws antiquated. In both cases, given the contextualization of Vietnam during the film's release, the narrative trope of slow, methodical advance implicates the imperial dimensions of American foreign policy during the post–World War II era, with military bases spreading all over the world, most notably Japan, Korea, England, and Germany. Who knows why the real Butch Cassidy (Robert Parker) and Sundance Kid (Harry Longabaugh) journeyed to South America? Their cinematic versions do so because there is no more domestic frontier left after a century of manifest destiny. In the absence of easy pickings when it comes to banks to rob and trains to hijack, they move on to less technologically sophisticated locations in Bolivia in order to maintain their acquisition. This plot device parallels America's move into Southeast Asia. As the American west has been conquered and its resources exploited, the United States moves on to international frontiers for exploitation.

24. Westerns during the 1990s included *Black Robe* (Beresford, 1991), *Thunderheart* (Apted, 1992), *Posse* (Van Peebles, 1993), *Tombstone* (Cosmatos, 1993), *Wyatt Earp* (Kasdan, 1994), *Legends of the Fall* (Zwick, 1994), *Maverick* (Donner, 1994), *Last of the Dogmen* (Murphy, 1995), *Dead Man* (Jarmusch, 1995), *The Quick & the Dead* (Raimi, 1995), and *Lone Star* (Sayles, 1996). Westerns on television included *Dr. Quinn, Medicine Woman* (1993–1998) and three mini-series follow-ups to *Lonesome Dove*: *Return to Lonesome Dove* (Robe, 1993), *The Streets of Laredo* (Sargent, 1995), and *Dead Man's Walk* (Simoneau, 1996).

25. The strength of the 9/11 referent in *Avatar* cannot entirely remove the importance of Vietnam. The specter of that war is still present throughout the film, although it has been pushed into the background. The appearance of technologies reminiscent of helicopters and daisy-cutter bombs during the final battle, not to mention the nature of the jungle fighting, more closely match Vietnam than post–9/11 conflicts.

26. Alfred Hitchcock discusses the plot device known as "the MacGuffin" during an interview conducted by Francois Truffaut in *Hitchcock*, pp. 137–139.

27. The fear that communism might spread throughout Southeast Asia, and eventually to Japan and India, was known as the "domino theory." The notion of sending either resources (money, weapons, or training) or armed forces to combat this spread was known as "containment." For a discussion of the forces that conspired to draw America into the Vietnam War, see Larry Addington's *America's War in Vietnam*.

28. One of the tribal elders of the Invisible People notes the encroachment of the expanding "civilization" by its consumption of trees: "When I was a boy the edge of the world was very far, but every year it comes closer."

29. For a brief discussion of the Black Hills, see *Bury My Heart at Wounded Knee*, p. 276.

30. In another part of the *Confidential Report*, Wilhelm records that nearly all of the resources on earth have been used up. Indeed, there are no more national parks; for instance, the sequoias and waterfalls of Yosemite have disappeared due to the need for wood and water, respectively (xiii). The planet's solution is apparently to move on to new vistas for exploration followed by exploitation, e.g., Pandora.

31. Declassified minutes from an FBI meeting a year after 9/11 indicated that the policy of blending in helped the Al-Qaeda operatives from attracting attention. According to FBI Director Robert Mueller, "They dressed and acted like Americans, shopping and eating at places like Wal-Mart and Pizza Hut" ("Hijackers").

32. Demonstrating the diverse manner in which cultural signs can be interpreted, Iraqi journalist Mamoon Alabassi argues that Iraqi viewers recognize them-

selves in Cameron's portrayal of the Na'vi: "[F]or a lot of Iraqis, *Avatar* is the film of the underdog. For many of them who feel dehumanized by some parts of the media, the positive depiction of blue non-humans is welcome."

Works Cited

Addington, Larry H. *America's War in Vietnam: A Short Narrative History*. Bloomington: Indiana University Press, 2000.

Alabbasi, Mamoon. "Iraqi View of *Hurt Locker, Avatar*." www.consortium.com/2010/022610a.html. Accessed September 1, 2011.

Anker, Elisabeth. "Villains, Victims and Heroes: Melodrama, Media, and September 11." *Journal of Communication* 55.1 (March 2005): 22–37.

Avatar. Directed by James Cameron. 20th Century Fox, 2009.

Bayers, Peter L. "Larry Watson's *Montana 1948* and Euroamerican Representation of Native/Euroamerican History." *Rocky Mountain Review* 61.1 (Spring 2007): 35–50.

———. "The US Mint, the Lewis and Clark Bicentennial, and the Perpetuation of the Frontier Myth." *Journal of Popular Culture* 44.1 (2011): 37–52.

Brown, Dee. *Bury My Heart at Wounded Knee: An Indian History of the American West*. New York: Holt, 1970.

Butch Cassidy and the Sundance Kid. Directed by George Roy Hill. 20th Century Fox, 1969.

Carey, Diane. *New Earth*. New York: Pocket Books, 2000.

Carmichael, Deborah A. *The Landscape of Hollywood Westerns: Ecocriticism in an American Film Genre*. Salt Lake City: Utah University Press, 2006.

Cawelti, John G. *The Six-Gun Mystique*. Bowling Green: Bowling Green University Popular Press, 1970.

———. *The Six-Gun Mystique Sequel*. Bowling Green: Bowling Green University Popular Press, 1999.

Chase, Averil. "The Sci Fi Channel, a History of the First Two Years." thethunderchild.com/Television/Networks/SciFiChannel.html. Accessed October 15, 2011.

Chomsky, Noam. *9–11*. Westminster: Seven Stories, 2003.

Clan of the Cave Bear. Directed by Michael Chapman. Warner Bros., 1986.

Clover, Joshua. "Marx and Coca-Cola: The Struggle for Space." *Film Quarterly* 63.3 (2010): 6–7.

Cooper, James Fenimore Cooper. *The Last of the Mohicans*. Project Gutenberg, www.gutenberg.org/ebooks/940. Accessed August 15, 2011.

Dances with Wolves. Directed by Kevin Costner. Orion Pictures, 1990.

Dixon, Winston Wheeler, ed. *Film and Television After 9/11*. Carbondale: Southern Illinois University Press, 2004.

The Emerald Forest. Directed by John Boorman. Embassy Films, 1985.

The Empire Strikes Back. Directed by George Lucas. 20th Century Fox, 1980.

Espenson, Jane, ed. *Finding Serenity: Anti-heroes, Lost Shepherds, and Space Hookers in Joss Whedon's Firefly*. Dallas: BenBella, 2004.

"Hijackers Conducted Surveillance Flights Ahead of 9/11." articles.cnn.com/2002/sep/27. Accessed August 15, 2011.

Kennedy, John F. "Special Message to Congress on Urgent National Needs." www.jfklibrary.org/Asset-Viewer/Archives/JFKPOF-034-030.aspx. Accessed October 1, 2011.

Kitses, Jim, and Gregg Rickman, eds. *The Western Film Reader*. New York: Limelight, 2004.

Kroeber, Karl. "American Indian Persistence and Resurgence." *boundary 2* 19.3 (Autumn 1992): 1–25.
Lenihan, John H. *Showdown: Confronting Modern America in the Western Film.* Urbana: University of Illinois Press, 1980.
Logsdon, John. "Ten Presidents and NASA." www.nasa.gov/50th/50th_magazine/10presidents.html. Accessed October 1, 2011.
McGee, Patrick. *From Shane to Kill Bill: Rethinking the Western.* Malden: Blackwell, 2007.
Newiz, Annalee. "When Will White People Stop Making Movies Like 'Avatar'?" io9.com/5422666/when-will-white-people-stop-making-movies-like-avatar. Accessed August 15, 2011.
Nichols, Roger. "Western Attractions: Europeans and America." *Pacific Historical Review* 74.1 (2005): 1–17.
Outland. Directed by Peter Hyams. Warner Bros., 1981.
Rickman, Gregg, ed. *The Science Fiction Film Reader.* New York: Limelight, 2004.
Saunders, John. *The Western Genre: From Lordsburg to Big Whiskey.* London: Wallflower, 2001.
Slotkin, Richard. *Gunfighter Nation: The Myth of the Frontier in Twentieth-Century America.* Norman: University of Oklahoma Press, 1992.
"Sputnik and the Dawn of the Space Age." history.nasa.org/sputnik. Accessed September 28, 2011.
Star Trek V: The Final Frontier. Directed by William Shatner. Paramount Pictures, 1989.
Star Wars: A New Hope. Directed by George Lucas. 20th Century Fox, 1977.
Truffaut, Francois. *Hitchcock.* New York: Simon & Schuster, 1983.
Turner, Frederick Jackson. *History, Frontier, and Section.* Albuquerque: University of New Mexico Press, 1993.
The Wild Bunch. Directed by Sam Peckinpah. Warner Bros., 1969.
Wilhelm, Maria, and Dirk Mathison. *Avatar: A Confidential Report on the Biological and Social History of Pandora.* New York: HarperCollins, 2009.

Security or Freedom
Joss Whedon's Science Fiction Westerns, Firefly *and* Serenity

J.P.C. BROWN

Joss Whedon's series, *Firefly*, was a fusion of Science Fiction (SF) and Western (something nicely registered in an iconic shot from the title sequence of horses being stampeded by a spaceship), of which Fox made fourteen episodes in 2002 (one a double) before cancelling it. The DVD sales were then so strong that Whedon was able to make a movie called *Serenity* (2005) for Universal, which continued some of the storylines of *Firefly*. So far as TV and film goes, that seems to be it. The movie did not do well enough for there to be hope for a sequel. But plenty of loose threads have been left hanging, and in multi-user games, other online activities, comics and so on, the story continues.

The show is set five hundred years in the future. Humanity, having used up "Earth-That-Was," has headed to another system in giant, sub-light generation-ships, and there set about colonizing many worlds and moons, adapting them by terraforming. Whedon extrapolated the political set-up from the present. He reckoned the two key global powers by the time of the departure from Earth would be the U.S. and China, and therefore imagines a Sino-American alliance accomplishing global evacuation, and remaining dominant thereafter. The show maintains a *Blade-Runner*-ish density of cultural allusion. Thus all the characters sprinkle their conversation with pungent Chinese phrases such as *Liou coe shway duh biao-tze huh hoe-tze duh bun ur-tze*, meaning "Stupid son of a drooling whore and monkey" (Sullivan 232). The idea was that knowing a bit of Chinese would be common. Much of the design is reminiscent of *Blade Runner*'s "retrofitting," so that elements of diverse eras and cultures end up superimposed in a palimpsestic present (on *Blade Runner*'s design see Sammon ch. 6).

America and China form the core of the Alliance, which runs a parliamentary but oppressive system that dominates the rich central planets, especially Londinium, which is mainly American, the UK having been annexed by the U.S. before the trek to the new system, and Sihnon, which is a new China. Shortly before the series is set, there had been a civil war in which the outer moons and planets had tried to assert their independence from the rich central planets, which wanted to control them in the name of unity (Whedon 12–14).

The hero of the show had been a sergeant in the independent Browncoat army in that war. In the wake of the independents' defeat in the Battle of Serenity Valley (which the original, double-length pilot starts by showing us), Sgt. Malcolm Reynolds (Nathan Fillion) scrapes together the money to buy a space freighter: a small firefly-class ship. This is how he aims to assert independence in the wake of defeat. The show's theme-song, also written by Whedon, invites one to identify with Mal's choice: "Take my life, take my land, take me where I cannot stand. I don't care. I'm still free. You can't take the sky from me." He then gathers around him a crew and passengers: we see exactly how over several episodes, sometimes in flashback. The crew comprises: Zoe (Gina Torres), who had been a corporal with Mal in the war; Wash (Alan Tudyk), the pilot, who is now married to Zoe; Jayne Cobb (Adam Baldwin), an unprincipled tough guy (his first name may connote J[ohn W]ayne, but also, by an irony typical of Whedon, is incongruously feminine); Kaylee (Jewel Staite), the mechanic; and then the passengers: Shepherd Book (Ron Glass), who appears to be a preacher; Simon Tam (Sean Maher), a brilliant surgeon on the run from the Alliance; and his sister River Tam (Summer Glau). The other regular is not exactly passenger or crew: Inara (Morena Baccarin) is a registered "companion," and hires one of the ship's shuttles to carry on her business as a—well, Mal says "whore," but the idea is that she is a courtesan or a *geisha* and that they are organized into a prestigious guild.

However, though Reynolds is the hero, given what we see of the story in the fourteen episodes of *Firefly* and in the film, *Serenity*, which is also the name of the ship, the story of the Tams comes closest to being a story arc spanning the whole thing. River Tam was sent to an Alliance-run academy for gifted children, where, as her brother discovered, she was experimented upon to change her. It becomes clear she is unstable and can read minds—talents to which the later stories add a flair for lethal, graceful violence. In the film that capacity for violence is triggered twice, the first time by a signal to which the Alliance scientists have programmed her to respond automatically. Afterwards Mal asks River (while she holds a gun on him), "Are you anything but a weapon? I've staked my crew's life on the theory that you're a person, actual and whole...." In the final episode of the TV series the crew discusses the threat River might pose, and Kaylee explains how in an earlier story, when River and herself were pinned down by armed guards, River had just glanced at the position of their three attackers, picked up a gun, closed her eyes, and shot them dead. Kaylee adds, "not nobody can shoot like that's a person." One question that this overarching storyline explores is whether an authentic, human individuality can survive the worst that modern science, in the service of an enslaving political system, can do to you (besides giving Whedon what he jokes, as the creator of *Buffy*, is the teenage girl with superpowers that is obligatory in all his shows). The story invites comparison between Mal and River in relation to a key preoccupation of the Western: can one wield violence righteously and retain both one's individuality and one's place in a community while doing so? It is a question on which the Western broods: think of Shane (Alan Ladd) exiling himself from the valley, having defended the homesteaders against Wilson (Jack Palance), or Ethan (John Wayne) turning back to the wilderness, having delivered Debbie (Natalie Wood), or Kemp (James Stewart) in *The Naked Spur* having to renounce the bounty he has used violent means to secure in order to open the possibility of a future with Lina (Janet Leigh) in California.

The Post–9/11 Western in Space

In considering the possibility that *Firefly* and *Serenity* might in some sense be post–9/11 Westerns there are at least a couple contextual issues to address. One concerns the nature of the Western as a genre: its mutations, its responses to history and its relations with other genres. The other concerns 9/11. What exactly did 9/11 change or reveal? It is an especially tricky question in relation to *Firefly* since the show was conceived prior to 9/11. Whedon traces his first inklings to reading Michael Shaara's book about the Civil War in 1999 (Whedon 8). But it was developed, shot and aired after 9/11, its initial (incomplete) run being from September to December 2002. If *Firefly* included an element of the post–9/11 Western, it must have done so in some degree presciently.

That is not as tall an order as it might sound, especially if one considers how 9/11 sits in the longer term. Horror burst upon al Qaeda's targets literally and metaphorically out of a blue sky. It broke into the normal activities of civilian life. The contrast between, on the one hand, the destruction, the loss of life and the monumental images of collapse, and, on the other, the quotidian normality of what everyone, including those in the World Trade Center, had been doing until 8:46 that morning, became the key feature of many narratives of survival or bereavement. Notwithstanding homicide rates that are high by the standards of other industrialized democracies (Singh 73–5, 77), for the U.S. there is a pronounced contrast between the pacified space within the polity and zones beyond it where violence may flourish on a large scale, albeit sometimes with the participation of forces deployed by the west.

The shocking contrast between daily normality and exceptional, bizarre violence points to a key feature of the attacks of September 11. They were horrifying but they were also highly *theatrical*. No al Qaeda planner can have imagined that they were going to bring the U.S. down by crashing four airliners into three targets, even if they had succeeded, and the heroic souls of United Airlines Flight 93 saw to it that, even on the 11th, the terrorists did not have things entirely their own way. This element of theatricality is intrinsic to terrorism: this is what multiplies the impact of terrorist violence to intensify the "subjective psychological pressure" through which terrorism works (Townshend 15). Publicity is a large part of what is being fought for. The al Qaeda brand was made by the coverage of that day's slaughter. The death toll was extraordinarily high for a single terrorist attack. However, an event that kills nearly 3,000 people is not, sad to say, exceptionally destructive by the terrible standards we have set for ourselves. It is dwarfed, for example, by the scale and rate of the killing in the Rwandan genocide of 1994 in which approximately half a million people were murdered in the space of about 100 days, with roughly another 300,000 dying by other means. A tenth of the population perished with relatively little attention from the rest of the world until it was too late. It is not even uniquely bloody for a single day's bloodshed on American soil. More men died at the Battle of Antietam on 17 September 1862. Nor is it necessarily an event that made the U.S. feel vulnerable in a way that it had *never* felt before (though it certainly did make the nation feel newly vulnerable). Just to confine oneself to events within living memory, the Japanese surprise attack on Pearl Harbor on 7 December 1941, the Soviet acquisition and testing of A- and H-bombs, allegations about communist infiltrators within the U.S. in the 1940s and 1950s, and the Vietnam War, in particular the Tet Offensive, all produced a widespread feeling of vulnerability among Americans. Nor was terrorist violence in itself a novelty in the U.S.: consider the Oklahoma City bombing of 1995, and before that the political assassinations and domestic terrorism associated with unrest in the 1960s and 1970s (perpetrated, for example, by the Weathermen). Admittedly, no individual terrorist atrocity in the U.S. has claimed anything like as many lives as the 9/11 attacks. Racially motivated lynching is one of very few categories of terrorist violence (assuming it qualifies as terrorism) in the U.S. to have claimed more lives, and its gruesome record of killing is spread over decades. However, the list of possible terrorist attacks on U.S. soil is long (see "Terrorism in the United States"). Terrorism in the U.S. and feelings of national insecurity were not new.

Some reactions to that insecurity, including reactions on the part of the authorities, have taken questionable forms. The felt need for security has seen the rights of some trampled upon: the rights, for example, of interned Japanese Americans after Pearl Harbor (one of whom noted that the result was more authentically Soviet than anything yet achieved in Russia, since the internment camp was a "truly classless community" in that people were "not recognized as individuals" [Ichihashi 255]), or the rights of some alleged communists brought before HUAC and then sometimes punished by extrajudicial means by being deprived of their livelihoods (Carroll and Noble 357–8). Almost inevitably, a sense of national vulnerability begets closer identification with the Federal Authorities, and especially with the President.

It can be argued that this is a pattern in U.S. history. Louis Fisher contends that the pattern goes back at least to the Sedition Act of 1798 (362). It is a pattern in which federal authorities overstep the bounds of constitutional propriety, and then have to be pulled back by public opinion (in elections or otherwise) or by the courts. Especially since World War II it is a pattern that has seen the executive power of the President expand in unconstitutional ways (364). The pattern derives from a recurrent temptation. Here Fisher describes it in relation to McCarthyism:

> McCarthyism, supposedly part of the conservative movement, elevates nativism, chauvinism, nationalism, and governmental power over individual rights. Ironically, it borrows from Communism: the State is all, the individual little. Its spirit flourished during the Alien and Sedition Acts of 1798, the Palmer raids after World War I, and many other periods that violated constitutional liberties. It surfaces in times of crisis and emergency when the government argues, in the name of national security, that it must forgo public trials, withdraw procedural safeguards, block access to evidence, and limit free speech and free association. Those forces reappeared after September 11, 2001 [Fisher 171].

In similar vein, in discussing human rights in the wake of 9/11, Stephen J. Toope remarks on "a sad but long tradition" of "Indiscriminate repression" (240).

Now, several years after 9/11, it is easier to see in what ways the federal government might have either overreacted or made improper use of the challenges the 9/11 attacks presented. The moment at which *Firefly* appeared in 2002 was very early in the 9/11 cycle of fear and deviation from constitutional norms, followed by second thoughts and partial reassertion of the constitution and of legal safeguards. It was possibly too early for its own good, given that it is a show in which a powerful, central government abuses its power in the name of the safety and improvement of the people: such criticism of government was out of fashion for a time. Nevertheless, it was possible for *Firefly* to be prescient about this process: to see what was happening and what was about to happen in the present, all the show's creators had to do was look back into the past. This was exactly how Whedon started to imagine *Firefly*: his earliest ideas for the show came from reading about the American Civil War.

Shifting Histories

In some ways the scene had been set ahead of time for aspects of 9/11. In the wake of the Cold War there had been various analyses of the USA's position in a changed world. Some were triumphalist, some concerned about the proliferation of threats; but one stood out as the book which academics, journalists and policy-makers could all allude to: Samuel Huntington's *The Clash of Civilizations* (1996), based on a thesis proposed in a lecture of 1992. The book's thesis is summarized by its title: in the wake of the Cold War, normal civilizational conflict will resume. The only crucial element that one needs to add is that the civilizations that are deemed most likely to clash are the west and Islam. There is a complex argument about civilizations usually needing to be stabilized by having a core state, and Islam lacking such a thing, which makes it difficult to deal with in the framework of a conventional diplomacy of states and their representatives. There is also an acceptance that the values of the west do not transcend history and difference: in other words, we have one way of life among others, rather than being the privileged torchbearers of an inevitable modernity. In Huntington's terms the west should value its European heritage of individual liberty, the rule of law, political democracy and so on, not because western civilization "is universal but because it *is* unique" (Huntington 311).

For Huntington history is not on anyone's side. However, if our values mean something to us (and he thinks they should and they do), we need to stick up for them. This is where the book's least impressive bit of conceptual underpinning became the key to its influence. As a child I was given *The Readers' Digest Great World Atlas*, in which there is a map showing the distribution of religions across the globe. I used to gaze at this trying to figure out who was where, never for a moment pausing to question the labels in the legend: Sunni Islam, Protestant, Catholic, Orthodox, etc. Huntington, in the midst of an absorbing and, in other respects, persuasive analysis, made the same mistake: he assumed that these labels correspond relatively unproblematically to essential differences. Those then draw the battlelines for his clashing civilizations. By the time of 9/11 Huntington's book had been around for five years and his doctrine for nearly ten. Not surprisingly, in the wake of 9/11 it was frequently cited. Huntington's book and the debate it occasioned anticipated key themes in post–9/11 discussion of global political order: universalism vs. difference, conflict vs. dialogue.

Even though President George W. Bush, to his credit, appealed for tolerance and respect for American Muslims, and drew a distinction between the extremist ideology of some Muslim terrorists and the religion of Islam, some proponents of the War on Terror took to denouncing Islamo-Fascism—a bizarre, concocted label, which ran the risk of appearing to denounce Islam *per se*, and which also made it harder than it should have been to enquire into the real nature of al Qaeda. In the event, the decision to attack Iraq in 2003 (after *Firefly* had been cancelled) as part of the "War on Terror" was so difficult to justify as a response to what had actually happened on and since 9/11, that it was easiest to assume the world was simply divided into good and evil, and Iraq was part of the Islamic "other." Such absolutist language had already appeared in the State of the Union address of 29 January 2002, which spoke of Iran, Iraq and North Korea "and their terrorist allies" constituting "an axis of evil" (Woodward 92), and this rhetorical flourish was then made to seem real by repeatedly implying a connection between Saddam Hussein and al Qaeda in the run-up to the 2003 invasion (Rich 69–70). This impatience with difference and complexity, along with a tendency to demonize a consolidated other and to posit a single pattern in history in which one's own values are destined to triumph, were among the things *Firefly* criticized. It did so in part by its revisionist reworking of the Western.

Firefly's *"Weapons of Mass Destruction"*

Though *Firefly* had ceased production by the time of the second Gulf War, in its portrayal of a wealthy, corporate political establishment that was capable of justifying violations of human rights in pursuit of security, it was touching on what by late 2002 (when it was in production) had already become a source of dismay for many Americans. "Special rendition" and the internment of alleged enemy combatants in Guantánamo Bay from 2002 onwards were especially controversial (on Guantánamo see Fisher, Chapter 7). Doubts were expressed about the legality of such internment under the U.S. Constitution and under international law, and stories started to leak out alleging the use of torture at Guantánamo. Other stories of human rights violations followed, including, most notoriously, the scandal of Abu Ghraib, news of which broke in April 2004. In *Firefly* River Tam has been interned inside a government institution and subjected to what amounts to torture, not to extract information from her, but to turn her into a superweapon. In *Serenity* (2005) we are actually shown what has been done to her, and the story creates a high-minded villain in the person of a government agent (the Operative) who is prepared to commit any crime in order to serve the Alliance and the future that he hopes for. Maintaining exclusive control of superweapons (the reason why River Tam is a wanted fugitive) or "Weapons of Mass Destruction" loomed large in the agenda for the 2003 invasion of Iraq. Whedon's portrayal of illegality and corruption in the Alliance government in *Firefly* had a long tradition in U.S. television to draw upon: since 1975 three out of five representations of the American political and legal process on prime time shows in the U.S. have portrayed it as corrupt (Lichter, Lichter and Amundson, 110). In 2002 and 2005 illegality on the part of the government was newly topical.

In Whedon's universe the government is actually *Sino*-American. Anyone looking at who was bankrolling the Federal debt in 2002 could have seen the point of what Whedon was doing. Now, in the wake of 9/11, with shifts in economic global power perhaps looming even larger than the threat of terrorism, Whedon's decision to link China and the U.S. seems acute and provocative. It helps to create a world in which the Western's use of East and West is reconceived. It also helps him to create a world in which what it is easy to assume (if one does not bother watching Westerns too closely) is the genre's black-and-white morality gets called into question. Given that this simplistic perception of the genre was deployed by the President in the wake of 9/11 (e.g., in the way in which he used his Prairie Chapel Ranch in Texas and his identity as an adoptive Texan in some press conferences (Woodward 65)), in the aftermath of 9/11 the Western, accordingly, became a source of legitmating accounts of righteous and even redemptive violence (Takacs 153–4). *Firefly*, in effect, re-presented elements of the Western in a way that made it possible to identify America not merely as the Westerner hero, which, with some qualification, is the role of Mal Reynolds, but *also* as the corporate Sino-American Alliance, against which Mal had fought and with which he remains at odds. In the process, it implicitly contested the attempt to use the iconography of the Western to justify the War on Terror.

Conceiving the Sci-Fi Western

Firefly is routinely referred to as an SF/Western. As Bruce Bethke remarks, SF that is really horse opera in space (hence "space opera") has a poor reputation in SF circles (177). However, chunks of *Firefly* are not just Westerns in new settings (in the way that Roddenberry pitched *Star Trek* as "*Wagon Train* to the stars"); it is possible to pick frames and even whole scenes from the show that look as if they actually come from a Western.

This inclusion of explicitly Western elements came about partly because there are frontier worlds in the solar system to which humanity has migrated. For example, in the double episode that was meant to start the series, Mal is trying to offload what we assume are bars of gold from the value everyone attaches to them, though they are actually foil-wrapped food rations. He has salvaged the goods from a space-wreck for Badger (Mark Sheppard), a small-time crook, who refuses to take them when he finds each bar bears the Alliance's stamp. After several scenes in space (including a close encounter with an Alliance cruiser which, in deference to the corporate character of the Alliance, looks like office-blocks in space), Mal and his crew arrive on a moon run by a woman called Patience (Bonnie Bartlett), who had shot Mal the last time they met. This time Patience and her boys are on horseback, and Patience looks as if she has just ridden in from the 1880s; Mal and Zoe are standing. When the talking stops and the shooting starts, Mal pulls his gun from an open leather holster, and we see a weapon that is not exactly like any handgun one has ever seen, but which resembles the 1851 Navy Colt in its profile and its octagonal barrel (Bernstein 1: 78–81). Whedon wanted it to look like the Civil War era handguns in *The Outlaw Josey Wales* (actually 1847 Colt Walker revolvers) (Whedon 62). Having got their money, Jayne, Mal and Zoe race back to Serenity on horseback, desperate to get airborne and outrun the Reavers who have followed them to the moon.

For science fiction, *Firefly* is unusual in boasting no aliens: the Reavers are Whedon's closest approach. They are creatures from a horror movie. Simon assumes the Reavers are just "campfire stories.... Men gone savage at the edge of space." Zoe explains, "if they take the ship, they'll rape us to death, eat our flesh and sew our skins into their clothing and if we're very very lucky they'll do it in that order." They are presented as simply other—no more "real" characters than legions of Orcs. In the following story, "Bushwhacked," Shepherd Book protests that Reavers are still men, "too long removed from civilization, perhaps—but men," but Mal insists "Reavers ain't men. Or they forgot how to be." Nothing we ever see (though they are kept at arm's length until the movie, *Serenity*) contradicts Mal's verdict. If the Reavers are simply savages, then, as Rabb and Robinson point out, in *Firefly*'s Western context, they are cast in the role often played by Native Americans in Westerns. In a sense the Reaver chase at the end of the pilot, "Serenity," is akin to the Apaches' pursuit in *Stagecoach*—except that there is no cavalry to ride to the rescue. On the face of it, then, *Firefly* accepts the idea of an "other" that is definitively other. Only at the end of the film will we learn more.

Having escaped the Reavers, the pilot episode ends with Mal offering Simon and River Tam a permanent place on Serenity. Simon wonders how he can be sure Mal will not shoot him in his sleep. Mal's answer recalls the credos of some other Westerners: "...if I ever kill you, you'll be awake, you'll be facing me, and you'll be armed." Compare J.B. Books' (John Wayne) credo in *The Shootist* (1976), "I won't be wronged. I won't be insulted. I won't be laid a hand on. I don't do these things to other people, and I require the same from them," or Tom Doniphon's (John Wayne) pronouncements on Western law in *Liberty Valance*. The encounter of Mal and Simon might remind one of Ransom Stoddard (James Stewart) and Tom Doniphon. Simon as a prodigiously talented and privileged doctor, who gives up everything to save his sister, has the learning, the status and the principles to make him resemble Ransom Stoddard. It sets up one of the many comparisons of Mal with other heroic or outlaw figures which the series invokes. In this case, one has what

Robert B. Ray considers the Western's most identifiable contrast: between the official, often "Eastern" hero, and the Western outlaw hero (Ray 59–66).

The next story, "The Train Job," was hastily written as an alternative series opener after Fox declined to use the original one. The "job" is pulled on a mining colony, and Mal and Zoe find themselves detained (along with the other passengers on the train) while Sheriff Bourne investigates the theft they have committed. Everyone is held in what looks like a frontier saloon. "Bushwhacked" concerns the survivor of a Reaver attack who tries to turn himself into a Reaver in order to cope with what he has seen, and raises again the possibility of seeing the Reavers in terms derived from Westerns' representations of native Americans as *other*. Tim Minnear, who wrote and directed the episode, explained that in moving between the aftermath of a Reaver attack to the Alliance cruiser which then stops and interrogates the passengers and crew of Serenity, he was deliberately moving from savagery to a civilization "*so* civilized that it becomes this collectivist, bureaucratic behemoth that ... [is] trying to control you too much." The survivor had been one of a party of settlers, and Minnear's account of the first half of the episode is accordingly derived from the Western: "...it's about homesteaders and regular people trying to get by. It's about the savagery of being too far away from civilization" (Bernstein 1: 84).

The Western (or, at least, nineteenth-century America) is visually present again in "Shindig" where Mal stumbles into a duel in a privileged society reminiscent of the old South, albeit with an expanded range of cultural reference and technology. Shawna Trpcic, the costume designer, acknowledges *Gone With the Wind* (Fleming, 1939) as an influence on the look of the episode (Bernstein 1: 111). "Shindig" leads directly to "Safe" which involves Mal in smuggling cattle, and presents a frontier settlement that is hopelessly backward and superstitious. Simon and River are kidnapped by villagers in need of a doctor, and when River's ability to read minds uncovers guilty secrets, they try to burn her as a witch. It is not the way the west is commonly portrayed in Westerns, though as early as *Bad Day at Black Rock* (Sturges, 1955), which was set in 1945, one finds the idea of a western town turned poisonously in upon itself in its guilt and hostility to the outer world. If one goes back to 1692 when the frontier was well to the east, one finds in Salem Village a community that faced alien cultures in its frontier conflicts and reacted by turning upon itself and burning witches (on the significance of the frontier wars as a factor in the witch trials, see Norton).

The obvious Western imagery gets thinner on the ground in the second half of the series, though there are hooped wagons in "Our Mrs. Reynolds" along with a religious community, the Triumph Settlers, seeking on the frontier of an outer world the freedom to worship by their own lights. "Heart of Gold" was caught between Whedon's impulse, "let's *do* a Western—let's do

Rio Bravo, let's do the siege," and Fox's instruction to make the show "less Western" (Bernstein 2: 174, 169). It features a rich landowner who aims to dominate his private world in the semi-feudal manner of Ryker in *Shane*, and a whorehouse that might put one in mind of *Unforgiven* (Eastwood, 1992) or *McCabe and Mrs. Miller* (Altman, 1971), save for its being wrapped in foil in an attempt to appease Fox.

There are, then, signficant and overt elements of the Western in *Firefly*. However, these overtly Western elements appear only in about half the show's fourteen episodes (save for a few shots in the title sequence). One could make a case for a couple more episodes including overtly Western elements. But in the movie, *Serenity*, except for the Reavers, they are less in evidence than they had been in the series, and the Reavers in *Serenity* owe as much to horror as to Westerns. As Whedon acknowledged, he omitted horses from *Serenity*, not because of external pressure (Universal did not share Fox's concerns over the Western aspects of the show), but because he "didn't see a place for them" (Whedon 25).

However, the explicitly Western visual elements in the show were never the whole story of the show's relationship to the genre. To understand the larger story of *Firefly*'s relation to the Western, and thus the ways in which it could be seen as implicitly contesting the government's appropriation of the genre after 9/11, it is necessary to look at the way the Western genre had informed other film genres to produce what one might call displaced Westerns, or, in Robert B. Ray's phrase, "disguised westerns" (75). These displaced Westerns emerged partly from the way in which the genre itself explored displacement (including literal loss of place, especially loss of wilderness) as a theme.

A Brief History of the Western

The heyday of the Western as a talkie approximately corresponds to the period of John Wayne's career in A-pictures, from c. 1939 to c. 1976 (there is a separate history of the silent Western). What one might call the "official" use of the idea of the Western corresponded to the perception of the genre that one might get if one assumed that what John Wayne said *about* his films was more truthful than his often superb performances *in* them (especially his insistence on the virtues of people on the frontier, which led him to condemn *High Noon*). Yet even in 1939 (and certainly by the 1950s), the Western was not only a film genre with a long history going back to *The Great Train Robbery* (Porter, 1903), but it was also capable of communicating a sense of displacement and belatedness. It is something Warshow touches on while discussing *Shane* in remarking, even in the early 1950s, on the Western's "endless repetitions" (121). Warshow comments that there is a sense of the film being a distillation of a long-established pattern. He speaks of "the legend of the West" being "reduced to its essentials and then fixed in the dreamy clarity of a fairy tale," and of Shane's opponent, Wilson, being cast as "a Spirit of Evil" (120). It makes one wonder what Warshow (who died in 1955) would have made of Leone's films or of Eastwood's *Pale Rider* (1985). Yet even in *Shane* the Westerner moves from history into the realm of myth. Thus early in the genre's great post-war period, it was formulating its characteristic way of meditating on heroism: as a phenomenon defined in myth, but awkwardly also located in a history which threatens to leave it behind. That is one sense in which many a Western feels belated. Accordingly, the Westerners at the core of the genre, such as Shane or Steve Judd (Joel McCrea) in *Ride the High Country* (Peckinpah, 1962), often acknowledge that their moment is passing.

It is one of the genre's achievements that it finds various ways of resolving the seeming contradiction between the eternal present of myth and the transformative onrush of history, especially of history in the form of paradigmatic change wrought by modernity. Shane accepts his redundancy once Wilson has been killed: his time is over. Yet the final image of Shane (wounded, perhaps dead in the saddle) riding up into the high places is surely the image eternally rooted in little Joey's mind: an image of an alternative father, the self-sacrificing hero who, in striking Joe Starrett with the butt of his revolver in order to get away to confront Wilson, has sacrificed even his personal honor in order to do the right thing and protect a future he cannot share. Shane is thus past and eternally present. Similarly in *The Man Who Shot Liberty Valance*, Tom Doniphon, the authentic western hero, has been so far left behind by the advent of modernity that he dies forgotten—except that the myth of "the man who shot Liberty Valance" lives on, albeit mistakenly attached to Ranse Stoddard rather than to Tom. In shooting Valance (Lee Marvin) from the shadows, and thus saving Ranse for Hallie (Vera Miles), Tom achieves the heroism of vanquishing the bad man and sacrificing himself for the good of others, but he violates his own code: he fails to confront Valance face to face. When Ranse expresses qualms about basing a political career on a killing, Tom explains who really killed Valance: "I can live with it," he tells Ranse, as he forces him back into the political meeting to accept the nomination and start his public career. But Wayne's ravaged, unshaven face tells a different story. Thus as an individual Doniphon dies forgotten, pushed aside by "progress," but, as a legend displaced onto Ranse, he lives on.

At the heart of the Western was the outlaw hero, who could be placed anywhere on a spectrum from heroism with no more than technical outlaw status (the Ringo Kid in *Stagecoach*) to figures that were essentially outlaws (Butch and Sundance, for instance). The outlaw hero was sometimes contrasted with the "official" hero, but the ambiguity of the genre derived from its preoccupation with the former. The Westerner may wield heroic violence guided only by his inner sense of natural law, but that tends to pave the way for official law. A world dominated by official law will have little space for the Westerner. It may, in fact, favor moral spinelessness (as it appears to do in *High Noon*). Yet the advent of law and order is commonly represented as a kind of inevitable progress, no matter what may have been lost along the way. It is a kind of progress the Westerner often acknowledges while seeking also to remain true to his own sense of himself, which sometimes means he has no place in the communities he protects. This may be accepted cheerfully (as at the end of *Dodge City* when Errol Flynn as Wade Hatton looks forward to taming other lawless towns, or of *Stagecoach*, when Ringo and Dallas head off for a new life across the border) or regretfully (as when Shane leaves to ensure there are no more guns in the valley).

This relation to progress means that the Western is caught between defining supposedly permanent values in its mythic side, and acknowledging its place in the unfolding of history. This points to ways in which the Western may be related to several other film genres. John Wayne became the archetypal Western hero, but the other genre in which he loomed large was the war film, notably in *Sands of Iwo Jima* (Dwan, 1949). Elements of the patriarchal figure he created in Sgt. Stryker informed almost all his subsequent roles (see Suid, Chapter 6). The war film finds the hero wielding violence to government order—an uncomfortable position for an authentic Westerner. Yet if there is any element of the maverick about the war hero, he starts to look like a displaced Westerner. Indeed, the war film as displaced Western is anticipated by Westerns set in the military, the key instances being John Ford's cavalry films.

The war film can head in two main directions: celebration of officially sanctioned heroism or exploration of the dissonance between military violence and the rule-bound civil society it serves. *Sands of Iwo Jima* does both at once: Wayne's Sgt. Stryker is tormented by family problems in civilian life that he cannot resolve, and even breaks the rules of the Marine Corps to punish a man he believes has got others killed; but he is also the embodiment of the Corps.

Thus the war hero may be the successor to the Westerner, but he serves a U.S. that dominates the continent, and where there is no more wilderness. Therefore the violence of the Western either has to turn inwards (as with some crime and gangster films) or be exported (as often with the war film or overseas adventures). This geographical displacement is sometimes seen within the Western, especially when stories shift south (in ways that might remind one of the USA's intermittent imperial ambitions in that direction, though these are commonly obscured, as they are in Wayne's film of *The Alamo*). It is a move that Kerouac's *On the Road* (1957)—a book obsessed with the old West and belatedness—makes ironically when Sal and Dean cross into Mexico, with Sal holding forth about the old outlaws of the west, and they head south for essentially the same reason than some Westerns head south: out west there is "no more land," as Dean puts it (Kerouac 276–7, 170). Similarly, fleeing the closure of the frontier, the advent of corporate power and the law-enforcement it pays for, Butch and Sundance head for Bolivia.

To summarize the case about the Western so far: in its heyday the Western managed to stabilize itself by two ploys. One was geo-historical, whereby movement west connoted progress. Even if personally doomed or displaced, the Westerner often evinces some sense of serving inevitable progress (though that can get strained, as in *High Noon*, and Butch and Sundance are set against the future). In particular, the tensions of the North-South conflict of the Civil War, where they surface, are apt to be resolved by East-West movement in quest of the future. The second ploy involved generic displacement, so that, even when one encounters dilemmas that are beyond the capacity of the Western as a genre to resolve within its own terms, elements of the Western can be displaced into other genres, such as war films, heist movies, and gangster films, and, Ray would add, some screwball comedies which involve the collision and eventual collusion of one partner of acknowledged status and another who is, if not exactly an *outlaw* hero, then from the wrong side of the tracks. Ray cites *It Happened One Night* (Capra, 1934), the founding movie of the screwball sub-genre, as an example: millionaire's daughter Ellie (Claudette Colbert) clashes and then falls in love with Clark Gable's streetwise reporter Peter. Among his other examples of disguised Westerns which transplant the Western's unofficial hero to new settings are adventures set outside the U.S. (*Red Dust* and *China Seas*), *Angels with Dirty Faces* (Curtiz, 1938) with Cagney as a basically decent hoodlum sacrificing even his personal sense of honor by feigning cowardice as he is led to his execution in the hope of reforming the Dead End Kids, and *Casablanca* (Curtiz, 1942), which involves Rick, an unofficial hero, seemingly cynical and unheroic, sacrificing himself to protect Victor Laszlo's official hero and uphold the sanctity of marriage. In the end, the accumulation of realities that the Western could not readily address in an undisguised form arguably contributed to the genre's partial eclipse from the mid–1970s in the wake of the Vietnam War and Watergate (Hoberman 88–92).

Firefly *and* Serenity *as Westerns*

Firefly and *Serenity* unravel these two moves by which the Western either stabilized itself or was displaced into other genres dealing with the Western's essential figure: the outlaw hero. One can see this, for example, in the way Mal is a defeated hero, with his Browncoat independents corresponding in some ways to the Confederacy (Vaughn 188–191). But there is no resolution.

The "West" of the frontier moons and planets does not represent an inevitable and singular progress into the future, where the defeated Browncoats can redeem themselves by fighting for the future in the manner of the former Confederate captain, Sgt. Tyree in *She Wore a Yellow Ribbon* (Ford, 1949), and there is no reconciliation with the victorious enemy in the manner of *The Undefeated* (McLaglen, 1969). The frontier worlds in *Firefly* represent *different* possible presents, although the Alliance attempts to compress them into its single vision.

At the same time the show's surface genres keep modulating. Of course, there is an element of pastiche in the fun the writers have with different genres. But there is also a logic to such variety: there being no singular destiny (except a self-reflexive one explored in "Out of Gas" which implies that there is a kind of destiny in the way these particular people have come together on the ship), the basic element of the Western that is constant in the Western proper and in displaced Westerns (the outlaw hero) engages in a series of nominally different genres. Thus one gets con movie ("Our Mrs. Reynolds" has Mal nearly falling victim to a heartless but sexually compelling grifter), crime story ("The Train Job"), heist movie (in "Ariel" the crew rob a hospital while Simon uses the hospital scanner to see what the Alliance has done to River, and in "Trash" the crew pulls off a robbery and out-grift the grifter who had nearly killed them in "Our Mrs. Reynolds"), and quite a dose of post–Vietnam war movie (especially in "War Stories" and "The Message"). To these genres, which clearly involve the outlaw hero, one can add other influences: horror movies (in the Reavers, especially), and, in Whedon's own view, 1930s Romantic Comedy in the unacknowledged attraction and friction between Mal and Inara (and 1930s comedy was one of Ray's more surprising candidates for a disguised Western), *film noir*, and Hong Kong cinema (Whedon 24–5). There is no ordained order to the history Whedon imagines, and so the Western moves easily between seeming to be itself and adopting the guise of the genres into which it has previously been displaced, but these are now all happening at once.

One thus gets a work which is clearly SF, but for which in a pervasive way the label "Western" is also apt. But it is a work which also challenges the Western's key element of the lone hero and its sense of history. Mal has a kind of family around him in the shape of his crew. Some commentators have linked the show with *Stagecoach* (including Whedon himself [Money, 116; Bernstein 1: 6]), where the entire party is the central character; but it recalls *The Outlaw Josey Wales* more strongly. In both stories the defeated rebel, who has lost everything, somehow reacquires a "family," and neither story puts any faith in large-scale socio-political processes, preferring to find modest hope in individuals resolving their differences, while remaining different and making common cause.

However, where Wales is in some sense the single, definitive outlaw hero, even with the support of his new "family" (he rescues them from the comancheros singlehandedly, and alone he negotiates an honorable peace with Ten Bears), Mal is repeatedly in need of the assistance of his "family," and he repays them with his loyalty. In "War Stories" he is captured and tortured by Nishka, the head of a crime operation, and the rest of the crew have to rescue him. In "Trash," having allowed "Saffron" (the con-woman) to get his weapon, he is left stranded and naked in the desert, dependent upon his fallback plan (having Inara surprise "Saffron") for success. His status survives such incidents partly because, though originally conceived as embittered and cynical, he is also a comic character, blessed with comedy's powers of flexibility and survival.

He is also presented with distorted mirror images of himself, which help to define him (often by showing us an outlaw without Mal's principles), but which also in the end qualify the kind of Western heroism that he embodies. In "Out of Gas," when the ship's power and life-support fail, Mal stays behind in case help comes. The Captain of a salvage ship shows up. The directions in the script make the parallel between them clear: the other Captain is "A serious sort; Mal without the funny" (Bernstein 2: 55). Each then seeks reassurances that the other will not ambush him. The Captain then establishes that Mal is alone, and shoots him in order to take his ship. When Mal recovers and pulls a gun on him, the Captain's hollow defense is "You would have done the same." The con-woman, "Saffron," who appears in "Our Mrs. Reynolds" and "Trash," is perhaps another counterpart to Mal, especially in "Trash," where Mal and herself seem to make common cause to steal an antique laser weapon. As has already been remarked, there is some sense in which Simon represents the "Easterner" hero by comparison with Mal's Westerner hero. But it is River who provides the most sustained and significant comparison with Mal, especially at the end of the series and in *Serenity*, where the meaning of what has happened to her turns out to be tied up with the film's revelation about the Reavers, and thus the show's handling of the Western's preoccupation with the theme of civilization vis-à-vis savagery.

I suggested earlier that the Reavers were as close as *Firefly* and *Serenity* come to including aliens, and noted that they are presented as absolutely other: they are savage beyond comprehension. They might appear, therefore, to be one element in the story that fits in with the logic of defining America against a consolidated, demonized alien threat, since the Reavers look like the kind of enemy that the Alliance and the outer planets need in order to make common cause. In other words, they might play the role some have sought to make communism and then al Qaeda play in real life. The revelation of *Serenity* is that the Alliance's experiments in social engineering by means of drug-induced contentment produced the Reavers in the first place: the drugs put into the atmosphere on the now hidden and dead colony of Miranda induced a passivity so complete that most died, drained of desire, where they sat. But in a tiny minority they produced the opposite effect: the bloodiest, basest cravings. Thus the Alliance is a Prospero that killed its own Miranda and *produced* its own Caliban (on the New World allusions to *The Tempest* in the handling of the Reavers, see Rabb and Douglas). The opposite poles of civilization and savagery presented in "Bushwhacked" prove to be linked. The corporate Alliance accidentally created its own antithesis while trying to render its subjects more governable. This is the Master-Slave dialectic with a vengeance. The implication is that the more unambiguously one seeks to define oneself *against* some other, the more likely it is that the other will resurface with all the disquieting force of the return of the repressed.

Perhaps this should not have come as a surprise: early in *Firefly* it is established that the Alliance has been experimenting on people to turn them into psychic super-weapons. River Tam is one of the subjects of these experiments. Though Whedon was not able to find room for horses in *Serenity*, he did include the Western's traditional *scène à faire*: the showdown. In fact, he had two of them at the same time: Mal takes on the Operative of the Alliance, while River Tam, who often seems strange to the point being inhuman, takes on the Reavers. Both these encounters qualify Mal's status as Western hero. The Operative is a "man with no name." Like some Westerners, the Operative uses violence in order to help a better world into being, but he does not expect to live in that promised land, any more than Shane can stay in the valley he has defended. Whedon notes a parallel, in that the hero of many a Western is "tying to create a world that can't include him," and cites Ethan in *The Searchers*, who, he acknowledges, is also "a big role model for Mal" (Whedon 21). In this respect the fight between Mal and the Operative at the end of *Serenity* is also about redefining the Westerner.

At the same time River is fighting the Reavers, whose name hers so eerily resembles; they are, after all, both products of government meddling. In "Objects in Space," having been marginalized by the crew's suspicions about her uncanny powers, she had protected them (and herself) against the bounty-hunter, Jubal Early, without using violence. At the end of *Serenity*, however, she finally appears to gain voluntary control of her lethal powers in order to defend her brother and the rest of the crew against the Reaver onslaught (compare her earlier, automatically triggered outbursts). She is now exercising heroic violence in order to protect the others who are wounded and defenseless, and is thus fulfilling the Westerner's traditional role. She does so in a way that is worryingly beautiful. The choreography of the fight exploits Summer Glau's skill as a dancer to produce a battle between beauty and the beasts. For the creator of *Buffy*, heroism is not only a masculine preserve.

Mal and River win. But winning does not bring final victory. The most Mal can hope for is to go on dodging the Alliance, avoiding defeat, and holding dystopian modernity at bay. The end of the film has River and Mal piloting

Serenity together (Wash having been killed). This suggests a sharing of the role of the Westerner, and thus a qualification of its normally masculine character. It is an ending at once more pessimistic and more optimistic than the endings of many an older Western. It is more pessimistic in that the Alliance remains, and, unlike the coming of modernity in the old West, this cannot, even ambiguously, be represented as progress. It is more optimistic in that they are still flying, and River has somehow reacquired the humanity the Alliance sought to steal. In words that Whedon quotes from *Angel* on the DVD commentary to "Objects in Space," "If nothing we do in this world matters, then the only thing that matters is what we do." In other words, no "metanarrative" will guarantee the meaning one's life: only the living of it.

Conclusion

The *Firefly / Serenity* story tells of a divided America. Whedon stages a clash between an America of lone heroes and small, improvised communities dependent mainly on themselves, and another America reflected in the giant, Sino-American, hi-tech, corporate Alliance. The implication is that America is in danger of becoming UnAmerican. Mal as the Western hero of the show shuns the institutionalized power of the Alliance.

He does so partly because he hates the idea of government trying to make people better. The Alliance may be Sino-American, but it was no communist (not even a Sino-capitalist one) who opined that government is to be judged "by what it makes of the citizens, and what it does with them; its tendency to improve or deteriorate the people themselves..." (Mill 170). This is the criterion for good government of John Stuart Mill, classical liberalism's most influential proponent of individual liberty. But he also wanted to believe in history as progress, and is therefore willing on occasion to regard people as the object and product of the government's activity.

Having discovered the dead world of Miranda, Mal insists that the people who created Miranda "will try again": "they'll swing back to the belief that they can make people ... better. And I do not hold to that." For us after 9/11 and in the midst of unfolding economic crises, it is the craving for physical, economic and perhaps psychological security that is most likely to induce us to submit to government control. It also goes along with the idea that other people can be *made* free and *made* democratic—and ultimately remade as we imagine ourselves to be. When everyone becomes reflections of ourselves, then, perhaps, we will feel secure.

Should such a thing ever come to pass, history will indeed have ended. "That'll be the day." On 9/11 history re-started with a vengeance, challenging the conception of modernity as single and convergent. John Gray argues that the assumption that modernity is an ultimately progressive condition, in which fundamental disagreements over values will inevitably melt away in the light of reason, is a myth that stems from the secularization of Christian concepts of history. While the transformations wrought by modernity are real enough, they do not, Gray contends, make societies more similar. Yet in some versions of modernity (Soviet Communism, Nazism, al Qaeda) there is a ghastly and distinctively modern redemptive hope: that "terror can remake the world" (118). It can be argued that a version of this hope is also locked into the myth of the West. In Richard Slotkin's words, in different ways for different groups, whether their main concerns were religious, political or economic, the myth of the western frontier "represented the redemption of American spirit or fortune as something to be achieved by playing through a scenario of separation, temporary regression to a more primitive or 'natural' state, and *regeneration through violence*" (Slotkin 12). In confronting the violence of 9/11 perhaps it was also necessary to confront something in the founding myths and history of the Republic, rather than merely acting on them.

It can be argued that for some time the west has been wedded to a flawed concept of security. One aspect of it is captured by Paul Rogers' coinage "liddism": keeping the lid on risk. Such containment tends to cause pressure to build up, and the greater the pressure, the more effort has to be devoted to containment in a self-defeating cycle, which Rogers speaks of as "keeping the violent peace" (130). This is partly a legacy of the Cold War. However, in Michael Dillon's view a metaphysically unattainable notion of security has informed the construction of western politics since Hobbes. It exhibits an impulse to render all calculable that seeks to get hold of dependable data, and to subject the future and all risks to quantifiable control. In this sense western politics has always been a security project, and also a project to escape politics proper (Dillon 28), in that it seeks largely to secure the *private* existences of its subjects. The means by which this is done can threaten the very freedoms one seeks to defend. Thus the attempt to achieve *absolute* security is self-defeating. Security can only be *relative*, which means one must always negotiate with some degree of *insecurity* (Dillon 33). To seek technical rather than specifically political ways of dealing with insecurity (i.e. accepting mortal existence and "mortal freedom always lived with others in Otherness" [Dillon 35]) is futile. The upshot is the practical dissociation of freedom from politics. Dillon's case has implications for post-9/11 projects for "security."

One of the more beguiling notions about western values and modernity suggests that economic self-interest on the part of individuals and states leads ultimately and inevitably to individual freedom and democracy. If this belief is true, then it might help to assuage our fears about security: in the long run, everyone's bound to wind up agreeing with us, and at that point, they will stop being a threat, and will themselves join in our kind of freedom and prosperity. That sort of thinking has played a role since 9/11 in, for example, prophecies of Iraq as a stable democracy and the US's natural ally. The obvious way of questioning such thinking is one Ernest Gellner invoked in *The Condition of Liberty* by asking about Asian economies in which economic success and individual freedom seem not to be naturally wedded to each other. What if it is possible to combine prosperity with a politically controlled society, so that economic power serves political oppression of a managed, controlled society, rather than individual freedom in a relatively autonomous civil society? Or, in Gellner's pungent phrase, "Whether we like it or not, the deadly angel who spells death to economic inefficiency is not always at the service of liberty" (199).

The world Whedon created in *Firefly* and *Serenity* lays down a similar challenge. There is no doubting the wealth of the Alliance's core planets. These are also intensely *managed* societies, passively condoning abuses of power for the sake of their own security and wealth. The TV series and the film have an unsettling question for post–9/11 America. What if freedom and security do not go together? Even if you have the courage to choose freedom, what will you do if most people prefer security, and are prepared to pay for it with their souls? It is, in other words, a saga that explores divided feelings about the world and about America and refurbishes the conventions of the Western to do so.

Works Cited

The Alamo. Dir. John Wayne. Perf. John Wayne, Richard Widmark. The Alamo Company / Batjac Productions. 1960. Film.
Bad Day at Black Rock. Dir. John Sturges. Perf. Spencer Tracy, Robert Ryan. MGM. 1955. Film.
Bernstein, Abbie, et al. *Firefly: The Official Companion*, vol. 1. London: Titan Books, 2006. Print.
_____. *Firefly: The Official Companion*, vol. 2. London: Titan Books, 2007. Print.
Bethke, Bruce. "Cut 'Em Off at the Horsehead Nebula!" *Serenity Found: More Unauthorized Essays on Joss Whedon's* Firefly *Universe*. Ed. Jane Espenson with Leah Wilson. Dallas: BenBella Books, 2007. 175–186. Print.
Butch Cassidy and the Sundance Kid. Dir. George Roy Hill. Perf. Paul Newman, Robert Redford. Twentieth Century Fox / Campanile Productions / Newman-Foreman Company. 1969. Film.
Carroll, Peter N., and David W. Noble. *The Free and the Unfree: a New History of the United States*, 2nd ed. Harmondsworth: Penguin, 1988. Print.
Dillon, Michael. *The Politics of Security: Towards a Political Philosophy of Continental Thought*. London: Routledge, 1997. Print.
Dodge City. Dir. Michael Curtiz. Perf. Errol Flynn. Warner Bros. 1939. Film.
Firefly. Dir. Joss Whedon, et al. 20th Century-Fox Television / Mutant Enemy. 2002. DVD. Television.
Fisher, Louis. *The Constitution and 9/11: Recurring Threats to America's Freedoms*. Lawrence: University Press of Kansas, 2008. Print.

Gellner, Ernest. *The Condition of Liberty*. London: Hamish Hamilton, 1994. Print.
Gone With the Wind. Dir. Victor Fleming. Perf. Clark Gable, Vivien Leigh. Selznick International / MGM. 1939. Film.
Gray, John. *Al Qaeda and What It Means to be Modern*. London: Faber & Faber, 2003. Print.
The Great Train Robbery. Dir. Edwin S. Porter. Edison Manufacturing Company. 1903. Film.
High Noon. Dir. Fred Zinnemann. Perf. Gary Cooper, Grace Kelly. Stanley Kramer Productions / United Artists. 1952.
Hoberman, J. "How the Western Was Lost" (1991). *The Western Reader*. Ed. Jim Kitses and Gregg Rickman. New York: Limelight Editions, 1998. 84–92. Print.
Huntington, Samuel P. *The Clash of Civilizations and the Remaking of World Order*. London: Simon & Schuster, 1997. Print.
Ichihashi, Yamato. "Stanford Professor Yamato Ichihashi Writes of His Internment" (June 7, 1942). *Problems in American History*, vol. 2. Ed. Elizabeth Cobbs Hoffman and Jon Gjerde. Boston: Houghton Mifflin, 2002. Print.
It Happened One Night. Dir. Frank Capra. Perf. Claudette Colbert and Clark Gable. Columbia Pictures. 1934,
Kerouac, Jack. *On the Road*. 1956. Intr. Anne Charters. Harmondsworth: Penguin, 1991. Print.
Lichter, S. Robert, Linda S. Lichter and Dan Amundson. *Images of Government in TV Entertainment*. Washington: Center for Media and Public Affairs, 1999. http://www.cmpa.com/pdf/Entertain/Images_of_Government_in_TV_Entertainment.pdf. Web. December 30, 2011.
The Man Who Shot Liberty Valance. Dir. John Ford. Perf. John Wayne, James Stewart, Lee Marvin, Vera Miles. John Ford Productions / Paramount. 1962. Film.
McCabe and Mrs. Miller. Dir. Robert Altman. Perf. Warren Beatty, Julie Christie. David Foster Productions / Warner Bros. 1971. Film.
Mill, John Stuart. *On Representative Government* in Mill, *Three Essays*, intr. Richard Wollheim. Oxford: Oxford University Press, 1975. Print.
Money, Mary Alice. "*Firefly*'s 'Out of Gas': Genre Echoes and the Hero's Journey." *Investigating Firefly and Serenity*. Ed. Rhonda V. Wilcox and Tanya R. Cochran. London: I.B. Tauris, 2008. 114–124. Print.
The Naked Spur. Dir. Anthony Mann. Perf. James Stewart, Janet Leigh, Robert Ryan. MGM. 1953. Film.
Norton, Mary Beth. *In the Devil's Snare: The Salem Witchcraft Crisis of 1692*. New York: Random House, 2002. Print.
The Outlaw Josey Wales. Dir. Clint Eastwood. Perf. Clint Eastwood, Chief Dan George, Sondra Locke. Warner Bros. / Malpaso. 1976. Film.
Pale Rider. Dir. Clint Eastwood. Perf. Clint Eastwood. Warner Bros. / Malpaso. 1985. Film.
Rabb, J. Douglas, and J. Michael Robinson. "Reavers and Redskins: Creating the Frontier Savage." *Investigating Firefly and Serenity*. Ed. Rhonda V. Wilcox and Tanya R. Cochran. London: I.B. Tauris, 2008. 127–138. Print.
Ray, Robert B. *A Certain Tendency of the Hollywood Cinema, 1930–1980*. Princeton: Princeton University Press, 1985. Print.
Rich, Frank. *The Greatest Story Ever Sold*. New York: Penguin, 2006. Print.
Ride the High Country. Dir. Sam Peckinpah. Perf. Joel McCrae, Randolph Scott. MGM. 1962. Film.
Rogers, Paul. *Losing Control: Global Security in the Twenty-first Century*, 3rd ed. London: Pluto Press, 2010. Print.

Sammon, Paul M. *Future Noir: The Making of Blade Runner*. London: Orion, 1996. Print.
Sands of Iwo Jima. Dir. Allan Dwan. Perf. John Wayne. Republic Pictures. 1949. Film.
The Searchers. Dir. John Ford. Perf. John Wayne, Ward Bond. Merian Cooper-C.V.Whitney / Warner Bros. 1956. Film.
Serenity. Dir. Joss Whedon. Perf. Nathan Fillion, Chiwetel Ejiofor, Summer Glau. Universal Pictures / Barry Mendel Productions. 2005. Film.
Shane. Dir. George Stevens. Perf. Alan Ladd, Jean Arthur, Van Heflin. Paramount. 1953. Film.
She Wore a Yellow Ribbon. Dir. John Ford. Perf. John Wayne, Ben Johnson. Argosy Pictures / RKO. 1949. Film.
Singh, Robert. *Contemporary American Politics and Society: Issues and Controversies*. London: Sage, 2003. Print.
Stagecoach. Dir. John Ford. Perf. John Wayne, Claire Trevor, Thomas Mitchell. Walter Wanger Productions / United Artists. 1939. Film.
The Shootist. Dir. Don Siegel. Perf. John Wayne, Lauren Bacall. Dino De Laurentis / Paramount. 1976. Film.
Slotkin, Richard. *Gunfighter Nation: The Myth of the Frontier in Twentieth-Century America*. New York: Atheneum, 1992. Print.
Suid, Lawrence H. *Guts and Glory: Great American War Movies*, intr. Charles Champlin. Reading, MA: Addison Wesley, 1978. Print.
Sullivan, Kevin M. "Unofficial Glossary of *Firefly* Chinese." *Finding Serenity: Anti-Heroes, Lost Shepherds and Space Hookers in Joss Whedon's Firefly*. Ed. Jane Espenson with Glenn Yeffeth. Dallas: BenBella Books. 229–238. Print.
Takacs, Stacy. "The Contemporary Politics of the Western Form: Bush, *Saving Jessica Lynch*, and *Deadwood*." *Reframing 9/11: Film, Popular Culture and the "War on Terror."* Ed. Jeff Birkenstein, Anna Froula and Karen Randell. New York: Continuum, 2010. 153–63. Print.
"Terrorism in the United States." *Wikipedia*. http://en.wikipedia.org/wiki/Terrorism_in_the_United_States#2000s. Web. October 28, 2011.
Toope, Stephen J. "Human Rights and the Use of Force after September 11th, 2001." *Terror, Culture, Politics: Rethinking 9/11*. Ed. Daniel J. Sherman and Terry Nardin. Bloomington: Indiana University Press, 2006. 236–258. Print.
Townshend, Charles. *Terrorism: A Very Short Introduction*. Oxford: Oxford University Press, 2002. Print.
The Undefeated. Dir. Andrew V. McLaglen. Perf. John Wayne, Rock Hudson. Twentieth Century Fox. 1969. Film.
Unforgiven. Dir. Clint Eastwood. Perf. Clint Eastwood, Gene Hackman, Morgan Freeman, Richard Harris. Warner Bros. / Malpaso. 1992. Film.
Vaughn, Evelyn. "The Bonnie Brown Flag." *Serenity Found: More Unauthorized Essays on Joss Whedon's* Firefly *Universe*. Ed. Jane Espenson with Leah Wilson. Dallas: BenBella Books, 2007. 187–202. Print.
Warshow, Robert. "Movie Chronicle: The Westerner" (1954) rptd. in *The Immediate Experience*, rev. ed. Cambridge: Harvard University Press, 2001. 105–124. Print.
Whedon, Joss, et al. *Serenity: The Official Visual Companion*. London: Titan Books, 2005. Print.
Woodward, Bob. *Plan of Attack*. New York: Simon & Schuster, 2004. Print.

Sixguns and the Shadowless Kick
Mythmaking and Generic Hybridization in Westerns and Martial Arts Fantasies

Fontaine Lien

Both the American Western and the Hong Kong "martial arts"[1] picture are enduring audience favorites that draw on firmly established national traditions and tell stories about quasi-mythical heroes from an allegorical past. Without neglecting the different ways with which their respective audiences engage with individual films, I would nevertheless observe that these two genres are accorded special statuses by Americans and the Chinese diaspora, both of which experienced a tumultuous and eventful twentieth century that dramatically altered the status quo. Will Wright shows in both of his works the ways in which the American Western has come to represent American identity, while the martial arts film, popular among Sinophone communities around the world, has posited a central axis of "Chineseness" for those affected by political schisms and geographical divisions.

Traditionally, film critics have attached the names of individual nations as prefixes to terms that designate both style and genre, and with good reason: Mexican Westerns and Latin-American Westerns endorse values distinct from that of the American Western despite also glorifying the cowboy figure (Wright, *Wild West* 190–91); the British New Wave movement emerged from a distinct national milieu despite borrowing stylistic attributes from the French New Wave movement.

We can see that the American Western and the martial arts film are similarly linked to national traditions. However, I would argue that the two genres are on a path of convergence: already similarly focused on a valorization of the outcast life, just violence, and heroic codes, they have evolved over time towards parallel "professional stages," a revision of the genres' seminal heroic types, and increased cross-pollination between the two genres. It is time for us to reconsider these genres in an age where film production and distribution are international endeavors, and it is now more difficult to discuss films strictly in terms of regional or national cinema (Grant 103). Michelle Bloom, for example, has explored the consequences of this trend in terms of what she calls "sinofrench" film.[2]

My initial concern here is not with how many cinematic conventions and codes Hong Kong has swiped from the American Westerns and, vice versa, how the popularity of Hong Kong cinema has influenced a new generation of American filmmakers who produce generic hybrids such as "Space Westerns" (a combination of Western, science fiction, and action-adventure) and westernized kung-fu dramas/action-adventures such as the *Rush Hour* series (1998–2007) featuring Hong Kong star Jackie Chan. Such intertextuality is certainly worth studying, but in this essay I will confine myself to the examination of how the two genres have evolved in parallel ways and are now converging, with an eye towards creating a tentative generic label, similar to "sinofrench," which draws on and incorporates Wright's organization of the Western into four categories (*Sixguns*). Throughout, I will assume that my reader has basic familiarity with the American Western and base my remarks on martial arts film on a comparison with that genre.

Stage One: National Myth

I will begin by briefly tracing the emergence of each filmic genre from their respective national traditions, validating the two genres' statuses as national myths by pointing out the continuity between them and newer genres and/or subgenres.

The American Western has its origin in the myth of Daniel Boone and James Fenimore Cooper's popular nineteenth-century novels, which featured frontier heroes, predecessors of the Westerns' cowboy hero (Wright, *Wild West* 6). Although the U.S. officially closed its western frontier in 1890, Hollywood ensured its continued popularity with the Western genre, which featured a West that most likely never existed as such (Wright, *Wild West* 56–57). Edward Buscombe notes that between 1926 and 1967, "Westerns consistently formed around a quarter of all feature films made in Hollywood" (35). Today, although the actual era of western settlement recedes ever further into the distant past, the cowboy's defiant individualism is an attribute shared among the heroes of contemporary non–Western films such as *Top Gun* (Scott, 1986), the *Die Hard* series (1988–2013), and *Armageddon* (Bay, 1998) (Wright, *Wild West* 192). Although the western frontier no longer exists, the cowboy figure continues to "do what a man's gotta do"[3] in outer space and in urban jungles, both of which are simply western frontiers transposed onto different times and circumstances. Wright's description of the "standard Western" might also describe most superhero movies:

> A new frontier community is threatened by greedy villains, and a stranger rides from the wilderness to help the decent citizens. He is detached from the social order ... and he has the skills of the wilderness, especially the skill of violence ... generally he must fight alone since the citizens are weak and fearful [*Wild West* 7].

Superheroes such as Superman and Batman, to name two of the most popular, must protect the "decent citizens" of Metropolis and Gotham City by fighting villains alone, but at the same time they are "detached from the social order" due to their superpowers and their concealed identities. Alan Moore's graphic novel *Watchmen* (1987), and to a lesser extent its 2009 film adaptation, is a more recent and cynical take on a superhero story that dramatizes its protagonists' alienation from the very society they seek to protect. Many consider superheroes to be contemporary mythic figures, and it is unsurprising that there is continuity between the Western and the superhero film.

The martial arts film similarly has its origins in canonical Chinese literature. Shanghai's Tianyi Film Company, founded by the Shaw Brothers, was responsible for jumpstarting the "wandering swordsman epic" (*wuxia* films)[4] genre with *Feifei* (1925) (J. Yang 9–10). However, *Feifei* and its successors could not have existed without the twelfth-century Chinese classic, *Water Margin* (*Shui hu zhuan* 水滸傳). It depicts a band of 108 outcast-heroes who, forced out of society by corrupt officials, find ways to serve their country from its "margins." The novel, taught as a classic in Chinese language and literature courses, popularized the code of the *jiang hu* 江湖, a term that literally means "rivers and lakes," but which designates a community with no actual physical boundaries (much like the Wild West) populated by "exiles and renegades" (J. Yang 48). These outcasts adhere to "an unwritten code of ethics—a chivalry of the outlaw brotherhood" (J. Yang 48) that calls for "fighting fair, respecting your opponent, and celebrating [a] shared bond" (J. Yang 49). The immensely successful and prolific writer Jin Yong (né Louis Cha) further popularized the *jiang hu* world with his best-selling martial arts novels published in the 1960s and 1970s, the plots of which are adapted over and over again for television series films, and video games. Most recently in 2013, Hunan Television aired a popular adaptation of Yong's *Xiao ao jiang hu* 笑傲江湖, one of his most beloved works whose title itself demonstrates the immediate evocative power of the term *jiang hu*. Jeff Yang credits Jin Yong as "perhaps the most popular Chinese writer ever, with some one *billion* books in print" (74).

The *jiang hu* code of ethics, as well as amazing displays of martial arts prowess, are prominent characteristics of many popular genres (or subgenres, if we want to say that the martial arts film is a genre by itself) in Chinese cinema.⁵ These include the aforementioned wandering swordsman epic, Bruce Lee's gritty kung fu sagas of the 1970s, John Woo's gangster films of the 1980s and 1990s which featured "heroic gunplay" (Bordwell 136), and the more fantastical flying swordsmen adventures launched into international fame by Ang Lee's *Crouching Tiger, Hidden Dragon* (2000) and Zhang Yimou's *Hero* (2002). For each of these (sub)genres, I borrow the terminology of David Bordwell, but as far as I am aware a consistent classification system does not exist. For the purposes of this essay and based on the previously mentioned shared characteristics, I will tentatively group all of these films under the term "martial arts films."⁶

Although both stem from fictional traditions, the codes of individuality and the *jiang hu* still hold currency for Americans and the Chinese diaspora respectively, and thus qualify as national myths—that is, fictionalized narrative vehicles for ideologies and principals that are strongly tied to one national identity. When Americans refer to someone as being a "cowboy," more often than not they mean that the person in question is acting rebelliously—Wright considers several examples of business and political figures that were referred to as "cowboys" (*Wild West* 7–8, 192). The imagery from that mythical frontier has created fashion trends and marketing icons (the ubiquitous cowboy hat and the Marlboro Man); John Wayne is synonymous with a particular brand of frontier masculinity. And during his 2000 campaign for the presidency, President George W. Bush once again recast the U.S. in terms of its one-time frontier, stating that "Western values of economic and personal freedom are the foundation of [the United States'] strength domestically—but also abroad" (Renshon 594–95). Obviously, some agree with Bush's "cowboy politics" and some do not, but that his politics are labeled as such attest to the durability of Western imagery.

The code of the *jiang hu* may be enduring because it has provided a sense of continuity and a possible means of achieving justice and closure during times of traumatic upheaval in China's history. As mentioned earlier, the heroes of *Water Margin* joined the *jiang hu* when they could no longer coexist with a corrupt (Song Dynasty) government. Similarly, Hector Rodriguez identifies nineteenth-century folk hero, martial artist, and physician Huang Feihong, popularized by many martial arts films of the twentieth century, as a patriotic Confucian hero whom colonial Hong Kong citizens looked to for reaffirmation of their cultural identities (6–8); Huang himself lived during a time when China was besieged by foreign powers, the latter years of the Qing Dynasty. The heroes of *Water Margin* and Huang adhere to an unofficial behavioral code because it ultimately stresses a brand of justice and chivalry that can be obtained by skill in the martial arts in an otherwise lawless *jiang hu*. The implicit assumption is that the law is powerless and unjust.⁷ One can imagine that such a worldview would prove appealing in times of social upheaval—in other words, when the ruling government becomes hopelessly corrupt or when one dynasty or regime replaces another by force. The Chinese could take additional pride from the way their corrective justices were obtained—by practicing traditional Chinese martial arts, in essence reaffirming tradition in adverse times.

Wright demonstrates in *Sixguns and Society* that although different variations of the cowboy hero have appeared in American Westerns, the hero's basic adherence to freedom and independence, and his "skill" (with guns) as derived from time spent in the wilderness, are the two characteristics that remained constant. Similarly, the typical plot of a *wuxia* novel or film features a young hero (oftentimes orphaned) who overcomes enormous odds to become a renowned martial arts master, dispatching various challengers during his ascension. In the process, he lives by the *jiang hu* code, sometimes with a handful of friends, but often alone. Like the Western hero, he will interfere on behalf of society if necessary, but afterwards he retreats into the mountains or to a martial arts temple to continue training, much as later Western heroes forsake society after restoring order. Essentially, however, these heroes live apart from societies that are frequently portrayed as ineffectual, corrupt, or irrelevant to their journey and maturation. The protagonist's journey in Jin Yong's *Xiao ao jiang hu*, for example, follows just such a development arc that is, of course, interrupted by many complications. This type of journey also echoes those in American superhero films as previously discussed, films whose ethos owes a strong debt to the individualistic frontier spirit of the Western.

Stage Two: The Cinematic Mirror Adjusts Itself

We have seen that the American Western and the martial arts film are dominant forms in their respective cultural spheres. However, they do not remain static. Instead, like all genres, they undergo shifts as filmmakers respond to changes in cultural landscapes and perceived changes in audience attitudes.

Wright's influential structural study of the American Western, *Sixguns and Society*, roughly divides the bestselling Westerns made between the years of 1930 and 1970 into four approximately chronological categories: classical, vengeance, transitional, and professional (13–15). The *classical* Western is "the prototype of all Westerns, the one people think of when they say, 'All Westerns are alike'" (32). In this form, the hero emerges from the wilderness and aids a society that is weak. Society then wishes to accept the hero, but the hero either loses or voluntarily relinquishes his status in society (48–49).

In the *vengeance* Western, the hero's trajectory is reversed—now he must leave the society he had initially belonged to in order to seek vengeance (69). Wright regards the *transitional* Western as somewhat of an anomaly or a prototype of the professional Western. In this category, society comes to represent the "evil" that is opposed to the cowboy's "good" (74–75).

Finally, in the *professional* Western, society becomes entirely incidental to the plot—the heroes are now "professionals" who work for compensation, absolutely dedicated to their "craft" and to one another. When the professional Western hero confronts a villain, it is "a contest of ability that is significant for its own sake ... divorced from ... social and ethical implications" (86). They are here, in effect, committed to a sort of *jiang hu* code, where loyalty is only owed to members of the *jiang hu* community.

Wright regarded the changing Western as a model for individual behaviors in a capitalistic society, macroeconomics reenacted on a smaller scale to which it is easier to relate. The Western hero begins as an individual committed to capitalistic necessity in an open frontier, but as the frontier closed and America shifted towards industry and corporate economy, the professional Western seemed to tell us, according to Wright, that "companionship and respect are to be achieved only by becoming a skilled technician" (186–87).

Thus far I have not read a similar structural study of the martial arts film,[8] but I have already outlined the ways in which it, too, has evolved over the years, but following a different pattern. Bordwell cites the Hong Kong film industry's unparalleled efficiency as well as its "midnight premiere" tradition, where filmmakers receive live (and sometimes quite vocal) feedback directly from the public, as bases for the more dialogic nature of Hong Kong cinema (32–38). Early in their careers, the most prolific (and thus most efficient) Hong Kong directors were pressed into service by the studios, so their œuvres tend to resemble that of Howard Hawks rather than that of John Ford—they usually worked in several (sub)genres rather than staying the course (Bordwell 115–18). Although John Woo is known for his stylish ultra-violent gangster films starring Chow Yun-Fat (*A Better Tomorrow*; *The Killer*; *Hard Boiled*), his fans outside of Asia may be surprised to know that he found early success in the 1980s as a director of cheesy slapstick comedies (J. Yang 83–87).

The Chinese martial arts genre is richer for the visions that each emergent director brings to the table—Woo, for example, has re-imagined the genre with gangster films where triad members live and die by the *jiang hu* code. The backdrop in these films is Hong Kong's urban jungle instead of China's mystical mountains, but the idea is the same—the heroes are isolated from society. I would posit, based on the evolutions on the subgeneric level cited earlier, that Hong Kong cinema has consistently adhered to what I call a professional model (after Wright's professional Western) even as the exact boundaries of the *jiang hu* change with each successive subgenre and each auteur.[9] As in the professional Western, the "brotherhoods" in these films are ultimately loyal to one another above all else.

Once Upon a Time in China and America: *The Martial Arts Western?*

It is intriguing that both the American Western and the martial arts film have eventually undergone deconstruction and revision. In progressing towards Wright's professional stage, the Western began to resemble the martial arts film in terms of its *jiang hu* ethos. Bishop, Dutch, and the Gorch brothers of *The Wild Bunch* (Peckinpah, 1969) decide to enter a fight they know they cannot win (Wright, *Sixguns* 93–95); Butch Cassidy and the Sundance Kid remain committed to their outlaw lifestyle and loyal to one another until the moment of their deaths (Wright, *Sixguns* 95–97). According to Wright, this particular variation of the Western is a reflection of "the emergence of a capitalist technology as a social and ideological force" (*Sixguns* 184) in 1960s and 1970s America, which deemphasized individuality and required that all workers become "professionals" who carried out their duties with no hesitation (*Sixguns* 180–81).

By the late 1980s, many Hong Kong directors also began to rethink the martial arts genre, "[turning] away from ... swordplay and gunplay spectaculars" (Bordwell 76). Instead, they "presented a modern Hong Kong inhabited by educated young men and women, working in business or the media, living in comfort" (Bordwell 76). This is the Hong Kong that is prominently on display in Wong Kar-Wai's celebrated urban jungle films *Chungking Express* (1994) and *Fallen Angels* (1995),[10] and in Steven Chow's audience favorite *Gambler*, his comedic film series (1990–1995).

Soon, legendary folk hero Huang Feihong, main character in a series of influential martial arts films made in the 1950s (Rodriguez 1),[11] would receive a makeover courtesy of Tsui Hark's *Once Upon a Time in China* series produced before and around the time of the Hong Kong Handover in 1997.[12] This immensely popular series starring Jet Li and Vincent Zhao is credited with "singlehandedly [reviving] the period kung fu genre" (J. Yang 97).[13] Tony Williams' insightful article, "Under 'Western Eyes': The Personal Odyssey of Huang Fei-Hong in *Once Upon a Time in China*," traces the ways in which the series depicts Huang "[moving] from a position of cultural certainty to confront twentieth-century encroachments affecting his previously secure sense of Chinese identity" (5). On the other hand, Yang Mingyu argues that the series can be read as a reflection of anxieties regarding Hong Kong's Handover. Although their precise interpretations of the series differ, Williams and Yang Mingyu are both drawing attention to the ways Tsui has updated a subgenre of the martial arts film.

Here I would like to briefly analyze the sixth and final film in Tsui's series, *Once Upon a Time in China and America* (Hung, 1997), and argue that it belongs to a new hybrid genre that I will tentatively call the "Martial Arts Western."[14] In the film, Huang (Jet Li) travels to the American West to help a former student celebrate the grand opening of his Chinese medicine shop. The film opens with a medium shot of a cowboy riding away from the camera towards the sunset. Director Sammo Hung then cuts to an extreme long shot of the rider, and we can now see that the majestic backdrop is Monument Valley (Williams 19). With only a couple of shots, the film signals that it will borrow heavily from the images and codes of the American Western, and this kind of visual homage to classic Westerns appears frequently throughout the film.

The unnamed rider turns out to be Billy (Jeff Wolfe), who in Wright's terms is the typical hero of a classical Western. He appears "out of the wilderness" and soon teams up with Huang (Jet Li) to drive out a town's corrupt mayor and his hired gunmen who rob the town's bank and massacre the townsfolk. After they successfully save the town, Huang returns to China while Billy is accepted into society as the town's new mayor. The film's instant alignment of the classical Western hero (Billy) with the traditional martial arts hero (Huang) suggests that there is a natural kinship between the two heroic types. Huang does not hesitate to rescue Billy from the desert despite his fiancée's assertion that they should not stop for strangers; Billy, in contrast to the white townsfolk, is guilelessly friendly towards Huang and the local Chinese laborers.

The film also initially appears to complicate the typical opposition between civilization and wilderness in Westerns by having Huang become a member of a Native American tribe—they take him in when he experiences amnesia after an accident and cannot remember his identity. However, during his time as a "native," Huang essentially becomes the hero of his own classical Western—he appears "out of the wilderness," helps the tribe defeat a savage rival tribe, and is nearly accepted into their society (a Native American girl is clearly interested in marrying him) before being recognized by his Chinese friends. This interlude only serves to underline the Huang's newly resonant identity as a classical Western hero.

Yet these cultural experiences are all brand new for Huang, whose attitude has changed remarkably since the first film in the series, *Once Upon a Time in China* (Tsui, 1991). In this film, Huang and his disciples are invited to an upscale western-style restaurant. Huang scrutinizes the unfamiliar dining utensils, the menu with dishes such as lobster bisque and salmon tartare, then politely asks for dim sum instead. Tsui also visually links Chinese food with discipline and honor, and western food with incivility and dishonor. In another scene, Huang admonishes his students for behaving without honor, then leads them through a lesson in discipline during their dinner of rice, eaten with chopsticks; in contrast, the treacherous group of Chinese mercenaries is shown boorishly wolfing down white bread and greasy chicken drumsticks while their leader celebrates his latest misdeed.

In *America*, Huang happily eats white bread and baked beans, has learned passable English, and befriends both the white man and the Native American. Huang is not the only classical hero who has experienced a change of heart. Wright has taken the Western to task for "separating the women" and "removing the Indians" (these are two fittingly named chapters in *Wild West*), but Tsui and Hung have transformed the classical Western hero (Billy) into a genial politician (mayor instead of sheriff) who stands in solidarity with the embattled Chinese workers. Thus Billy is not entirely the classical Western hero he initially appeared to be; nor is Huang, who formed a genuine (though perhaps temporary) bond with both Billy and the Native-American tribe. Notably, according to this hybrid film, both the martial arts hero and the Western hero are shown to have undergone these transformations *prior* to their alliance. Indeed, it is their softened stance toward outsiders and willingness to form a new kind of brotherhood that has enabled this partnership.

Certainly, while the Native American tribe that briefly becomes Huang's family in the film is depicted in a reasonably nuanced and sympathetic manner, it is nonetheless problematic that they are still relegated to the status of secondary characters that exist only to help Huang complete his hero's journey.[15] In this sense, this film remains guilty of "removing the Indians," possibly because it leans so heavily on established Western tropes. Is such a removal deliberate and significant in this age of "mature," evolving Westerns and Western hybrids? Or is it simply a regrettable consequence of global cinematic intertextuality? What happens to the traditional Other in Westerns when another foreign presence (Huang) is introduced—and what contemporary relevance such a depiction has, if any—could well serve as the subject of another essay.

Despite these reservations, *Once Upon a Time in China and America* is true to the implication of cooperation suggested in its title—for its two *jiang hu* heroes, at least. It demonstrates how two heroes from different, evolving national mythologies might be linked with one another in visual, narrative, and ideological ways in a martial arts Western.

Conclusion

It is easy to say that Hollywood films like the Western—and its generic successors—are popular around the world because audiences everywhere derive enjoyment from watching good triumph over evil, and from the voyeuristic pleasure derived from traditional narrative cinema and its increasingly realistic special effects (Metz 93–95). My investigation shows that there is another possibility—that we simply derive pleasure from the familiar, as the American Western has increasingly come to resemble the Hong Kong martial arts film.

The generic interplay has continued with the aforementioned *Once Upon a Time in China and America*, one of the first films to transplant a traditional martial arts hero to a Western milieu. Many other more recent productions could potentially be classified as martial arts Westerns or variations thereof. *Shanghai Noon* (Dey, 2000) is a more recent example where a Chinese martial arts expert must re-orient himself in the Wild West. In the science fiction genre, the *Firefly* television series (2002), Japan's *Cowboy Bebop* (1998) from which the former arguably borrows,[16] and the hybrid omnibus film *Cloud Atlas* (Tykwer, Wachowski, and Wachowski, 2012) all allow previously ignored minorities a place in the space frontier, examining heroic codes and glorifying the life of the outcast who must operate outside of society. Their manner of doing so, however, remains problematic and worthy of examination. Also worthy of consideration alongside the martial arts Western is Japan's important samurai cinema, whose kinship with the Western was emblematized in *The Magnificent Seven* (Sturges, 1960), a remake of *Seven Samurai* (Kurosawa, 1954), and more recently in the two-volume *Kill Bill* (Tarantino, 2003).

These are but a few representative examples that come to mind, but the films (and television series) that might be considered examples of the genre are too numerous to enumerate here. Their numbers continue to grow as filmmakers and film viewers alike continually rediscover and reorient themselves against a newly globalized romantic ethos that might serve as a source of reassurance as their own worlds continue to change at a breathless pace. The meaning and significance of that ethos—the *jiang hu* or "professional" code—and the "skills" required to adhere to it are also continuously evolving and given fresh perspective by today's filmmakers. Further investigation is required to determine what other films might complicate the parameters of the martial arts Western, and how the genre is influenced by and dialogues with its parent genres in an age of globalized cinema.

NOTES

1. See below for additional clarification of this generic label.
2. Bloom deliberately leaves the word un-capitalized "in an effort to avoid conveying the priority of the first term ['sino']" (4).
3. John Wayne's original line from *Stagecoach* (1939) is "A man's gotta do what a man's gotta do."
4. The character *wu* 武 denotes the martial arts, and *xia* 俠 can either refer to a knight-errant or, approximately, the chivalrous quality that such a person would possess. Eric Yin, whose website provides an excellent overview of the term, translates

"*wuxia* fiction" as "martial-chivalric fiction." See both Liu and Ruhlmann for in-depth studies of the heroic knight-errant character type.

5. For a more complete over view of the cinematic martial arts genre and its related kung-fu genre, see Lau and Glaessner, respectively.

6. The development of a comprehensive classification scheme that takes into account generic labels currently in circulation is a worthwhile project, but evidently beyond the scope of this essay.

7. Huang is an intriguing figure to study in this context because he prefers to achieve justice through the law, but the universe he exists in effectively denies him this possibility, and thus Huang eventually resorts to the codes of the *jiang hu* (Rodriguez 4).

8. At the time of this writing, I have not been able to obtain a copy of Ma's thesis, which is titled "A Structural Study of Hero Films in Hong Kong." Bordwell points out that Ma, too, has found continuity in Hong Kong cinema: "[Ma] has shown ... that the swordplay films of the 1960s, the kung-fu films of the 1970s, and the 1980s gangster sagas all tend to adhere to the chivalric conception of heroism" (42).

9. Obviously, this is a general observation. Much work remains to be done in this area in terms of classifying these subgenres and finding anomalies, after which a clearer picture of the martial arts film's evolution may emerge.

10. Incidentally, one of Wong's most celebrated films is also a martial arts fantasy based on a Jin Yong novel, *Ashes of Time* (1994).

11. His signature fighting technique is called the "shadowless kick," *wuyingjiao*.

12. Tsui produced all six films in the series and directed four of them. Yuan Bun and Sammo Hung directed the fourth and sixth films in the series, respectively.

13. For consideration of the series as a whole, see Courtiad, Hwang, and Lo. See Yu for an examination of the historical figure Huang Feihong in comparison with his fictionalized representation.

14. The film is not the first work (nor the last) to combine genres in this way— a notable predecessor is the popular American television series *Kung Fu* (1972) starring David Carradine as a half–Chinese Shaolin master who journeys to the American West. Williams also catalogues some "[historical] and cinematic precedents" of "Hong Kong cinema's interest in the Wild West" in a footnote (no. 27) (24). All of these will have to be considered in a more comprehensive survey of the martial arts Western.

15. See Churchill's *Fantasies of the Master Race* for a consideration of problematic representations of Native Americans in sociological discourse, literature, and film. Both Slotkin and Tompkins are more complete considerations of the role of the Native American in cinematic Westerns.

16. Both of these series saw their stories continue in film, in *Serenity* (2005) and *Cowboy Bebop: The Movie* (2001), respectively.

Works Cited

Bloom, Michelle. "Chinese Cinema with a French Twist: Contemporary Sinofrench Films of Emily Tang Xiaobai and Jia Zhangke." Unpublished manuscript, 2008.

Bordwell, David. *Planet Hong Kong: Popular Cinema and the Art of Entertainment.* Cambridge: Harvard University Press, 2000.

Buscombe, Edward, ed. *The BFI Companion to the Western.* New York: Atheneum, 1988.

Churchill, Ward. *Fantasies of the Master Race: Literature, Cinema, and the Colonization of American Indians.* San Francisco: City Lights Books, 1998.

Courtiad, Laurent. "Wong Fei-hung par Tsui Hark." *HK Orient Extrême Cinéma* no. 6 (March 1998): 40–47, 95.

Glaessner, Verina. *Kung Fu: Cinema of Vengeance*. London: Bounty, 1974.
Grant, Barry Keith. *Film Genre: From Iconography to Ideology*. London: Wallflower, 2007.
Hark, Tsui, prod. *Once Upon a Time in China*. Dir. Tsui Hark. Golden Harvest, 2001.
_____. *Once Upon a Time in China and America*. Dir. Sammo Hung. China Star Entertainment, 1997.
Ho, Ng. "The Three Heroic Transformations of Huang Feihong." *Wong Fei Hung: The Invincible Master*. Hong Kong: Urban Council, 1996.
Hwang, Ange. "The Irresistible: Hong Kong Movie *Once Upon a Time in China* Series." *Asian Cinema* 10, no. 1 (Fall 1998): 10–23.
Lau Shing-hon, ed. *A Study of the Hong Kong Martial Arts Film*. Hong Kong: Urban Council, 1980.
Liu, James J. Y. *The Chinese Knight-Errant*. London: Routledge and Kegan Paul, 1967.
Lo, Kwai-Cheung, "*Once Upon a Time*: Technology Comes to Presence in China." *Modern Chinese Literature* 7 (1993): 83.
Ma, Ka-fai. "Hero, Hong Kong Style: A Structural Study of Hero Films in Hong Kong." MA thesis, University of Chicago, 1990.
Metz, Christian. *The Imaginary Signifier: Psychoanalysis and the Cinema*. Trans. Celia Britton et al. Bloomington: Indiana University Press, 1982.
Renshon, Stanley A. "Presidential Address: George W. Bush's Cowboy Politics: An Inquiry." *Political Psychology* 26 (2005): 585–614.
Rodriguez, Hector. "Hong Kong Popular Culture as an Interpretive Arena: The Huang Feihong Film Series." *Screen* 38 (1997): 1–24.
Ruhlmann, Robert. "Traditional Heroes in Chinese Popular Fiction." *The Confucian Persuasion*. Ed. Arthur C. Wright. Stanford: Stanford UP, 1960. 169–70.
Slotkin, Richard. *Gunfighter Nation: The Myth of the Frontier in Twentieth-Century America*. New York: Atheneum, 1992.
Tompkins, Jane. *West of Everything: The Inner Life of Westerns*. Oxford: Oxford University Press, 1992.
Turner, Graeme. *Film as Social Practice*, 3d ed. London: Routledge, 1999.
Williams, Tony. "Under 'Western Eyes': The Personal Odyssey of Huang Fei-Hong in *Once Upon a Time in China*." *Cinema Journal* 40.1 (2000): 3–24.
Wright, Will. *Sixguns and Society: A Structural Study of the Western*. Berkeley: University of California Press, 1975.
_____. *The Wild West: The Mythical Cowboy & Social Theory*. London: Sage, 2001.
Wu, Jiaqi. "性別、殖民變異及流行知識：論徐克之黃飛鴻系列作品 [Gender, Colonial Mutation, and Popular Knowledge: On Tsui Hark's Huang Feihong Series]." Working paper, n.d. 7 Dec. 2008. http://140.122.100.145/ebook/eb9/g5c/g5c18.doc.
Yang, Jeff. *Once Upon a Time in China: A Guide to Hong Kong, Taiwanese, and Mainland Chinese Cinema*. New York: Atria, 2003.
Yang, Mingyu. "China: *Once Upon a Time*/*Hong Kong*: 1997: A Critical Study of Contemporary Hong Kong Martial Arts Films." Diss., University of Maryland, 1995.
Yin, Eric. "An Introduction to the Wuxia Genre." *Once Upon a Time in China*. Heroic Cinema. 8 Dec. 2008. http://www.heroic-cinema.com/eric/xia.html.
Yu, Mo-Wan. "The Prodigious Cinema of Huang Fei-Hong: An Introduction." *A Study of the Hong Kong Martial Arts Film*. Ed. Lau Shing-hon. Hong Kong: Urban Council, 1980.

Part IV
New Visions

Reclaiming Past, Resisting Progression
Existential Tensions in Rockstar's Red Dead Redemption

MICHAEL SAMUEL

In Memory of Roy Rhodes

The Western genre, for all of its identifiable conventions, narrative strategies, character archetypes and other recognizable attributes (visual and aural grammar) is—as it always has been—in a perpetual state of becoming. Within its cyclical re-emergences, alterations and generic variations, the Western genre has proven an effective vehicle for channeling meaning in response to social, political and cultural issues affecting America at specific points of reference in their history: from John Ford's *Stagecoach* (1939); Howard Hawks's *Red River* (1948); George Stevens's *Shane* (1953) and Sam Peckinpah's *The Wild Bunch* (1969); through to more recent examples such as Clint Eastwood's *Unforgiven* (1992); Andrew Dominik's *The Assassination of Jesse James by the Coward Robert Ford* (2007) and Joel and Ethan Coen's *True Grit* [2010]. Subtextual strategies in the writing and direction of these Westerns subvert themes such as identity, which can include national, generational and gender; commentaries that are social, cultural and political; and representations of time and place. In regard to form, the Western is versatile; it has the potential to be adopted, referenced, remade, experimented with and borrowed from, yet it remains, in essence, distinct and purposeful. Despite what might be considered as a restriction to the number of narratives belonging to the Western genre, it is still able to subvert meaning: subsuming context and inviting interpretation. John Saunders, in *The Western Genre* (2001) features the opinion of Frank Grüber who writes that the genre has only seven "basic plots"

Advertisement for *Red Dead Redemption*. Rockstar Games, 2010.

(Saunders 5-6). These include "the Cavalry and Indians story; the Union Pacific or Pony Express story; the Homesteaders or Squatters theme; the Cattle Empire story; the Lawman story; the Revenge story; and the Outlaw story" (Cawelti 34-5). Imperative to the impact of the meaning(s) that might be interpreted in the Western narrative, is the use and clarification of setting and location, along with approaches to the concept of the Frontier myth and its significance in American history and culture. On the Frontier, Saunders aligns his work with that of the historian Frederick Jackson Turner. Turner, in a lecture on "The Significance of the Frontier in American History" in 1893, argues "the striking characteristics of the American intellect—restless energy, practical expediency, exuberance, and individualism among them– are the product of the highly charged encounter between civilization and the wilderness, East and West." From Turner, Saunders calls attention to what he defines as 'the frontier experience which lies behind so many Western films'" (6).

The creation of the Western myth is sustained by the idea of "characteristics and values" that are "uniquely American." The myth includes tradition, "individualism, self-reliance and an instinctive commitment to democracy" (Murdoch vii). Regardless of production choices, characteristics and the place of the author in meaning, message is conveyed through the communal and collective experience of watching, and interpreting the codes embedded within the Western genre. Saunders brings into line his opinion of the Western myth with Will Wright's definition of it as "a communication from society to its members" (Wright 16). The Western myth is "the embodiment of social meaning rather than personal message" and "promises a useful approach to a species of entertainment which, in practice, is usually experienced communally and in ignorance of a particular author" (Saunders 8). This is relevant as it will contribute to the intended outcome for the argument for *Red Dead Redemption* (Rockstar San Diego, 2010) as a text that is meant to be experienced during a specific context, for which it carries a particular message or expression about *that* particular time of reference.

The Western genre certainly becomes popular during times of crisis, however it is also presented during times of transition and change, highlighting tensions, and existing between movements where the reinforcement of identity and the comfort of a recognizable film grammar serve to ease audiences into a sense of security. Through generic conventions, tropes and characteristics that are distinct in their form, genres such as the Western experience a collective response that is usually critically divided. In contemporary cinema the genre can experience great success, such is the case with *The Assassination of Jesse James*; *3:10 to Yuma* (Mangold, 2007); *No Country for Old Men* (Coen and Coen, 2007); remake *True Grit*; *Django Unchained* (Tarantino, 2013); *Lawless* (Hillcoat, 2012). However, the genre can also fall victim to mediocre critical opinion and ratings, and achieve average box office success. Such is the case with *Once Upon a Time in Mexico* (Rodriguez, 2003); *Seraphim Falls* (Ancken, 2006) and *Cowboys & Aliens* (Favreau, 2011); and in certain cases, as with the revamp of *The Lone Ranger* (Verbinski, 2013), the Western can result in box office failure. The contemporary Western distorts and diverts—subverts even—the codes that explicitly distinguish the Western genre based on context and other external popular genres. In reaction, the Western can be seen to blur generic distinctions; reformatting and reworking the form for expression, through themes and film grammar.

Considering these factors, we can begin to see emergences and evolutions in the Western genre in and through a diversity of forms beyond cinema such as television, with series' such as *Deadwood* (Milch, 2004–2006); particular episodes of *Breaking Bad* (Gilligan, 2008–2013); *Hell on Wheels* (Gayton and Gayton, 2011–); and the History Channel miniseries *Hatfields and McCoys* (Reynolds, 2012). Given consideration to genre hybridity and the multi-platform versatility of the Western genre, developments have paved way for what we might now categorize as the Neo-Western genre, which includes *The Three Burials of Melquiades Estrada* (Jones, 2005); *No Country for Old Men* and *There Will Be Blood* (Anderson, 2007). The Western genre also extends to the horror–Western with *Near Dark* (Bigelow, 1987) and *Vampires* (Carpenter, 1998); the comedy Western genre, which includes *Shanghai Noon* (Dey, 2000) and *Bandidas* (Rønning and Sandberg, 2006); the animated

Western genre, *Spirit: Stallion of the* Cimarron, (Asbury and Cook, 2002) and *Rango* (Verbinski, 2011); and importantly, for the focus of this essay, the Western's embrace in the context of computer games, with titles such as *Red Dead Revolver* (Rockstar Games and Take 2 Interactive, 2004); *Call of Juarez* (Techland and Ascaron, 2007) and *Red Dead Redemption*. Moreover, in the context of video games, a similar hybridity of genres has become increasingly evident. Generic traits of the Western feature dominantly in what might be perceived as games belonging to other (game) genres. Examples of this are the drifter in Rockstar's *Grand Theft Auto* series; the frontier and vast landscape to be explored in the *Mass Effect* (Bioware, 2007–) and *Fallout* (Interplay Entertainment, Edusoft, 1997–) series; the lawman at the center of first-person shooter series *Call of Juarez*; through the deployment of visual and aural characteristics, such as the soundtrack to the *Borderlands* franchise (Gearbox Software, 2009–) and Ennio Morricone's score to *Red Dead Redemption;* and in the intricate narrative re-imagining of early twentieth-century American history and reworking of historical events belonging to *that* period in *Bioshock Infinite* (Irrational Games and 2K Australia, 2013).

Returning to an overview of the Western genre, in all of its variations, certain themes are recurrent and prevalent. For the American Western in particular, a sense of twenty-first century historicity and identity provides the foundation. There is an existential allure that rests at the core of the character of "the drifter" and in the vast strangeness and impossibility of the landscape. Examples of this is relationship between "the drifter" and the town or place can be found in *Shane*; *Hondo* (Farrow, 1953) and *The Searchers* (Ford, 1956), and in hybrid and cross platform Westerns. Mentionably, these include Travis Bickle (Robert De Niro) and New York City in *Taxi Driver* (Scorsese, 1976); Travis Henderson (Harry Dean Stanton) and Texas in *Paris, Texas* (Wendes, 1984); and Walter White (Bryan Cranston) and Albuquerque in television series *Breaking Bad*. Stanley Corkin, on the "drifter" and the Western myth—moreover the relation between the "drifter" and a particular place and space—writes, "This myth defines "the West" as a condition that removes the artifices of civilization from social life. Within the resulting state of nature, individuals show their essential qualities of character." Corkin concludes, "Such a view relies on a kind of biological determinism, as well as on a simplified concept of nature and civilization" (67).

Interpretations of the characteristics of the Western, be it character, landscape, themes, narratives, audio-visual codes, might vary in perception based on context, depending on when *that* text was made. For instance, the optimistic west of wartime and post-war America is presented in the characters that John Wayne portrays, whereas post–Vietnam critique rots away at the center of *The Wild Bunch;* likewise, shame eats away at the psyche of the old West in the Western genre during the period after the Nixon presidency, as Nixon was an advocator of the old West myth; *Unforgiven* followed with a portrait of a dying, or dead West; and after the 9/11 attacks, the American myth is revisited and reinforced through the characters and iconography of America's past—examples of this include John Dillinger in *Public Enemies* (Mann, 2009) and Jesse James in *The Assassination of Jesse James by the Coward Robert Ford*. *Public Enemies* traces the story of Dillinger and reignites and reasserts the legend that powers the myth, while *The Assassination of Jesse James* reflects upon and rejects its icon, and progresses through the moments leading to James' murder at the hands of Ford. Revisiting the Western myth, the Western Genre has played a significant role in many, varying points of reference in American history, historic and recent. It is through these revisits that a re-education takes place: the education of what it is to be an American in increasing times of social, cultural, political and national stress and ambiguity. It is with this opinion where I rest this analysis of *Red Dead Redemption* as a transitory text.

Concentrating on the idea of identity, this essay will examine, in-depth, aspects of the game *Red Dead Redemption* with the goal of attempting to provide evidence for the claim of existential tension as its premise. Existentialism is the modern philosophy movement used for identifying and highlighting uniqueness, and seeking self-definition in times of individual situation, often during times of indifference and ambiguity. It is responsible for stressing one's importance as an individual and is related with finding identity and meaning in what might be perceived as an existence that is seemingly without meaning.

Pursuing this definition of existentialism, I will analyze the framed character John Marston at the center of *Red Dead Redemption* with the idea that he is symbolic of the contemporary American—seeking identification while conflicted with the existentialist realization of America in a perpetual state of becoming. One intended objective is to argue the case for computer games' dependence on the intertextual play between history, novel and film. Another is to call for the subtextual recognition of *Red Dead Redemption* as an historical document, which, through the genre of the Western, channels contemporary concerns; references key points for national identification in a time of dramatic progression; and, through case studies of elements of the game *Red Dead Redemption,* addresses the idea of existentialism during a context that is in a state of flux.

Red Dead Redemption is the product of developer Rockstar San Diego and published by Rockstar Games. Rockstar, as a game developer has a synonymous reputation with controversy, their games are generally explicit and intended for an adult audience. Titles reputable with the Rockstar Games brand include the "sandbox" game series *Grand Theft Auto/GTA* (1997–present), which are open world in nature and allow for a great degree of gamer freedom and interaction; the *Midnight Club* racing series (2000–2010); the neo-noir detective *Max Payne* series (2001–2012); the disturbing stealth/psychological horror *Manhunt* (2003–2007); and the Western *Red Dead* series, which includes *Red Dead Revolver* (2004), *Red Dead Redemption* and *Red Dead Redemption: Undead Nightmare* (2010). Other standalone features from Rockstar include 2006's *Bully* (also titled *Canis Canem Edit*) and 1940s Hollywood detective thriller *L.A. Noire* (2011). Rockstar games, despite their provocative nature are financially and critically successful, earning many top ratings with reputable game companies and critics, such as IGN (Imagine Game Network), IMDB (Internet Movie Database) and audiences alike. Their diverse titles are post-modern and provide rich references to contemporary society, politics and culture; they have an awareness of genre, but most importantly they are deeply intertextual and include reference to their film and television heritage. Examples of this include *Grand Theft Auto IV*'s commentary on capitalism and racial policy in the wake of 9/11 terrorist attacks on New York, and economic climb during times of economic downturn. This is best exploited in *Grand Theft Auto: Vice City* (2002)—a spin off from *GTA3* which features the fictional Vice City (mirroring Miami) during the 1980s boom of cocaine-fueled wealth and tourism. *Vice City* pays homage to television series *Miami Vice* (Yerkovich, 1984–1990) as well as Brian De Palma's film *Scarface* (1983). Other examples of Rockstar's references include *Midnight Club*'s relation with the racing genre, made popular by the road movie and recently by the *Fast* and Furious series (2001–); *Manhunt*'s reference to the psychological thriller, with references to *The Silence of the Lambs* (Demme, 1991) and *Saw* (Wan, 2004); and *L.A. Noire*'s reformatting of the film noir, which rests on homages to the novels of the late James Elroy, whose books provided the source of films *L.A. Confidential* (Hanson, 1997) and *The Black Dahlia* (De Palma, 2006). Other pulp fiction references include the novels of Raymond Chandler and the films of Humphrey Bogart.

Of Rockstar's primary influences, it can be contended that the Western genre plays a huge part in providing reference to American culture and society for the benefit of exposé and critique; this features dominantly within Rockstar's narratives. Character Niko Belic in 2008's *Grand Theft Auto IV*, for instance, comes to the fictional Liberty City (modeled on present-day New York) from Yugoslavia to seek revenge on two men who betrayed him in "the wars." While in Liberty City, he aspires to climb and integrate socially in spite of rising social and racial tensions and increasing economic decline. Niko very much conforms to the "drifter" paradigm in the "revenge" or "outlaw» stories, to revisit Grüber. Similarly the *Max* Payne series traces the arc of detective Max Payne who, after experiencing the corruption and betrayal in law enforcement, and following the murder of his family (for which he is framed), becomes the hunted. With *Max Payne* there are references to the "lawman" and "outlaw" stories.

Red Dead Redemption was released on the Playstation 3 and Microsoft Xbox 360 consoles in 2010. It is the successor to *Red Dead Revolver*, which appeared on the previous generation of games consoles, the Playstation 2 and Microsoft Xbox, and in 2012 it (*Red Dead Revolver*) was made available on the Playstation 3, via the Playstation Store. *Red Dead Redemption* chronicles the story of John Marston, a former gang member and outlaw, as he operates with the government as a bounty hunter tracking his former gang members in exchange for the safe return of his wife (Abigail) and son (Jack) who are being held hostage by the government. It is set in 1911 against the dissolving American Frontier, and in the expansive and conflicted borderlands between America and Mexico. Like the *Grand Theft Auto* series and *L.A. Noire*, *Red Dead Redemption* is concerned with space, and the setting of the game is fully realized: it is vast and open; optimistic yet constrained. It gives reverence to America's Wild West past, while struggling in the progressive present, where the emergence and development of technologies and society (such as automobiles, weaponry, economy and law) are obstacles. As the setting influences for the *Grand Theft Auto* series pay reference to the internal dynamics and issues affecting factual contemporary cities, along with cinematic references—for example, Liberty City's replication of New York post–9/11, Vice City's impression of Miami during the 1980s and San Andreas's depiction of 1990s Los Angeles, San Francisco, Las Vegas and Nevada—the setting for *Red Dead Redemption* pays visual reference to the John Ford landscape in *Stagecoach* and *The Searchers*—a landscape still healing from the American Civil War, while being compromised with the invasion of technology (the railway), which cautiously lingers in the final frames of *Once Upon a Time in the West* (Leone, 1968). In order to arrive to the point of challenging the assertion that *Red Dead Redemption* is an existentialist expression and allegory of an America presently in a state of flux, I will look at three aspects in particular: the importance of landscape and context in response to character emotion and self-realization; the expression of opposing states of time within the narrative of *Red Dead Redemption* and comparisons of forms of the Western genre; and a visit to the idea of the death of the west as emphasized in a key scene of the game's narrative.

Through the Western from earlier examples to recent titles, "the landscape," according to Saunders, "has been one of the most expressive codes available to the genre, and the association of high mountains with lofty feelings and moral elevation was deeply rooted, long before the West was won" (15). Players are able to exist in the world of *Red Dead Redemption* during and between missions; they have to cross borders and take on the expansive frontier on horse-back, and in later missions, as a passenger in the first motor vehicle, which is owned by the government officials; they can participate in side-missions, such as shootouts, poker games and games of horse shoes, visit cinemas or chase bounties. Keeping with the "homesteader" and "cattle" stories as outlined by Grüber, a narrative thread follows the re-building and maintaining of the Marston ranch, where missions include buying livestock and aiding in their survival, hunting foxes and wolves who pose threat to smaller livestock (chickens), to picking herbs and acquiring pelt, all with the aim of aspiring to the idea of the sustainability of life. As the narrative progresses in *Red Dead Redemption,* so do the pressures of the central objective, to catch and kill the surviving members of Marston's previous gang, along with their leader, Dutch van der Linde.

While generic traits such as the outlaw and lawman characters, along with relatable narrative story *types* can be found in Rockstar's catalogue, the Western genre is debatably the most prevalent. Each game drifts away from a mere reproduction or impression of the Western genre, and instead, as is the case with certain films of the Western genre, it (*Red Dead Redemption*) *presents* the player with a self-conscious Western which has a duty to homage without compromising the Western genre in its complete state. In reference to film *Shane* (Stevens, 1953), with a similar conclusion in mind, Saunders remembers it "as the archetypal Western, a self-conscious attempt to reproduce the familiar themes and characters in a classically pure state" (13). This is what *Red Dead Redemption* aspires to, and Rockstar games alike. Rockstar's games are complicated and subversive genre hybrids, post-modern in their approach to film grammar and characteristics of a variety of genres. While their homages are explicit, Rockstar is experimental in using more than one generic reference to influence a particular reading of the text. An example of this is the playful approach to the Western and zombie B-movie genres in *Red Dead Redemption: Undead Nightmare*. *Undead Nightmare*'s narrative follows the death of Marston, the protagonist in *Red Dead Redemption,* and players control the resurrected zombie version—retracing the Wild West arc of *Red Dead Redemption*. While superficially *Undead Nightmare* might be perceived as having fun with genres, another possible reading might suggest that the dying West of *Red Dead Redemption,* is depicted in *Undead Nightmare* as being dead, literally. Despite attempting to revive figures from the past (as zombies), and arguably the resurrection of the Wild West myth along with it, *Undead Nightmare* expresses concerns, and a sense of hopelessness, over the inability to recover and continue the genre, and perpetuate the myth in a constantly changing environment and time state.

Returning to the argument regarding *Red Dead Redemption* as an existential piece portraying an America in shift, the first element that this essay will concern itself with is the location and context behind the narrative, the American Frontier of 1911. To revisit Saunders' assertion that the landscape is the "most expressive code available to the genre" (15) for its association with "feelings" and reasons for emotional relation; the landscape's scale, in proportion to the character(s) subject to the narrative, usually works as a catalyst for character reflection on their position in the world around them. Saunders writes: "Effects of scale and perspective work both to suggest the subservience of the merely human to some larger, more permanent order and to endow the figures in the landscape with comparable stature and impressiveness" (15). *Red Dead Redemption*, like *Once Upon a Time in the West, The Wild Bunch, McCabe & Mrs. Miller* (Altman, 1968) and other Westerns after the 1960s, is concerned with putting the landscape into perspective: it is scarred and its scale, though vastly exaggerated in the game, is background, and is not overwhelming in comparison with the internal, character narrative, whereas in the cinema of Ford the landscape appears "permanent and impressive" (Saunders 15). The conflicting seasons and terrain, developing landscape (railways, roads and the erecting of towns) and internalized narrative within the Marston ranch mean that this scale is compromised. The synergy between landscape and character in the Western genre is reflective of the character's persona, and emotional place. Saunders calls attention to the landscape within John Ford's Westerns as framing "John Wayne's equally craggy persona," thus creating a "truly monumental effect" (15). In *Red Dead Redemption* there is a sense of opposition to this; as the landscape changes and evolves, and life within it evolves accordingly (people operate differently, society is formed, business supply and demand is formalized and industrialized), for John Marston, unlike Wayne, the landscape suggests displacement and an uncompromising shift, which threatens Marston's place. Thus, the assertion that there is a synergy between location and character persona is pivotal in response to existentialism.

In regard to the function of the landscape and context within *Red Dead Redemption*, there is a sense of belonging with reference to the waves of development within the Western genre. Whereas the familiarity of the landscape is visible and relatable with the Ford, Huston and Hawkes Westerns, the conflict between character and surroundings emphasizes that *Red Dead Redemption* belongs also to the post 1960s Western—the films of Peckinpah, Leone, Eastwood, and more recent examples in the genre. Thus, we arrive at our first checkpoint in debating *Red Dead Redemption* as the embodiment and expression of a transitory text with regard to form.

In cinema the Western has shifted, disappeared and re-emerged in times of social, political and cultural transition, to varying popularity and significance. The Western genre during transition—between the Wild West to the contemporary reality, or from the frontier myth to reality—is an effective device for communicating the tensions confronted when existentially questioning one's placement in the grand scheme. Marston consistently wrestles with such questions: does he stay faithful to his "outlaw" past with Dutch's gang? Or can he sustain a life in the transition between past and future, investing in the present in order to prepare his family for the future? Does he indeed have a place in the future, considering his criminal past? Can the old values of the West that he, along with other characters such as Professor Harold MacDougal and Dutch uphold, survive an American landscape in a state of progression, which is departing from tradition and bringing with it a new set of oppositional values? Significantly, the Western can be expressive through form, as mentioned previously with regard to "waves" or movements within the Western genre.

This segment will gather such ideas, along with modes for conveying meaning in the Western genre firstly by highlighting the form of *Red Dead Redemption*, using cinema as a reference point; secondly, focusing in further detail on the character Marston as a transitory figure; and lastly, by analyzing the themes in relation to the missions/activities/tasks that Marston involves himself with and how they reflect his present situation.

In times of tensions, between the old and the new in the Western, explicit arguments are often made for the death of the West. There is a sense of departure from the myth of the Wild West, the image of "uniqueness" that promotes "individualism, self-reliance and an instinctive commitment to democracy" that Murdoch records (vii), and an acceptance of the constant shift and impacting future. While certain Westerns project optimism toward change, for example *Rio Bravo*'s (Hawkes, 1959) drunk, shamed deputy sheriff Dude (Dean Martin) comes out of depression to rediscover his power and worth with the help of Sheriff John T. Chance (John Wayne); others react and reinvent myth. Quentin Tarantino is a recent example of this, confronting wartime perspectives in *Inglorious Basterds* (2009) and African American history in *Django Unchained* (2012). Whereas others might seem oblivious and reclaim myth without future concern, some dismiss future altogether and are nihilistic—*McCabe & Mrs. Miller, The Wild Bunch, Unforgiven*—succumbing to the inescapably dying West. In *McCabe & Mrs. Miller*, this idea of the dying West is immortalized in the final sequence to the film. The narrative leading up which tells the story of a business partnership between gambler John McCabe (Warren Beatty) and Constance Miller (Julie Christie) in a remote mining town before the arrival of a large corporation. Altman's narrative attacks are the same concerns central to *Red Dead Redemption*, the tension between past and progression. McCabe and Miller very much exist in this tension and the business that they have is the victim of dramatic social and industrial change. The penultimate scene results with a shot of McCabe collapsing, and remaining hunched, seated and dying in the snow; meanwhile the town and church carry on. There is no alarm or grievance for the dying man; McCabe is without hope and without legacy. He is emblematic of the old world, the old West, accepting its fate in an increasing progressing world. Very much so, *McCabe & Mrs. Miller*'s theme of death of the West is frequently deployed in the post 1960 Western narrative, with references including lead characters in *Bonnie and Clyde* (Penn, 1967), Dennis Hopper in *Easy Rider* (Hopper, 1969), to Tony Soprano in *The Sopranos* (Chase, 1999–2006). *McCabe*, like the other aforementioned titles, paints a bleak portrait of character fate, but also a collective consciousness of death in transition, to comment on Mrs. Miller, who mourns McCabe even before his death, because she understands his fate and the fate of the old West. Altman understands form with reference to *McCabe*, and through key characters and scenes, produces an allegory, not to mention an elegy to the dissolving old West, and perhaps to the Western genre in general. Altman does so, with this scene, by deconstructing the myth and confronting audiences with the fact that it has no place in the future. *McCabe* provides a staple reference for the wonderfully empty or absent, introspective Westerns that follow decades later, such as *Meek's Cutoff* (Reichardt, 2010).

As re-emerging trends within the Western genre appear, this idea is consistently featured. *Red Dead Redemption* marginally opposes such defeatism, in that Marston is aware of the future and prepares for progression, yet for the character of Marston, this idea is inescapable and he gradually succumbs to it; he does not belong to the changing landscape, nor the imminent West. Like *McCabe*, *Red Dead Redemption*'s protagonist is presented with a similar fate. Sometime after the death of Dutch, Marston's missions include farming, herding cattle and horses, teaching son Jack to hunt and provide, and several moral lessons from the "old West," with the vision of living a relatively peaceful and resourceful, sustainable life on the ranch. However, in the mission entitled "The Last Enemy That Shall Be Destroyed," Marston and Jack are engaged in a discussion about the future, which is optimistic in tone; they speak of family, the ranch and about an airplane demonstration that is going to happen in the near future. Uncle, one of the members of the Marston Ranch family, shouts for John who tells Jack to go to the house and lock the doors and not to come out. John knows what's coming, he expects it, and it is probable that he has been expecting this for some time. Approaching the ranch are the American soldiers and government agents, coming to kill him. Like McCabe throughout *McCabe & Mrs. Miller*, Marston is aware of his destiny and the pending shift, and surrenders, not before putting up a fight however. John and Uncle arm themselves and defend the ranch from the first group of soldiers. Jack comes out to help John and Uncle and, after a smaller gunfight, Uncle is shot and John and Jack continue. After this wave, John orders Jack and Abigail to ride away on horseback. He knows the outcome of this battle, that it is his last fight. In order for Jack and Abigail to get away, he must confront the posse. Opening the barn door to around two dozen soldiers, the player enters "dead eye" shooting mode. The fight is impossible and after an attempt, John is gunned down with multiple gunshot wounds. For his sacrifice, the government will not chase down Jack and Abigail and thus, John's redemption for his earlier sins and previous life is achieved. The final shot of the mission, unlike the non-existent scene of *McCabe*'s finale, depicts a nineteen-year-old Jack staring over John's gravestone, his mother Abigail buried beside. Whereas with *McCabe* the film ends with the death of the West and the transition toward, and start of the new generation continues, Marston is mourned by family and avenged by his son Jack, who the player immediately assumes control of. As a result of the lessons Marston taught his son, Jack, he continues the values of the "old West" forward into the new and follows a path of vengeance. These analyses demonstrate two attitudes toward the West, with particular focus on the idea of the death of the West. While in *McCabe* this idea is relatively bleak, in *Red Dead Redemption* there is hope. In *McCabe*, progression is inevitable and is relentless, discarding memory and replacing the Wild West generation with the new. In *Red Dead Redemption* progression, while John was alive, is approached with optimism and is prepared for, if not for the character John, then for future generations: values are continued and memory is significant in the becoming identities that will be shaped with the transition, and there is a responsibility toward the myth. The only possible signifier to be considered when interpreting these two readings in response to the idea of the death of the West is context. *McCabe*, made in the 1971, comes during a time after a decade of prominent social and political shifts and confrontations (black civil rights movement, the assassination of Dr. Martin Luther King, Jr., Vietnam). American cinema approached this in instances, pessimistically, with portrayals of a shamed nation and the death of the "American" ideal. *Easy Rider* is the embodiment of this, using the road movie as a vehicle, as well as *Bonnie and Clyde* and *McCabe & Mrs. Miller*. *Red Dead Redemption* is produced during an equally turbulent time, approaching the topic of progress from a reflective angle, it carries with it a subtext of an America healing from the wound of the 9/11 terrorist attacks, struggling with critical responses to the invasion of Afghanistan and the media war that followed, wrestling still with issues regarding identity (equal rights, attitudes toward people of other backgrounds) and generally, a context ridden with insecurity. Whereas *McCabe* might suggest a defeatist stance and an incapability to change, *Red Dead Redemption*, in light of the social, cultural, political and temporal tensions that it presents, proposes hope in the idea of redeeming, and (re)discovering oneself.

Reverting ever so slightly back in *Red Dead Redemption*'s narrative to a scene of dialogue in the cut-scene mission entitled "The Prodigal Son Returns (To Yale)," nostalgia for the West is expressed and instantly dismissed. In a conversation between Professor Harold MacDougal and Marston, MacDougal comments, "You know, I dreamt of documenting the last days of the old West.

The romance, the honor, the nobility! But it turns out it is just people killing each other." To which, Marston replies, "It always was, Professor." This simple conversation highlights a realization and, in part, admittance to the myth of the West depicted in many Westerns. Whilst Marston abides to a "code" of the "old West," ultimately he understands the reality. This reality is expressed in the mission between Marston and Dutch entitled "And the Truth Will Set You Free." This mission shortly follows the previous mission "At Home with Dutch" in which Marston, along with MacDougal and Native American Nastas investigate a lead that points to the location of Dutch, at a fort called Cochinay. Before infiltrating the camp's guard, MacDougal says to Nastas: "We must try to reason with them, sir. Van Der Linde's gang contains several Natives. We must meet them and try to save them from disaster," to which Nastas responds, "My people have already endured many disasters. Before, this was all our land." Like the dialogue between Marston and MacDougal, this conversation follows in similar vein in admitting to the faults on behalf of the old West American, but also highlights the perpetual idea of change, which is forced and where a generation is destroyed to make way for the next. In the mission "And the Truth Will Set You Free," Marston's battles his way to Dutch's camp after the character/player is confronted with many of Dutch's guards. Marston is forced to pursue Dutch to a cliff's edge where a standoff between the two characters takes place. Marston and Dutch's dialogue is monumental in expressing the idea of inescapable change. In Dutch's omission to Marston, he says, "We can't always fight nature John ... we can't always fight change," before finishing his sentence with, "Our time has passed, John." After this line, Dutch jumps to his death, before Marston has the opportunity to shoot him. Dutch accepts his fate, and with complete control, decides to end his life. There is a sense of understanding at the core of Dutch's character, and a sense of belonging: he is aware that he belongs to the old West and that the pending West has no room for him. And, although he attempts to teach Marston this, while Marston understands it deep down, he perseveres in his search for identity and thus, Marston exists between the past and present modes, where he can neither go backward, nor forward.

In conclusion, I want to make one final attempt at relating the essence of John Marston's character and the context of contemporary America. It might be assumed that America, like the America background to Westerns of the 1960s, the 1970s, the 1990s and the 2000s, experienced a time of introspection. When faced with its self, the American Western has provided reassurance by presenting the myth of the West. Likewise, it has been brutally honest in mirroring a social, political and cultural critique and with reference to *Red Dead Redemption*, it presents both past and future and a character held in stasis between two poles of movement. Intentionally, I think, the objective in presenting Marston's position this way is to promote reflection—

honest reflection on the myth while accepting change—as a commentary and suggestion of how America might use the Western genre. By the additional element of gameplay, there is a further level of interactivity with the myth that is not permitted through other mediums such as film and television. Where in *Easy Rider, McCabe & Mrs. Miller* and *The Sopranos*, the viewer experiences the myth of the West as a spectator, with *Red Dead Redemption* there is a degree of immersion in and interactivity with this myth.

The myth, along with generic identifiers, signs and symbols—such as the drifter, landscape, the gunfighter—are significant of and to "the field of cultural history," according to Slotkin, who describes the field as an exploration of "the ways in which human cultures develop over time" (5). Cultural sources can be examined to form an "historical account" that documents the "activities and processes through which human societies produce systems of value and meaning by which they live and through which they explain and interpret the world and themselves" (5). According to Slotkin's ideas, one might distinguish Rockstar, the developer of *Red Dead Redemption*, as assuming the role and responsibilities of the "cultural historian" in that they try "to construct a historical account of the development of *meaning* and to show how the activities of symbol-making, interpretation, and imaginative projection continuously interlock with the political and material processes of social existence" (5). The "culture making" process that Slotkin describes can be assigned to *Red Dead Redemption* in that it, as a text, highlights three "different, but closely related aspects": "ideology, myth and genre" (5). Ideology is explained as the "system" by which "concepts, beliefs, and values that defines a society's way of interpreting its place in the cosmos and meaning of its history" (Slotkin 5); myths are significant of the stories that are "drawn from a society's history that have acquired through persistent usage the power of symbolizing that society's ideology" and is used for "dramatizing its moral consciousness" (Slotkin 5); and genre is the means by which "ideological concepts" can be "directly and explicitly" communicated (Slotkin 5). Arguably, *Red Dead Redemption* deploys these three aspects—ideology, myth and genre; they are woven in the narrative and interaction that the player has with the text and, in response, *Red Dead Redemption* has the potential to create, or at least inspire such impact upon an intended culture.

Slotkin has discussed the constant deployment and reinvention of the "frontier myth" to re-establish or re-assert America's identity in eras of uncertainty or change. Concerning America at present, which is in an arguably in this kind of existential state and unaware of its own identity, the use of these myths and symbols within sources like *Red Dead Redemption* aligns with Slotkin's ideas. Like Marston in *Red Dead Redemption*, it is proposed that America needs to involve itself with journeys of discovery and change; confronting myths of the past to realize its place in the future.

186　Part IV. New Visions

FILMOGRAPHY

Altman, Robert. *McCabe & Mrs. Miller*. David Foster Productions & Warner Bros., 1971. Film.
Ancken, David Von. *Seraphim Falls*. Icon Productions, 2006. Film.
Ashbury, Kelly, and Lorna Cook. *Spirit: Stallion of the Cimarron*. Dreamworks Animation, 2002. Film.
Bigelow, Kathryn. *Near Dark*. F/M, Near Dark Joint Venture, 1987. Film.
Carpenter, John. *Vampires*. Film Office, JVC Entertainment Networks, Largo Entertainment, 1998. Film.
Chase, David. *The Sopranos* Home Box Office (HBO), Brillstein Entertainment Partners, Park Entertainment, 1999–2007. Television.
Coen, Joel, and Ethan Coen. *No Country for Old Men*. Paramount Vantage. Miramax Films, Scott Rudin Productions, 2007. Film.
Coen, Joel, and Ethan Coen. *True Grit*. Paramount Vantage, Skydance Productions, Scott Rudin Productions, 2010. Film.
De Palma, Brian. *Scarface*. Universal Pictures, 1983. Film.
De Palma, Brian. *The Black Dahlia*. Universal Pictures, Millennium Films, Signature Pictures, 2006. Film.
Dey, Tom. *Shanghai Noon*. Touchstone Pictures, Spyglass Entertainment, Roger Birnbaum Productions, 2000. Film.
Demme, Jonathan. *The Silence of the Lambs*. Strong Heart/Demme Production, Orion Pictures Corporation, 1991. Film.
Dominik, Andrew. *The Assassination of Jesse James by the Coward Robert Ford*. Warner Bros., Jesse Films Inc., Scott Free Productions, 2007. Film.
Eastwood, Clint. *Unforgiven*. Warner Bros., Malpaso Productions, 1992. Film.
Farrow, John. *Hondo*. Warner Bros., Wayne-Fellows Productions, 1953. Film.
Favreau, John. *Cowboys & Aliens*. Universal Pictures, DreamWorks SKG, Reliance Entertainment, 2011. Film.
Ford, John. *The Searchers*. Warner Bros., C.V. Whitney Pictures, 1956. Film.
Ford, John. *Stagecoach*. Walter Wanger Productions, 1939. Film.
Gilligan, Vince. *Breaking Bad*. High Bridge Productions, Gran Via Production, Sony Pictures Television, 2008–2013. Television.
Hanson, Curtis. *L.A. Confidential*. Regency Enterprises, Wolper Organization, Warner Bros., 1997. Film.
Gayton, Joe, and Tony Gayton. *Hell on Wheels*. Entertainment One Television, Nomadic Pictures, (gayton),[2] 2011–. Television.
Hawkes, Howard. *Rio Bravo*. Warner Bros., Armada Productions, 1959. Film.
Hillcoat, John. *Lawless*. Benaroya Pictures, FilmNation Entertainment, Annapurna Pictures, 2012. Film.
Hopper, Dennis. *Easy Rider*. Columbia Pictures Corporation, Pando Company, Inc., Raybert Productions, 1969. Film.
Jones, Tommy Lee. *The Three Burials of Melquiades Estrada*. EuropaCorp, Javelina Film Company, 2005. Film.
Leone, Sergio. *Once Upon a Time in the West*. Finanzia San Marco, Rafran Cinematografica, Paramount Pictures, 1968. Film.
Mangold, John. *3:10 to Yuma*. Lionsgate, Tree Line Film, Relativity Media, 2007. Film.
Mann, Michael. *Public Enemies*. Universal Pictures, Relativity Media, Forward Pass, 2009. Film.

Milch, David. *Deadwood*. CBS Paramount Network Television, Home Box Office (HBO), Paramount Network Television, 2004–2006. Television.
Peckinpah, Sam. *The Wild Bunch*. Warner Bros./Seven Arts, 1969. Film.
Penn, Arthur. *Bonnie and Clyde*. Warner Bros./Seven Arts, Tatira-Hiller Productions, 1967. Film.
Reichardt, Kelly. *Meek's Cutoff*. Evenstar Films, Film Science, Harmony Productions, 2010. Film
Reynolds, Kevin. *Hatfields and McCoys*. Thinkfactory Media, History Channel, Sony Pictures Television, 2012. Television mini-series.
Rodriguez, Robert. *Once Upon a Time in Mexico*. Columbia Pictures Corporations, Dimension Films, Troublemaker Studios, 2003. Film.
Rønning, Joachim, and Espen Sandberg. *Bandidas*. Eurocorp, TF1 Films Production, A.J. O. Z. Films, 2006. Film.
Tarantino, Quentin. *Django Unchained*. Weinstein Company, Columbia Pictures, 2013. Film.
Tarantino, Quentin. *Inglorious Basterds*. Universal Pictures, Weinstein Company, A Band Apart, 2009. Film
Verbinski, Gore. *Rango*. Paramount Pictures, Nickelodeon Movies, Blind Wink Productions, 2011. Film.
Verbinski, Gore. *The Lone Ranger*. Walt Disney Pictures, Jerry Bruckheimer Films, Bling Wink Productions, 2013. Film.
Wan, James. *Saw*. Evolution Entertainment, Saw Productions Inc., Twisted Pictures, 2004. Film.
Wendes, Wim. *Paris, Texas*. Road Movies Filmproduktion, Argos Films, Westdeutscher Rundfunk (WDR), 1984. Film.
Stevens, George. *Shane*. Pictures Corporation, 1953. Film
Yerkovich, Anthony. *Miami Vice*. Michael Mann Productions, Universal TV, 1984–1990. Television.

WORKS CITED

Cawelti, John G. *The Six-Gun Mystique*. Bowling Green: Bowling Green University Popular Press, 1971. Print.
Corkin, Stanley. "Cowboys and Free Markets: Post-World War II Westerns and U.S. Hegemony." *Cinema Journal* 39.3 (2000): 66–91. Print.
Murdoch, David H. *The American West: The Invention of a Myth*. Cardiff: Welsh Academic Press, 2001. Print
Saunders, John. *The Western Genre: From Lordsburg to Big Whiskey*. London: Wallflower Press, 2001. Print.
Slotkin, Richard. *Gunfighter Nation: The Myth of the Frontier in Twentieth-Century America*. Norman: University of Oklahoma Press, 1998. Print.
Turner, Frederic Jackson. "The Significance of the Frontier in American History." *Frontier and Section: Selected Essays of Frederick Jackson Turner*. Ed. Ray Allen Billington. Englewood Cliffs, NJ: Prentice-Hall, 1961. Print.
Wright, Will. *Sixguns and Society: A Structural Study of the Western*. Berkley: University of California Press, 1975. Print.

Alex Cox and the Hybrid Western

Matthew Sorrento

In a 2006 article, filmmaker Alex Cox described the Western as long dead; as an active critic who authored books on "Spaghetti Westerns,"[1] his stance is compelling. Recent scholarship on Cox would suggest as much, even if the Western genre has been integral to his films. Essays on Cox tend to discuss either his "punk" aesthetic (see Davies, Mendik), or his 2002 film version of Thomas Middleton's *The Revenger's Tragedy* in drama-to-film adaptation studies (see Minton, Wray). A closer look at his career lends insight on his view of the Western's presence in recent films, and the genre's demise.

While Cox argues that the death occurred in the 1970s, the 1980s—when he made his filmmaking debut—would become the darkest decade for the Western. The heavy revisionism of the New Hollywood era, from 1967 through the 1970s, reworked the genre for the youth audiences in light of the Vietnam War and the Civil Rights Movement to the point of often estranging the results from classicism. In the shadow of George Lucas, Steven Spielberg, and their tastes for tradition, the Western was too mythical for the 1980s, save direct tribute (Clint Eastwood's *Pale Rider*, 1985, a retelling of George Stevens' *Shane*; and Robert Zemeckis' *Back to the Future Part III*, 1990) or parody (John Landis' *Three Amigos* and Paul Bartel's *Lust in the Dust*, both 1985). We wonder if this mini-cycle geared more to established fans (by then, aged) than the youngsters—Lucas' target—accompanying them to the theater. The best high-profile fantasies of the 1980s, like the first *Back to the Future* film (Zemeckis, 1985), mix traditions (for Zemeckis, teen romance with science fiction time travel, parts '50s and '80s) to refresh traditional, myth-based storytelling (Shail and Shoate 23–29).

Many filmmakers flourished during the era of Lucas and Spielberg's influence, but more prevalent for our discussion are those who rebelled against the popular myths. These "rebels" occupied the traditional generic styles to hijack them. We cannot describe this approach of revisionism to be like that of the New Hollywood, since the 1980s artists were not exposing the premises behind the genres as faulty (for example, Arthur Penn's *Little Big Man*, 1970, which treats Native Americans with sympathy). The 1980s "rebels" used the fantasy frameworks for anarchism, a more reactive version of what Zemeckis does in *Back to the Future*. The horror film serves as a fine example. After the launch of the slasher movement in the 1970s, which mainstreamed a strict structure (killer preys upon small group of teens, many of them lustful and dying as a result, until a final tomboyish girl rises to defeat the threat), horror needed a new style within classical expectations. John Landis' *American Werewolf in London* (1981) uses a classical movie monster, the werewolf, while intensifying the existential plight of Universal Studios' *The Wolf Man* (George Waggner, 1941). The antihero, David (David Naughton), plagued with the curse, grows delusional; his friend, who dies early on, "returns" in David's nightmares to urge his friend's suicide. David's other chaotic nightmares, like a bizarre raid of Nazi ghouls, characterize Landis' clever entry of anti-myth based in tradition. Similarly, a filmmaker from Canada, David Cronenberg, uses the horror genre to focus on our fear of bodily decay. His standout work from the early 1980s, *Videodrome* (1983), remains subjective to reflect the antihero's descent into madness, which is putatively the result of a video-delivered infection, but essentially a means to drive the suspense narrative. While adhering to cause-and-effect, linear narration, Cronenberg brings the viewer's experience to various forms of fear: suspense, paranoia, gore, destruction.

The Western, meanwhile, remained firmly in the traditionalist or parodic modes, save for the work of Alex Cox. A British emigre with an American film school education and sensibility, Cox broke into feature filmmaking in the early 1980s, when Lucasian fantasy and Spielbergian "innocent" dreams were en vogue. Instead of resisting this style and limiting himself to underground status—though he would return there after a major studio claimed that he took a high-budget project, *Walker* (1987), too far—Cox fashioned a frenetic entry in Western-crime-science fiction hybridity, *Repo Man* (1984). It is ironic that he pronounced the Western dead before the 1980s, since the genre's motifs are so integral to his film's framework that it would crumble were they removed. While a grounding reference point throughout his career, the Western was a direct focus for Cox later in the 1980s, in two films that play more as New Hollywood revisionist entries and removed him from studio filmmaking. Since then, Cox has continued to employ the Western, though he would eventually depict the genre's decay.

This essay will trace Cox's use of the Western genre as an engine for hybridity with other forms. After his two Westerns from 1987, *Straight to Hell* and *Walker*, Cox fused the genre with the police film (*Highway Patrolman*, 1991), dystopian noir (*Death and the Compass*, 1996), and Jacobean/dystopian tragedy (*Revengers Tragedy*, 2002). In doing so, he avoids the vogue of Spaghetti Western associations (though an avid lover of the style) by invoking, instead, American "revenge Westerns" of the 1950s directed by Anthony Mann and Budd Boetticher. I will conclude by discussing how, in a film released one year after he wrote about the Western's demise, Cox acknowledges his sentiment in his post–Western, *Searchers 2.0* (2007), which agonizes over the loss of a tradition in the film's content, style, and narrative pace. This statement comes after a 20-year career which began with a fervent use of the genre's motifs. His films post–*Walker* signal the thematic of *Searchers 2.0* approaching. For his elegy of the West, Cox uses a desolate road movie released post–9/11, a time that favored narrative resolutions of loss and confusion. He occupies a popular style of despair to declare another kind of loss.

Lucas, Spielberg and the Other *Rebel Forces*

While Cox would eventually accept this "death" and bear witness to it, he began making films when traditional genres reclaimed popularity, at times in overdrive. It is hardly worth repeating how enormous an impact George Lucas' *Star Wars: A New Hope* (1977) had on the film industry, popular culture, and American—hence, global—pop-psychology. Its use of mythical characters and story arc, based on Joseph Campbell's *Hero with a Thousand Faces* (1949), Buck Rogers serials, and samurai films, drew from audiences a latent passion. The project's promotional strategy changed the marketing of films, by introducing "action figure" tie-ins, a best-selling soundtrack of classical Hollywood-style orchestration (which also became a disco hit), and even a laughable "Holiday Special" for television. The film invokes a premise familiar to the New Hollywood, if only to abandon its other conceits. The story of Luke Skywalker (Mark Hamill), on Planet Tattooine, begins as a tale of a potential drop out, a youth discontent with the limits of his home. In style as well as pacing, the film plays languidly, especially if one can mentally remove the score. (In the same year, Spielberg released *Close Encounters of the Third Kind*, about a rebel who discovers that the arrival of aliens is something wonderful.) *Star Wars*' narrative redirects Luke toward adventure, as a warrior in training under a mentor, with a princess to rescue. An armored presence of ultimate evil, Darth Vadar (David Prowse), is the villain, while Luke is assisted by a hardened man-of-action, Han Solo (Harrison Ford), who's paired with a version of Leslie Fiedler's non-white-male companion (here, alien).

In "Papering the Cracks: Fantasy and Ideology in the Reagan Era," Robin Wood notes that the style of the fantastic journey reduces us to a child-like state, "for Uncle George (or Uncle Stephen) [to] take you by the hand and lead you through Wonderland" (147). With the association to theme parks, and their simplicity, Wood indicates the paternal authority reassuming power after the countercultural triumph of the 1970s. Wood describes imagination, in Blakean terms, as "a force that strives to grasp and transform the world, not restore 'good old values'" (148). One could say that Alex Cox was destined to begin his career during a rebirth of such mythical storytelling, since he was the answer to Wood's call for a new Whitman of American cinema. As he writes in the revised version of his book on Spaghetti Westerns, *10,000 Ways to Die*, Cox was drawn to the Westerns and action stories as a youth who found himself in rough English schoolyards where violence seemed to be everywhere (10). And yet, to Cox, the straight paternal-/traditionalism of Lucas signaled a call to rebellion.

Lucas' *Star Wars*, with the help of Spielberg, helped usher in old-time heroism like Richard Donner's *Superman* (1978) and Robert Wise's *Star Trek: The Motion Picture* (1979), while Lucas and Spielberg would collaborate on *Raiders of the Lost Ark* (1981), itself more in kind with the early Saturday serials that inspired *Star Wars*. Many horror entries of the decade even use a child's point of view (*Poltergeist*, Tobe Hooper, 1982; *Gremlins*, Joe Dante, 1984; *The Lost Boys*, Joel Schumacher, 1987). Through producing many of these films, including hits like *Back to the Future* and Richard Donner's *The Goonies* (both 1985), Spielberg capitalized beyond his own reach while Lucas largely stepped away from directing as the father of one of the most influential film series of all time. Often discussed as members of the "movie brat" generation, Lucas and Spielberg occupy a different place than directors like Martin Scorsese and Francis Ford Coppola, who also came of age in New Hollywood but maintained that sensibility.

The movie genre consciousness of Lucas created a vogue of multi-genre treatment within an action/adventure film (Shail and Stoate 27). Such movie-craziness appeared in the work of Robert Zemeckis, Chris Columbus, Richard Donner, and Joe Dante. Though hardly enough for this new fervor, straight tribute was all that the scant number of 1980s Westerns could muster. A popular adventure could contain teen romance, slapstick comedy, and science fiction exploration (in *Back to the Future*, produced by Spielberg and written/directed by Robert Zemeckis); Peter Pan, gangsters on the lam, and atomic-age movie monsters (in *The Goonies*, produced by Spielberg with his scenario and directed by *Superman's* Richard Donner); American family comedy, the haunted house film, and paranormal studies in *Poltergeist* (written and produced by Spielberg and directed by Tobe Hooper). And yet, the traditionalist craze was not the only element to influence such genre blending. We must consider developments occurring earlier in the 1970s, in the tradition of popular comedy.

As the most inherently ironic of styles, comedy uses disorientation to upset expectation. In the 1970s, slapstick comedy began to fold in various styles to highlight its anarchic approach. The popular films of the Monty Python team used sketch comedy to develop feature film narratives, their practice of concocting a number of bits into a feature narrative making for rambunctious entertainment. In *Monty Python and The Holy Grail* (Terry Gilliam and Terry Jones, 1975) an absurd King Arthur (wisely played straight by Graham Chapman), is on a journey back to his kingdom and onward to the eponymous prize. Along the way, he encounters a black knight who won't die, a killer rabbit, and other nonsensical parodies of Arthuriana. Tim the Enchanter (John Cleese), in a restored scene, urges the principal characters to "get on with (the story)," before he appears in the film proper; this scene brings the universe into a meta-consciousness. The comical activities amount to an absurd universe that leads to an anti-diegetic conclusion, in which contemporary police nab the medieval characters. The film uses sundry inspirations to offer a unique take on the Theater of the Absurd. Having learned much from their first feature, the Python's 1979 release *Life of Brian* mastered the approach by tightening the narrative line without sacrificing the zany inspiration. The fatalistic journey of Brian (Chapman again), beloved as the new messiah but with little chance of surviving the narrative, ends crucified in a show-tune set piece that celebrates such a tradition though really commenting on Brian's life and fate.

Python's popularity in the U.S. and abroad—thanks to their prominence on television, which bolstered their work on film—injected a loose-cannon style of inspiration into the gestalt. One member, Terry Gilliam, would continue the Python style of uniting sundry inspiration into narrative drama (more on him below). The American writer-director Mel Brooks used an approach similar to the Pythons, though more focused on punch-line delivery (verbal or visual, however silly) in lieu of the latter's gag delivery. Woody Allen, even in his early farcical features, relied on storylines, likely from his alliance to well-made stage dramas of the 1930s and 40s, which would be a more direct approach in his later career (Lax 240–41). Though he would contribute to various forms of comedy in the coming years, Allen revised narrative shape less than the Pythons and Brooks, even if Allen's works seem more satisfying overall. John Landis' *National Lampoon's Animal House* (1978), the clever "slob" comedy that launched a cycle, inherits the revisionist power of the new ironic style, though many of the following films remained conservative on the structural level (like Ivan Reitman's *Stripes*, 1981, in spite of Bill Murray's brilliant performance).

Though we could read Cox as spinning from the Lucas mold, or perhaps as a renegade who caught his own form of the Lucas bug, Cox is a product of the comical/ironic style, which lends its own form of new mythical treatment. This alternate form of new myths helped bring horror towards comedy, though the comic scenes in *Dawn of the Dead* (George A. Romero, 1978) set a vogue as well. Standout works like Frank Henenlotter's *Basket Case* (1982) and Stuart Gordon's *Re-Animator* (1985) display a style informed by the Python approach, maximizing potential of effect by including more generic elements. (In *Laughing Screaming*, William Paul discusses the horror genre's connections to late 1970s/1980s comedy, under a style he describes as the "gross-out" film.) Gilliam offered comical, intricate treatments of the fantastic journey aligned to Lucas/Spielberg only on the surface. British-born filmmaker Ridley Scott, who entered the filmmaking scene with a nearly absurdist take on two nineteenth-century *Duellists* (1977)—sharing little with the Lucas/Spielberg hits of the year save its facade of heroism—then followed the inspiration of Gilliam and company with dark fantasies informed by the revisionist narration. Scott's *Alien* (1979) plays as the 1950s style of monster movie returning, post–*Star Wars*, by including a statement on body horror, *They Drive by Night*-style cargo films, and a feminist hero. James Cameron mirrors *Alien*'s mix in *The Terminator* (1984), a blend of time travel, science fiction-horror, and slasher films, with a Lucas-sized backstory. Scott's *Blade Runner* (1982; a dystopian work of science fiction and noir) presents a reality that may not be actual, while *Legend* (1985) realizes a sense of evil and decay distant from the Lucas bandwagon.

This style of mythic regeneration via comedy is where Cox enters the scene. In a tradition independent of the blockbuster, it undoubtedly rode the mainstream's wake.

Repo Man: *A Range of Traditions*

Like the film brats before him, Cox entered filmmaking via film school at UCLA. And like Lucas and Coppola, Cox initially dovetailed with the New Hollywood irreverence in his debuting work, the self-produced short film *Edge City*, a.k.a. *Sleep is for Sissies* (1980). While finishing with an abortive heist, fodder for high-concept storytelling, *City*'s narrative concerns societal drop outs, a drug overdose, and a road trip—ironic occurrences reflecting the chaotic anti-plots of the late 60s/70s. Cox describes his script as "written in the fragmented fashion in the style of director Nick Roeg," whose 1970s British films *Performance* (1970), *Don't Look Now* (1973), and *The Man Who Fell to Earth* (1976) were inspirations to, and informed by, the resistance to narrative conventions in America at the time (Cox, *X Films* 10).[2] With assistance from Mike Nesmith, a musician-turned-producer like George Harrison for Gilliam's *Time Bandits* (1981), Cox's feature debut, *Repo Man*, offers a similar narrative style and can be appreciated alongside the colorful madness of The Monkee's television series (1966–68) and their feature, *Head* (1968).

Judging by his first film, Cox would seem ignorant to the popular movie milieu, while committed to the sentiments of fellow UCLA students, notably Charles Burnett (*Killer of Sheep*, 1979). While Cox's biographical information leaves scant insights on or ties to popular films of the time,[3] *Repo Man* shows that he acknowledged the new Spielbergian currents to work against them. British by birth (like the Python crew) and still identifying with the culture (though in love with America's), Cox is the kind of cultural outsider able to reassess American cinema so keenly. With the Western genre proper disappearing, Cox employs its motifs, with those of other genres, to fashion *Repo's* sundry styles into an ironic (bomb)shell of a classical narrative.

The variety of influences makes sense, when hearing of Cox's preoccupations during scriptwriting. In *X Films*, Cox notes that he was mulling over the repetition of coincidences in the news (41)[4] how various elements intermix, similar to how the crime and Western genres were related from their beginnings (Witschi 381) and how Dashiell Hammett's noirs inspired Akira Kurosawa's nihilistic samurai film *Yojimbo* (1961), which begat the beginning of the Spaghetti Western movement, Sergio Leone's *Fistful of Dollars* (1964). Miller (Tracey Walter), a repo shop employee who doesn't drive, notes that "People are hung up on specifics." Cox shows how American viewers possess this hang-up, to their detriment, when preferring broad narrative strokes to his complexities. While capturing such alluring chaos during scripting, Cox heard tales from actual repo men, a profession holding the status of both "official" and "outsider." The resulting iconoclastic style has been described as "punk cinema," since Cox became exposed to the Los Angeles scene in the late 1970s and songs from the movement became essential to the film's soundtrack (*X-Films* 68–9). And yet Cox's debut feature uses various motifs of popular genres—with the Western a running, if at times latent, inspiration—to construct its mix. Here the Western offers vitality to a yarn about a prized, missing Chevy Malibu.

Cox originally conceived the work as a road movie—beginning in Los Angeles (the on-location setting of *Edge City*) and ending in New Mexico (Cox, *X Films* 31). After further rewrites, his script would end in apocalypse— the trunk of the Chevy opening for its contents to obliterate the city, an idea that Cox admits he borrowed from the "Great Whatsit," radioactive material, in Robert Aldrich's film noir, *Kiss Me Deadly* (1955). Late in the production, Cox's producers thought up a new ending: instead of the explosion, which made Universal Studios wary, the trunk would contain a vague alien device that sends the car flying into space, with Miller, the film's trickster, and Otto (Emilio Estevez), the palindromic antihero, seated therein. That repairman Miller, who never drives a car, and Otto, who *officially steals* them, are the passengers is subversive: after strolling in air over the city, the vehicle enters an anti–Lucas version of warp speed into the stars, to nowhere specific—the final nebulous step in narrative delivery. That it could be a shot to another world, or blissful moments before their annihilation, makes it all the more celebratory.

A Westerner avenger re-imagined for the city, Bud (Harry Dean Stanton) ends the film injured and removed from his service. As a repo man who brings Otto into the profession, he serves the narrative as an ironic mentor figure, Machiavellian and cocaine-snorting. He instructs Otto that the job of reclaiming prized autos from an urban wasteland, where all food is generic save for liquor bottles, is full of tense situations, in which they must act swiftly to escape. By repossessing cars, they put instincts into action to drive Cox's narrative, if less coherently. Bud is the filmmaker's pure holdover from Italian Westerns of the 1960s. For Cox, within these films is "a world of arbitrary, stupid violence with a protagonist who deal(s) with it and survive(s) it" (*10,000 Ways* 11). As a Man of Action, Bud uses his own auto little, while reclaiming others. The classical Man of Action's land to claim is reduced to mechanized transportation. Salvation in Reagan America is reclaiming property, not land and the beginnings of community. Civilization has reached its post-communal state, an element of apocalypse remaining after the original ending was cut, and a theme that Cox would continue using. The title *Repo Man*, in fact, connotes both the titular profession and that Otto and his ilk are men reclaimed, repossessed by whichever diegetic/generic device presently occupies them.

As the putative central character, Estevez delivers a minimalistic portrayal, saying few words with intensity. Dispossessed at the film's start—his girlfriend, job, and nest egg from parents, all gone—he enters a new role with action more than reflection. His sparse language, the antithesis of Bud's verbose musings, shows him inhabiting the Man of Action's traits, naturally. He moves from buddy pic rides to repos, heist film hokum (the car constantly stolen; encountering liquor store robberies), to science fiction espionage (men in white after the Malibu and its contents) with spare, incising remarks. "Fuck that!" and "This is intense!" reflect his swift, simple denial or acceptance of an occurrence facing him.

The film's villains—punks/former friends of Otto and the Rodriguez brothers (rival repos also after the Malibu)—reflect, respectively, the frontier bandits and native marauders, the racial "others" of the Western. Though a "white suburban punk" himself, Otto has taken up with a brotherhood that redirects rebellion towards its own kind of justice. Along with Otto's affinity to the punk hoods, the rivalry between Bud's posse and the Rodriguez brothers is fraternal as much as combative: Bud's call to those "damn Rodriguezes!" signals familiarity through the frustration. The visual style throughout the chases and antics is contained, the viewer unable to imagine a universe existing outside the frame. It's Cox's clever formality to suggest that the city is already wasted, like the film's punks. The LA River, that filmically overused though probing urban feature, shows the desertion behind a truly desert city, as it does in quiet investigative scenes in Roman Polanski's *Chinatown* (1974).

This take on Hitchcock's *The Trouble with Harry* (1955), about a car that wouldn't stay possessed by the same driver, uses the Western to ground its sundry inspirations. Cox's two 1987 films show his negotiation, or struggle, with a genre that he would later pronounce "dead."

Straight to Bleak Frontiers

Cox's punk associations made his following project, a biopic about Sex Pistols bassist/alleged killer Sid Vicious, a natural move. With its loose structure, *Sid and Nancy*, a.k.a. *Love Kills* (1986), continued Cox's use of Roegian storytelling, albeit more chronological. The film's true standout connection to *Repo* is the final scene, a dance with Sid (Gary Oldman) and a group of kids that reads as sublimely as the Malibu taking flight.

Cox's two following films, *Straight to Hell* and *Walker* (both 1987), drew him back to the Western. The former film, a tribute to the Spaghetti West that was written and filmed quickly, brings a contemporary heist narrative into a bizarre frontier of the past and present. When a pack of hoods, post-bank robbery, enters a desert town, they are met with a gang of coffee addicts, often framed in close-ups akin to the Italian West. Coffee as the choice of drink may seem like parody, with the classic frontiers of the screen full of whiskey. And yet, the caffeinated drink is a fitting choice for Cox's energetic style, though in this misfire of a film, the element is like one of many bullets ricocheting in a dull canister. In George Stevens' *Shane* (1953), coffee fuels the master-killer Wilson (Jack Palance), while the drink prevalent in revenge Westerns of Anthony Mann. Wilson chooses to drink something intensifying, not dulling, to the senses—even if Shane's skill proves better. *Straight's* caffeine guzzlers spell heat-borne death for all, with irony: here they wield espresso machines, alongside a shirtless, *Rambo*-esque shop owner and a jingle-obsessed hot dog vendor, to hint at contemporary chic malaise (Beliveau). More comes when a Farben Oil truck arrives to town after the film's final death toll. Reaganite corporate groupthink, and its strangle on humanity, sends this frontier town towards demise.

The fate of the frontier in *Walker* isn't as dire: 1850's Nicaragua survives after the eventual capture and execution of a Man-of-Action-gone-awry. Loosely based on an historical figure, Cox's William Walker (Ed Harris), an American soldier of fortune traveling after a failed insurrection in Mexico, arrives to Nicaragua to overthrow the government and establish a trade route from the Atlantic to the Pacific. As a tragicomic portrait, *Walker* features one gringo's evil in lieu of *Straight*'s sundry. The former film thus attacks America's colonial policies towards Latin America. As a film of the 1980s, the ordeal relates to the past and present.

Walker has industry behind him, with backing from filthy-rich Cornelius Vanderbilt (Peter Boyle). And yet Walker's belief in Manifest Destiny, described by journalist John O'Sullivan, drives Walker to maniacal power, as he rejects Vanderbilt's claim for the trade route after overthrowing the government, killing any objectors, and eventually installing himself as president. Hardly the classical Man of Action to solidify the community and defeat it threats, Walker forces his influence through a fascist takeover. That he directly addresses Manifest Destiny, in lieu of the idea's place as a premise in John Ford's post-war Westerns, highlights the misfortune in light of 1980s American colonialism, as the film was made in Nicaragua during the Contra War.

The film's style stands out as a surrealist take on historical biography (Beliveau). Though structurally, it mirrors a style of the horror film in which a monstrous threat aims to assume power as well as instill fear/death, ranging from Tod Browning's *Dracula* (1931) to Brian Yuzna's *The Dentist* (1996). Responses to Cox's use of anachronisms—brief appearances of helicopters, automobiles, and contemporary magazines—have been mixed, though the underlying claim, that America during the film's release was doing something similar to Nicaragua through foreign policy, resounds regardless of how jarring the references seem. Cox rethinks the Spaghetti Western in his two 1987 films that are more blunt and brutal than the energetic hybridity of *Repo Man*. His use of the genre reflects chaos and a sense of loss greater than Leone's take on the West. In his two late 80s Westerns, Cox reveals a tradition in decay; he proclaims its demise twenty years later in *Searchers 2.0*.

Banished to Strangelands

Bankrolled by a major studio that became disappointed with the film's financial failure, *Walker* was Cox's last project within the studio system. His next film, a Spanish-language Mexican feature, *El Paturello* (a.k.a. *Highway Patrolman*, 1991), allowed Cox to work within another national cinema to critique the United States' "occupation" of a Latin American frontier. (He would continue to work outside of the U.S. through the 1990s.) His avenger enlists in the Mexican highway patrol, in which his job should concern local issues, but proves broader when he encounters a gringo in a bar who turns out to be a drug trafficker. Cox's patrolman, Pedro Rojas (Roberto Sosa), is slight in build and seems self-conscious about his presence. He compensates with focus, while his paraphernalia inspires professionalism. The performance plays as something like a Mexican (and clear headed) Dick Rude, a leading man in *Hell* and punk antagonist in *Repo*.

This version of the frontier avenger largely concerns the genre's take on women. With a wife at home, Pedro takes up with a prostitute who begins her job when he does his. The film follows the standard Western schoolmarm-saloon gal binary, a generic variation of Freud's Madonna-Whore complex, through Pedro's emotionally taxing wife and a side girl; the latter is his release, until she demands support. Cox has written of the widespread desire for Mexican patrolmen to reform a prostitute (*X Films* 179), which aligns to the mythos of the classical Western, as in Ringo Kid's (John Wayne) confirming the heart in ex-prostitute Dallas (Claire Trevor) in John Ford's *Stagecoach* (1939). Cox's vision proves more complex, as Pedro keeps both relationships and aims to maintain two households. On the job, he is similarly overburdened. A work injury leaves him with a bum leg and hobbling like the title character in the dystopian Western *Mad Max* (George Miller, 1979). And like Max, Pedro quits his job to transport laborers for his wife, an act he nearly arrests her for earlier, when they first meet. After his friend dies on the job, Pedro takes his automatic weapon to inherit rapid fire against his threats. They turn out to be Americans fueling drug trade, the inversions of the common American narrative of Mexicans smuggling drugs into the United States (see the Coen brothers' *No Country for Old Men*, 2007).

Highway Patrolman uses the West for a tale of an innocent avenger. Though when the film brings Rojas into rugged terrain, Cox employs the landscapes of psychological Westerns by Anthony Mann and Budd Boetticher. The landscapes that made Ford's prized monuments into reflections of torment show Cox moving away from the Italian West of the 1960s, and toward an earlier revenge strain of the American Western. During the time he made his next two features—both of which reached completion after the release of Quentin Tarantino's *Pulp Fiction* (1994)—Cox undoubtedly noticed a new vogue of heavy violence and nihilism. Tarantino, another devotee of the Spaghetti West, reprocessed the style's motifs successfully, granted, but into commercialization. This 90s wave of intense-cool was so broad that critics argued (wrongly) that the work of Mexican novelist-turned-screenwriter Guillermo Arriaga was inspired by it (Sorrento). Cox has said little about his stance on Tarantino and his prominence, save for the former's distaste for mainstream films overall. Likely acknowledging Tarantino's "claim" over the Italian Westerns in the popular eye, Cox began to use motifs of the 1950s psychological Western, thus avoiding swift, populist nihilism for treatments of revenge on the frontier. (While the Spaghetti Westerns *Fistful of Dollars* and Sergio Corbucci's *Johnny Oro* [1966] have revenge elements, the theme is not a unifying motif, as it is for the central Men of Action in the 50's Western style predating them.) To resist further commercialization, Cox's tales of vengeance have literary origins.

Though not the subject of Cox's book on the genre, the psychological Western and its directors, Anthony Mann and Budd Boetticher, are referenced throughout. As a modification of the classical style, the revenge Western thrived when the genre was facing what Andre Bazin argued was the advent of the "super Western": entries like *Shane* and Fred Zinneman's *High Noon* (1955), according to the famed French critic, attempted to become something greater than their tradition (51). The psychological Western still highlights a Man of Action, though here very alone on a quest to vengeance. In Budd Boetticher's films starring Randolph Scott, the Man of Action avenges the murder of his wife, an act indicating his severance from close relations and desire for action. With his community lost, the avenger has little interest in saving many, but merely himself from his own obsession. Though headed towards a nihilistic theme, the revenge Western has the goal-oriented duty of the classical tradition. While critic Lee Russell argues that the style offers the truest sense of individualism in the genre (197), the avenger is driven by an obsession almost against himself. As Anthony Mann noted, the ideal avenger, to him, was a man who is "able to kill his own brother" (Willeman 209). By often employing familial battles, Mann highlights the avenger's removal from the communal and lack of a collective cause. In a sense, the psychological Western offers its own despair, in which morality is grounded by individual choice (Russell 196), while rooting the narrative with a cause and something else to win through the quest (a new love, or a potential community). Cox was clever to adjust his inspiration, thus continuing his commitment to a style by referencing an earlier, post–Classical movement.

Cox's *Death and the Compass* (*DC*) began as a television program for BBC that he expanded into a feature; the "completed" longer narrative employs a noir/dystopian style in its hybridity with the revenge Western. An adaptation of a Jorge Luis Borges short story of the same name (1942; English translation, 1954), the film highlights the noir elements reflected in the title, which indicates initially, the threat/misfortune of noir and then the aim for solving and interpreting the intricate ordeals. The title suits the narrative, which is conscious of the style to the point of parody.

The film's framing device, appearing throughout the running time, features Trevanius (Miguel Sandoval), who rambles to the camera details about a now deceased investigator, Lönnrot (Peter Boyle). In the noir tradition, Trevanius reflects an obsession with the past, the kind of narration from the first-person accounts of Raymond Chandler's Philip Marlowe or Billy Wilder's Walter Neff (Fred McMurray) in *Double Indemnity* (1944). Simultaneously, Trevanius's direct address suggests a dramatic monologue, which appears proper in Cox's following project, *Revengers Tragedy*. Boyle's Lönnrot is a gumshoe who's aged but lively and obsessed with belief systems, especially the one associated to the film's first murder investigation: the Jewish Kabbalistic tradition. Lönnrot is legendary, according to the narrative surrounding him, while Boyle wisely plays him as reserved and knowing. Opposing Lönnrot is an extreme version of villainy, Red Scharlach (Christopher Eccelston), a demonic punk. The feature version added an extended black-and-white scene early in the narrative to explain Lönnrot's feud with his antagonist. Here Scharlach stages a robbery with the pace of the gang in John Carpenter's *Assault on Precinct 13* (1976) and the eerie presence of the beings in E. Elias Merhige's *Begotten* (1991). The murder of the blind but sharpshooting Commandant Borges (Cox in a cameo) sets Lönnrot towards revenge with a trace of James Stewart's aw-shucks-gone-renegade roles he played for director Anthony Mann.

Left in decay where unexplained bombs continue to fall, the city needs Lönnrot's help, though he ignores everything to investigate the murder of a rabbi/Jewish Mysticism expert, which points to Red Scharlach. In this apocalyptic revenge Western, the Man of Action uses his Ahab-like obsession to find one that has wronged him. *DC*'s initial murder should urge Lönnrot's duty to serve and protect, and yet piques his intellectual drive for revenge. Trevanius, who accompanies him, argues that the rabbi was an incorrect mark for robbery, a theory that Lönnrot says is "possible, but not interesting." This point is not to suggest that Lönnrot has lost the heart of a classical Man of Action: he is able to bring two would-be robbers/Scharlach impersonators to their knees for penance. In line with Lönnrot's prior career interest to become a priest, his presence takes on a religious dimension, as he occupies the special status of a savior like George Stevens' title character in *Shane*; Lönnrot trails a villain whose dread equals the former's glory, though he won't have Shane's success. A clue left in a typewriter page, "The first letter of the name has been spoken," indicates a serial killer motif in *DC*, though Cox, true to the source story, places the device as fuel for excessive vengeance, as a serial murderer fuels the post–Civil Rights rogue avenger Dirty Harry. While *DC*'s matchup is tied to personal gain and interest, the film's vengeance holds traces of Cox's taste for the Spaghetti West, and yet is rooted in 1950s "psychological" frontier revenge. That a newspaper editor discovers the body suggests the presence of a different avenger (like the reporter characters of early Hollywood), though he's a barely concealed foil.

Cox's vision of Borges' unnamed city could not hope for much more than what Lönnrot offers. The police station, shot in Mexico City's cavernous Palacio de Correos (which Cox, in Brechtian fashion, does not hide from view), is as dark as the bleakest street corner. The office rows are overrun with bureaucratic materials and the tone of dialog snippets, a claim to the city employing 3000 detectives (with Lönnrot the standout), along with public surgery (the collapse of public institutions suggested by comments by present-day Trevanius), and stylized torture (seemingly reserved for women). Cox's use of the plano secuencias style of shooting, which involves long takes to establish and vary composition—having learned the style in Mexico from Arturo Ripstein, Cox employed it for the first time in *Highway Patrolman* (*X Films* 76)—captures sundry bizarre bits and channels the style of his fellow mythical rebel, Terry Gilliam.

The avenger meets his aim as the film wraps, though Lönnrot is doomed, as Trevanius of the present narrative indicates early on. Lönnrot uses strategy to find the location of a potential fourth murder, thus completing the fourth letter of the name indicated by the clues, which reflects the fourth point of the eponymous compass. And yet the end proves to be a prank by the trickster Scharlach, who's revealed to be Zunz (also played by Christopher Eccelston) toying with Lönnrot all along. The hunt for ultimate evil critiques viewers' faith in detection. The film is, essentially, a parody of noir and, with Cox's sly treatment, an unsuspecting parody of the revenge Western. The city in need of a modern savior ails, while it's divided over the old king of a new one, a conflict akin to that between homesteaders and cattlemen. With Lönnrot's theory having failed him at his moment of death, Scharlach notes that Lönnrot's idea of a traditional plot was all his own invention, and that *next time* (beyond Lönnrot's logical understanding of time and space) the path will be a single straight line, invisible, everlasting. In so many words, the trickster-villain offers an empty promise for a return to the classical sleuth/avenger tradition that, Cox indicates, is gone in the era of the "post–Western" (see below for further discussion).

DC proves to be a revenge Western that surprises viewers as a tragedy. Elements of the latter style are hidden in *DC*, unlike Cox's next film, an adaptation of Thomas Middleton's *The Revenger's Tragedy*. The source Jacobean stage play is spare in its psychology and more focused on action than the more reflective *Spanish Tragedy* by Thomas Kyd, the benchmark of English revenge tragedy and inspiration to Shakespeare's *Titus Andronicus* and *Hamlet*, in which the genre is a foil for humanistic rhapsody. Like its title, Middleton's play parodies the established genre. The antihero Vindice muses to a skull a la *Hamlet*, though it occurs immediately in the text and calls forth revenge instead of Hamlet's opportunity for philosophy.[5]

The backstory of Vindice (Christopher Eccleston), partially revealed in flashback, lays down the psychology for Cox's purest rendition of revenge. His wife poisoned on his wedding day, Vindice is set to take revenge against her killer, The Duke (Derek Jacobi). Here Cox channels the Boetticher Western by connection to a Jacobean text that was archetypal to the latter Western style. Having spurned the Duke's advances, Gloriana (Jean Butler), along with the rest of the wedding, fall from the poison, while Vindice and his sister

Castiza (Carla Henry), have not drank from the glasses. The prominent flashback signals a Spaghetti Western element, though here invoking Leone's 1968 epic Western, *Once Upon a Time in the West* (in which the character Harmonica avenges the death of a brother), a celebration of the Western overall which borrows heavily from Mann, Boetticher, and countless other Westerns (see Fawell 23–40). To begin the narrative, Vindice arrives on a bus that has been ambushed. In this futuristic take on the stagecoach, in which various parties band together during frontier travel to represent civilization and spread its glory (most famously in John Ford's 1939 film bearing the name), Vindice is the sole survivor. No longer part of a roaming group, he departs the transport a sole Man of Action bent on his goal. To remove distraction in an act of purifying, he shaves his head, before meeting a gang of street rogues/roadside bandits asking him if he's a cockney. Vindice's disposal of them, in a choreographed fight scene, underscores his action over pondering. Cox's film, true to the play he's adapting, will continue vengeful moments. The developing futuristic narrative, in light of the filmmaker's earlier use of revenge Western motifs, reveals his final (at the time of this writing) use of the genre as an agent of energy.

Vindice's address to Gloriana's skull (red hair still intact) indicates his sure path to death beyond the present aim. His attachments to family, his sister and mother, assure only the same. Castiza assists Vindice in killing of the Duke by luring his clouded view to Gloriana's skull, which bears poison on its teeth from which the Duke dies, after a misplanted kiss. Like Vindice, she meets her fate from bullets fired by powers that extend far beyond her and her brother's control. Their mother, blind in this version of the story, chooses to offer Castiza to the Duke's son; Vindice impersonates the messenger for the deal to test his mother. The weak familial bonds present in the Duke's clan—with his wife's incest with her son, and the son's conspiring to take down Lussurioso (Eddie Izzard), heir to the title—indicate the same for Vindice. His vengeance, according to fate spelled through a portentous comet, will save nothing in the Coxian wasteland. By Vindice setting Lussurioso against his own parents, we find traces of *Yojimbo/Fistful of Dollars* and hence, Cox's commitment to the Spaghetti West. And yet, by choosing an alternate to Shakespeare, a Middleton revenge tragedy, Cox opposes the endorsed source, and thus minimizes further Italian West associations for the 50s revenge style.

The film blends the classic text with contemporary and extra literary language (which suggests a connection to Anthony Burgess' novel *A Clockwork Orange*, 1962, and Stanley Kubrick's 1971 film adaptation) (Minton 133) to suggest that past conflicts are part of the present, like the anachronisms in *Walker*. Cox includes a handful of satiric elements—media sensationalism, including one reflecting Princess Diana's death (133), surveillance, sports violence, and the 9/11 cultural shift, all violent energy that fuels revenge. The media scandal urges more blood, while the sports violence notes how conflict on the field breeds more by fans. Imagery of the nuclear bomb at the film's end, after Vindice and Castiza die offscreen in a hail of bullets, plays with Vindice's voicing the word revenge through Gloriana's skull. Originally wanting to include the twin towers falling at this moment (Cox, *X Films* 269), Cox sees the military conflict following the September 11, 2001, attacks as a severe case of revenge, which consumes Americans as well as their "enemies." Similarly, the Western—America's tradition of the past that has always mediated for the present—has grown exhausted after trying to deliver such themes to contemporary viewers. All that's left of a rich cultural tradition is elegy.

The Western Wasteland: Searchers 2.0

With the release of Cox's 2007 "microfeature" (made with digital video on a small budget and proud of its minimal production scale), it seems that his Western obsession erupted into a film continually conscious of the genre. This film signals the genre's end, even if Cox had been well aware of previous attempts to bury it, such as Tonino Valerii and Sergio Leone's Western-comedy *My Name is Nobody* (1973). Cox's *Searchers 2.0* serves as a textbook example of Neil Campbell's concept of the "post–Western," a sub-genre "fascinated by the *afterlife* of the classic Western's *afterlife*"—i.e., what transpires after the Men of Action establish order, ride off into the sunset, and are no longer needed. Campbell uses John Sturges' noir–Western *Bad Day at Black Rock* (1955) as an example, and adds other recent works in a 2013 book-length expansion of the idea. While not a focus for Campbell, *Searchers 2.0* exemplifies the anti–Western in that the genre occupies the film as ethereal nostalgia.

Searchers 2.0 is full of generic references and contains characters who had acted in a Western; they are driven to revenge because of the experience. Thus Cox offers a postmodern take on the psychological Western, which offers tragedy due to a back-story crime; here, the violation occurs during the making of a bit of genre myth. Mel Torres (Del Zamora) has a chance encounter with Fred Fletcher (Ed Pansullo), when both realize that, as children, they acted in the same film during which they were abused by screenwriter Fritz Frobisher (Sy Richardson).[6] Sharing an obsession with things West, with a poster of Leone's post-classical epic *Once Upon a Time in the West* in Fred's living room, they decide to travel to a fan event that Frobisher will attend, to get a piece of him. By depicting characters who experienced real pain when making a revisionist genre piece, Cox recalls the new violence of films like Sam Peckinpah's *The Wild Bunch* (1969) as the beginning of when the genre started killing itself, if with insight. That Mel and Fred are clueless as to how to get back at Frobisher—it's unclear as to whether they aim to beat him up, or worse—adds to the irony of this journey. Of all the quotes, faux dictums, and debates that Mel and Fred share, on movies, politics, and Americana, none of the scenes can drive them to action. On their journey, they are snared by various roadblocks, underscored by a dream of getting caught in bear trap, a rendering of frontier travel reduced to inaction.

These unlikely but inevitable buddies lead the film into a road movie/ Western hybrid (the former genre a New Hollywood favorite), even if Mel's daughter, Delilah (Jaclyn Jonet), accompanies them as their driver. Naturally, she's the antithesis of the commonality among the two men, bored with Westerns and, in a deviously ironic moment, wrongfully trying to distinguish literary revenge as superior to the filmic treatments (as the discussion earlier shows, *Revengers Tragedy* asserts they are one and the same). Cox's title invokes Ford's 1956 classic as one of the earliest to question the genre's myths, even if Boetticher and Mann did it prior, as Cox knows. The title also moves the genre into a world of digitized hyper-technology, which forever reproduces information, often glanced over and forgotten, while the Western genre maintained its own strength for the first half of the twentieth century. Cox's use of digital video underscores his film's abandonment from the putative genre, which had captured landscapes and travel with celluloid's fluidity. Cox maximizes use of the new filming technology while noting that other developments have fractured the past, in which fans, like Mel and Fred, regurgitate movie factoids that are so easily accessed they've lost their power. Access sans memory—i.e., obsessive web *searches*—captures the surface without the heart.

While once part of the tradition, these men have lived after the Western's "apocalypse" where many, like Delilah, think the film tradition to be ridiculous, and a veteran like Frobisher (when they finally encounter him) is more concerned with profiting through memorabilia sales. (While George W. Bush is heard on a radio, urging Americans to buy, spend, and fuel the economy, a character picks up day laborers, implicating consumerism to be maximizing on the "racial other" of today: "purchased" Mexican immigrants.) The information coming from Fred leaves Pansullo an awkward presence, like Cox's use of Dick Rude, who is directed to unsettle viewers. While overloaded with information about the films he loves, Fred struggles to articulate his stance against the war, though loathing Michael Moore. When arriving to the event that Frobisher was to attend, the two former actors find an inflatable movie screen, looking like state fair bouncing amusement for children. Cox offers an absurdist note of where the film tradition lies in the age of technological and information overload. The film's final mock shootout, to end the film proper, is a relay of trivia challenges that reducing a genre tradition into verbose spectacle. And when we learn, post-"shootout," that Fred is an impostor, actually an investigator out to nail Frobisher on copyright infringement (he sold off the rights to his paraphernalia long ago), Fred had acquired his stock of information with ease for his mission. Using technology, information offers the chance for deception in the hands of corporate interests.

Cox loves the many details of the genre to which he's devoted his work. But he's none too pleased about the tradition eating itself away with excessive availability that leaves little understanding. Many exploit the genre while lamenting its demise, while the tradition has informed Cox's unique blends of filmmaking.

NOTES

1. Cox wrote his first version of the text (originally unpublished but now available as a free PDF on his Web site, alexcox.com) in 1978 while still in graduate school; he revised the text into a substantially different book in 2009.

2. Roeg himself enjoyed the film, having accepted a special invitation to a London screening.

3. In an interview with *X Films*, Cox later admitted to his loathing for mainstream films (247).

4. Still intrigued by coincidences, Cox recently published *The President and the Provocateur: The Parallel Lives of JFK and Lee Harvey Oswald* (Feral House 2013).

5. Unlike Hamlet's hesitant hero, Vindice is ready to kill the penitent Duke during a funeral scene.

6. While such abuse may seem the stuff of legend, filmmaker Allan Dwan admitted to abusing a child actor as early as 1931 (Mandelbaum and Morris 13).

WORKS CITED

Bazin, Andre. "The Evolution of the Western." Kitses and Rickman 49–56.
Beliveau, Ralph. "Great Directors: Alex Cox." *Senses of Cinema* 48 (2008). Web. 29 August 2013. http://sensesofcinema.com/2008/great-directors/alex-cox/.
Campbell, Neil. "Post-Western Cinema." Witschi 409–424.
Cox, Alex. *10,000 Ways to Die: A Director's Take on the Spaghetti Western*. Harpenden: Kamera, 2009. Print.
_____. *X Films: True Confessions of a Radical Filmmaker*. Brooklyn: Soft Skull, 2008. Print.
Fawell, John. *The Art of Sergio Leone's Once Upon a Time in the West: A Critical Appreciation*. Jefferson, NC: McFarland, 2005. Print.
Fiedler, Leslie A. "Come Back to the Raft Ag'in, Huck Honey!" *Partisan Review* (June 1948): 664–71. Print.
Kitses, Jim, and Gregg Rickman, eds. *The Western Reader*. New York: Limelight, 1998. Print.
Lax, Eric. *Woody Allen: A Biography*. Cambridge: Da Capo, 2000. Print.
Mendik, Xavier. "*Repo Man*: Reclaiming the Spirit of Punk with Alex Cox." *Punk Cinema*. Ed. Nicholas Rombes. Edinburgh: Edinburgh University Press, 2005: 193–203. Print.
Minton, Gretchen E. "*The Revenger's Tragedy* in 2002: Alex Cox's Punk Apocalypse." *Apocalyptic Shakespeare: Essays on Visions of Chaos and Revelation in Recent*

Film Adaptations. Ed. Melissa Croteau and Carolyn Jess-Cooke. Jefferson, NC: McFarland, 2009: 132–147. Print.

Mandelbaum, Howard, and Gary Morris. "Angel in Exile: Allan Dwan." *Action! Interviews with Directors from Classical Hollywood to Contemporary Iran*. Ed. Gary Morris. London: Anthem, 2009: 3–15. Print.

Paul, William. *Laughing Screaming: Modern Hollywood Horror and Comedy*. New York: Columbia University Press, 1994. Print.

Russell, Lee. "Budd Boetticher." Kitses and Rickman 195–200.

Shail, Andrew, and Robin Stoate. *Back to the Future: BFI Film Classics*. London: Palgrave Macmillan/British Film Institute, 2010. Print.

Sorrento, Matthew. "Writing (and Filming) the Memories: An Interview with Guillermo Arriaga on *The Burning Plain*." *Bright Lights Film Journal* 67 (2010). Web. 31 August 2013. http://brightlightsfilm.com/67/67ivarriaga.php#.Uke7l1OoiVo.

Witschi, Nicolas S. "Detective Fiction." Witschi 380–394.

____, ed. *A Companion to the Literature and Culture of the American West*. Chichester: Wiley-Blackwell, 2011. Print.

Willeman, Paul. "Anthony Mann: Looking at the Male." Kitses and Rickman 209–212.

Wood, Robin. *Hollywood from Vietnam to Reagan ... and Beyond*. New York: Columbia University Press, 1986 (2003). Print.

Wray, Ramona. "*Revengers Tragedy*: Jacobean Drama, Kenneth Branagh's Cinema and the Politics of the Not-Shakespearean." *Shakespeare Bulletin* 29.4 (2011): 543–558. Print.

The Vertical Frontier
Amir Naderi's Vegas *and the End of American Dream After 9/11*

MARCO GROSOLI

In 2001, Lincoln Center in New York City organized a retrospective called "The Films of Amir Naderi and Iranian Cinema: New Directors, New Directions." Its main focus was Amir Naderi, born in 1945, a crucial figure of New Iranian Cinema who emigrated to New York at the end of the 1980s after a dozen motion pictures directed in his homeland, and has lived there ever since, making five others.[1] The retrospective never took place: it started on 10 September, but had to be canceled the next day for obvious reasons.[2]

Such a coincidence would have eventually proved quite fatal. A stubbornly independent, low-budget working filmmaker, Amir Naderi arguably never faced social and political topics in a direct, full frontal way. Yet *Vegas: Based on a True Story*, the film he presented at Venice Film Festival in 2008 (and at the Tribeca Film Festival in New York the following year, among other worldwide venues), has indeed a lot to say about post 9/11 United States, even though this was perhaps not Naderi's intention, or at least not primarily.

Although not a Western movie in the narrow sense, *Vegas* shares many traits with the Western genre. Naderi never mentioned his work belonged to that genre, but he did declare (in an interview with Bilge Ebiri), "I looked at the great American masters to find a style. People like John Ford, George Stevens, Howard Hawks, Raoul Walsh." Notoriously, they all made Westerns, especially the first of the list. Its recourse to the genre that probably more than any other has dealt with the historical roots of American society makes *Vegas* an attempt to question the place of 9/11, as well as of America itself after that attack, inside the broader course of national History.

Echoes of 9/11 are not to be sought exclusively in mainstream films: the American independent, experimental scene bears traces of it as well. The following essay closely analyzes *Vegas* in order to identify to what extent it can be said to unexpectedly rejoin Hollywood's Western tradition, and what this implies in relation to the 9/11 attacks, to which the film quite overtly, albeit marginally, alludes.

A Few Introductory Remarks About *Vegas* and Naderi

Vegas is set in the Nevada city of the same name, and unsurprisingly deals with gambling. Two of the three main characters (husband and wife— the other is their son Mitch, played by Zach Thomas) are former compulsive gamblers. After having lost everything they owned because of it, the Parkers now live a decent but rather poor life. They live in a small house derived somehow from a caravan in the extreme periphery of Las Vegas; approximately where the city finishes and the desert begins. Eddie (Mark Greenfield) works in a used tire store (and occasionally still gambles small sums without telling his wife), while Tracy (Nancy La Scala) is a waitress in a diner. One day, a stranger comes and visits them. He tells them his name is Brian Watson (Walt Turner), a U.S. Army soldier who just came back from Iraq to bury his father, who used to own the house the Parkers now live in. After a while, he makes the puzzled family a shocking proposal: $150,000 for their little home (being patently worth much less than this). They refuse, so he raises (still in vain) the sum to $180,000. Why is that house so important for him? The mystery is soon revealed: a suitcase containing one million dollars is believed to be deep in their yard, buried there by the "Gibson gang" some decades before. Eddie wants to dig their land in order to find it. Tracy is reluctant, but finally lets him do it, as long as he does not touch her flowers or her tomatoes. The metal detector indicates a particular spot the suitcase might be in—but even after a lot of digging, nothing is found. They are about to give in—but after some research in a local library, Tracy finds out that the handle they found under their yard seems to be the actual one of the original Gibson gang's suitcase. So she starts digging again, even more vigorously than her husband. House and yards are soon increasingly, and then almost completely destroyed because of the digging. They even start to employ a power shovel to dig more effectively. But then, an unexpected visit occurs. A detective tells them that they are the victim of a cruel deceit. They are the unaware protagonists of a kind of gambling called *reality gambling*: some people, mostly gathering in the small casino on the opposite side of the road Eddie's house is on, bet on other people doing or not doing certain things for money. The supposed soldier was just someone they hired to get them into destroying their own house for the hope of money. Some bet the Parkers would have done it, some others they would not. However, Eddie does not believe him: obsessive and paranoiac as he now is, he thinks that it is all a stratagem created so that they would stop searching. Exhausted, his wife leaves to live in a motel. The relationship with his son quickly deteriorating, Eddie as well leaves shortly thereafter. Only Mitch remains in the now completely ravaged home, and starts cleaning up the huge mess his parents have made.

Vegas is, like most films by Naderi, a tale of obsession. *Water, Wind and Dust* (1989), the last motion picture he made in Iran, follows a young boy (Majid Niroumand) desperately looking for water in his drought-devastated village. It shows little more than his repetitive efforts, again and again, with an astounding attention to natural settings (it has been almost entirely shot in the desert) and especially to the *rhythm* that his actions and gestures end up composing onscreen: *Water, Wind and Dust* can easily be defined as a visual *symphony,* indicatively culminating with the first notes of Ludwig van Beethoven's Fifth bursting out during the final sequence. A seemingly realistic way of staging soon turns to wild abstraction: "realistic images of the decomposed body of a cow and of a man digging in search of water soon change into surrealistic collages, among them a jar of water containing two red fish dropping to the ground and a watermelon that has been placed on the burning sands of the desert" (Mirbakhtyar 28). *Manhattan by Numbers* (1993), the first film of his American period, stages a very similar search: this time it is George Murphy (John Wojda) who has 24 hours to find the money for his rent. It is the last call: if he fails, he is thrown out of his flat. The desert is now New York City; the streets and places George wanders through are filmed again with impeccable accurateness and precision. Repetitiveness is transformed into rhythm thanks to virtuoso editing. In *Marathon* (2002), montage is much less minimalistic and more furiously quick instead, attempting to suggest the impression of multiple moving objects intersecting in the same place. Once again, the main character (Sara Paul) has only one goal in mind and she is entirely absorbed in this obsessive pursuit: completing 77 crossword puzzles in 24 hours. She says that subway chaos helps her concentrating, so this is where she stays (almost) throughout the film. Naderi here tries to give an order to the chaos infesting the place by composing an impressively refined and neat (albeit intricate) metropolitan symphony mixing together multiple visual and sound sources.

The structure of Naderi's films often consists in one character doing one single thing over and over again (with a significant set of variations stemming from this incessant repetition). As a rule, his characters' monomaniac challenges mirror his own. The conditions of his shootings are more often than not impervious and extreme. In order to hold a flagrant contact with the specific places involved in the story, Naderi has stubbornly filmed in the middle of the desert, in the New York subways at night without any municipal authorization and exposing the production to a consistent risk in terms of security (various materials, camera included, have been stolen in the process), and so on. Naderi is an obsessive perfectionist. He makes films with strenuous independence, total creative control, very little money and plans far in advance: he needs it to exhaust the actors with his impossible requests (by his own admission), to work out every little detail, to polish his cinematography and his editing up to reaching an extraordinarily tidy and exact quality. Naderi is like an artisan intensely focused on the object he is creating, obsessively working on it again and again until the wished-for result is reached.

Vegas is no exception. All he asks of his crew is to endure a full immersion inside the actual situation the film revolves around, in order to depict it more efficiently. Starting from Naderi himself. As he declared in the already mentioned interview by Bilge Ebiri, residing in Las Vegas for some months before was not enough: he had to bet the entire production money ($25,000) at the gambling table—and slowly lose it all. And the whole crew (actors included) had to engage in a 24-hour work experience on location with almost no spare time for six months. Filmmaking as a veritable *idée fixe*.

No More Frontiers

The affectionate portrait of Amir Naderi made by Hamid Dabashi confirms the impression these brief remarks should suggest. Naderi devotes his life entirely to his films, almost like a monk would devote his life entirely to prayer. He is so obsessed with visual perfection that he often tends to isolate himself completely from the rest of the world in order to reach it. "He once saw me on national television (it was PBS) commenting on one thing or another. He called me up and said he liked the color combination of my tie and shirt. This was his way of disapproving of my having anything to do with politics, and ever since I rarely accept television appearances" (Dabashi, "Amir Naderi" 222). The paradox of Naderi's cinema, according to Dabashi, is that *through* this sternly-pursued and strictly aesthetic visual quality something straight-forwardly political often appears:

> One can neither forget his politics nor make it paramount in his cinema. He is first and foremost an aesthetician, and then a metaphysician. He turns reality on to its visual awareness of the sublime, and from there he commences a metaphysical reflection on reality—and yet all in terms characteristic of his visual realism. I am absolutely convinced that Naderi's solitude is by choice, not by accident. He chooses to be a tabula rasa, to reflect the troubled world of his nation, and with his nation the world at large. His politics are apolitical. His art is his politics. Having abandoned the realm of ideology and Utopia, in his cinema Naderi has detected a miraculous take on reality, a visual awareness of its absolutism [223].

The specific way this operates in *Vegas* will be inquired later; for the moment, I want to focus on the two very marginal (but very important) points in the film where something like a direct political reference seems to blink somehow at the viewer.

The first is the Iraqi War. The man that starts the whole hell is a (fake) marine who fought in Iraq. The second is 2008 stock market crash.[3] This latter reference is perhaps a bit more hidden than the former, but hardly questionable. The turning point of the plot regards people who gamble on the fate of *other gamblers*: a definition that could also (relatively, of course) apply to *financial futures speculation*. *Vegas* is by no means the first motion picture to employ casino gambling as a metaphor for financial speculation: suffice it to mention Steven Soderbergh's *Ocean's Eleven, Twelve* and *Thirteen* (2001, 2004 and 2007), not to mention his later *Contagion* (2011). Besides, what happens to the Parkers themselves can recall (even though a bit less poignantly) the subprime loans crisis, since they are compelled to abandon their own household as a result of their wanting more and more without being able to afford it.

The September 11 attacks (along with all that came from it—the Iraqi War included) and world economic crisis ideally frame (although not exactly in a chronological fashion) the first decade of the third millennium. In those years, United States' world leadership has been severely weakened—primarily because of these traumatic events. *Vegas* epitomizes the disorientation characterizing that decade. It is also worth noticing that Eddie, Tracy and Mitch are the unaware protagonists of "reality gambling," which easily relates to *reality television*, probably the single most successful TV format of the 2000s, and without any doubt the most paradigmatic token of the ways television has changed during those years.

These two moments in the film also point at the main connection between *Vegas* and the Western universe: the *frontier*. Ever since Frederick Jackson Turner's famous 1893 speech acknowledging the strong bond between the development of America and the existence of an ever-moving frontier, "the 'end of the West' as a theme, the effective end of the Western as a popular genre, and the end of American supremacy as a historical development seem to be more than coincidentally related" (Countryman 125). Westerns have often and variously been seen as a particularly explicit expression (and a not-so-implicit ideological justification) of America's imperialism, for instance by Patricia Limerick in her *The Legacy of Conquest*. And the soldier coming from Iraq to reclaim the family's attention with unheard-of promises of wealth intertwines America's expansionism and Western genre in both form and content. On the one hand, this apparition perfectly matches the Western stereotype of the mysterious stranger coming from nowhere to haunt the settled community with his ambiguous presence: will he be helpful or harmful?

On the other hand, the direct mention of Iraq unfailingly recalls United States' territorial expansionism—and especially its limits, the dead ends it is made to bang against lately—especially after 9/11. In *Vegas*, a recent, very critical phase of America's persisting effort to enlarge its own influence (The Iraqi War) is mentioned in a directly analogical relation to the false, sterile horizons of hope decisively triggering the plot (the suitcase full of money supposedly lying under the garden). Westerns have often been read as "foundational rituals" (Cawelti 72) through which the original compromise between nature and culture is reaffirmed—meaning also a certain form of legitimation of violence as an active support of civilization. As soon as the United States begins to ruthlessly enlarge their military influence,

> to preserve the self-image, it has been necessary to disguise the aggressive impulses in these historical realities under the mask of moral purity and social redemption through violence. Thus, there has always been an observable similarity between the pattern of justifying rhetoric used to defend American military policy and the Western drama [84].

So *Vegas* is one of the many examples (indirectly) suggesting that this kind of ritualistic legitimation of violence is breaking apart and falling to pieces—certainly in an utterly different fashion from the films testifying a similar social disruption in the 1960s or 1970s. Times change, and so do frontiers and cinematic forms and manners.

Indeed, the military one is not the only frontier in *Vegas* to contravene the promises of wealth and conquest it used to stand for. There is also a *non-territorial* frontier: the financial one, the potentially infinite virtual self-increase of capital through exchange alluded in *Vegas* by the "meta-gambling" (people speculating on other people's speculations) substantiating its narrative denouement. This kind of increase ultimately has limits too, and it is periodically doomed to collapse. As demonstrated by several scholarly works on the subject, this non-territorial, strictly economic frontier is no less related to Western genre. For instance, in his "Cowboys and Free Markets," Stanley Corkin has analyzed the abundant traces of America's postwar effort to export and impose its own economical pattern worldwide in *My Darling Clementine* (Ford, 1946) and *Red River* (Hawks, 1948). And Will Wright (130–153 and 174–190) has analytically described in a structuralist fashion how the gradual shift from the "classical plot" narrative model to the "revenge plot" and "professional plot" ones in postwar Western films mirrors the passage from "market capitalism" to "corporate capitalism" in the U.S. in approximately the same period.[4] With regard to this, *Vegas* seems to (also) point quite clearly at so-called "bubble economy." The little house of the main characters, halfway between the big city and the desert, almost leveled to the ground by their own greed, looks like the extreme point of a schematic historical-economical parable: after the desert has made way for the city (the traditional Western dynamics), and after the city has been abandoned for the suburbs (like in the second part of twentieth century), the suburbia single-family mansion is about to become a desert again.⁵ Ironically enough, an (Iranian) *immigrant*, an enthusiastic pioneer who did go west signs this parable. New York was the New World he had to reach so that his filmmaking could fully blossom. This makes *Vegas*, paradoxically, an *inherent* critique of Westerns rather than one simply coming from a non–American director.⁶

To put it differently, *Vegas* enacts a *vertical* quest. The main characters do not have to go far west anymore to find their fortune: it is underground, right under their feet. They do not have to ride, but to dig. In the film, this quest is placed between the allusion to the horizontal, territorial frontier (Iraq) and the one to the non-territorial (financial speculation). This is what such a structure suggests: a compulsive, *more and more immaterial* search for money (strictly similar to the gambling the Parkers were addicted to) is the obvious continuation of the pioneers' explorations once they have run out of disposable land. Indeed, the couple's vertical search is halfway between the material and the immaterial: on the one hand huge physical efforts are made, but on the other the treasure they are looking for is only imaginary. Now that the actual resources beyond the frontier are gone, along with the frontier itself and more broadly with U.S. hegemony (especially after 9/11), the automatic, obsessive perseverance in that quest and the perverse and self-destructive accumulation of capital only remains. The family's furious (vertical) digging represents America's perseverance in still being itself when it cannot be it anymore, since there is no longer any (horizontal) frontier—and trying to raise quick money through stock market speculation ("gambling") is not one either. Their digging is the prolongation of the logic of the frontier when it is no longer in place. The financial crack appears to be only the extreme consequence of it.

The Garden and the Desert

At this point, the actual analysis of the film can begin. *Vegas* is not so much concerned by plot development or thickness: there are some rare, sparse events which, although coherently concatenated, seem to float amidst emptiness. This rarefaction also indirectly justifies the claim according to which *Vegas* could have to do with Westerns, although it is certainly not one in the narrow sense: no doubt this is not at all a genre movie. This is a film based on just *a few* elements, but *most* of them relate to the Western in a basic, recognizable way. The film is *relatively* rich in Western references.

Naderi "is a visual physicist, and not a storytelling engineer"⁷ (Dabashi, "La New York" 151). What *Vegas* lingers over the most, while narrative solidity and compactness vacate, is *places*. And places in *Vegas* remind us of the most basic Western dichotomy: civilization vs. wilderness. Las Vegas is never shown in the film, except for a number of wide views of its skyline from a very far distance—basically, from Eddie's house. The main characters do not really live in that city: they live at the farthest margins of it, almost at the beginning of the desert. Ideally, their house lies *on* the frontier between wilderness and civilization, between the desert and the city. If one of the most famous and valid definitions of a Western is "a story which takes place on or near a frontier, and consequently, ... generally set at a particular moment in the past" (Cawelti 35), nonetheless this very frontier can rightfully pop up in films set in the present as well, when certain conditions are met. Naderi visually emphasizes this spatial situation from the very beginning, during the first dialogue between husband and wife: an overtly *introductory* moment, one that is supposed to introduce the situation the rest of the movie will be about. It takes place in the passenger compartment of a pick-up: Eddie is driving on the highway, with Tracy. They are talking about their daily efforts to get rid of the addiction to gambling, by betting only five dollars a day. The camera is on the trunk. First, it frames Las Vegas's skyline, on its left. Then it moves a little to the right, until it frames the passenger compartment from the outside (and from behind) straight ahead. After a while, it moves to the right again, to frame the quasi-desert on the other side of the street. Although subdivided and segmented into three "phases," each lasting a few seconds, this pan has no editing cuts, and it underlines that the Parkers' place is *in between* those two radically divergent environments, just like the Western's place is in between civilization and wilderness. Later in the film, there is another shot from the point of view of the trunk, but this time *a pickax* (the infernal tool of destruction) lying over the trunk, framed *from above*. These two shots, from different moments in the film, suggest a spatial dynamic that we have already mentioned: the passage from the horizontal to the vertical.

The binary couple "civilization vs. wilderness" notoriously recalls another one: the garden vs. the desert. According to Henry Nash Smith's notorious formulation,

> The imaginary figure of the wild horseman of the plains would have to be replaced by that of the stout yeoman who had for so long been the protagonist of the myth of the garden. As settlement moved up the valleys of the Platte and the Kansas rivers, the myth of the desert was destroyed and in its stead the myth of the garden of the world was projected out across the plains. The crux of the matter was rainfall, since it was rainfall alone that distinguished the abundantly fertile prairies of eastern Kansas and Iowa from the bleak uplands farther west. The imaginative conquest of the desert accordingly took the form of a proliferation of notions about an increase of rainfall on the plains [179].

According to many (mainly Eastern) opinions from the nineteenth century collected by Smith, the wild desert was something so inhuman that it was thought to *infect* whoever ventured into it. Therefore, the desert had to become a civilized garden. But in order to do so, rain had to fall. A *deeper* contact with nature (than the one mere wilderness could have) had to be found and established, so that rain could fall and the desert could become a garden. The whole Western mythology has relied on this interconnection between the myth of the wildly natural desert and that of the civilized garden. But this is hardly anything new for Naderi, whose last Iranian film (*Water, Wind and Dust*) revolved precisely around man's desperate, delirious, ultimately de-humanizing efforts to force nature into making water finally grace the desert's sand.

In *Vegas*, the house is essentially the garden at the edge of a vast desert. Tracy dedicates all her free time to lovingly care for her garden, her flowers, her tomatoes. "Women are primary symbols of civilization in the Western" (Cawelti 47), and indeed Tracy's role is to keep their household clean, respectable, orderly. She tells her son all the time to put away his bike and not to play football in the living room she tells her husband not to smoke inside and she insists on having dinner at a proper time. Eddie is more on the side of the desert. For him, his own yard is like the desert Land of Opportunities of his ancestors: a place whose resources must be wildly explored and exploited. The hope of reaching wealth justifies the total destruction of his wife's garden. There is no family reconciliation now, unlike in *God's Little Acre* (Mann, 1958),[8] a non–Western film by a director who owed his fame particularly to his Westerns. There, a man (Robert Ryan) was about to entirely ravage his own mansion looking for gold—but his family, at last, managed to make him change his mind. But times change, America changes, and the family in *Vegas* is ravaged even more than their garden, *which has become a desert itself* after it has been completely devastated by a pickax, a shovel, a jackhammer and eventually even an excavator. If, following Cawelti's classic text again (35–37), Western's interplay between civilization and wilderness ultimately reaffirms the control of the former over the latter, here this dialectic is completely upside-down. Soon, the main characters are no more in control of their gambling fever, which quickly takes over: greed wastes everything away. If "it is possible to have Westerns without Indians or outlaws, but not without someone playing the role of savage for the antithesis between townspeople and savagery is the source of the plot" (53), the Indians here are *Eddie and Tracy themselves*. The citizen and the savage here are no more in opposition: they collapse on each other. It is no more (as in classic Westerns) a matter of reaffirming our own identity by harming some Other: now the Other is us and the fury is strictly self-destructive. Individualism (one of the key features of the whole Western universe) is no more traditionally opposed to the community,[9] but stands now *against the individuals themselves.*

In order to properly identify this "collapse of the Western dialectic," it is important to notice that Tracy's moderate ambition to keep the household safe is *not* simply defeated by Eddie's greed. Eddie craves for the money the earliest, but Tracy follows shortly, showing more and more signs of "domestic capitulation," such as giving up cooking (unless with a microwave oven) or telling her husband and son to use Scottex sheets for napkins. Their *common* fall is just another way to represent the dead end the logic of Western genre has come to, the fatal vicious circle between the garden and the desert. In his well-known study, Jim Kitses (24–25) has defined (following especially Northrop Frye) the Western genre as a complex interaction among four elements: history, themes, archetype, icons. As for the second and the third, we have already seen where *Vegas* stands: the most basic element of the genre ("themes") in this film tend to present themselves in its unadorned "nakedness," with very little narrative, melodramatic and/or novelistic "thickening" ("archetype"). As for the fourth, it consists of the moral tones thanks to which even the most contradictory contents of Western narratives shine of a special light and appeal to the viewer as self-justified and incontrovertibly right.[10] Someone else would have used the term "myth," but Kitses maintains that this word is misleading in the case of Westerns. Whatever way one wants to name it, this aspect is dialectically related to the first one in Kitses's definition: history. Ever since Bazin's seminal essay "The Western, or the American Film *Par Excellence*," the relationship between myth and history in this genre has often been seen (although in many different possible ways) as essentially dialectical.

In *Vegas*, Eddie believes Brian thanks to the *emblematic power* of his uniform and of the lies he tells: after having fought for the country, he would like to settle down on the land once owned by his father. Eventually, Tracy is deceived by a photograph in an ancient newspaper found at a local library, attesting that the handle they found in their yard belongs to one of Gibson gang's suitcase. In other words, they are both duped: one from myth, and the other from history. So, in this respect as well, the logic of Western (the one binding together history and myth) finds itself stuck in a vicious circle. Mitch (the child of the concerned couple) represents a possible hope, a vague yet urgent way out of the vicious circle of that logic.

Mitch

Fredric Jameson's *The Political Unconscious* underlines the double-sided nature of cultural texts—that is, ideological and utopian—along with their strong, hard-to-pin-down reciprocity. "Even hegemonic or ruling-class culture and ideology are Utopian, not in spite of their instrumental function to secure and perpetuate class privilege and power, but rather precisely because that function is also in and of itself the affirmation of collective solidarity" (281). More broadly, not only a text manifests at some more or less implicit level the social contradictions it is produced by, but it also might contain some hints pointing somehow at the ideal resolution of these very contradictions.[11] Therefore, "a Marxist practice of ideological analysis proper, must in the practical work of reading and interpretation be exercised simultaneously with a Marxist positive hermeneutic, or a decipherment of the Utopian impulses of these same still ideological cultural texts" (286). Detecting in the tissue of a cultural text some formal contradictions mirroring the contradictions of society is not enough: one must also detect the points within the plies of the text where this "ideological" side is converted into the "utopian" one.

The Man Who Shot Liberty Valance (Ford, 1962) offers a clear example of such a "conversion." At the end of a film that many have read as the ultimate depiction of the contradiction grounding the ideology of Western genre—that is, civilization vs. wilderness—the very last shot shows *a cactus rose*, symbolizing the utopian harmony between what grows in the desert and what (usually) grows in a garden. Very similarly, and perhaps even more explicitly, the very last shot in *Vegas* shows a flowerpot (rescued and hidden by Mitch away from his parents' devastating fury) on the desert. Indeed, *Vegas* not only deals with the dead ends of the Western genre, but also lets the utopian possibility of conciliating the opposites filter through.

Mitch notably embodies this utopian function. *Vegas*'s very first shot is dedicated to him, as if the film was recommending us to pay attention specifically to him, because, although shadowed by his parents' more serious business and misfortunes, *he* is the actual focus of the story. If, as a rule, Westerns start with an extreme long shot of a man (or some men) riding his/their horse(s), on the vast plains or across the mountains, *Vegas* starts with Mitch on his bike, followed by the camera (equally through an extreme long shot) as he rides somewhere between the city and the desert.

He does not really cover an active role in the story. Most of the time, he just stands by the side of his parents, or spies or eavesdrops on them from behind some door or window. In one scene, at night, he gets up, walks to the living room and stares perplexedly at his father, nervously smoking by the yard outside, thinking about whether minding Brian or not. More generally, throughout the film the camera espouses Mitch's point of view: it looks at the family the same detached, emotionless way he does. The camera documents—phase by phase—the terrible degradation of his parents, who basically lose any kind of humanity along their obsessive pursuit,—almost shovel blow by shovel blow—with relentless gradualness and aplomb. Medium shots and semi-pans observe very quietly the unceasing devastation. Mitch himself seems to be very little moved, even when in the end he, alone, takes control of the now totally ruined house, after both his parents leave. Neither happy nor sad, he just keeps on being as tranquil, indifferent and clear-headed as ever. There is one particular shot that seemingly confirms this ideal symbiosis between him and Naderi's camera. Tracy and Eddie talk outside. The camera stares at them from inside the house, through an opened door. After some seconds, Mitch comes and stares at them unseen from aside the door (exactly like the camera short before that).

After a while, Mitch starts silently dissociating himself from his parents' efforts, initially just staying inside the house while they dig, but then more and more decidedly. When the detective comes to tell them that the suitcase story was a lie, Naderi cuts a few times from a large shot of all of them to a close-up of Mitch, showing no particular reaction. These close-ups are as neutral as they can be, not really serving any narrative purpose. They just signal that the boy is *aside* from his parents' doom. It is only *their* business. These close-ups do not really convey any narrative information strictly speaking: through the usual exactness of his staging, Naderi focuses on Mitch just to confirm that the point of view of the film is his. And this apparently neutral point of view turns the whole matter into something different.

Mitch cannot be entirely read as an only-passive presence. After all, he has a key responsibility in his family's fall. He is the one convincing his mother to start digging, while a jubilant Eddie spies on their dialogue from behind the window: one of the several moments in the film the father is depicted as a grown-up child. Initially, Mitch is very happy with the perspective of digging to find the money. So where is the difference from his parents then? The difference is in the spirit of *play*. Mitch does not want to dig out of greed, but as it were a game. When the game turns monomaniac, he is off. What he rejects is the obsessively goal-oriented attitude his parents (and all they symbolically stand for at a broader social-historical level) are stuck on. In other words, what divides him from them is the little, and yet abysmal, difference between *gambling* and *playing*. Indicatively, we see him playing around with the metal detector all over the garden, while his parents keep digging by the spot the suitcase is supposed to be (and Eddie attempts twice, in two different scenes, to prevent his son from using it as it were a toy). The only thing Brian left him is not some precious information to make profit of, but a ball to play with when the house is already half-destroyed. And Naderi lingers lengthily over the *unnecessary, non-finalized* movements of Mitch just riding a bike (an object he cares about more than any other thing *or person*, he says) for the sake of it.

More generally, the parents' obsessive pursuit and the child's playing around are strictly interconnected, although ultimately different, like two sides of the same coin. In other words, the game is the utopian side of the frontier ideology embodied by Eddie and Tracy. It points at a possible, even hopeful way out of the vicious circle they ended up in, by persevering in a historical frame (and, one could even say, in a form of life), by now completely worn out. There are no more frontiers to conquer (nor gardens to be well-kept), but only ruins to play with. Like those in *Germany Year Zero* (Rossellini, 1948) for the little Edmund (Edmund Moeschke)—but now the ruins are America's, hence the ruins of the Western. Barely a character, little more than a vacuous, opaque presence merely standing around (precisely like the child in Rossellini's film), Mitch is, as it were, nothing in itself, but also *nothing more than* the blind spot where his parents' obsession for easy money gets reflected and converted into something (potentially) different. The access to the other, utopian side of ideology.

This is by no means the first time Naderi identifies with a child—so often the main character in his stories. Many accounts on *The Runner* (1985) stressed an overt semi-autobiographical aspect (Mirbakhtyar 123–129). It is about Amiro (Majid Niroumand), "a ten- or twelve-year-old boy who lives alone in an abandoned ship on the coast of the Persian Gulf. To stay alive, he has to run and fight" (123), and do all sorts of small odd jobs. Nonetheless, he strives hard to self-educate. His life is thus extremely harsh—but at the same time, he lives it with an astonishingly *serene levity*, potently underlined by the similar tone assumed by Naderi's camera, which here, more than ever, focuses on *surfaces* (rather than in what one could call the "objective life conditions" of the main character) in search of beautiful, appealing visual shapes. Amiro's life is both very hard and *a game*. And Naderi (in his childhood also an orphan) plays along with his camera, looking for gorgeous, highly stylized cinematic forms. "He is poor below any poverty line, but his simple existence projects a profile of grace and beauty inherent to the material evidence of his own manner and making" (Dabashi, "Amir Naderi" 240).

In fact, according to Cawelti (71–73), the game is part and parcel of the ritual confirmation of the myth the Western genre is based upon. By referring especially to Piaget's famous studies (32), he affirms that through game conflicts are virtually transcended and overcome—and as such its function looks quite akin to that of myth. But if, in traditional Westerns, game and myth are intertwined by virtue of the perpetual confirmation of the basic assumptions of the genre through difference and repetition, in *Vegas* the playful part tends to *split apart* from myth, and to become a value in itself.

This does not mean, of course, that Naderi plays *with* myth. He does not at all play with the by now obsolete surfaces of Western genre. Nothing could be farther from his cinema than the postmodernist "playing with something that used to be (supposedly) taken seriously." Naderi does not and could not share this postmodernist euphoria and lightness, simply because game is to him a very serious matter. As *The Runner* would easily confirm, playing is a matter of life and death, literally a reason to live.

Mitch looks too indifferent to suggest that the total doom of his family and home was something like a "trauma" for him. Anyway, whether these events are felt that way by him or not, his reaction consists in transfiguring the supposedly traumatic events into their image. The only thing Mitch seems to care about and wishes to protect is the cage imprisoning three little birds he keeps in his room. A patently metaphoric transfiguration of the situation of his own family, they are "transitional objects" in pediatrician Donald Winnicott's sense: a sort of imaginary mediation whereby the child manages to face an otherwise intolerable external reality. As such, they are almost as revealing with regard to Naderi's cinema as *The Runner*'s Amiro was: "'There was an outside world,' he [Naderi] once told me, 'that to me was ugly and intolerable. And then there was a world inside my mind, full of movies made and movies waiting to be made, which was beautiful and exciting'" (Dabashi, "Amir Naderi" 250).

Dabashi himself insists that stubbornly focusing on the visual surface of reality is for Naderi (whether he is conscious about it or not) a very *political* reaction to the world. This is all the more significant in *Vegas*, a film facing the genre (Western) that perhaps more than any other demands the conflicts it is based on (say, man vs. nature) to be *visually* represented in a vivid, evident fashion. But while the Western genre tends to subordinate appearances to the *mythic* appeal of the involved elements (Cawelti 39–43), Naderi turns his visual approach *away* from myth, making it a value in its own terms. *This* is the playful utopia that Mitch and Naderi oppose to a collapsing utilitarian civilization (the American one): a formalism not to be intended as a mere aesthetic whim, but rather an active passion for beauty so close to one's living and breathing to be literally a *form of life*.

In other words, it is the *aura* (in Walter Benjamin's terms) of the Western genre that is defused here, to be re-worked in a direction far away from myth, and much closer to ordinary experience.[12] Naderi's camera and editing work shifts the visual dimension away from myth to appear as a very serious game not *with* but *of* life. *Vegas*'s style lies entirely in this "utopian" transfiguration.

Sound should never be forgotten, when dealing with Naderi's cinema. Its role is as important as that of the image. The wind blows abundantly and noisily in most exterior scenes. This is almost all the soundtrack *Vegas* counts on. However, every once in a while (actually quite frequently) another sound can be heard: the strange, dissonant, barely perceptible ring of a wind chime softly whispering. The relationship between these two sounds is very much the one between what has been called here "ideology" and "utopia": the wind chime marimba-like "chords" as an aesthetic transfiguration of the wind noise, while remaining very close to that sound. This little difference corresponds precisely to the shift from ideology to utopia, from contradiction to its utopian resolution. No wonder that the sound which is, by far, the closest to that of the pervasive wind chime in *Vegas* is the repetitive, screeching "eek" noise produced by Eddie's shovel in the penultimate scene of the film, sadly scrubbing on the ground as he walks away from what used to be his home. The collapse of an entire civilization (symbolized by the Parkers' misfortunes), lost in greed, is the quickest way to utopia.

Mise en Scène

Naderi's low budget minimalism is a triumph of cleanliness and precision. The limpid and compositional quality of his shots could hardly go unnoticed. In this film, he especially uses large shots. As always, his way of directing focuses on the sheer, photogenic materiality of places, and on movement. He is not so concerned about directorial choices underlining this or that element pertaining to drama (reactions to lines of dialogues, emotional U-turns and so on), but he is very much concerned about stressing the being-there of things and beings at their most elementarily physical level, and finding for them some kind of order they fit in, either in terms or frame composition and montage. His typical shot (at least here) is probably a large shot focusing on a character from quite a big distance, following his/her movement so precisely that he/she does not seem to move; in other words; he/she tends to occupy always the same place inside the frame, moving along with it. Also, large shots of the yard (arguably the most employed location in the film) are often framed from slightly above the average camera height, so that all the characters could not only enter the frame, but also fully manifest the spatial relationship through which they are connected to their environment. Rhythm is calm; pace is slow.

In his cinema, meanings often tend to be conveyed in purely cinematic terms, by virtue of his way of staging. What strikes the viewer the most is probably the relentless gradualness through which devastation is depicted: shot after shot and scene after scene, each time a new hint of the ongoing increasing degradation is suggested (another flower bed being torn apart; Tracy starting to sleep in the truck rather than in her bed; water refusing to go down the basin tap; Eddie's beard growing longer and longer). Another example: an extreme large shot shows a very small Eddie in a corner of the frame, while the rest of it is overwhelmed by a huge pawn shop building— indicating in a very graphic way Eddie's subordination to gambling and its consequences. In another early shot, Tracy is seen in the lower part of the frame, while a casino is seen in the upper one, more or less one mile ahead, in the far depth of the framed space. A large empty space lies between Tracy and the casino: it is the "frontier" the Parkers have chosen not to cross in order to regain a decent life. This is why, when Tracy moves to the left towards home shortly thereafter, while remaining in approximately the same position inside the (moving) frame, in the upper side of it Mitch at the window can now be seen: his stare towards his mother indicates that the casino-life has been replaced by the responsibility towards him.

Western movies often rely on a similar way to make meaning through composition inside larger shots. Another, even more Western-like token of this is the symmetrical shot/countershot facing (from the camera-closest element to the farthest) Eddie, his family and the house in one shot, and Brian, his car and the casino in the other. It is civilization vs. wilderness again, the settled ones vs. the mysterious cowboy (even if a car replaces the horse).

Regarding the Western dialectic, it is important to notice that there are many recurrent large shots (seemingly "candid" shots) showing people standing by the casino looking towards the camera—that is, towards the Parkers' house (probably they are the "reality gamblers" mentioned by the detective). This makes the filmic space even more *centripetal*; it virtually closes the characters inside their home, implying that any gaze addressing to the outside is sent back to where it came from (by a gaze into the camera), so there is no horizon to stare at, there is no "beyond" out of the main characters' house. In other words: *no more frontier*. Horizontal movement is thus virtually impeded, frustrated, denied.

This means that only the vertical one is left. And indeed, *Vegas* emphasizes a lot the vertical nature of the Parkers' research. If ever there is a fourth main character apart Eddie, Tracy and Mitch, it would certainly be Eddie's pickax. In the film, *more than one hundred and twenty* blows on the ground are seen and heard[13] (sometimes only heard, while the image shows something else). And most of them are not just "background": they are the focus itself of the shot. These blows are often followed closely by the camera, panning from the top-down and from down-top.

More precisely, the film builds up a structure more and more dependent from these blows, and less and less from narration. From minute 36 (when the very first blow hits the ground, much to Tracy's horror) until the end, any possible scheme of narrative progression is given up, and replaced by a systematical alternation of what one might call a "pickax segment" and a "story segment." In the former, we witness a series of blows (sometimes a little less than ten, sometimes more than twenty), either through a large shot depicting the characters digging, or through a much closer one where the camera goes up and down to keep the tool inside the frame at each blow. Or even both kinds in a row. In the latter, a few shots indicate something narratively relevant (for instance, Mitch falling asleep at school out of tiredness).

There are also some transitional shots, in the "pickax segments," in which something narrative is conveyed by the image while we hear the sound of the pickax nearby. It is important to notice that these shots are *never* isolated: they are always part of a consistent series of consecutive pickax shots (either just heard or heard-and-seen) in a "pickax segment." They are never placed within a "story segment." Their nature is, precisely, strictly transitional: they do not affect the distinctness of the two kinds of segment. Consequently, "pickax segments" and "story segments" are all the more the backbone of the structure; as the alternation goes, it gets complicated by various differences. For instance, horizontal movement exceptionally occurs when, during one particular "pickax segment," Tracy takes the clay out of the yard by a wheelbarrow (*all* the other horizontal movements are instead in the "story segments"). Or, in another shot, Eddie's pickax goes up and down in a little corner of a close-up of Tracy staring at him.

In the past, Naderi has made a few movies entirely built on a non-narrative (or only marginally narrative) pattern of difference and repetition of structural elements. *Sound Barrier* (2005) was one of them, perhaps the most extreme. *Vegas* is not. Its structure is a hybrid one. For the first thirty minutes or so, it looks like a narrative movie; the focus is very much on the delicate relationship between the three characters: both parents want to "use" the child in order to impose his/her own idea to his/her husband/wife. But then, after the first blow, the alternation between "pickax segments" and "story segments" begins and goes on until the end, albeit through an intricate system of repetition and difference. And as this alternation goes, Mitch is more and more apart from his father and mother, who are instead more and more "allied" with each other in order to find the money.

Indicatively, the scene containing the very first thirty blows is quite unlike the other ones that follow: it is the only one where the editing alternates among the three characters to show their emotions and reactions about the incipient digging. As such, this scene looks like "a threshold" between *Vegas*'s two "souls": the narrative/intersubjective film and the experimental, pattern-oriented film.

We should consider this "suspension of drama" in direct relation to *gambling*: in gambling, victory is not the result of a clearly definable cause-effect step-by-step chain (in other words: a narrative), but a possibility *always indeterminately open*—and this very non-determination provokes and justifies the (sometimes pathological) compulsion to repeat over and over the attempts to win. By embracing and reproducing his characters' compulsion to repeat (and to gamble) instead of drama, Naderi, one of the most obsessive filmmakers around, sets himself in between obsession and play. More precisely, he shows that obsession can be transfigured into play, just like ideology in utopia, just like a glimpse of playful hope (Mitch) can stem from a family of compulsive gamblers. The perfectionist frenzy of his compulsively repetitive style is a goal-freed, gratuitous, gloriously futile game with structures and patterns, which *forgets about* the standard, structural, dramaturgic needs of storytelling (although it does tell a story, in its own particular way). Notably, the camera documents all that physical and human devastation in a completely cool and uninvolved manner, without any trace of emotion. Repetition becomes an end in itself, a source of pleasure in itself.

In one particular scene, Tracy stares with melancholy at her last flowerpots. Then, she throws one away. Then a second. A third. Then a dozen or so, more and more angrily. She is possessed by obsession, greed, rage. Yet, there is something beautiful in her gestures. A regularity of movements, the harmonious way she moves from the right to the left and back, the gradualness of an imperceptibly accelerating rhythm. It is a matter of *form*. By virtue of his formal work, Naderi plunges into obsession, namely into the obsession for visual perfection and tidiness, up to find himself stuck in the infernal circle of compulsory repetition. But there, he manages to turn it to a quasi-musical harmony, a formal arabesque *never* separated from a sheer, flagrant, down-to-earth realism. It is his way to convert (by subtracting any goal-oriented purposes—including narrative functionality) the ideology of progress and of perpetual increase of capital (the ideology of *frontier*) into a game, the terrible but pleasurable game with one's own life.

Conclusion

The fact that *Vegas* is not a genre movie is an evidence which has no need to be proved. However, saying that it has nothing to do with genre (and with the Western genre in particular) would be too simplistic. There is a strange, negative relation with genre that is not "nothing," and needs to be duly traced.

Undeniably, a film that shows more than 120 pickax blows has more than something to do with repetition. Genres too, in their own way, "are instances of repetition and difference" (Neale 48): a fixed scheme is repeated each time along with a certain difference. And in doing so, countless "shocks" are thrown at the spectator only to make him/her more comfortably capable to reabsorb them by means of the perpetual return of the same (20–25). "Each genre also, therefore, engages and structures differently the two basic subjective mechanisms which any form of the balance involves: the want for the pleasure of the process, and the want for the pleasure of its closure" (26). In *Vegas*, only *the former* applies: we lack the pleasure for the closure (the suitcase is not found), but repetition becomes a pleasure in itself, an exquisitely formal play. Thus, genre is not simply absent from *Vegas*: repetition, i.e., one of genre's most important components, takes a completely different function.

In *Vegas*, there are certainly some "semantic" and "syntactic" elements belonging to the Western. Quite obviously, what the film lacks for Rick Altman's "semantic/syntactic/pragmatic approach" to be suitable here is precisely the pragmatic dimension: *Vegas* does certainly not belong to the kind of commercial cinematic dimension that would establish a "discourse" between producers, audiences, promoters and so on. This "discourse" can be formed and established only through and around the repeated attempts to provide the tokens of the genre (the single films), i.e., to the ritualistic confirmation through difference of the basic assumptions of the myth grounding a certain genre. Of course *Vegas* does not take part in this complex, multifaceted, commercial "rite." But repetition is detoured away from rite and made into the fundamental element of the film.

This "detour" qualifies pretty much *Vegas*'s relationship with the Western. The post 9/11 America depicted in the film is lost, empty, desperately and obsessively attached to an ambitious ideology of perpetual growth and expansion that can no longer be in place. But this very obsession, this very ideology (here embodied by some sparse remnants of the Western genre's *Weltanschauung*), in Naderi's hands can be transformed into something different, a glimpse of hope beyond this bleak impasse. Western traits, by now devoid of any mythic appeal, turn into the elements of a vital, very serious (and, as such, by no means postmodern) *play* with form.

Notes

1. His latest *Cut* (2011), which has been produced and shot in Japan, should also be added.

2. http://filmlinccom.siteprotect.net/archive/wrt/programs/9-2001/iran/iran.htm.

3. Another curious coincidence: *Vegas* premiered at Venice Film Festival in the first days of September 2008, only a few days before the explosion of the financial crisis.

4. At any rate, we should also mind Tag Gallagher's objection to Wright's argument: this kind of mirroring by no means applies exclusively to the postwar years. As early as 1913, and even before, "any news event or fashion trend—labor actions, bloomers, Apaches, prohibition, female suffrage, Balkan crises, and a myriad of forgotten issues of the day—were zealously incorporated not only into Westerns but into whatever other genres were currently popular, the Western hero and the nature of his struggles altering accordingly" (Gallagher 266).

5. Just a few months before *Vegas*' Venetian premiere, Steven Spielberg showed an apocalyptic atomic explosion devastating a very typically American suburbia in his *Indiana Jones and the Kingdom of the Crystal Skull* (2008), arguably with very similar sociological implications regarding the contemporary age.

6. National identity does not really seem to be the point here. Naderi never came back to his homeland, and he often declares that he does not want to. As a rule, when interviewed, Naderi never shows much attachment to either the Iranian or the American identities. He feels like a New Yorker but, as far as what he says, nothing more than this.

7. My translation.
8. I owe this remark to Maurizio Buquicchio, whom I thank.
9. More precisely, the community is left out of the film (focusing on a single family), until the moment it is revealed to be staring from the beginning at the unaware main characters. Hence, this is yet another Western dichotomy (individual vs. community) popping up from a film seemingly having nothing to do with "genre movies."
10. With regard to this, it is indicative that the suitcase under their garden is supposed to belong to a band of gangsters, the Gibson gang. As Robert Warshow demonstrated in a very famous essay ("The Westerner"), gangster movies are the specular reversal of Westerns, so this little detail appears to be a "reverse" symptom of the film's affinity with Western. What both genres have in common is a hero secluded from society, who relies on violence to achieve success. What differs is especially *how* they do this. Nonetheless, they still have in common the importance of *style* as such: it is style (corresponding more broadly to what Kitses called "icon"), the way he gloriously appears, that provides an implicit justification for the way both the gangster and the Westerner are.
11. Jameson's stance overtly relies on one of the most famous definition of myth given by Claude Lévi-Strauss: an imaginary solution of a real contradiction.
12. Walter Benjamin's work gave birth to a number of discording interpretations. Hence, referring to Benjamin is always an ambiguous move: *which* (or *whose*) Benjamin is at stake here? As far as this "reworking" of the visual appeal ("aura") of myth towards a more general, common and participated re-appropriation of the appearances is concerned, I refer especially to Bruno Tackels's *L'Œuvre d'art à l'époque de W. Benjamin*.
13. It is not possible to provide the exact number of the blows because for some of them there are some technical doubts as to whether they can be counted in. At any rate, the total is very unlikely to be under 120.

Works Cited

Altman, Rick. *Film/Genre*. London: British Film Institute, 1999. Print.
Bazin, André. "The Western, or the American Film *Par Excellence*." *What Is Cinema?* Vol. 2. Ed. and trans. Hugh Gray. Berkeley: University of California Press, 1971. 140–148. Print.
Cawelti, John. *The Six-Gun Mystique*. Bowling Green: Bowling Green University Popular Press, 1971. Print.
Contagion. Dir. Steven Soderbergh. Perf. Matt Damon, Gwineth Paltrow, Jude Law, Lawrence Fishburne, Kate Winslet. Warner Bros., 2011. Film.
Corkin, Stanley. "Cowboys and Free Markets: Post-World War II Westerns and the U.S. Hegemony." *Cinema Journal* 39.3 (2000): 66–91. Print.
Countryman, Edward. "Frontier." *The BFI Companion to the Western*. Ed. Edward Buscombe. London: British Film Institute, 1993. 124–125. Print.
Cut. Dir. Amir Naderi. Tokyo Story/Bitters End/cut, 2011. Film.
Dabashi, Hamid. "Amir Naderi: The Runner." *Masters & Masterpieces of Iranian Cinema*. Waldorf: Mage Publishers, 2007. 221–250. Print.
_____. "La New York di Amir Naderi." *Il vento e la città: il cinema di Amir Naderi*. Ed. Massimo Causo and Grazia Paganelli. Milano: Il Castoro, 2006. 133–154. Print.
Ebiri, Bilge. "*Vegas: Based on a True Story*: Director Amir Naderi on Gambling Away His Budget." *New York Magazine*. New York Media, 1 May 2009. Web. 1 October

2011. http://nymag.com/daily/entertainment/2009/05/vegas_based_on_a_true_story_di.html.
Gallagher, Tag. "Shoot-Out at the Genre Corral: Problems in the 'Evolution' of the Western." *Film Genre Reader 3*. Ed. Barry Keith Grant. Austin: University of Texas Press, 2003. 262–275. Print.
Germany Year Zero. Dir. Roberto Rossellini. Salvo D'Angelo/Tevere Film, 1948. Film.
God's Little Acre. Dir. Anthony Mann. Perf. Robert Ryan, Aldo Ray. United Artists, 1958.
Kitses, Jim. *Horizons West. Anthony Mann, Budd Boetticher, Sam Peckinpah: Studies of Authorship Within the Western*. London: Thames and Hudson and the British Film Institute, 1969. Print.
Jameson, Fredric. *The Political Unconscious*. Ithaca: Cornell University Press, 1981. Print.
Limerick, Patricia. *The Legacy of Conquest: The Unbroken Past of the American West*. London: Norton, 1987. Print.
The Man Who Shot Liberty Valance. Dir. John Ford. Perf. John Wayne, James Stewart, Vera Miles, Lee Marvin. Paramount, 1962.
Manhattan by Numbers. Dir. Amir Naderi. International Film and Video Center/Pardis/Rising Star Productions, 1993.
Marathon. Dir. Amir Naderi. Alphaville Productions, 2002. Film.
Mirbakhtyar, Shayla. *Iranian cinema and the Islamic Revolution*. Jefferson: McFarland, 2006. Print.
My Darling Clementine. Dir. John Ford. Perf. Henry Fonda, Victor Mature. 20th Century Fox, 1946.
Neale, Stephen. *Genre*. London: British Film Institute, 1980. Print.
Ocean's Eleven. Dir. Steven Soderbergh. Perf. George Clooney, Brad Pitt, Matt Damon, Andy Garcia. Warner Bros., 2001.
Ocean's Twelve. Dir. Steven Soderbergh. Perf. George Clooney, Brad Pitt, Matt Damon, Andy Garcia. Warner Bros., 2004.
Ocean's Thirteen. Dir. Steven Soderbergh. Perf. George Clooney, Brad Pitt, Matt Damon, Andy Garcia. Warner Bros., 2007.
Red River. Dir. Howard Hawks. Perf. John Wayne, Montgomery Clift, Walter Brennan. United Artists, 1948.
The Runner [Davandeh]. Dir. Amir Naderi. Studio of the Voice and Portrait of the Islamic Revolution of Iran, 1985.
Smith, Henry Nash. *Virgin Land. The American West as Symbol and Myth*. Cambridge: Harvard University Press, 1970.
Sound Barrier. Dir. Amir Naderi. Alphaville Films, 2005.
Tackels, Bruno. *L'oeuvre d'art à l'époque de W. Benjamin. Histoire d'aura*. Paris: L'Harmattan, 2000. Print.
Warshow, Robert. "The Westerner." *Film: An Anthology*. Ed. Daniel Talbot. Berkeley: University of California, 1969. 148–162. Print.
Water, Wind and Dust [Aab, baad, khaak]. Dir. Amir Naderi. Islamic Republic of Iran Broadcasting Channel, 1989.
Wright, Will. *Six Guns and Society: A Structural Study of the Western*. Berkeley: University of California, 1975. Print.

Epilogue—New Visions / New Vistas
Christopher Nolan's Batman *Trilogy* and the New Western

Scott F. Stoddart

In examining the Western, David Lusted links its history with the evolution of the film industry, comparing the genre to something akin to comfort food for contemporary audiences—it's a story form that the industry returns to at a time of crisis or self-doubt. He believes the Western "diminishes" and falls "out of favor" at times when "history is largely settled" (6); he finds that it resurfaces in times of national crisis. At the time that he wrote his introduction in 1999, the Western had experienced one of these lulls, becoming, in some estimations, similar to "the British heritage film" (6), a way for America to experience its once glorious dominance in the global sphere.

As *The New Western* proves, revisiting this truly American form within the context of 9/11 offers a new point of reflection. The Western not only regained serious popularity during the past years since 9/11, but has resurfaced in newly vibrant ways with directors revisiting older films and reshaping them with more violent undertones, including, James Mangold's *3:10 to Yuma* and the Coen brothers' *True Grit* (both discussed in this volume). Furthermore, the mythology of its central figure, the cowboy—on film with the Coen brothers' Oscar-winning *No Country for Old Men* or on television through *Deadwood* or *Justified*—with its anti-heroes and nerve-wracking attention to violence, seemed to re-invent the genre all on its own. And as this book has shown, the Western blended with other generic forms to contemplate the state of the world reaching to outer space (Cameron's *Avatar*; Whedon's *Firefly* and *Serenity*).

Therefore, it appears most fitting to end a collection examining this

Poster for *The Dark Knight*. A Warner Bros. Entertainment release with Legendary Pictures and Syncopy, Inc., directed by Christopher Nolan, 2008.

newly re-conceived version of a Hollywood staple with a dissection of Christopher Nolan's Batman Trilogy (2005–2012) because its apocalyptic take on the Caped Crusader is steeped in the tropes of the Western, and awash in the anxieties facing America in the aftermath of 9/11. Radically different in tone from Batman's first filmic incarnation, Leslie Martinson's 1966 camp riot, and dramatically separate from the four films of the 1990s directed by Tim Burton and Joel Schumacher, Nolan's Batman Trilogy employs the generic undertones of the Western to radically rethink the mythology of Batman and his fight to save America against the unthinkable.

Batman Begins

The Western imaginary revolves around two broad concepts, space and its relation to the hero—a hero whose purpose appears to be preserving said space from whatever antagonism thwarts its interests. In re-conceiving Batman for the post 9/11 age, Nolan uses this basic ideology to ground Batman's journey from disillusioned orphan to responsible hero. "He's a mythic figure, rather than just a conventional action protagonist ... you're having to deal with somebody wrestling with issues that it seems important to wrestle with" (ix). While no one would mistake Nolan's vision of Gotham City for Ford's Monument Valley, the city becomes the territory fought over, and the various villains seek to corrupt "the soul" of its people. Gotham is the site of much pain for Wayne, but it is also the center of his existence, as pointed out by his father, in a flashback that explains his solitary state in the film's present. While riding downtown aboard a newly constructed monorail, Thomas Wayne (Linus Roache), Bruce's father, explains, "Gotham's been good to our family ... but now the city's suffering. People less fortunate than us are enduring very hard times ... so ... we built a new, cheap public transportation system to unite the city ... and at the center.... Wayne Tower" (14). The city, in essence, is Bruce's legacy—the only real community the orphan knows once his parents are murdered. In each of the Dark Knight films, Batman finds himself rescuing the very city that he hates and loves, defending the territory against villains who seek to possess it and destroy its ideological foundations, to create a new territory based in their own twisted traditions.

In establishing a foundation for this new re-birthing of the Caped Crusader, Nolan used the Western to add an American dimension to his Dark Knight. *The Searchers* offers a solid basis of comparison because the character of Ethan Edwards (John Wayne) becomes the iconic vigilante in a manner similar to Nolan's Bruce Wayne (Christian Bale). Ford opens his film not only with establishing shots of Monument Valley, but by placing Ethan within the context of an American family—Ethan's brother, Aaron (Walter Coy), his nieces Lucy

(Pippa Scott) and Debbie (Natalie Wood), a nephew, Ben (Robert Lyden) and the beloved Martha (Dorothy Edwards)—who chose the promisingly practical brother Aaron over the individualist Ethan. As outlined by Edward Buscombe, "It's a film about family, as many of Ford's films are" (18), and while the opening sequence might seem long in its detail—reuniting the family after the Civil War, preparing for the evening meal, stolen kisses between now lovelorn Ethan and Martha—Ford's method establishes the domestic tranquility and sophistication missing from Ethan's life—a life that his spirited wanderlust prevents him from readily admitting he desires.

In *Batman Begins* (2005), Bruce Wayne grows "step-by-step ... from an orphaned child to a man with a hole in his heart, to eventually become this mythic figure" (ix)—a misguided youth who returns to Gotham City—his domestic space—to only discover how much the shattered city is a part of him. We witness the seminal moment that prepares us for Wayne's transformation into the classic frontier loner: His fall down an abandoned well, causing him to be frightened by a bevvy of bats, ultimately rescued by his doting father and Alfred Pennyworth (Michael Caine), the family's trusted servant. This glimpse into Bruce's bucolic beginning is similar in nature to *The Searchers*' opening as it establishes the family ties that mold the psyche of the central figure—a life that promises a version of the American Dream resplendent with familial wealth.

However, violence intrudes on both films and destroys the promise of heteronormative homogeneity. Ford orchestrates his violence off screen, Ethan returning to his familial homestead to find his family murdered, their home burned, and the youngest niece Debby abducted by Comanches, headed by Scar (Henry Brandon)—whose blue eyes and linguistic acumen with English make him a mirror image, of sorts, for Ethan. Nolan allows us to witness Bruce's jolt into adulthood when his concerned parents leave a production of Boito's *Mefistofele* at the Gotham Opera House with him via a back exit, causing them to be shot in an abandoned alley by a petty thief. In robbing the Waynes of their jewels and their lives, the thief leaves the young Bruce orphaned to fend for himself in this violent world, setting him on a course of discovery that fuels the trilogy. Guilt is the central motivator in both films. Ethan secretly lusts for his brother's wife—his former sweetheart further idolatrized after her death during the Indian rampage; his guilt fuels his vengeance. The staging of the opera's winged demons is what causes the young Bruce to ask his parents to leave the opera; similarly, he finds himself ravaged by grief—believing his fear caused his parents' deaths. With these acts of violence against the family, both Ford and Nolan create missions of vengeance for their heroes, guilt justifying, in essence, the vigilante spirit. Each protagonist alone—except for a lone confidante—seeks revenge in their effort to re-establish the order wrested away from them by antagonists that create chaos.

Ethan's mission takes him roughly seven years as he follows Scar's trail in order to "rescue" Debby, the lone survivor of the Edwards family. Given Ethan's singular mission, his vengeance replaces the romance he once thought might be his, and his quest to rescue Debby by killing her—now that she has certainly been possessed by her Native American captors—makes his journey all the more powerful. Ford's film, taking its lead from the newly emerging field of psychology in the 1950s, makes for a multi-dimensional protagonist—Ethan is not the "good" cowboy of older Westerns; instead, he is complicated by his racism which takes the form of a maniacal misogyny, despite the protestations of Martin Pawley (Jeffrey Hunter), Lucy's fiancée, who just so happens to be one-eighth Indian. Martin slowly becomes a conscience for Ethan, and his actions—it is he who eventually kills Scar, in return for raping and murdering Lucy—leave Ethan clean—able to embrace Debby and return her to the Jorgensens—an immigrant family who now takes up the mantle of being her new American family of the plains.

In a similar manner, Alfred Pennyworth emerges as Bruce's conscience, reminding the young Bruce that his family name is synonymous with Gotham's good fortunes, and tied to its future. For instance, when the petulant Bruce returns from Princeton set on avenging his parents by shooting their murderer upon his release from prison, Alfred steps in to remind his master of what is important:

> This house, *Master Wayne*, has sheltered six generations of the Wayne family.... I give a damn, sir, because a good man once made me responsible for what was most precious to him in the whole world.... I don't presume to tell you what to do with the past, sir. Just know that here are those of us who care what you do with your future [24–25].

Upon Bruce's return from his travels abroad, Alfred reminds his young master that he will never "give up" on him, mainly because Alfred feels secure in the notion that Bruce *is* Gotham, just as the Wayne legacy represents the very soul of the frontier.

Wayne's own seven-year journey removes him from Gotham, taking him to Himalayas where Ducard (Liam Neeson), an emissary for Ra's Al Ghul (Ken Watanabe) and his League of Shadows releases him from an Asian prison to turn his anger into something more productive: "You have learned to bury your guilt with anger. I will teach you to confront it. And to face the truth" (19). Just as Ethan uses his vengeance to fuel his journey, Bruce learns to channel his anger to the League's ends, particularly after Ghul assigns his mission: "Gotham's time has come. Like Constantinople or Rome before it ... the city has become a breeding ground for suffering and injustice ... it is beyond saving and must be allowed to die" (40). Neither Bruce nor Ethan feels the deep pull of home until it has been threatened, and Bruce strikes back just as Ethan does—destroying Ghul and his headquarters, returning to Gotham and his familial empire to restore order.

Bruce returns to a corrupt Gotham, run by a powerful mob presence overseen by Carmine Falcone (Tom Wilkinson), who is quickly usurped by Dr. Jonathan Crane (Cillian Murphy) who moonlights as The Scarecrow, a villainous emissary of Ducard's. Just as Scar's terror causes Ethan's id to surface, Scarecrow's toxic mask releases a "weaponized hallucinogen, administered in aerosol form" (88) that paralyzes its victims with their inner most fears. The weapon's use on Batman forces Wayne to take Alfred into his confidence, in addition to Lucius Fox (Morgan Freeman), to assist the millionaire vigilante to take on Scarecrow. Alfred becomes Bruce's conscience, as much as Martin becomes Ethan's—it is Alfred's reserved love for the Wayne family that causes him to devote himself to "Master Bruce," ensuring that the crusader's myopic vigilance is always focused on the good. In this brand of Western, villains and sidekicks take on more complex roles; rather than simply destroying civilization—the villain becomes representative of the hero's inner struggle with their instinctive ideology; they mirror the inner lives of the protagonist who has to set aside personal pain to restore the greater good. In this light, the sidekick becomes central to retaining the audience's empathy for the protagonist, keeping them on the path to the greater good.

In preserving the democratic way of life in epic showdowns—Ethan by fighting off another Comanche attack and rescuing Debby; Batman by thwarting Ducard's final efforts to destroy Gotham through its mass transit system—each protagonist adheres to the primary goal of the Western, restoring law and order to the territory. Douglas Pye, in his *The Movie Book of the Western* (1990) posits four closures for the conventional Western "which express the possibilities for the Western hero: the hero rides off, dies, or forms a couple who then ride off together or remain in the community" (33). However, *The Searchers* poses an option that has been written about by scholars ad infinitum, and it's a closure that Nolan employs for *Batman Begins*. As composed by Ford,

> looking from the dark interior of the house we see Ethan approach, carrying Debbie. He sets her down in front of the Jorgensens, who take her inside. Ethan looks to join them, but as he moves forward, Marty and Laurie come from behind him. He moves aside to let them pass into the house. Then he stands on the porch, feet astride.... He turns and walks straight out into the desert. The door closes on him [Buscombe 65].

As read by David Lusted, "the final image of *The Searchers* pre-empts the tragic irony of heroism in the elegiac Western—the hero is not just alone, but unwanted and unnecessary" (209).

Nolan ends *Batman Begins* with a seeming nod to the ending of *The Searchers*, Bruce and Rachel (Katie Holmes) discussing the newly saved

Gotham amidst the burned rubble of Wayne Manor, destroyed in an effort to save the city. Rather than setting off the torturous journey, this ruined home sets the stage for pushing past the pain to establish a new order—one that will honor the family, and reconstitute the value of the established order. However, the calm is fleeting, as the final scene echoes the end of *The Searchers*. Even though Commissioner Gordon (Gary Oldman) shows Batman evidence of a new threat (setting the stage for the sequel), the final image is of the lone warrior perched atop the spires of Gotham, the camera circling the crusader in an effort to set him apart from his fellow man. In saving Gotham, Batman helps the disillusioned Wayne to become socially responsible, isolating him as the only hope against the forces that will continue to threaten humanity—an ominous parallel to the American conscience in the aftermath of 9/11.

The Dark Knight

With *The Dark Knight* (2008), Nolan set his newly re-envisioned protagonist against another threat to Gotham in the guise of The Joker (Heath Ledger). While some critics read the second film as a response to the global war on terror, Nolan believes it is simpler:

> The Joker's an anarchist; a completely different mindset. He lacked a plan, which energized the question of, "Well, what's he going to do? Why's he going to do it? Does he have a plan? Does he not have a plan?" That's really the crux of the character throughout, in terms of his backstory, in terms of what he wants, right up until he moment he burns that pile of money. And even after that, you still think, "Is there a method or is there just madness?" [xiii–xiv].

With this reading, it is easier to see how *The Dark Knight* takes on the Western's patina as it puts Bruce Wayne/Batman, now a politically active member of Gotham society and confidante to Commissioner Gordon, against the uncontrolled villainy of The Joker, a corrupt force of unexplainable evil.

In *Batman Begins*, the criminal terrorism brought on by mastermind Ducard/Rah-al Ghul—an obvious nod to Al Qaeda—represented an almost invisible terrorist threat, the citizens of Gotham never fully aware of who or what was attacking their way of life. However, in using The Joker in *The Dark Knight*, Nolan moves from tropes embodied in *The Searchers* to more generic tropes that concern the outlaw. The Joker is no abstraction like Scar. Instead, he is a full-blown personality whose psychosis is bent toward random annihilation. Therefore, Batman's struggle for Gotham in taking on The Joker becomes more personal; the villain's outrageous antics make Batman's routine vigilantism secondary, as The Joker's reign of terror becomes a test for the purity of Gotham's soul. Each front that The Joker takes on, starting with

Gotham's criminal world, moving gradually through its commercial and political enterprises, ending with a city-wide morality lesson, tests the soul of this civilization. It takes the lone pioneer who has removed himself from the day-to-day operations of the city to gain the perspective necessary to combat this brand of outlaw.

The outlaw is one whose actions set themselves "outside" the parameters of the law, the guiding force of civil behavior. In the Western, it has taken the form of an antagonist who constantly disrupts the action of a story, complicating the progress of the main protagonist, whose central goal becomes restoring order to the newly civilized territory. In the form of one man, as opposed to the more abstract embodiment of outlaw, such as *The Searchers'* Comanches, the Western becomes more psychological, pitting the man of the law against the man outside the law in a moral struggle. It is this trope that Nolan developed in his screenplay for *The Dark Knight*, "It's The Joker's film for so much of the movie because he's an electric sort of presence" (xvi), and developing the outlaw in such an open-ended manner heightens the terror that he brings to the city. "It's a very genuine thing to have suffered in that way and see him [Batman] trying to pull himself out of that and do something for the good" (xvi). Being the haunted protagonist aligns Batman, once more, with the loner frontiersman who wants to strike out on his own to find his own moral perfection yet ends up remaining with civilization to serve the greater human good.

In his assault against Gotham, the Joker takes no prisoners, acting alone against crime lords and upstanding citizens alike. He robs the mob of their funds; disrupts a Harvey Dent (Aaron Eckhart) fundraiser and blows up Gotham General; murdering Rachel Dawes (Maggie Gyllenhaal), Bruce's oldest friend and love object. What makes the struggle frightening is that there appears to be no logic to The Joker's assault on the territory. However, while he claims to be a "man with no plan," his manic brand of anarchy does reveal a logic. The Joker does not simply want money—he desires the soul of the city. And corrupting Gotham's leaders, the foundation of its civil system, allows him to rule the city through panic—a form of outlaw—a spiritual terrorist who uses fear to rot the soul as it breeds mayhem.

Of course, The Joker's sense of humor is part of what makes for the electric performance. Like most outlaws, he has a sense of self-deprecation that makes for memorable one-liners, revealing his wry sense of humor—the most disturbing aspect of his personality—because it resonates with the spectator. For instance, while being interrogated by Harvey Dent, The Joker admits, "Do I look like a guy with a plan, Harvey? I don't have a plan … the mob has plans, the cops have plans. You know what I am, Harvey? I'm a dog chasing cars…. I wouldn't know what to do with one if I caught it. I just *do* things" (286). Of course, by admitting he has no plans, The Joker reveals he, in fact, has a master plan. Just like the outlaws of the West, The Joker wants to rule the territory on his terms. In explaining his reasons for killing Rachel, The Joker reveals his simple philosophy to the anguished Dent:

> It's the schemers who put you where you are. You were a schemer. You had plans. Look where it got you. I just did what I do best—I took your plan, and I turned it on itself. Look what I've done for this city with a few drums of gas and a couple of bullets. Nobody panics when the *expected* people get killed. Nobody panics when things go according to plan, even if the plan is horrifying. If I tell the press tomorrow a gangbanger will get shot, or a truckload of soldiers will be blown up, nobody panics. Because it is all part of the plan. But when I say that one little old mayor will die, everybody loses their minds! Introduce a little anarchy, you upset the established order and everything becomes chaos. I'm an agent of chaos. And you know the thing about chaos, Harvey? It's fair [287].

Again, The Joker's seemingly random thoughts reveal a super-structure that is slowly strangling the community of Gotham, and controlling it through terror. The Joker wreaks havoc in a manner similar to the outlaw's use of terrorist tactics to wrest civility from nobility.

Another way that The Joker takes on the guise of a Western outlaw is through his inescapable bond with the lawman—exemplifying the societal id, the outlaw's philosophy articulating what is held in check by the lawful protagonist. In the film's version of a showdown, The Joker admits as much when Batman interrogates him:

> THE JOKER: Those mob fools want you gone so they can get back to the way things were. But I know the truth—there's no going back. You've changed things. Forever.
> BATMAN: Then why do you want to kill me?
> The Joker: Kill you? I don't want to kill you. What would I do without you? Go back to ripping off mob dealers? No, *you*.... You. Complete. Me.
> BATMAN: You're garbage who kills for money.
> THE JOKER: Don't talk like one of them—you're not, even if you'd like to be. To them you're a freak like me ... they just *need* you right now. But as soon as they don't they'll cast you out like a leper. Their morals, their code ... it's a bad joke. Dropped at the first sign of trouble. They're only as good as the world *allows* them to be. You'll see—I'll show you ... when the chips are down, these civilized people ... they'll *eat each other*. See, I'm no monster.... I'm just ahead of the curve [262].

The Joker's language here is crucial, as it details how the outlaw/criminal mind ingratiates itself with the mind of the law/hero. The Joker knows Batman is another form of vigilante—understood as an outlaw himself because of his unorthodox methods. However, while *Batman Begins* focuses on Batman's vigilante birth, *The Dark Knight* emphasizes Batman's struggle to remain an individual (in the Western sense—free of societal responsibility) and a doer of good (in his efforts to stop The Joker). But The Joker's point is a valid one: as we saw with *The Searchers*, there is no room in the heteronormative world for vigilante activity—no matter how "good" the hero might be. Being "ahead of the curve" proves The Joker's prescience, as his final scheme makes Batman a true outlaw.

In his penultimate display of criminality, The Joker plays maniacal ethics professor with "a social experiment" involving two boatloads of Gothamites, one carrying an ordinary set of refined, hard-working commuters trying simply to get home; the other with a cargo of inmates from Arkham Asylum. Both ferries are outfitted with the means for destroying the other. This test of who will perpetrate violence on one another—the privileged citizenry or the savage criminals—not only questions the role of violence in a post 9/11 world hungry for revenge, but it mirrors the plight of the lone Western hero, solitary in his fight to preserve the dignity of the newly tamed West. In order to track The Joker, Batman leads Lucius Fox into a moral quandary with the harnessing of a sonar concept (used earlier in the film) to log on to every cell phone in the city to triangulate The Joker's position once he uses a phone. While the morally horrified Lucius reluctantly agrees to assist, The Joker continues to taunt the bridge-and-tunnel crowd to detonate the other ship. What The Joker plays off of here is the fear that manifests itself in revenge—which group will hurt the other first. Like most outlaws, The Joker puts his faith in humanity—certainly the commuters will argue that the men from the Asylum have had their chance with society; the inmates, having no moral judgment, will simply detonate the other ship. However, his faith is misplaced, because the inmates toss the detonator out the window, and the commuters, try as they might, cannot fathom the courage to destroy the others.

However, one aspect of The Joker's overall scheme come to fruition—in murdering Rachel, he unleashes a monster in Harvey Dent, who seeks revenge of his own against Commissioner Gordon. Just as Batman apprehends The Joker, he must contend with the grossly disfigured Dent, who now raves in a maniacal manner since losing his bride-to-be. When Dent threatens to kill Gordon's young son, Batman takes him down, killing the former D. A. hero in an effort to save the Gordons. What resonates is Batman's actions after Dent plunges to his death—he exits the film by taking on the costume of vigilante criminal, allowing Dent to be seen as the hero who saved the Gordons from Batman. His reasons are simple: If Harvey, destroyed by madness, is viewed as a criminal, and does not maintain the patina of a hero, then The Joker wins. Gordon agrees:

> Harvey's prosecutions, everything he fought for, everything Rachel died for. Undone. Whatever chance Gotham had of fixing itself—whatever chance you gave us of fixing our city—dies with Harvey's reputation. We bet it all on him. The Joker took the best of us and tore him down. People will lose all hope [320].

Batman fixes this by relinquishing his claim to heroism, and donning the cloak of the criminal: "You either die a hero or live long enough to see yourself become the villain. I can do those things because I'm not a hero, like Dent. *I* killed those people. That's what I can be" (321). In telling Gordon and his son this, and by leaving in a blaze of inter-cutting that involves Alfred, Lucius, police and reporters, Batman lights out for the territory—in essence, leaving the front door of civilization open as he exits, to exist as "the hero that Gotham deserves ... but not the one it needs right now" (323). A dark knight who must exit the civilized world because "sometimes the people deserve more" (322), meaning that they need their mythologies in the civilized world so as to cope with the extraordinary pressures that terrorism—in whatever form—brings. Like Ethan, Batman understands there is no place for him in this Gotham; only when the wounds caused by The Joker's murderous rampage heal can the Dark Knight return to become a part of the culture, but not before.

The Dark Knight Rises

The final installment of the trilogy, *The Dark Knight Rises* (2012), colors my reading further by laying an extra-textual layer onto its Western terrain. On the night that the film opened, 20 July 2012, James Eagan Holmes, a local resident of Aurora, Colorado, dressed in tactical clothing, and armed with assault arms and tear gas, opened fire in a movie theatre, killing 12 and injuring 70. Holmes has never offered any explanation as to why he chose *The Dark Knight Rises* for his random act of violence, but his decision to dye his hair a shade of green triggered in some thoughts of The Joker. Whatever the motives for orchestrating this random act of terror, the incident triggers an uncomfortable recognition in how palpable our American mythologies can be for the individual.

The Dark Knight Rises opens with its own act of terror, a dazzling midair skyjacking of a CIA plane by Bane (Tom Hardy), a new enemy of Gotham. Much the opposite of The Joker, Bane is an outlaw *with* a simple plan—to make an apocalyptic example of Gotham, which to him represents a city rotting from within. The struggle for Bruce Wayne/Batman is that he does not totally disagree. Wayne is disillusioned by the world since The Joker's rampage eight years before that took the life of his beloved Rachel, and Gotham suffers from a crippling depression brought on by the death of Harvey Dent, supposedly at the hands of The Batman. Bane, with the covert assistance of Miranda Tate/Talia (Marion Cotillard) wages a revolution within Gotham, perpetrating "the willing surrender of power, the fracturing of the paradigm by which power would matter and changing it to something else" (xiv–xv). On the surface, *The Dark Knight Rises* does not seem to follow the Western, seeming more like an apocalyptic adventure. However, in creating a sham revolution to enlist the common man to destroy the city, the civilized center law and order controls, Bane uses the lies created by the patriarchy to shift the allegiance of Gotham's citizenry, creating an army that seeks a new territory. In true outlaw fashion, his own plan is much more heinous, placing the essence of Gotham at risk.

Many of the events that take place in this film appear to have been birthed in the pages of recent newspapers; however, Nolan, returning to the mythologies that fueled his desire to re-tell The Dark Knight's tale, refutes this idea. For instance, with Bane's assault on Gotham's financial district, which disarms the greedy capitalists who have exploited the less fortunate, the film appears to shift to providing commentary on the collapse of Lehman Brothers and the "Occupy Wall Street" movement, which brought the fragility of America's economic system to the forefront. But reading this from the vantage point of the Western, Bane's actions—the outlaw riding into town, disrupting the once wild territory's new sense of order with the promise of something better, plays to the heart of the Western—the struggle for law and order over the wild. Like many outlaws, Bane instills fear while offering a ray of hope. As he tells Batman before leaving him to watch helplessly from The Hole—the most heinous of prison fortresses:

> Hope. Every man who has rotted here over the centuries has looked up to the light and imagined climbing to freedom. So simple, so easy. And, like shipwrecked men turning to sea water from an uncontrollable thirst, many have died trying. I learned here that there can be no true despair without hope. So as I terrorize Gotham, I will feed its people hope so as to poison their souls. I will let them believe they can survive so that you can watch them clamber over each other to stay in the sun.... You will watch as I torture an entire city to cause you pain you thought you could never feel again. Then, when you have truly understood the depths of your failure.... We will destroy Gotham. And when it is done ... when Gotham is in ashes ... *then* you will have my permission to die [439].

Bane's language rings similarly to that of Western outlaws, hyperbole that grandly categorizes the masses as cattle, willing to follow anyone who offers the promise of a better life. After rendering the elite impotent, Bane uses the information he has found to expose Harvey Dent, who is now lauded as the hero of "The Dent Act." The act, a piece of legislation passed in Harvey's memory designed to incarcerate hundreds of criminals, is founded on myth, and its exposure brings Gotham out of the darkened twilight and in to the harsher realities of daylight. Calling himself a "liberator" in his televised address (453), Bane tells Gothamites that their hero is nothing more than a fabrication created by Commissioner Gordon and others, to make Gotham feel more secure in their new found civilized state; in exposing the truth, Bane deigns chaos as his guiding principle: "We take Gotham from the corrupt. The rich. The oppressors of generations who've kept you down with the myth of opportunity. And we give it to you, the people. Gotham is yours—none shall interfere. Do as you please" (459). And as he sets the city aflame, he takes control of the Wayne Foundation's nuclear reactor to carry out his final plan, the utter annihilation of Gotham along side his trusted outlaw companion, Miranda, who is actually Talia, daughter of Ras al Ghul.

Bane's brand of brutal corruption works to expose how fragile the tradition of American democracy is—a mainstay of the Western. Batman's gradual shifting from a dazed, hurting human to his determined, superhuman hero is a binary shift that comes to play as in the traditional Western, where the disillusioned cowboy has to make a choice between his self-imposed exile and his determination to see civilization—in essence America—preserved in all of its positive attributes.

In a manner distinct from the previous films, Batman has his own posse—one comrade more than willing, the other a reluctant warrior—who helps, along with the stalwart Commissioner Gordon, to restore order to the territory. Blake/Robin (Joseph Gordon Levitt) works through the system—the police force—to shine as a crusader in his own right, gradually putting the pieces of Bane's puzzle together and jolting the depressed Wayne into action. Selena Kyle/Catwoman (Anne Hathaway) works against the system as a jewel thief, but gradually comes around once Batman enters the foray and shows her that what she thought she wanted to see—Gotham in chaos—was not all that it was thought to be. She joins the fight for Gotham once Batman shows her good faith by offering her a "Clean Slate"—the computer program she seeks to start her life anew. This cadre joins forces to disengage the plot of Ras al Ghul, saving the civilized world of Gotham from the renegade outlaws who seek its soul.

Critics of this new Batman Trilogy have written extensively on the use of masks in the first two films. However, masks appear to be much more central to this third entry, mainly because of the trilogy's adherence to the principles of The Western. Recall that the mask is a symbol of the outlaw in the Western's traditional plot schema, obscuring the identity of the villain from being recognized while committing a crime. However, in this film masks complicate because not only do both Bane and Catwoman wear masks, but the hero does as well. In Laurie Dudenhoffer's psychoanalytic discussion, the mask hides the "inner nature" of the hero, allowing Batman to shine as both everyman and superhero. Brent Holmes contends in another psychological study that Batman's mask hides the pain that has created the superhero, allowing him more liberty to expose the pain within the criminals he fights. However I think these scholars have only hit part of the point, as the Trilogy abounds in masks—not only do The Scarecrow (*BB*) and The Joker (*DK*) wear masks, but also Ducard, who masquerades as a friend of Wayne's until Bruce decides he cannot join the evil Army of Shadows; Harvey Dent, who is transformed into Two-Face by the Joker, and who hides behind the mask of political crusader through most of the film, even taking on the guise of Batman at one point; and Talia al Ghul, who not only masquerades as Miranda Tate, champion of free and clean energy, and who even wears a physical mask to her own fundraiser. In fact, Batman's inability to see beyond his own mask at times causes him much more trouble. Returning to the generic roots of The Western, we can see that outlaws wear masks to hide their motives; heroes wear masks to obscure their emotions, thereby protecting loved ones who might be in peril should the hero's identity be revealed. Therefore, Nolan's masks are not simply the psychoanalytic calling cards to inner souls in torment (even though it is fair to argue that Bruce's soul does suffer from guilt in that he caused the death of his parents in the first film and Rachel Dawes, in the second); instead, they mask motivation.

Take, for instance, The Joker, who hides behind his "war paint." Throughout *The Dark Knight*, he tells three different stories explaining where he got the scars that form his mask and each story he tells contributes to making him sound loonier as he proceeds to his next diabolical event. His mask, paired with a wild tale, disarms his critics—both criminal and civil—who think he's a simple lunatic. That is what makes him so dangerous. Or take Selena Kyle, who disguises herself at various times throughout *The Dark Knight Rises* as a maid, as a socialite, as a tourist, as an outlaw, and finally as a vigilante. Each time she presents a new personality, she obscures the real Selena—a side she only reveals to Bruce / Batman as she grows to trust him. Remember, when Blake boldly asks Batman why he wears the mask, the crusader offers a simple explanation: "To protect the people closest to me" (425). Harkening back to the Western, the mask is a necessary item, obscuring the harsh realities of life on the plains—adding to the mystique of the cowboy who seeks to tame the wilderness, and ride the open range.

In bringing the Trilogy to a close, Nolan comes full circle with Bane and Talia's linear insistence on making their mentor and benefactor Rha al Ghul's dream a reality. Batman's efforts to prevent villainy from destroying Gotham become the archetypical tale of the prairie frontiersman removed from civilization seeking solace for his own wounded psyche; but because of his humanity, he is drawn into the battle for civilization, ultimately saving it from annihilation. It is therefore fitting that once Bane and Talia are defeated, and order is restored to Gotham once more, Batman can leave his cowl to Blake/Robin and light out for the territory with Selina—just as Alfred had always dreamed.

Given the parallel histories of American cinema and the Western, it is fitting to see that Nolan's approach to Batman takes its ideological underpinnings from the genre, and uses them to create a new approach to the Caped Crusader. In this way, Batman not only becomes further ingrained in the mythology of American popular culture, he helps to make the spirit of the Western relevant in the post 9/11 world.

WORKS CITED

Buscombe, Edward. *The Searchers*. London: British Film Institute, 2004.
Dudenhoeffer, Laurie. "Masks of Infamy: The About-faces in Christopher Nolan's *The Dark Knight*." *Forum* 12 (2011).
Lusted, David. *The Western*. New York: Pearson/Longman, 2003.
Holmes, Brent. "Why They Wear the Mask: The Mouthpieces of Nolan's Batman Trilogy." *Kino: The Western Undergraduate Journal of Film Studies* 4.1 (2013).
Nolan, Christopher, with Jonathan Nolan and David S. Goyer. *The Dark Knight Trilogy: The Complete Screenplays*. New York: Opus, 2013.

About the Contributors

J.P.C. **Brown** taught English and film at Middlesex University between 1992 and 2011, and social and political theory at Birkbeck, University of London, from 1997 to 2011. He is an associate research fellow in the Department of Politics at Birkbeck and a lecturer in theatre for IES (Abroad) in London.

Patrick **Condliffe** is a PhD candidate at the University of Sydney. His thesis research delves into the issues of hoax literature and fraudulent composers and the impacts these have upon Indigenous cultures and our appreciation of their art.

Marco **Grosoli** is a British Academy Postdoctoral Fellow at the University of Kent, where he is completing a monograph on the "Politique des auteurs." His research interests include André Bazin's integral corpus of writings (2600 articles).

Andrew **Howe** is an associate professor of history at La Sierra University, where he teaches courses in film history and theory, popular culture, and American history. Recent publications include articles on race and racism in *Star Wars* and the depiction of Latino identity in *Breaking Bad*.

Jenna **Hunnef** is a doctoral candidate in the Department of English at the University of Toronto. Her research interests include American studies, Indigenous literatures, western American fiction, animals and affect and intersections between law and literature.

Fontaine **Lien** is a PhD candidate at the University of California, Riverside. Her dissertation focuses on literature, television and cinema of the fantastic. She teaches Chinese, French and cinema at Eastern Connecticut State University.

Vincent **Piturro** is an assistant professor of English and cinema studies at Metropolitan State University of Denver. His areas of study include Westerns, science fiction, documentaries and Italian-American cinema.

Arthur **Redding** is the author of three books on American culture, literature and politics. He is a professor of English at York University in Toronto.

Michael **Samuel** is pursuing a PhD at the University of Leeds. His thesis analyzes the relationship between heritage film, tourism and historical buildings. He has published in the *Birmingham Journal of Literature and Language* and in several edited collections.

Matthew **Sorrento** teaches film studies and media journalism at Rutgers University. He regularly contributes to *Film International, Senses of Cinema* and other publications and is editing a collection on the Zodiac Killer in popular culture for McFarland.

Scott F. **Stoddart** is an associate professor of English at John Jay College, SUNY. He is the editor of *Analyzing Mad Men: Critical Essays on the Television Series* (McFarland, 2011) and has published on a diverse range of topics in film and literature.

Joseph S. **Walker** received his PhD in contemporary American literature from Purdue University. His recent work has examined popular culture and television in essays on programs including *The Sopranos, Mystery Science Theater 3000, Veronica Mars, Community* and *Arrested Development*.

Index

Abu Ghraib Scandal 143
The Abyss 121
Academy Awards 52, 81
Acland, Charles R. 49
Al Qaeda 129, 139–40, 142, 152
The Alamo 149
Alamogordo, NM 120
Aldrich, Robert 194
Aldrin, Buzz 120
Alien 193
Allen, Woody 192
Altman, Robert 70, 147, 180, 182
American Historical Association 10
An American Werewolf in London 189
Amos and Andrew 16
Ancken, David von 174
Anderson, Flora 25, 30
Anderson, Paul Michael 174
Angels with Dirty Faces 150
Anker, Elizabeth 122
Appaloosa 75
Archbold, Jason 19
Arkham Asylum 238
Armageddon 160
Armstrong, Neil 120
Arriaga, Guillermo 198
Assassination of Jesse James 8, 11, 74, 172
Assault on Precinct 13 200
Aurora, CO, shooting 239
Avatar 7, 116–34, 229

Ba'ath Party 129
Baccario, Morena 138
Back to the Future 188–89
Bad Day at Black Rock 146, 203
Bal, Mieke 15
Baldwin, Adam 138
Bale, Christian 91, 231–43
The Ballad of Little Jo 89
Bandidas 174
Bane 239–42

Barnes, Justus D. 2
Bartel, Paul 188
Bartlett, Bonnie 145
Basket Case 193
The Batman 161
Batman (1966 television series) 230
Batman Begins 231–35, 237
The Batman Trilogy 8, 229–44
Battle of Antietam 140
Battle of Chickamauga 55
Battle of Little Big Horn 130
Battle of Wounded Knee 130
Battlestar Galactica 122
Baxter, Denton 65
Bay, Michael 160
Bayers, Peter 125
Bazin, Andre 3, 199, 216
Beatty, Warren 181
Beethoven, Ludwig von 209
Begotten 200
Belic, Niko 177
Bell, David 17
Bell, Kristen 25
Bell, Lilly 28
Belmont, Frank 67
Bening, Annette 66
Benjamin, Walter 220
Bennett, Mags 33
Bernstein, Matthew 16, 17
Bethke, Bruce 143
A Better Tomorrow 164
Bickle, Travis 175
Big Jake 70
Bigelow, Kathryn 174
Billy Jack 13
bin Laden, Osama 11
Bioshock Infinite 175
Birth of a Nation 124
The Black Dahlia 177
Blade Runner 137, 193
Blake, aka Robin 241–42

247

Index

Blazing Saddles 4, 97
Bloom, Michelle 160
Boetticher, Budd 7, 81, 84, 190
Bogart, Humphrey 150, 177
Bohannon, Cullen 28–9
Bonanza 21
Bonnie and Clyde 3, 182–83
Boone, Daniel 160
Boorman, Charley 126
Boorman, John 126
Booth, Powers 25
Bordwell, David 162, 164
Borges, Jorge Luis 199
Boyle, Peter 197, 199
Bragg, Randall 75
Brandon, Henry 232
Breaking Bad 174–75
Bridges, Jeff 49, 51, 52, 54
British New Wave 159
Brod, Henry 97
Brokeback Mountain 7, 64, 81–94, 95–115
Brolin, Josh 51
Brook, Shepherd 137
Brooks, Mel 4, 192
Brooks, Peter 96
Brown, Clarence 124
Browning, Tod 197
Buck Rogers 21
Buckley, Thomas 33
Buffy the Vampire Slayer 139, 153
Bullfighter and the Lady 7, 81
Bullock, Seth 23, 25
Bully 177
Bumpo, Natty 7, 123–34
Burgess, Anthony 202
The Buried Letters 84
Burn After Reading 70
Burnett, Charles 194
Burton, Tim 230
Burwell, Carter 51
Buscome, Edward 84–85, 86–88, 160
Bush, George W. 11, 64, 142, 162
Butch Cassidy and the Sundance Kid 4, 7, 86, 118
Butler, Jean 201

Cagney, James 150
Caine, Michael 232–33
Call of Juarez 175
Cameron, James 7, 116, 121, 193
Campbell, Glen 50, 71
Campbell, Joseph 190
Campbell, Neil 203
Capra, Frank 150
Carmichael, Deborah 119
Carpenter, John 121, 174, 200
Carradine, Keith 25

Casablanca 16, 150
Cawelti, John 118
Celido, Julio 66
The Challenger 121
Chan, Jackie 160
Chance, John T. 181
Chandler, Raymond 177, 199
Chaney, Tom 51, 54–56
Chapman, Graham 126, 192
Chase, David 181
Chaucer, Geoffrey 46
Cheyenne 29–31
Chicago World's Fair 10
Chihuahua 85
China Seas 150
Chinatown 196
Chingachgook 123
Chow, Steven 165
Christie, Julie 181
Chungking Express 165
Cimarron 4
City Slickers 4
Civil Rights Movement 188
Civil War 19, 140–41
Clan of the Cave Bear 126
The Clash of Civilizations 142
Cleese, John 192
A Clockwork Orange 202
Close Encounters of the Third Kind 190
Clothier, William H. 100
Cloud Atlas 168
Cobb, Jayne 137
Cochran, Doc 24
Coen brothers 6, 21, 40–62, 62–80, 172, 198, 229
Cogburn, Rooster, 40–62, 62, 80
Cohn, Jan 43, 44
Colbert, Claudette 150
Cold War 12–15, 17, 62, 64, 142, 155
USS *Cole* 130
Columbus, Chris 191
Common 29
Conan the Barbarian 13
The Condition of Liberty 156
Contagion 211
Cooper, James Fenimore 7, 116, 123–36, 160
Coppola, Francis Ford 23, 191
Corbin, Ed 76
Corbucci, Sergio 198
Corkin, Stanley 175, 212
Cornell, Drucilla 17
Cosmopolitan 16
Costner, Kevin 4, 11, 63–64, 87, 116
Cotillard, Marion 239
Cowboy Bebop 168
Cowboys and Aliens 12, 174

Index 249

Cox, Alex 8, 188–206
Coy, Walter 231
Craig, Daniel 12
Crane, Jonathan, aka Scarecrow 234, 241
Cranston, Bryan 175
Crichton, Michael, 12
Cronenberg, David 189
Crouching Tiger, Hidden Dragon 161
Crowe, Russell 11, 12, 90, 92
Crowther, Bosley 97
CSI Franchise 121

Dabashi, Hamid 210–20
Daggett, Little Bill 5
Damon, Matt 50, 51, 71
Dances with Wolves 4, 5, 7, 63, 65, 123, 127
Dante, Joe 191
Darby, Kim 57, 71
The Dark Knight 235–39
Dark Knight Rises 239–43
Darnell, Linda 85
Darth Vader 190
Dawes, Rachel 234, 236–38, 242
Dawn of the Dead 193
Dead End Kids 150
Dead Man 11, 12
Deadwood 6, 19–27, 174, 229
Deakins, Roger 45
Death and the Compass 190, 199–203
Deep Space Nine 121
The Deerslayer 123
Del Mar, Ennis 87, 90, 95–115
DeMille, Cecil B. 17
Demme, Jonathan 177
Denby, David 83
DeNiro, Robert 175
The Dentist 197
DePalma, Brian 177
Depp, Johnny 11, 12, 176
Diana, Princess of Wales 202
Diaz, Junot 15
Dickens, Kim 25
Die Hard 160
Dillinger, John 175
Dillon, Michael 155
Dirty Harry 200
Ditsky, John 46
Django Unchained 21, 174, 181
Dodge City 149
The Dog of the South 45
Doherty, Thomas 49
Dolly, Ree 46
Dominik, Andrew 8, 74, 172
Doniphon, Tom 96–101, 144, 148
Donner, Richard 191
Don't Look Now 193
Dourif, Brad 24

Downs, Cathy 85
Dracula (1931) 197
Ducard, Henri 233, 235
Ducat, Stephen J. 42
Dudenhoffer, Laurie 241
Duelists 193
Dunbar, John 116, 126
Dune 128
Durant, Thomas 31
Duvall, Robert 65, 151

Earp, Wyatt 84–86
Eastwood, Clint 5, 11, 17–18, 26, 63, 147–48, 172, 188
Easy Rider 4, 181, 183
Ebert, Roger 45, 83, 97
Ebiri, Bilge 207
Eccleston, Christopher 200–01
Eckhart, Aaron 236
Edge, Rod 7
Edge City or *Sleep Is for Sissies* 193
Edwards, Dorothy 232
Edwards, Ethan 16, 73, 74, 231–33
Elam, Jack 29, 30, 31
Elsaesser, Thomas 96
The Emerald Forest 126, 128
The Empire Strikes Back 120
Estevez, Emilio 194–95
Estrada, Melquiades 66–68
Evans, Ann 92
Evans, Dan 91
Everdeen, Katniss 46
Exxon Valdez Oil Spill 128

Fabrizio, Lisa 44
Falcone, Carmine 234
Fallen Angels 165
Fallout 175
Faludi, Susan 43, 57
Fargo 45, 69, 72
Fast and Furious 177
Feifei 161
Feihong, Huang 165
Fillon, Nathan 138
Film Noir 151
Fine, Kerry 46–47
Firefly 7, 121, 137–58, 168, 229
First Blood 13
Fisher, Louis 141
Fistful of Dollars 194, 198, 202
Five Came Back 3
Fleming, Victor 146
Fletcher, Fred 203, 204
Flynn, Errol 149
Focus Features 7, 88, 101
Fonda, Henry 16, 84
Fonda, Peter 91

250 Index

Ford, Harrison 112, 190
Ford, John 3, 6, 10–12, 63, 73, 81, 84, 95–101, 149, 172, 178, 180, 202, 204, 207, 231
Fort Apache 3
Fort Apache, the Bronx 13
Foster, Ben 83
Foucault, Michel 21
Fox, Lucius 234, 238–39
Frankenstein 119
Freeman, Morgan 5, 234
Frobisher, Fritz 203
Frye, E. Max 16
Frye, Northrop 216

Gable, Clark 150
Gambler 165
Gambon, Michael 65
Gandolfini, James 181
Gellner, Ernest 156
Germany Year Zero 219
Geronimo: An American Legend 125
Ghosts of Mars 121
Gilbert, James 42
Gill, Brendan 97
Gilliam, Terry 192
Girard, Rene 22, 32
Givens, Raylan 31–34
Glass, Ron 138
Glau, Summer 138
Gledhill, Christine 97
God's Little Acre 214
Gone with the Wind 146
The Good, the Bad and the Ugly 21, 77
The Goonies 191
Gopnik, Larry 69
Gordon, James 234–35, 238, 240
Gordon, Stuart 193
Gotham City 8, 161, 231
Gran Torino 17 -18
Grand Theft Auto 175 -77
Gray, John 154–55
The Great Train Robbery 2, 63, 147
The Green Berets 70
Greene, Peter 33
Greenfield, Mark 208
Greenwald, Maggie 89
Greenwood, Bruce 77
Gremlins 191
Griffith, D.W. 124
Gruber, Frank 172
Guantanamo Bay 143
Gulf War 4, 35, 143
Gunfighter Nation 13, 19, 143
Gunsmoke 11
Gyllenhaal, Jake 87
Gyllenhaal, Maggie 236

Hackman, Gene 5
Hamill, Mark 190
Hamlet 201
Hammett, Dashiell 194
Hanna 46
Hannah, Darryl 126
Hanson, Curtis 177
Hard Boiled 164
Hardy, Tom 239
Hark, Tsui 165
Harris, Ed 75, 196
Harris, Mark 2–3
Harrison, George 193
Harvey, Dent, aka Two Face 236–38, 240
Hatfields and McCoys 174
Hathaway, Ann 99
Hathaway, Henry 40–62, 62–80
Hatton, Wade 149
Hawkes, John 24
Hawkeye (Natty Bumpo) 123
Hawks, Howard 3, 14–15, 95, 164, 172, 207
Head 193
Heart of Darkness 118
Hell on Wheels 6, 21, 28–31, 174
Henderson, Travis 175
Henenlotter, Frank 193
Henried, Paul 150
Henry, Carla 202
Herbert, Frank 193
Hero 162
Hero with a Thousand Faces 190
Hickock, Wild Bill 25
High Noon 120, 147, 149–50, 199
Highway Patrolman 190, 197–99, 201
Hill, George Roy 4, 7
Hillcoat 174
Hitchcock, Alfred 196
Hoberman, J. 97
Holliday, Doc 84 -6
Holmes, Brent 241
Holmes, James Eagan 239
Holmes, Katie 234
Homer 14
Homosexuality 81–93
Hondo 175
Hong Kong martial arts picture 7, 151, 159–70
Hooper, Tobe 191
Hopper, Dennis 4, 181
Houston, John 180
HUAC 141
Hubble Telescope 121
Hunan Television 161
The Hunger Games 46
Hunter, Jeffrey 233

Huntington, Samuel 142
Hussein, Saddam 143
Hyams, Peter 120

In Plain Sight 47
Inglorious Baterds 29, 181
Iraq War 211
Irons, Jeremy 75
Islam 142
It Happened One Night 150
Izzard, Eddie 202

Jacobi, Derek 201
Jaeckel, Richard 92
James, Frank 48, 72
James, William 18
Jameson, Fredric 216
Jarmusch, Jim 11
Jiang Hu 161–64
"Jihad Jane" (Colleen LaRose) 129
The Joker 235–39, 241–42
Jones, Tommy Lee 6, 66
Jonet, Jaclyn 204
Joyce, Justin 32–3
Judd, Steve 86, 148
Justified 6, 31–5

Kar-Wai, Wong 165
Katharos 22
Kaylee 138–9
Keegan, Rebecca 46
Keith, Toby 11
Kennedy, John F. 120
Kennedy, Robert F. 43
Kerouac, Jack 149
Kershner, Irvin 120
Kick-Ass 46
Kill Bill 168
Killer of Sheep 194
The Killers 164
King, Dr. Martin Luther 183
King Philip's War 122
Kirkwood, R. Cort 45
Kiss Me Deadly 194
Kitses, Jim 216
Kneivel, Evel 15
Kowalski, Walt 18
Kroeber, Karl 123–24
Kubrick, Stanley 202
Kurosawa, Akira 168, 194
Kurds 129
Kurtiz, Michael 16, 150
Kyd, Thomas 201
Kyle, Selena, aka Catwoman 241–42

L.A. Confidential 177
L.A. Noire 177

LaBoeuf 43, 48–51, 53, 57–8, 70–1, 75
Lacan, Jacques 99–100
Ladd, Alan 139
Landis, John 188–89, 192
Lane, Anthony 69
Lang, Stephen 119
La Scala, Nancy 208
The Last of the Mohicans 123–36
Laszlo, Victor 150
Laughing Screaming 193
Laughlin, Tom 13
Lavery, David 69
Law & Order 121
Lawless 174
Leatherstocking (Natty Bumpo) 123
Ledger, Heath 87, 235
Lee, Ang 83–94, 95–115, 162
Lee, Bruce 162
The Legacy of Conquest 211
Legend 193
Lehman Brothers 240
Leigh, Janet 139
Lenihan, John 118
Leo, Melissa 67
Leone, Sergio 5, 1, 21, 26, 65, 70, 148, 194, 203
Lethem, Jonathan 44
Levitt, Joseph Gordon 241
Li, Jet 165–66
Libby, Bill 16
Life of Brian 192
Limehouse, Ellstin 34
Limerick, Patricia 12, 211
Lincoln, Abraham 16, 28
Lindh, John Walker 129
Little Big Man 13, 125, 188
Little Blackie 52–3
Livingston, Reb 15
Logan, Ned 5
The Lone Ranger (film) 12, 65, 174
The Lone Ranger (television series) 11
Lonesome Dove 66, 126
Lorimer, George Horace 43–4
The Lost Boys 191
Lucas, George 120, 188, 190–92
Lust in the Dust 188
Lusted, David 84, 92, 229, 234
Lyden, Robert 58

Macbeth 58
MacCurday, Carol 91
MacDougal, Prof. Harold 181–84
Macready, Mindy (Hit Girl) 46
Mad Max 198
Madsen, Michael 34
The Magnificent Seven 7, 121
Maher, Kevin 45, 168

Maher, Sean 138
Maland, Charles J. 17
Malcomson, Paula 24
A Man Called Horse 125
The Man from Laramie 3
The Man Who Fell to Earth 193
The Man Who Shot Liberty Valance 3, 7, 14, 16, 95–101, 144, 148, 217
The Man Who Wasn't There 70
Man with No Name 26
Man Without a Name Trilogy 70
Mangold, James 83, 229
Manhattan by Numbers 209
Manhunt 177
"Manifest Apology" 125, 130
Manifest Destiny 62
Mankiewicz, Joseph L. 17
Mann, Anthony 3, 190, 196, 199, 215
Mann, Michael 124
Marathon 209
Marlowe, Philip 199
Marquand, John P. 120
Marston, John 176
Martin, Dean 181
Martin, Trayvon 32, 34
Martindale, Margo 33
Martinson, Leslie 230
Marvin, Lee 96
Mass Effect 175
Massey, Joseph 15
Mathison, Dirk 128
Mature, Victor 84
Max Payne 177
May, Karl 11
McCabe, John 181
McCabe and Mrs. Miller 70, 147, 180–83
McCarthyism 141
McCrea, Joel 86, 148
McDonough, Neal 34
McElligott, Dominique 28
McElroy, Byron 91
McGee, Patrick 130
McKellan, Ian 89
McKinney, Devin 22–3, 30, 32, 34
McLaglen, Victor 151
McMurtry, Larry 95
McShane, Ian 24
Meaney, Colm 31
Meek, Stephen 77
Meek's Cutoff 77–80
Meeuf, Russell 44
The Melodramatic Imagination 96
Merhige, E. Elias 200
Metropolis 161
Middle East 64, 127–29
Middleton, Thomas 188, 201
Midge, Ray 45–6

Midnight Club racing series 176
Midnight Cowboy 4
Milch, David 19, 27, 35
Miles, Vera 98, 148
Mill, John Stuart 154
Millar, Darren 12
Miller, Constance 181
Miller, George 198
Mingyu, Yang 165
Minnear, Tim 146
Mister, Andrew 15
Mr. Blond 34
Mitchell, Lee Clark 10, 33
Mix, Tom 11
Moeschke, Edmund 219
"Mohican Syndrome" 123
Mol, Gretchen 92
Moloney, Robert 28
The Monkees 193
Monty Python and The Holy Grail 192
Moore, Michael 204
Morricone, Ennio 175
Morrow, Gemma Teller 47
Mortensen, Viggo 75
Mount, Anson 28
The Movie Book of the Western 234
Mumford & Sons 30
Munny, William 5
Munro, Cora 123
Murphy, Cillian 234
Murphy, George 209
Murray, Bill 192
My Darling Clementine 3, 7, 84–6, 212
My Name Is Nobody 203

Naderi, Amir 207–28
The Naked Spur 139
National Lampoon's Animal House 192
Native Americans 4, 29, 65, 166–67
Naughton, David 189
Na'vi 116–31
Near Dark 174
Neeson, Liam 233
Neff, Walter 199
Nesmith, Mike 193
New Iranian Cinema 207
The New Serenity Manifesto 15
Newman, Paul 86–7
Neytiri 122
Nichols, Dudley 3
Niroumand, Majid 209, 219
Nixon, Richard M. 174–75
No Country for Old Men 21, 45, 64, 77, 174, 198, 229
Nolan, Christopher 8, 229–44
Norton, Mike 66–8
Nugent, Frank S. 17

Index

Obama, Barack 34, 122
Occupy Wall Street 240
Ocean's Eleven 211
Oklahoma City Bombing 140
The Old Wrangler Rides Again 16
Oldman, Gary 196, 234–5
Olyphant, Timothy 23, 31
On the Road 149–50
Once Upon a Time in China 165–67
Once Upon a Time in China and America 166–67
Once Upon a Time in Mexico 174
Once Upon a Time in the West 178, 180, 202–03
Open Range 6, 11, 64–6, 87
Oro, Johnny 198
Ossana, Diana 95
O'Sullivan, John 197
Otto, Rudolph 24, 27
Outland 120
The Outlaw Josie Wales 144, 151

Palance, Jack 139, 196
Pale Rider 148, 188
Pansullo, Ed 203
Paris, Texas 175
Park, Ed 45
The Pathfinder 123
Paul, Sara 209
Paul, William 193
Pawley, Martin 233
Pearl Harbor 140–41
Peckinpah, Sam 3, 5, 13, 65, 70, 148, 172, 203
Penn, Arthur 3, 189
Pennyworth, Alfred 232, 238–39, 242
Peoples, David Webb 5
Pepper, Barry 51, 66, 75
Pepper, Lucky Ned 49, 54, 70, 75
Performance 193
Perkins, Pete 66–8, 80
Petrie, Daniel 13
The Pioneers 123
Piontek, Thomas 87–8, 90
Pirl, Don 72
Pitch Black 121
Pitt, Brad 11
Pocahontas 122, 125
Polanski, Roman 196
The Political Unconscious 216
Poltergeist 191
Porter, Edwin S. 2, 63, 147
Portis, Charles 6, 40–62, 62–80
Prairie Chapel Ranch 143
Prieto, Rodrigo 95
Prince, Charlie 83, 89, 91–3
Production Code 2–3, 84, 86

Proulx, Annie 87, 96
Prowse, David 190
Public Enemies 175
Pulp Fiction 198
Pumphrey, Martin 92
Pye, Douglas 234

Qualen, John 97
Quaritch, Miles 119
Quarles, Robert 34

Raiders of the Lost Ark 13, 191
Rambo: First Blood II 13
Rambo III 13
Rango 12, 17, 21, 175
Ra's Al Ghul 233, 235, 241
Ray, Robert B. 146–47
Readers' Digest Great World Affairs 142
Reagan, Ronald 11, 15, 120
Re-Animator 193
Red Dead Redemption 7, 172–87
Red Dead Redemption: Undead Nightmare 177, 179
Red Dead Revolver 175, 178
Red Dust 150
Red River 3, 8, 95, 172, 212
Red Scare 120
Redford, Robert 86–7
Reichardt, Kelly 77
Reitman, Ivan 192
Repo Man 189, 193–96
Reservoir Dogs 34
The Return of the Jedi 120
The Revenger's Tragedy 188, 201, 204
Reynolds, Malcolm 137–39
Rhetoric of Sincerity 15
Rialto Films 11
Ribisi, Giovanni 128
Richardson, Sy 203
Rickman, Gregg 11
Ride the High Country 3, 86, 148
Ringo Kid 148–49, 198
Rio Bravo 3, 95, 147, 181
Roache, Linus 231
Roberts, Marguerite 62
Robinson, Anthony 15
Rockstar San Diego/Rockstar Games 176
Roddenberry, Gene 120, 144
Rodriguez, Richard 174
Roeg, Nicholas 193
Rogers, Paul 155
Rogers, Will 16
Rojas, Pedro 197
Roland, Gilbert 81
Romero, George A. 193
Rondeaux, Ron 78
Roosevelt, Theodore 42

Rooster Cogburn (film) 70
Ross, Frank 51, 54–6, 72
Ross, Katharine 86
Ross, Mattie 6, 40–62, 62–80
Rossellini, Roberto 219
Rough Riders 42
Rowlandson, Mary 122
Rudin, Scott 40
The Runner 219–20
Rush Hour 160
Russell, Lee 199
Rwandan Genocide 140
Ryan, Robert 215

St. Crispin's Day 130
Saldana, Zoe 122
Salem, MA 146
Sandoval, Miguel 199
The Sands of Iwo Jima 149
Sarkeesian, Anita 47
The Saturday Evening Post 17, 43
Saunders, John 172–73
Saw 177
Scarface 177
Scharlach, Red 200
Schlesinger, John 4
Schumacher, Joel 191, 231
Schwarzenegger, Arnold 13, 49
Sci-Fi Channel 121
Scorsese, Martin 23, 191
Scott, A.O. 96
Scott, Pippa 232
Scott, Randolph 86, 199
Scott, Ridley 193
Scott, Tony 160
Screen Actors' Guild Awards 52
The Searchers 3, 16, 48, 73, 95, 175, 178, 231–35
Searchers 2.0 8, 190, 203–05
Sedition Act of 1798 141
Seitz, George 124
Selfridge, Parker 128
Seraphim Falls 174
Serenity 137–58
A Serious Man 69
Seven Samurai 168
Seven Years War 127
The Sex Pistols 196
Shaara, Michael 139
Shane 63, 79, 95, 139, 147–48, 172, 179, 188, 196, 200
Shanghai Noon 168, 174
Shannon, Mary 47
"Share Your Story" 101–15
Shatner, William 120
Shaw Brothers 161
She Wore a Yellow Ribbon 3, 151

Shelley, Mary 119
Sheppard, Mark 144
The Shootist 70, 145
Sid and Nancy aka Love Kills 196
The Silence of the Lambs 177
Silverstein 125
Simon & Schuster 43, 150
The Sixgun Mystique 118
Sixguns and Society 162
Skywalker, Luke 190
Slotkin, Richard 10, 12–14, 19, 34, 89, 118, 155, 185
Smith, Henry Nash 214
Snipes, Greg 25
Soderbergh, Steven 211
Soldier Blue 13
Solo, Han 190
Sons of Anarchy 47
Soprano, Tony 181
The Sopranos 181, 185
Sosa, Roberto 197
Sound Barrier 223
Spaghetti Westerns 21
The Spanish Tragedy 201
Spearman, Boss 65
Speilberg, Steven 13, 188, 190, 194
Sperling, Nicole 52
Spirit: Stallion of the Cimarron 175
Sputnik 120
Stack, Robert 81
Stagecoach 2–3, 8, 16 77, 145, 148–49, 151, 171, 178, 198
Staite, Jewel 138
Stallone, Sylvester 13
Stam, Robert 63
Stanfield, Peter 3
Stanton, Henry Dean 175, 195
Star, Sol 24
Star Trek 21, 144
Star Trek V: The Final Frontier 120
Star Trek: The Motion Picture 191
"Star Wars" 13
Star Wars: A New Hope 120, 190
Stargate SG-1 121
Steinfeld, Hallie 46, 51–2, 71
Stevens, George 95, 172, 200, 207
Stewart, James 16, 96, 139, 200
Stoddard, Ransom 16, 96–101, 145, 148
Stonehill, Colonel 47–8, 53, 55
Straight to Hell 189, 196–97
Strategic Defense Initiative 120
Stripes 192
Stubbs, Joanie 25
Studlar, Gaylyn 16–17
Sturges, John 7, 146, 168, 203
Sully, Jake 116
Superman (film) 191

Superman (television series) 161
Survivor 12
Swearengen, Al 24–26

Taken 122
Taliban 129
Tam, River 137–39, 143
Tam, Simon 137–39
Tarantino, Quentin 29, 93, 168, 174, 181, 198
Tate, Miranda, aka Talia 239, 241–42
Taxi Driver 23, 175
The Tempest 153
10,000 Ways to Die 191
The Terminator 121, 193
Tet Offensive 140
Tetherow, Emily 78–9
Thelma and Louise 11
There Will Be Blood 174
They Drive by Night 193
Thomas, Zach 207
Thorn, Jesse 15
The Three Amigos 188
Three Bad Men 16
Three Burials of Melquiades Estrada 6, 66–9
3:10 to Yuma 7, 12, 21, 174
3:10 to Yuma (1957) 92
Tianyi Film Company 161
Titus Andronicus 201
Tolliver, Cy 25–6
Tompkins, Jane 12, 14, 26, 53, 55
Top Gun 160
Torres, Gina 138
Torres, Mel 203–04
Toruk 130
Total Recall 13
Tourneur, Maurice 124
Trevor, Claire 198
The Trouble with Harry 196
Trpcic, Shawna 146
True Grit (Coen brothers) 6, 40–62, 62–80, 172, 229
True Grit (Hathaway) 6, 40–62, 62–80
True Grit (novel) 40–62
Tudyk, Alan 138
Turan, Kenneth 97
Turner, Frederick Jackson 10, 12, 42, 118–19, 173, 211
Turner, Walt 208
Twain, Mark 46
Twin Towers/11 September 2001 attacks 1, 5, 42–3, 65–6, 118, 122, 129–30, 140–42, 154, 177, 183, 203, 211–13, 229
Twist, Jack 87, 90, 95–115, 126
Twoby, David 121

Uncas 123
The Undefeated 151
Unforgiven 5, 21, 63, 65, 147, 172, 176, 181
United Flight 93 140

Valance, Liberty 96, 148
Valerii, Tonio 203
Vampires 174
vanAlphen, Ernst 15
Vanderbilt, Cornelius 197
Van der Linde, Dutch 179–84
Vegas 207–28
Verbinski, Gore 17
Verne, Jules 119
Videodrome 189
Vietnam War 3, 19, 35, 42, 48, 63, 70, 116, 118, 122, 128–29
The Village People 13
The Virginian 10, 14, 42, 118

Wachhorst, Wyn 58
Wade, Ben 90–2
Waggner, George 189
Wagon Train (television series) 120
Waite, Charlie 65
Walker 189, 196–97
Wallace, David Foster 15
Walsh, Monte 87
Walsh, Raoul 207
Walter, Tracey 194
Wantanabe, Ken 233
"War on Terror" 66, 143–44
Warshow, Robert 12
The Watchmen 161
Water Margin 161–62
Water, Wind and Dust 209, 215
Watergate 120
Watson, Brian 208
Wayne, Bruce 231–42
Wayne, John 6, 1, 14–15, 40–62, 62–81, 137, 145, 147, 149, 162, 175, 180–81, 231
Wayne, Thomas 231
"Weapons of Mass Destruction" 143
The Weathermen 140
Weber, Christina D. 48
Weiler, A.H. 97
Wells, H.G. 119
West of Everything 26
Westchester '73 3
The Western Genre 172
Westerns: Making the Man in Fiction and Film 10
Westrum, Gil 86
Westworld 12
Whedon, Joss 7, 121, 137, 229
White, Walter 175
Whitehead, Colson 15

The Wild Bunch 3–4, 8, 13, 70, 125, 165, 172, 175, 181, 203
Wilder, Billy 199
Wilhelm, Maria 128
Wilkinson, Tom 234
Williams, Michelle 78, 89
Williams, Tony 165
Williamson, Mykelti 34
Wills, Gary 70
Winnicott, Donald 220
Winter's Bone 46
Wise, Robert 191
Wister, Owen 6, 10, 14, 42
Wojda, John 209
The Wolf Man 189
Wolfe, Jeff 166
Woo, John 166, 64
Wood, Natalie 73, 232
Wood, Robin 88, 90, 190–91
Worthington, Sam 116
Wright, Will 159–62, 174, 212

Wyatt Earp 11

X Films 194

Yimou, Zhang 162
Yoakam, Dwight 67
Yojimbo 202
Yong, Jin 161–62
Young, Keone 26
Young Mr. Lincoln 16
Younger, Cole 72
Yun-Fat, Chow 164
Yuzna, Brian 197

Zamora, Del 203
Zellweger, Renee 75
Zemeckis, Robert 188–89
Zhao, Vincent 165
Zimmerman, George 32, 199
Zinnemann, Fred 120
Zurhellen, John 7

www.ingramcontent.com/pod-product-compliance
Ingram Content Group UK Ltd.
Pitfield, Milton Keynes, MK11 3LW, UK
UKHW041934140426
5217IPUK00014B/469